empty tomb®, inc.

Executive Summary:

The State of Church Giving through 2007:
What Are Our Christian Billionaires Thinking—Or Are They?

(19th Edition in the series, Oct. 2009)

"So if you have not been trustworthy in handling worldly wealth, who will trust you with true riches?" Jesus Christ quoted in Luke 16:11 (NIV)

Updates on Church Member Giving and Membership Trends through 2007

Chapters 1-5 update church member giving from various perspectives.

Giving as a percent of income to Total Contributions and Congregational Finances (the internal operations of the congregation) increased from 2006-2007. Giving as a percent of income to Benevolences (causes outside the local congregation's operations) declined again in 2007, reaching its lowest point in the 1968-2007 period (Table 1, p. 13).

If the trends continue, Benevolences will reflect a small portion of income in the future (pp. 44-45).

Membership as a percent of U.S. population in 37 Protestant denominations and the Roman Catholic Church, combined, continued to decline in 2007 (Fig. 14, p. 48).

Overseas Missions Support in 34 Denominations

Data is updated through 2007 (Tables 16-21, pages 59-65).

Foreign-Born Remittances Compared to Native-Born Church Member Overseas Giving

In 2007, foreign-born people living in the U.S. sent $79 billion overseas. If native-born church members had supported overseas ministries similarly, churches would have sent $314 billion more (pp. 72-73).

Calculated Per Member Additional Cost to Expand Global Evangelism and Impact Deed Need

General discussion of the calculations of the cost of expanding missions in cents per day for selected church populations is presented (pp. 66-70, including Tables 23 and 24).

Roman Catholic Potential Giving in Nine Archdioceses

Discussion of current and potential giving in nine archdioceses that have, or traditionally have had, a cardinal is presented (pp. 71-72, including Table 25).

U.S. Bureau of Labor Statistics Consumer Expenditure Survey 2007 Charitable Spending

An analysis of the data by age, income, and region of residence, including 1987-2007 data in terms of region of residence, is presented (pages 80-89, including Tables 26-32).

What Are Our Christian Billionaires Thinking—Or Are They?

"Wholesale billionaire philanthropists" (high-capacity donors) could help mobilize "retail billionaire philanthropists" (individual donors who combine to support multi-billion church institutions) to expand missions outreach (pp. 108-110, 144-147).

Wholesale billionaire philanthropist efforts could engender resistance from church leaders at all levels, but there are solid reasons to pursue church member mobilization (pp. 110-122).

A Model to Calculate Country-Specific Costs for Preventing Child Deaths

Using available data, a model calculates country-specific costs to address eight causes of death in children under five years of age in 68 countries that account for 95% of under-5 deaths (pp. 123-134).

The Wycliffe Model

Wycliffe Bible Translators set a goal to begin the last Bible translation by the year 2025, and has stated a timeframe and dollar-cost goal that is succeeding in its early phase (pp. 135-137).

A Case Study: The Southern Baptist Convention

The second largest communion in the U.S., the Southern Baptist Convention (SBC) stated a clear goal that is at a scale designed to meet a global need. Since 2007, the communion has announced a need for 2,800 more missionaries, but not the dollar cost, to engage unreached people groups. The SBC's approach to its goal is reviewed and analyzed, based on public documents (pp. 137-147).

empty tomb®, inc.

Executive Analysis of the Implications of Findings:

The State of Church Giving through 2007:
What Are Our Christian Billionaires Thinking—Or Are They?

(19th Edition in the series, October 2009)

"So if you have not been trustworthy in handling worldly wealth, who will trust you with true riches?" Jesus Christ quoted in Luke 16:11 (NIV)

"From Jesus' perspective, apparently when we're handling 'worldly wealth' we're actually trundling along on training wheels and not, as we picture ourselves, cruising along in something like the most expensive car in production, a Bugatti Veyron, having zoomed to 60 mph in 2.5 seconds" (p. 7).

The Consequences of Church Member Giving Trends Both In and Outside the Church

Table 40 (p. 114) presents quotes from various church leaders that highlight the "lukewarmness" present across the theological spectrum. Youth, both in and outside the church, may be particularly impacted by lukewarm church member giving trends (pp. 84, 120-122, 127, 130-134).

Globally, both word and deed needs continue unmet. Although endorsed by both government and church groups, Millennium Development 4, "To reduce by two-thirds the number of under-5 child deaths between 1990 and 2015," is behind schedule (Fig. 21, p. 123). The two maps by Mark Newman (p. 124) display an inverse relationship between Gross Domestic Product (Fig. 22) and Child Mortality (Fig. 23) in many countries. The global evangelization progress map (Fig. 24, p. 135), prepared by the Joshua Project, adds another dimension in its commonality with the Child Mortality map and its differences with the Gross Domestic Product map.

The Implications of the Wycliffe Model and the Southern Baptist Convention Case Study

The Wycliffe Bible Translators Model is a good example of an organization not only setting a goal, but also developing specific strategies and taking active steps to achieve that goal.

As discussed in *The State of Church Giving through 2004: Will We Will?* (SCG04) 16th Edition (2006), denominations may be as likely to "provide cathartic drama at a maintenance level" as to fulfill their potential to lead renewal through discipleship (pp. 107-110). The specific example considered was The United Methodist Church's Initiative on Children and Poverty that, the Bishops announced in 1997, demanded "Nothing less than the reshaping of The United Methodist Church…" By 2004, the Bishops announced the Initiative was "discontinued" but would still be an "emphasis" (SCG04, p. 110).

In *The State of Church Giving through 2007*, the Southern Baptist Convention (SBC)'s announcement of the need for 2,800 additional missionaries to engage the world's unreached people groups provides another case study. The SBC announced the need for those missionaries beginning in 2007. However, the SBC did not tell its members the specific dollar cost to field the new missionaries. Possible reasons for the lack of that dollar cost information are considered (p. 138). The result to date is that the denomination has received numerous qualified missionary applicants, but funding to support the missionaries has decreased. Consequently, some missionaries, at least one couple having sold their home and given away their pet, are on indefinite hold (p. 139).

The SBC may be fairly unique in having a clearly stated goal that is at a scale needed to address a particular global need. However, the presence of dynamics that may run counter to actually achieving the stated goal does not appear to be uncommon, judging by denominations' statements and the results.

The proposal in *The State of Church Giving through 2007* is that one or more wholesale billionaire philanthropists could offer to match 2009 SBC Lottie Moon Christmas Offering donations that exceed last year's offering total, in order to raise the needed funds (pp. 144-146). The Lottie Moon Christmas Offering funds the SBC mission effort in combination with denominational unified giving allocations.

The SBC has a choice as to whether to rise to the occasion in 2009 and take creative and bold action. The communion could not only achieve its stated goal, but also provide both inspiration and a model for other leaders who want to guide their churches into deeper discipleship.

Nineteenth Edition 2009

The State
of
Church Giving
through 2007

What Are Our Christian Billionaires Thinking — Or Are They?

John L. Ronsvalle

Sylvia Ronsvalle

empty tomb®, inc.
Champaign, Illinois

The State of Church Giving through 2007:
What Are Our Christian Billionaires Thinking —
Or Are They?
by John and Sylvia Ronsvalle
Published by empty tomb, inc.
First printing, September 2009

empty tomb, inc.
301 N. Fourth Street
P.O. Box 2404
Champaign, IL 61825-2404
Phone: (217) 356-9519
Fax: (217) 356-2344
www.emptytomb.org

ISBN 978-0-9679633-9-6
ISSN 1097-3192

CONTENTS

TABLES AND FIGURES

PREFACE _____

As noted on the following pages, the number of verses throughout the Bible that address the topic of money suggests that it is an important topic for the church. Therefore, the officials who document congregational and denominational giving provide a valuable service to the entire church. We are grateful for the faithful work of these individuals, who have compiled the data analyzed in this volume, and for their ministry of numbers.

The *Yearbook of American and Canadian Churches* is an essential resource for anyone interested in learning more about the church in the United States. Eileen W. Lindner, as editor, has sustained this series started in 1916. The church owes her a debt of gratitude for her twelve years of service. She is ably assisted by Marcel Welty and Tenny Thomas, who interact with many denominations to extend the historical data stream. The collegial working relationship we have with the *Yearbook* office is both a professional and personal pleasure.

The National Council of the Churches of Christ in the U.S.A. has provided a home for the *Yearbook* for many years. The General Secretary, Michael Kinnamon, is to be commended for his leadership in sustaining this valuable publication series.

This year we extend special thanks to Mark Newman, physics professor at the University of Michigan, and Dan Scribner of the Joshua Project, for permission to reprint the maps they have designed.

The writing of this publication occurs even while other activities of empty tomb, inc. are carried out. The team of individuals who have chosen to live out their Christian discipleship as staff of empty tomb have provided support, encouragement, and the necessary energy to sustain the local works even while challenging the church throughout the U.S. to consider the importance of giving to the mission of God. The support from these coworkers, coordinated by Shannon Cook while we were deep in the writing process, as well as from volunteers and financial supporters of empty tomb, inc.. is critical to this effort. For the production of the volume, we are very grateful for the work of Britta Miller. Jana Waite volunteered many hours. Mark and Rachel Smith, Nya Winfrey, Don and Linda Garrett, and Peter Helfrich also assisted in the production process.

As the months of work come to a close, and this edition in the series is completed, our prayer is that the information in this volume will inspire and challenge Christians so that God may receive glory through Jesus Christ and the church (Ephesians 3:20-21).

John L. Ronsvalle, Ph.D.
Sylvia Ronsvalle

Champaign, Illinois
September 2009

SUMMARY _____

Summary

The State of Church Giving through 2007 is the most recent report in an annual series that began with *The State of Church Giving through 1989.* These analyses consider denominational giving data for a set of denominations first analyzed in a study published in 1988. The present report reviews data for a composite set of denominations from 1968 to 2007 that includes 28 million full or confirmed members, and just over 100,000 of the estimated 350,000 religious congregations in the U.S.

The findings of the present church member giving analysis include the following.

- Per member giving for the composite set of denominations was analyzed for 1968 through 2007. As a portion of income, giving to Total Contributions and Congregational Finances increased, while Benevolences decreased from 2006 to 2007.

- Data for an additional 18 denominations was available for 2006-2007, allowing an analysis that included 44 Protestant communions for those two years. Giving as a portion of income in the expanded group followed the pattern of the composite set.

- An analysis of data for a subset of mainline Protestant denominations and a subset of evangelical Protestant denominations found giving higher in the evangelical Protestant denominations, but a steeper decline in giving patterns among the evangelicals over the 1968-2007 period. Evangelical denominations were increasing in membership during these years, but their members were giving a smaller contribution as a portion of income. In the mainline denominations, giving as a portion of income to Congregational Finances was higher in 2007 than in 1985; however, Benevolences and membership continued to decline in these denominations.

- A review of giving and membership patterns in 11 Protestant denominations from 1921 to 2007 found that per member giving as a portion of income began to decline in 1961, and membership began to decline as a percent of U.S. population in 1962. Giving as a percentage of income was lower in 2007 than in either 1921 or 1933.

- Data was analyzed using both linear and exponential regression. Both giving and membership data were reviewed for how past patterns may influence the future for various sets of denominational groups.

1

- A survey of 34 denominations' overseas missions income in 2003 through 2007 found that, for the group as a whole, denominations' overseas ministries income was 2¢ for every dollar donated to congregations in 2007. The cost per church member for addressing global needs, such as world evangelization and helping to stop, in Jesus' name, global child deaths, were calculated.

- If church members were to reach a congregation-wide average of 10% giving, an additional $161 billion dollars would be available to assist both local and global neighbors in need.

- Charitable giving data for the U.S. Bureau of Labor Statistics Consumer Expenditure Survey, 2007, was analyzed by age, income level, and region of residence. Three estimates for Total Giving by Living Individuals in 2005 were compared, the latest year for which the three sources had available data. The data in the analysis was obtained from the U.S. Bureau of Labor Statistics Consumer Expenditure Survey, the Internal Revenue Service Form 990 series, and the *Giving USA* publication, based on IRS charitable deduction information. The numbers differed by as much as 56%, totaling $61 billion.

- Chapter 8 explores the concept of "wholesale billionaire philanthropists" and "retail billionaire philanthropists." A model is presented for calculating the cost on a country-specific basis to address under-5 child deaths due to eight causes. A model and a case study explore two efforts to complete the task of global evangelization.

INTRODUCTION _____

A historical series of financial and membership data in the United States extends back to 1916. Church statesmen took a broad overview of organized religion as a major social institution. They collected and preserved the data through publications and archives.

This information tradition continues through the present. Individual congregations initially provide the data to the regional or national denominational office with which the congregation is affiliated. The denominational offices then compile the data. The *Yearbook of American and Canadian Churches* (*YACC*), of the National Council of the Churches of Christ in the U.S.A., requests the data from the national denominational offices, publishing it in annual *YACC* editions.

The data published by the *YACC*, in some cases combined with data obtained directly in conjunction with the present study from a denominational source (as noted in the series of tables in Appendix B), serves as the basis for the present report. The numbers on the following pages are not survey reports. Rather, they represent the actual dollar records included in reports submitted by pastors and lay congregational leaders to their own denominational offices.

By following the same data set of denominations over a period of years, trends can be seen among a broad group of church members. In addition, since the data set includes communions from across the theological spectrum, subsets of denominations within the larger grouping provide a basis for comparing patterns between communions with different perspectives.

In an ongoing fashion, efforts are made to use the latest information available. As a result, *The State of Church Giving through 2007* provides information available to date.

Definition of Terms. The analyses in this report use certain terms that are defined as follows.

Full or Confirmed Members are used in the present analysis because it is a relatively consistent category among the reporting denominations. Certain denominations also report a larger figure for Inclusive Membership, which may include, for example, children who have been baptized but are not yet eligible for confirmation in that denomination. In this report, when the term "per member" is used, it refers to Full or Confirmed Members, unless otherwise noted.

The terms "denomination" and "communion" are used interchangeably. Both refer to a group of church people who share a common identity defined by traditions and stated beliefs.

The phrase "historically Christian church" refers to that combination of believers with a historically acknowledged confession of the faith. The broad spectrum of communions represented in the National Church Leaders Response Form list indicates the breadth of this definition.[1]

Total Contributions Per Member refers to the average contribution in either dollars or as a percent of income which is donated to the denominations' affiliated congregations by Full or Confirmed Members in a given year.

Total Contributions combines the two subcategories of Congregational Finances and Benevolences. The definitions used in this report for these two subcategories are consistent with the standardized *YACC* data request questionnaire.

The first subcategory of Congregational Finances includes contributions directed to the internal operations of the individual congregation, including such items as the utility bills and salaries for the pastor and office staff, as well as Sunday school materials and capital programs.

The second subcategory is Benevolences. This category includes contributions for the congregation's external expenditures, beyond its own operations, for what might be termed the larger mission of the church. Benevolences includes international missions as well as national and local charities, through denominational channels as well as programs of nondenominational organizations to which the congregation contributes directly. Benevolences also includes support of denominational administration at all levels, as well as donations to denominational seminaries and schools.

As those familiar with congregational dynamics know, an individual generally donates an amount to the congregation which underwrites both Congregational Finances and Benevolences. During the budget preparation process, congregational leadership considers allocations to these categories. The budget may or may not be reviewed by all the congregation's members, depending on the communion's polity. However, the sum of the congregation's activities serves as a basis for members' decisions about whether to increase or decrease giving from one year to the next. Also, many congregations provide opportunities to designate directly to either Congregational Finances or Benevolences, through fundraising drives, capital campaigns, and special offerings. Therefore, the allocations between Congregational Finances and Benevolences can be seen to fairly represent the priorities of church members.

When the terms "income," "per capita income," and "giving as a percent of income" are used, they refer to the U.S. Per Capita Disposable (after-tax) Personal Income series from the U.S. Department of Commerce Bureau of Economic Analysis (BEA), unless otherwise noted.

The Implicit Price Deflator for Gross National Product was used to convert current dollars to 2000 dollars, thus factoring out inflation, unless otherwise specified.

Appendix C includes both U.S. Per Capita Disposable Personal Income figures and the Implicit Price Deflator for Gross National Product figures used in this study.

Analysis Factors. *Chained Dollars.* The analyses in *The State of Church Giving through 2007* are keyed to the U.S. BEA series of "chained (2000) dollars."

Income Series. The U.S. Department of Commerce Bureau of Economic Analysis has published the 12th comprehensive revision of the national income and product accounts, with the reference year being 2000. The U.S. Per Capita Disposable Personal Income series used in the present *The State of Church Giving through 2007* is drawn from this national accounts data.

Rate of Change Calculations, 1985-2007. The following methodology is used to calculate the rate of change between 1985 and the most recent calendar year for which data is available, in the present case, 2007.

The rate of change between 1968 and 1985 was calculated by subtracting the 1968 giving as a percent of income figure from the 1985 figure and then dividing the result by the 1968 figure.

The rate of change between 1985 and 2007 was calculated as follows. The 1968 giving as a percent of income figure was subtracted from the 2007 figure and divided by the 1968 figure, producing a 1968-2007 rate of change. Then, the 1968-1985 rate of change was subtracted from the 1968-2007 figure. The result is the 1985-2007 rate of change, which may then be compared to the 1968-1985 figure.

Rounding Calculations. In most cases, Total Contributions, Total Congregational Finances, and Total Benevolences for the denominations being considered were divided by Full or Confirmed Membership in order to obtain per capita, or per member, data for that set of denominations. This procedure occasionally led to a small rounding discrepancy in one of the three related figures. That is, by a small margin, rounded per capita Total Contributions did not equal per capita Congregational Finances plus per capita Benevolences. Similarly, rounding data to the nearest dollar for use in tables and graphics led on occasion to a small rounding error in the data presented in tabular or graphic form.

Giving as a Percent of Income. The most useful way to look at church member giving is in terms of giving as a percent of income. Considering what percent or portion of income is donated to the religious congregation provides a different perspective. Rather than indicating how much money the congregation has to spend, as when one considers dollars donated, giving as a percent of income indicates how the congregation rates in light of church members' total available incomes. Has the church sustained the same level of support from its members in comparison to previous years, as measured by what portion of income is being donated by members from the total resources available to them?

Percent of income is a valuable measure because incomes change. Just as inflation changes the value of the dollar so $5 in 1968 is not the same as $5 in 2007, incomes, influenced by inflation and real growth, also change. For example, per capita income in 1968 was $3,114 in current dollars; if a church member gave $311 that year, that member would have been tithing, or giving the standard of ten percent. In contrast, 2007 per capita income had increased to $33,706 in current dollars; and if that church member had still given $311, the member would have been giving less than 1% of income. The church would have commanded a smaller portion of the member's overall resources.

Thus, while dollars donated provide a limited picture of how much the church has to spend, giving as a percent of income provides both a measure of the church member's level of commitment to the church in comparison to other spending priorities, as well as a measure of whether the church's income is keeping up with inflation and growth in the economy. One might say that giving as a percent of income is an indication of the church's "market share" of church members' lives.

In most cases, to obtain giving as a percent of income, total income to a set of denominations was divided by the number of Full or Confirmed Members in the set. This yielded the per member giving amount in dollars. This per member giving amount was divided by per capita disposable personal income.

Giving in Dollars. Per member giving to churches can be measured in dollars. The dollar measure indicates, among other information, how much money religious institutions have to spend.

Current dollars indicate the value of the dollar in the year it was donated. However, since inflation changes the amount of goods or services that can be purchased with that dollar, data provided in current dollars has limited information value over a time span. If someone donated $5 in 1968 and $5 in 2007, on one level that person is donating the same amount of money. On another level, however, the buying power of that $5 has changed a great deal. Since less can be bought with the $5 donated in 2007 because of inflation in the economy, on a practical level the value of the donation has shrunk.

To account for the changes caused by inflation in the value of the dollar, a deflator can be applied. The result is inflation-adjusted 2000 dollars. Dollars adjusted to their chain-type, annual-weighted measure through the use of a deflator can be compared in terms of real growth over a time span since inflation has been factored out.

The deflator most commonly applied in this analysis designated the base period as 2000, with levels in 2000 set equal to 100. Thus, when adjusted by the deflator, the 1968 gift of $5 was worth $20.09 in inflation-adjusted 2000 dollars, and the 2007 gift of $5 was worth $4.17 in inflation-adjusted 2000 dollars.

Data Appendix and Revisions. Appendix B includes the aggregate denominational data used in the analyses in this study. In general, the data for the denominations included in these analyses appears as it was reported in editions of the *YACC*. In some cases, data for one or more years for a specific denomination was obtained directly from the denominational office. Also, the denominational giving data set has been refined and revised as additional information has become available. Where relevant, this information is noted in the appendix.

---

[1] John Ronsvalle and Sylvia Ronsvalle; "National Church Leaders Response Form"; *The State of Church Giving through 1998* (2000 edition); <http://www.emptytomb.org/survey1.html>.

chapter 1

Church Member Giving, 1968-2007

"So if you have not been trustworthy in handling worldly
wealth, who will trust you with true riches?"

— Jesus Christ, quoted in Luke 16:11 (NIV)

Church Giving as a Measurement Standard

Luke 16:11 introduces a noble-sounding sentiment by contrasting "worldly wealth" with "true riches."

On a practical level, does this religious theme have any implications for a study of church giving patterns?

In the context of Jesus' statement, it appears that money is important as a gauge of the church's heart condition. Money, rather than an end in itself, serves as a measurement of spiritual maturity, a testing mechanism to judge the readiness, on the part of the individual Christian and of the church as a whole, to move to a next level of service.

Patterns in church giving and church spending, then, are a vital means of measurement of whether the church is prepared to take on an increased level of responsibility, beyond maintenance, for "truly" important matters that reflect God's bigger priorities.

The perspective that "worldly wealth" is not the ultimate achievement in life is certainly not a standard view outside, or for that matter often inside, the church. Bigger incomes, whether individual, congregational, or denominational, are regarded as an important sign of success.

However, Jesus' statement in Luke 16:11 suggests another standard. From Jesus' perspective, apparently when we're handling "worldly wealth" we're actually trundling along on training wheels and not, as we picture ourselves, cruising along in something like the most expensive car in production, a Bugatti Veyron, having zoomed to 60 mph in 2.5 seconds.

If that's the case, an evaluation of how money given to the church ranks with members' other spending choices, and of how donations to the church are distributed, reveals more than whether the church can pay its bills. Church giving patterns reveal the development level of both church members and church structures.

In this chapter, as in chapters 2 through 5 and chapter 7, the discussion will focus on church members' use of "worldly wealth." In chapters 6 and, especially, chapter 8, the discussion will explore possible relationships between "worldly wealth" and "true riches."

Overview of Church Member Giving, 1968 through 2007

Giving Categories. When a dollar is given to the church, it is allocated into one of two major subcategories, as defined by the annual reporting form of the *Yearbook of American and Canadian Churches.*

The first subcategory is Congregational Finances. This subcategory refers to those expenditures that support the operations of the local congregation, such as building and utilities, pastor and staff salaries, insurance, music and Sunday school materials.

The second is Benevolences, which refers to expenditures for what might be termed the broader mission of the church, beyond the local congregation. Benevolences includes everything from support of regional and national denominational offices to the local soup kitchen, from seminaries to international ministries.

As suggested by Luke 16:11, how a church member allocates his or her resources is an important thermometer of the member's heart.

Total Contributions is the sum of Congregational Finances and Benevolences.

Giving as a Percentage of Income, 1968-2007. As suggested by Luke 16:11, how a church member allocates his or her resources is an important thermometer of the member's heart. What does the church member value most? Where is the church member placing emphasis, as evident in the allocation of resources? What is the church member achieving as a result of the money spent?

The level of giving to the church is, in this context, an important gauge. The measurement tool can be the number of dollars given, or the portion of income given. The percent of income given provides a more precise measure of what individual church members value.

Even factoring out inflation, few people had the same amount of income in 2007 as in 1968. This real growth in income is taken into account when the number of dollars given is placed in the context of the total amount of resources available to the donor. If income goes up faster than the amount of dollars given, in a very real sense giving has decreased in the donor's priorities, because the dollars given represent a smaller percent of the donor's total spending.

If the rate of increase in income slows, and yet church giving remains steady or even increases, then the percent of income given will increase, thus suggesting a sustained commitment to the church even in difficult economic times.

Considering giving as a percent of income provides insight not only into the amount given by church members, but also into the priority that the members are placing on those donations, compared to other categories that attract the church member's spending.

Figure 1 presents per member giving as a portion of income to the church among the members of the basic set of denominations in this analysis, referred to as the composite data set. As can be observed from this chart, giving as a portion of income declined in all three categories of Total Contributions, Congregational Finances, and Benevolences between 1968 and 2007. The overall decline in giving as a portion of income from 1968 to 2007 suggests that the church is commanding less of church members' attention compared to other spending priorities.

The portion of income contributed to the church, as represented in Total Contributions, decreased from 3.11% in 1968 to 2.56% in 2007, a decline of 18% from the 1968 base.

Overall, giving as a percent of income to Congregational Finances decreased from 2.45% in 1968 of income to 2.20%, a decline of 10%. Giving to Congregational Finances began to recover from a low point in 1992, and the trend continued through 2007.

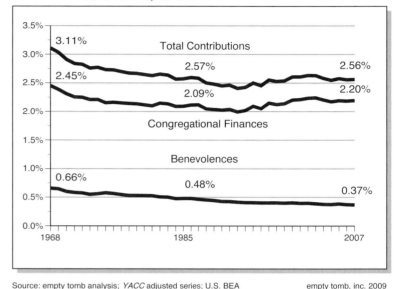

Figure 1: Per Member Giving as a Percent of Income to Total Contributions, Congregational Finances and Benevolences, 1968-2007

Source: empty tomb analysis; *YACC* adjusted series; U.S. BEA   empty tomb, inc. 2009

The portion of income directed to Benevolences demonstrated a fairly steady decline throughout the period. Beginning in 1968, the portion of income directed to Benevolences was 0.66%. By 2007, the level had declined to 0.37%, the lowest in the 1968-2007 period. This change represented a decrease of 44% in the portion of income directed to the category of Benevolences.

After declining three years in a row, 2002-2004, an increase in the portion of income to Benevolences occurred from 2004 to 2005.

The year 2005 included appeals for response to the December 26, 2004, Indian Ocean earthquake and tsunami, the devastation of Hurricanes Katrina, Rita and Wilma, and the major earthquake centered in Pakistan. The increase in Benevolences giving in 2005 appears to have been in response to the disasters, since the portion of income given to Benevolences in both 2006 and 2007 declined, rather than sustained the 2005 increase.

Implications of Giving in 2006 Compared to 2007. Giving as a percent of income increased from 2006 to 2007 to Total Contributions and Congregational Finances.

However, giving as a percent of income decreased to Benevolences from 2006 to 2007. Sometimes the change in the portion of income given can be very small from one year to the next. Yet, because there are so many members involved, even small changes are magnified. To explore the implications of these changes, consider the impact of the difference in the portion of income given to Benevolences between 2006 and 2007.

In 2006, per member giving to Benevolences as a portion of income measured 0.37%. In 2007, the amount decreased to the lowest point in the 1968 to 2007 period, but also measured 0.37% in numbers rounded to the second decimal.

The implications of this change, minuscule though it appears, can be understood when translated to dollars. To compare data for 2006 and 2007 more precisely, information from denominations that reported numbers for both years was considered. The unrounded difference between 2006 and 2007 Benevolences as a portion of income was -0.0042805% of per capita income. When multiplied by the 2007 current dollar U.S. per capita income figure of $33,706, that change translated into a decrease in 2007 of $1.44 given by each of the 28,520,026 members in these denominations. The combination of these individual dollar decreases meant that the composite communions had $41.1 million less to spend in 2007 on the larger mission of the church, compared to the 2006 level.

Consider that in chapter 6 of *The State of Church Giving through 2002*, it was estimated that $688.77 could save the life of one child under five who is dying from preventable causes somewhere around the globe. Taking the change in the amount of Benevolences income in 2007 as an example, the $41.1 million not given in 2007 as a result of the decrease in giving to Benevolences from 2006 to 2007, if applied to address child deaths through the denominations' already established programs, could have prevented the deaths of 59,742 children in 2007, representing a little more than the entire population of Bismarck, the capital of North Dakota.

The difference
between the
potential and the
actual amounts
given impacts the
ministry of the
church in very real
ways.

Potential Giving. Another approach is to consider what would have been the situation in 2007 if giving had at least maintained the 1968 percentages of income donated.

The implications of the difference become clearer when aggregate totals are calculated. The levels of giving as a percent of income in 1968 were multiplied by 2007 income. The resulting per member dollar figure was then multiplied by the number of members reported by these denominations in 2007. If the same portion of income had been donated in 2007 as in 1968, aggregate Total Contributions would have been $29.6 billion rather than the actual amount given of $24.6 billion, a difference of $5 billion, or an increase of 20%.

Aggregate Congregational Finances would have been $23.4 billion rather than $21.1 billion, a difference of $2.3 billion, or an increase of 11%.

There would have been a 76% increase in the total amount received for Benevolences. Instead of receiving $3.5 billion in 2007, as these church structures did, they would have received $6.2 billion, a difference of $2.7 billion available for the larger mission of the church.

The difference between the potential and the actual amounts given impacts the ministry of the church in very real ways.

Chapters 6 and 8 of this volume consider some of the implications and consequences of the difference between actual and potential giving levels among church members.

Giving in Dollars, 1968 through 2007. Per member giving measured in current dollars (the value the dollar had in the year it was given) increased every year. This increase was evident in giving to Total Contributions, and to the two subcategories of Congregational Finances and Benevolences.

Of course, dollars did not have the same purchasing power in both 1968 and 2007. To be able to compare dollars across different years, a deflator is used to factor out the effects of inflation. When inflation is factored out, the value that the dollars had in the same year the dollars were given ("current" dollar value) is converted to the value those adjusted dollars have in a standard year ("inflation-adjusted" dollar value).

The year 2000 serves as the standard year for the deflator series used in these analyses. Applying this deflator series, a gift of $5.00 in 1968 has the value, or purchasing power, of $20.09 in the year 2000, and a gift of $5.00 in the year 2007 has the value of $4.17 in the year 2000. By factoring out inflation, gifts in dollars can be compared across years in a more meaningful way.

Figure 2 presents the changes in inflation-adjusted dollar contributions to the three categories of Total Contributions, Congregational Finances, and Benevolences. As can be observed in Figure 2, giving to each of the categories of Total Contributions, Congregational Finances, and Benevolences declined in some years. For example, giving to Benevolences declined 11 out of 39 possible times, when measured in inflation-adjusted dollars.

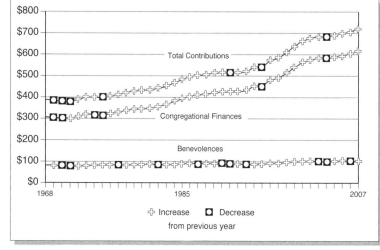

Figure 2: Changes in Per Member Giving in Inflation-Adjusted 2000 Dollars, Total Contributions, Congregational Finances, and Benevolences, 1968-2007

Source: empty tomb analysis; *YACC*, adjusted series; U.S. BEA   empty tomb, inc. 2009

Of the total inflation-adjusted dollar increase between 1968 and 2007, 94% was directed to Congregational Finances. Stated another way, of each additional inflation-adjusted dollar donated in 2007 compared to 1968, 94¢ was directed to Congregational Finances. This emphasis on the internal operations of the congregation helps explain the finding that Benevolences represented 21% of all church activity in 1968, and 14% in 2007.

From 1968 to 2007, per member giving to Total Contributions increased 85% in inflation-adjusted dollars. However, during this same period, U.S. Per Capita Disposable (after-tax) Personal Income increased 125%. The fact that incomes increased faster than giving explains why per member giving increased overall from 1968 through 2007 in dollars, but shrank as a portion of income.

Figure 3 provides a comparison of per member giving to the categories of Congregational Finances and Benevolences with changes in U.S. per capita DPI, both in inflation-adjusted 2000 dollars.

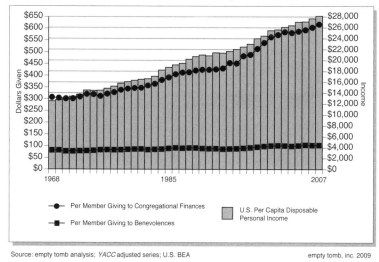

Figure 3: Per Member Giving to Congregational Finances and Benevolences, and U.S. Per Capita Disposable Personal Income, 1968-2007, Inflation-Adjusted 2000 Dollars

Source: empty tomb analysis; *YACC* adjusted series; U.S. BEA   empty tomb, inc. 2009

Details of Church Member Giving, 1968 through 2007

The Composite Denominations The first study that provided a basis for the present series was published in 1988. The *Yearbook of American and Canadian*

Churches (*YACC*) series publishes church member giving data. Data for the years 1968 and 1985 could be confirmed for 31 denominations.[1] The data year 1968 was selected because, beginning that year, a consistent distinction was made between Full or Confirmed Membership and Inclusive Membership in the *YACC* series. The denominations that published data for both 1968 and 1985 included 29,476,782 Full or Confirmed Members in 1985. The current composite denomination set comprises approximately 100,000 of the estimated 350,000 religious congregations in the U.S.

The present church member giving report series extended the analysis for the original set of denominations beyond 1985. The current report analyzes the data set through 2007, the most recent year for which data was available at the time the report was written.[2] Also, data for the intervening years of 1969 through 1984, and 1986 through 2006, was included in the composite data set, as available.[3]

Financial Categories. Calculating contributions on a per member basis accounts for any changes in membership, either through growth or decline, which might have taken place during the period under review. The dollars given can be considered from two points of view. The *number of dollars given* by members indicates how much money the church has to spend. On the other hand, *giving as a percentage of income* places donations in the larger context of the income available to church members, and demonstrates how the church fared compared to other church member spending priorities.

The key general category is giving as a percent of income. This category considers not only the dollars given, but also what portion those dollars represent of the resources available to the church member who gave them. One might say that considering giving as a percent of income reflects how the donation rated in the donor church member's overall lifestyle choices, a sort of thermometer to gauge the member's commitment. Therefore, since the point of interest is in what priority members place on their church giving, giving as a percent of income is the more useful category.

Giving as a percent of income is, of course, based on the dollars given, set in the context of dollars available as income. Within the category of dollars given, there are two approaches: (1) current dollars; and (2) inflation-adjusted dollars.

Current dollars refers to the value that the dollar had in the year it was donated. However, inflation affects the value of dollars. A dollar in 2007 bought fewer goods or services than it did in 1968. In order to account for this factor, a deflator is applied to the current dollar values, to translate the dollars into the value they have in a standard year, thereby neutralizing the economic impact of inflation.

Giving as a Percent of Income, 1968-2007. The first approach to considering giving is giving as a portion of income. Unlike dollars, there is no distinction between current or inflation-adjusted when one is considering giving as a percent of income. So long as one compares current dollar giving to current dollar income when calculating the percent of income—or inflation-adjusted giving to inflation-adjusted income—the percent will be the same.

In Table 1, giving as a percent of income is presented for per member Total Contributions, and the two subcategories of Congregational Finances and Benevolences. The arrows indicate whether the percent of income in that category increased or decreased from the previous year. Inasmuch as the percent figures are

...giving as a percentage of income places donations in the larger context of the income available to church members, and demonstrates how the church fared compared to other church member spending priorities.

rounded to the second decimal place, the arrows indicate the direction of a slight increase or decrease, including for those values in which the percent provided appears to be the same numerical figure as the previous year.

A review of Table 1 yields the following information.

Overall, per member giving as a percent of income to Total Contributions decreased from 3.11% in 1968 to 2.56% in 2007, a decline of 18% in the portion of income donated to the church. Giving as a percentage of income to Total Contributions decreased 25 times out of a possible 39 times, or 64% of the time.

The decline in giving as a percent of income to Total Contributions is in contrast to the increase to Total Contributions in both current and inflation-adjusted dollars between 1968 and 2007 (see Tables 2 and 3 below). Unlike measuring only the dollars given, considering giving as a percent of income takes into account changes in the resources available to the donor as well. U.S. per capita Disposable (after-tax) Personal Income (DPI) serves as an average income figure for the broad spectrum of church members included in the composite denominations data set.

U.S. per capita DPI was $3,114 in current dollars in 1968. When that figure was calculated in inflation-adjusted 2000 dollars, U.S. per capita DPI in 1968 was $12,510.

The current-dollar DPI figure for 2007 was $33,706. When inflation was factored out, 2007 U.S. per capita DPI was $28,132.

Thus, after-tax per capita income in inflation-adjusted dollars increased by $15,623, an increase of 125% from 1968 to 2007. Even though per member Total Contributions increased 85% in inflation-adjusted dollars

Table 1: Per Member Giving as a Percent of Income, 1968-2007

Year	Per Full or Confirmed Member Giving as a Percentage of Income					
	Total Contributions	↑↓	Congregational Finances	↑↓	Benevolences	↑↓
1968	3.11%	—	2.45%	—	0.66%	—
1969	3.03%	↓	2.39%	↓	0.65%	↓
1970	2.91%	↓	2.31%	↓	0.60%	↓
1971	2.84%	↓	2.26%	↓	0.58%	↓
1972	2.83%	↓	2.25%	↓	0.58%	↓
1973	2.76%	↓	2.21%	↓	0.55%	↓
1974	2.77%	↑	2.21%	↑	0.56%	↑
1975	2.73%	↓	2.15%	↓	0.58%	↑
1976	2.73%	↓	2.16%	↑	0.56%	↓
1977	2.70%	↓	2.15%	↓	0.55%	↓
1978	2.67%	↓	2.14%	↓	0.53%	↓
1979	2.67%	↓	2.14%	↓	0.53%	↑
1980	2.65%	↓	2.12%	↓	0.53%	↓
1981	2.63%	↓	2.10%	↓	0.53%	↓
1982	2.65%	↑	2.15%	↑	0.51%	↓
1983	2.64%	↓	2.14%	↓	0.50%	↓
1984	2.57%	↓	2.09%	↓	0.48%	↓
1985	2.57%	↑	2.09%	↑	0.48%	↑
1986	2.60%	↑	2.12%	↑	0.48%	↑
1987	2.58%	↓	2.12%	↑	0.46%	↓
1988	2.50%	↓	2.05%	↓	0.45%	↓
1989	2.48%	↓	2.04%	↓	0.44%	↓
1990	2.45%	↓	2.02%	↓	0.43%	↓
1991	2.46%	↑	2.04%	↑	0.43%	↓
1992	2.41%	↓	1.99%	↓	0.41%	↓
1993	2.42%	↑	2.02%	↑	0.41%	↓
1994	2.50%	↑	2.09%	↑	0.41%	↓
1995	2.45%	↓	2.05%	↓	0.40%	↓
1996	2.55%	↑	2.15%	↑	0.40%	↑
1997	2.53%	↓	2.12%	↓	0.40%	↑
1998	2.54%	↑	2.14%	↑	0.40%	↓
1999	2.61%	↑	2.20%	↑	0.40%	↑
2000	2.61%	↑	2.21%	↑	0.40%	↓
2001	2.63%	↑	2.24%	↑	0.40%	↑
2002	2.63%	↓	2.24%	↑	0.39%	↓
2003	2.58%	↓	2.20%	↓	0.38%	↓
2004	2.55%	↓	2.17%	↓	0.37%	↓
2005	2.58%	↑	2.19%	↑	0.38%	↑
2006	2.56%	↓	2.19%	↓	0.37%	↓
2007	2.56%	↑	2.20%	↑	0.37%	↓

Details in the above table may not compute to the numbers shown due to rounding.

from 1968 to 2007, income increased 125% during the same period. This difference explains how church member contributions could be increasing in inflation-adjusted dollars in most of the years from 1968 to 2007, and yet decreasing as a percent of income in most of the years from 1968 to 2007.

As a percent of income, giving to Congregational Finances, the amount spent to maintain the operations of the local congregation, decreased 22 times during the 39 two-year sets in the 1968-2007 period, or 56% of the time. Congregational Finances declined from 2.45% in 1968 to 2.20% in 2007, a percent change of -10% from the 1968 base in giving as a percent of income. It may be noted that giving as a percent of income to Congregational Finances declined in more than twice as many years than it increased between 1968 and 1992. In 1993, an intermittent increase in this category began, with giving as a percent of income to Congregational Finances increasing in twice as many years as it declined in 1993 through 2007. By 2007, Congregational Finances as a portion of income had recovered to the level given in the mid-1970s.

As a percent of income, giving to Benevolences, church members' investment in the larger mission of the church, declined from 0.66% of income in 1968 to 0.37% in 2007, a decline of 44% as a portion of income. Out of the 39 two-year sets in the 1968-2007 interval, the portion of income that went to Benevolences declined 29 times, or 74% of the time. The decline in giving as a percent of income to Benevolences was fairly steady in the 1968 to 2007 period, never increasing more than two years in a row. The level of giving as a percent of income to Benevolences in 2007 was at its lowest level in the 1968-2007 period.

> The level of giving as a percent of income to Benevolences in 2007 was at its lowest level in the 1968-2007 period.

An increase may be noted in giving to Benevolences as a percent of income in 2005. This increase appears to have been a function of the disaster response opportunities that year. The year 2005 included the Indian Ocean earthquake and related tsunami that occurred the day after Christmas in 2004, Hurricanes Katrina, Rita and Wilma, and the Pakistani earthquake, all presented as opportunities for compassionate response in churches. The decline in this category in 2006, and then reaching in 2007 the lowest point in giving as a percent of income to Benevolences in the 1968-2007 period, suggests that the 2005 giving was crisis-oriented, and did not represent a change in the pattern of long-term decline.

Giving in Current Dollars, 1968-2007. Table 2 presents per member contributions in current dollars for the composite denominations data set. Per member giving is presented as Total Contributions, and the two subcategories of Congregational Finances and Benevolences. U.S. per capita DPI is also included. The last column includes the Benevolences dollar figures divided by the DPI, yielding Benevolences as a percent of income, which are also presented in Table 1.

As can be seen in Table 2, the per member amount given to Total Contributions, Congregational Finances, and Benevolences increased in current dollars each year during the 1968-2007 period.

Overall, from 1968 to 2007, Total Contributions to the church in current dollars increased $767.01 on a per member basis. That amounted to an increase of 792% from the 1968 base.

Of this amount, $663.55 was allocated to Congregational Finances, for the benefit of members within the congregation, an increase of 869% for this category from its 1968 base.

Benevolences, or outreach activities of the congregation, increased by $103.46, an increase of 506% over the 1968 base level for the category.

Meanwhile, U.S. per capita DPI increased from $3,114 in 1968, to $33,706 in 2007, an increase of 982% from the 1968 base.

Therefore, even though Benevolences increased by 506% in current dollars, this subcategory shrank 44% as a portion of income because U.S. per capita DPI increased at a higher rate than did giving to Benevolences.

While a congregation or denomination might accurately state that members gave more dollars from one year to the next, the reality of inflation's impact should be taken into account, to understand the practical value of those dollars given.

Giving in Inflation-Adjusted Dollars, 1968-2007.

The U.S. Bureau of Economic Analysis (U.S. BEA) publishes the deflator series used to factor out inflation. These deflators allow dollar figures to be compared more precisely across years. The current year of base comparison in the U.S. BEA series is 2000. By applying the Implicit Price Deflator for Gross National Product to the current-dollar church member giving data, the data can be reviewed across years with the effects of inflation factored out.

Table 3 presents per member giving in inflation-adjusted dollars, as well as U.S. per capita DPI, also in inflation-adjusted dollars. The arrows next to the three inflation-adjusted giving category columns are included to provide a quick reference as to whether giving increased or decreased from one year to the next.

Table 2: Per Member Giving to Total Contributions, Congregational Finances, and Benevolences, U.S. Per Capita Disposable Personal Income, Current Dollars, and Per Member Giving to Benevolences as a Percent of Income, 1968-2007

| | Current Dollars | | | | |
| | Per Full or Confirmed Member Giving | | | U.S. Per Capita Disposable Personal Income | Per Member Giving to Benevolences as % of Income |
Year	Total Contrib.	Cong. Finances	Benevol.		
1968	$96.79	$76.35	$20.44	$3,114	0.66%
1969	$100.82	$79.34	$21.47	$3,324	0.65%
1970	$104.36	$82.87	$21.49	$3,587	0.60%
1971	$109.55	$87.08	$22.48	$3,860	0.58%
1972	$116.97	$93.16	$23.81	$4,140	0.58%
1973	$127.37	$102.01	$25.36	$4,616	0.55%
1974	$138.87	$110.79	$28.08	$5,010	0.56%
1975	$150.19	$118.45	$31.73	$5,498	0.58%
1976	$162.87	$129.15	$33.72	$5,972	0.56%
1977	$175.82	$140.23	$35.60	$6,517	0.55%
1978	$193.05	$154.74	$38.31	$7,224	0.53%
1979	$212.42	$170.17	$42.25	$7,967	0.53%
1980	$233.57	$186.90	$46.67	$8,822	0.53%
1981	$256.59	$205.15	$51.44	$9,765	0.53%
1982	$276.72	$223.93	$52.79	$10,426	0.51%
1983	$293.52	$237.68	$55.83	$11,131	0.50%
1984	$316.25	$257.63	$58.62	$12,319	0.48%
1985	$335.43	$272.95	$62.48	$13,037	0.48%
1986	$354.20	$288.73	$65.47	$13,649	0.48%
1987	$367.87	$301.73	$66.14	$14,241	0.46%
1988	$382.54	$313.15	$69.40	$15,297	0.45%
1989	$403.23	$331.06	$72.16	$16,257	0.44%
1990	$419.65	$346.48	$73.17	$17,131	0.43%
1991	$433.57	$358.67	$74.90	$17,609	0.43%
1992	$445.00	$368.28	$76.72	$18,494	0.41%
1993	$457.47	$380.54	$76.94	$18,872	0.41%
1994	$488.83	$409.35	$79.48	$19,555	0.41%
1995	$497.71	$416.00	$81.71	$20,287	0.40%
1996	$538.39	$453.34	$85.05	$21,091	0.40%
1997	$554.59	$466.07	$88.52	$21,940	0.40%
1998	$587.90	$495.56	$92.34	$23,161	0.40%
1999	$624.81	$527.99	$96.82	$23,968	0.40%
2000	$664.25	$563.52	$100.72	$25,473	0.40%
2001	$690.79	$586.58	$104.22	$26,243	0.40%
2002	$714.79	$609.46	$105.33	$27,183	0.39%
2003	$724.64	$618.85	$105.80	$28,076	0.38%
2004	$754.08	$643.18	$110.90	$29,592	0.37%
2005	$788.78	$671.11	$117.67	$30,611	0.38%
2006	$825.11	$704.99	$120.12	$32,263	0.37%
2007	$863.80	$739.90	$123.89	$33,706	0.37%

Details in the above table may not compute to the numbers shown due to rounding.

When the effects of inflation were removed, one may note that per member giving decreased in some years, unlike in the Table 2 current dollar columns. For example, although per member contributions to Total Contributions increased in the majority of years, the seven years of 1969, 1970, 1971, 1975, 1991, 1995, and 2003 posted declines from the previous year. Per member giving to Total Contributions did increase overall from 1968. However, when inflation was factored out, the percent increase was smaller than in current dollars. Per member giving to Total Contributions in inflation-adjusted dollars increased from $388.82 in 1968 to $720.95 in 2007, an increase of 85% from the 1968 base.

Congregational Finances also generally increased in inflation-adjusted 2000 dollars. Declines appear in six years: 1969, 1970, 1974, 1975, 1995, and 2003. Overall, per member giving to Congregational Finances increased from $306.72 in inflation-adjusted dollars to $617.55 in 2007, an increase of $310.83, or 101%.

Benevolences also increased in the majority of years when adjusted for inflation. Decreases occurred in 11 years in the 1968-2007 period, in the years 1970, 1971, 1977, 1982, 1987, 1990, 1991, 1993, 2002, 2003, and 2006. From 1968 to 2007, per member giving to Benevolences in inflation-adjusted dollars increased $21.31, an increase of 26% from the 1968 base.

U.S. per capita DPI, considered in inflation-adjusted dollars, increased from $12,510 in 1968, to $28,132 in 2007, an increase of 125%.

Per member giving as a percent of income to Benevolences is again included in Table 3. The figures for this category are the same in both Tables 2 and 3. Because the same deflator is applied to both the giving dollars and the income dollars, per member giving to Benevolences as a percent of income is proportionally the same, whether the information is considered as current or inflation-adjusted dollars. As long as current dollar giving is compared

Table 3: Per Member Giving to Total Contributions, Congregational Finances, and Benevolences, U.S. Per Capita Disposable Personal Income, Inflation-Adjusted 2000 Dollars, and Per Member Giving to Benevolences as a Percent of Income, 1968-2007

	Inflation-Adjusted 2000 Dollars							U.S. PerCapita Disposable Personal Income	Per Member Giving to Benevolences as % of Income
	Per Full or Confirmed Member Giving								
Year	Total Contrib.	↑↓	Cong. Finances	↑↓	Benevol.	↑↓			
1968	$388.82	—	$306.72	—	$82.10	—	$12,510	0.66%
1969	$385.87	↓	$303.68	↓	$82.19	↑	$12,722	0.65%
1970	$379.34	↓	$301.22	↓	$78.11	↓	$13,038	0.60%
1971	$379.22	↓	$301.41	↑	$77.81	↓	$13,361	0.58%
1972	$388.03	↑	$309.05	↑	$78.98	↑	$13,734	0.58%
1973	$400.14	↑	$320.47	↑	$79.67	↑	$14,502	0.55%
1974	$400.20	↑	$319.28	↓	$80.92	↑	$14,438	0.56%
1975	$395.48	↓	$311.91	↓	$83.56	↑	$14,478	0.58%
1976	$405.40	↑	$321.46	↑	$83.94	↑	$14,865	0.56%
1977	$411.47	↑	$328.16	↑	$83.31	↓	$15,251	0.55%
1978	$422.08	↑	$338.33	↑	$83.75	↑	$15,795	0.53%
1979	$428.89	↑	$343.58	↑	$85.31	↑	$16,086	0.53%
1980	$432.41	↑	$346.02	↑	$86.39	↑	$16,333	0.53%
1981	$434.20	↑	$347.16	↑	$87.05	↑	$16,524	0.53%
1982	$441.34	↑	$357.15	↑	$84.19	↓	$16,629	0.51%
1983	$450.29	↑	$364.63	↑	$85.65	↑	$17,076	0.50%
1984	$467.61	↑	$380.93	↑	$86.68	↑	$18,215	0.48%
1985	$481.28	↑	$391.63	↑	$89.65	↑	$18,706	0.48%
1986	$497.28	↑	$405.37	↑	$91.91	↑	$19,163	0.48%
1987	$502.68	↑	$412.31	↑	$90.38	↓	$19,460	0.46%
1988	$505.48	↑	$413.78	↑	$91.70	↑	$20,213	0.45%
1989	$513.34	↑	$421.48	↑	$91.87	↑	$20,697	0.44%
1990	$514.34	↑	$424.66	↑	$89.68	↓	$20,997	0.43%
1991	$513.47	↓	$424.76	↑	$88.71	↓	$20,854	0.43%
1992	$515.19	↑	$426.37	↑	$88.82	↑	$21,411	0.41%
1993	$517.61	↑	$430.56	↑	$87.05	↓	$21,353	0.41%
1994	$541.57	↑	$453.52	↑	$88.05	↑	$21,665	0.41%
1995	$540.32	↓	$451.61	↓	$88.70	↑	$22,024	0.40%
1996	$573.59	↑	$482.98	↑	$90.61	↑	$22,470	0.40%
1997	$581.21	↑	$488.44	↑	$92.77	↑	$22,993	0.40%
1998	$609.38	↑	$513.66	↑	$95.72	↑	$24,007	0.40%
1999	$638.41	↑	$539.48	↑	$98.93	↑	$24,490	0.40%
2000	$664.25	↑	$563.52	↑	$100.72	↑	$25,473	0.40%
2001	$674.63	↑	$572.85	↑	$101.78	↑	$25,629	0.40%
2002	$686.11	↑	$585.01	↑	$101.10	↓	$26,093	0.39%
2003	$681.08	↓	$581.64	↓	$99.44	↓	$26,388	0.38%
2004	$688.94	↑	$587.62	↑	$101.32	↑	$27,036	0.37%
2005	$697.84	↑	$593.74	↑	$104.10	↑	$27,082	0.38%
2006	$707.20	↑	$604.25	↑	$102.96	↓	$27,653	0.37%
2007	$720.95	↑	$617.55	↑	$103.41	↑	$28,132	0.37%

Details in the above table may not compute to the numbers shown due to rounding.

to current dollar income, or inflation-adjusted giving is compared to inflation-adjusted income, giving as a percent of income will be the same for both series.

One may observe the consequences of the fact that U.S. per capita DPI increased 125% from 1968 to 2007, while per member giving to Benevolences increased 26%. The result was the overall decline of 44% to Benevolences in the portion of income given, from the 1968 base.

Giving in Inflation-adjusted Dollars, 1968 and 2007. The first report, which served as the basis for the present series on church member giving, considered data for the denominations in the composite data set for the years 1968 and 1985. With data now available through 2007, a broader trend can be reviewed for the period under discussion, the 40-year range from 1968 through 2007.

The per member amount donated to Total Contributions in inflation-adjusted 2000 dollars was $332.13 greater in 2007 than it was in 1968 for the denominations in the composite data set. This amount represented an average increase of $8.52 a year in per member contributions over this 40-year period.

Gifts to Congregational Finances also increased between 1968 and 2007. Per member contributions to Congregational Finances were $306.72 in 1968, in inflation-adjusted 2000 dollars, and increased to $617.55 in 2007, a total increase of $310.83, with an average annual rate of change of $7.97.

In inflation-adjusted 2000 dollars, gifts to Benevolences were $82.10 in 1968 and grew to $103.41 in 2007, an increase of $21.31, with an annual average rate of change of $0.55.

Table 4: Total Contributions, Congregational Finances and Benevolences, Per Member Giving in Inflation-Adjusted 2000 Dollars, 1968 and 2007

	Per Member Giving in Inflation-Adjusted 2000 Dollars								
	Total Contributions			Congregational Finances			Benevolences		
Year	Per Member Giving	Difference from 1968 Base	Average Annual Diff. in $s Given	Per Member Giving	Difference from 1968 Base	Average Annual Diff. in $s Given	Per Member Giving	Difference from 1968 Base	Average Annual Diff. in $s Given
1968	$388.82			$306.72			$82.10		
2007	$720.95	$332.13	$8.52	$617.55	$310.83	$7.97	$103.41	$21.31	$0.55

Details in the above table may not compute to the numbers shown due to rounding

Table 4 presents per member gifts to Total Contributions, Congregational Finances, and Benevolences in inflation-adjusted 2000 dollars for the years 1968 and 2007.

Giving as a Percentage of Income, 1968 and 2007. Between 1968 and 2007, Total Contributions declined from 3.11% to 2.56% as a portion of income, an absolute decline of 0.55%, or one-half percent of income donated to the church. The percent change in the portion of income donated to the church in the 40-year period was -18%.

Per member gifts to Congregational Finances measured 2.45% of income in 1968, and 2.20% in 2007. The absolute change in giving as a percentage of income was –0.26%. The percent change in the portion of income to Congregational Finances, from the 1968 base, was -10%.

From 1968 to 2007, the portion of member income directed to Benevolences decreased from 0.66% to 0.37%, an absolute difference of –0.29%, a larger figure than the decline in Congregational Finances, even though Benevolences began from a

Table 5: Per Member Giving as a Percent of Income to Total Contributions, Congregational Finances, and Benevolences, 1968 and 2007

| Year | Per Member Giving as a Percentage of Income | | |
	Total Contributions	Congregational Finances	Benevolences
1968	3.11%	2.45%	0.66%
2007	2.56%	2.20%	0.37%
Absolute Difference in Per Member Giving as a Percent of Income from 1968 Base	-0.55%	-0.26%	-0.29%
Percent Change in Giving as a Percent of Income, Calculated from 1968 Base	-18%	-10%	-44%

Details in the above table may not compute to the numbers shown due to rounding

smaller base. The decline in the portion of income given to Benevolences translated to a percent change in giving as a percent of income of -44% from the 1968 base.

Table 5 presents per member giving to Total Contributions, Congregational Finances, and Benevolences as a percentage of income in 1968 and 2007.

Notes for Chapter 1

[1] John Ronsvalle and Sylvia Ronsvalle, *A Comparison of the Growth in Church Contributions with United States Per Capita Income* (Champaign, IL: empty tomb, inc., 1988).

[2] Two of the original 31 denominations merged in 1987, bringing the total number of denominations in the original data set to 30. As of 1991, one denomination reported that it no longer had the staff to collect national financial data, resulting in a maximum of 29 denominations from the original set, which could provide data for 1991 through 2007. Of these 29 denominations, one reported data for 1968 through 1997, but did not have financial data for 1998 through 2007, although dialogue continues. A second denomination merged with another communion not included in the original composite set but that has since been added; having merged, this new denomination has not collected financial data for 2001-2007 from its congregations, although it did do a survey of congregations for one year. Finally, one denomination indicated that the national office would no longer provide data after 2006 in order to focus on other priorities. Therefore, the composite data for 2007 includes information from 26 communions in the data set. Throughout this report, what was an original set of 31 denominations in 1985 will be referred to as the composite denominations. Data for 31 denominations will be included for 1968 and 1985, as well as for intervening years, as available.

[3] For 1986 through 2007, annual denominational data has been obtained which represented for any given year at least 98.78% (the 2005 and 2007 percentage) of the 1985 Full or Confirmed Membership of the denominations included in the 1968-1985 study. For 1986 through 2007, the number of denominations for which data was available varied from a low of 26 denominations of a possible 30 in 2005 and 2007 to a high of 29 in 1987 through 1997. For the years 1969 through 1984, the number of denominations varied from a low of 28 denominations of a possible 31 in 1971-1972 and 1974-1975 to 31 in 1983, representing at least 99.59% of the membership in the data set. The denominational giving data considered in this analysis was obtained either from the *Yearbook of American and Canadian Churches* series, or directly in correspondence with a denominational office. For a full listing of the data used in this analysis, including the sources, see Appendix B-1.

chapter 2

Church Member Giving for 44 Denominations, 2006-2007

Overview of Giving for 44 Denominations, 2006-2007

The composite denominations data set considered in chapter 1 was expanded to include eighteen additional denominations for which 2006 and 2007 data was also available.

In the composite set, from 2006 to 2007, giving as a portion of income increased to Total Contributions and Congregational Finances, and decreased to Benevolences.

When the data set was enlarged to a total of 44 denominations, from 2006 to 2007, giving as a portion of income also increased to Total Contributions and Congregational Finances, and decreased to Benevolences.

Although both the composite and the expanded data sets evidenced the same trends, the level of giving as a percentage of income was higher in the expanded set of communions than in the composite set.

Details of Giving for 44 Denominations, 2006-2007

The 1968-2007 analysis in chapter 1 considers data for a group of denominations that published their membership and financial information for 1968 and 1985 in the *YACC* series. That initial set of communions, considered in the first report on which the present series on church giving is based, has served as a denominational composite set analyzed for subsequent data years.

The goal of chapter 1 is to provide a comprehensive estimate of giving over the years from 1968 through the latest year with available data, for example 2007, in the composite set of denominations. Therefore, each year's data includes all the denominations that reported that year in the composite set. However, when the two most recent years are being compared, a more exacting measure is available and may be helpful. Therefore, in chapter 2, as in the 2006 to 2007 comparison in chapter 1, the comparison made will include only those denominations in the composite set that had comparable available data for both years.

Data for both 2006 and 2007 for an additional eighteen denominations was either published in the relevant editions of the *YACC* series, or obtained directly from denominational offices. By adding the data for these 18 denominations to that of the composite group for these two years, giving patterns in an expanded set of 44 communions can be considered.

In this enlarged comparison, the number of 2007 Full or Confirmed Members increased from 28.5 million in the composite set to 39,714,821 in the expanded set, a 39% increase in the number of members considered. The number of denominations increased from 26 to 44. The larger group of denominations included both The United Methodist Church and The Episcopal Church, which were not included in the original 1968-1985 analysis because of the unavailability of confirmed 1968 data at the time of that study. A list of the denominations included in the present analysis is contained in Appendix A.

Table 6 presents the data for the 44 denominations in tabular form, including per member giving in current and inflation-adjusted dollars, and giving as a percent of income.

Table 6: **Per Member Giving in 44 Denominations, 2006 and 2007, in Current, Inflation-Adjusted 2000 Dollars, and as a Percent of Income**

Year	Total Contributions			Congregational Finances			Benevolences		
	$s Given in Current $	$s Given in Inflation Adj. '00 $	Giving as % of Income	$s Given in Current $	$s Given in Inflation Adj. '00 $	Giving as % of Income	$s Given in Current $	$s Given in Inflation Adj. '00 $	Giving as % of Income
2006	$839.42	$719.47	2.60%	$708.49	$607.25	2.20%	$130.93	$112.22	0.41%
2007	$879.85	$734.35	2.61%	$744.72	$621.57	2.21%	$135.13	$112.78	0.40%
Difference from the 2006 Base	$40.43	$14.88	0.01%	$36.23	$14.32	0.01%	$4.20	$0.56	0.00%
% Change in Giving as % of Income from the 2006 Base			0.33%			0.61%			-1.21%

Details in the above table may not compute to the numbers shown due to rounding.

Per Member Giving as a Percent of Income.

In the composite denominations set, from 2006 to 2007, giving as a percent of income increased to Total Contributions and Congregational Finances, and decreased to Benevolences.

The percent given to Total Contributions increased from 2.55% in 2006 to 2.56% in 2007, a percent change of 0.3% in giving as a percent of income from the 2006 base.

Congregational Finances increased from 2.18% in 2006 to 2.20% in 2007, a percent change of 0.6% from the 2006 base.

Benevolences measured 0.37% in 2006 and also rounded to 0.37% in 2007. The percent change was -1.15% from the 2006 base.

In the expanded group of 44 denominations, giving as a percent of income followed the same pattern as the composite set.

In this expanded set, the percent of income given on a per member basis to Total Contributions measured 2.60% in 2006 and 2.61% in 2007, a percent change of 0.3% in giving as a percent of income from the 2006 base.

Congregational Finances was 2.20% in 2006 and increased to 2.21% in 2007, a change of 0.6% from the 2006 base.

Benevolences measured 0.41% in 2006 and 0.40% in 2007, resulting in a change of -1.21% from the 2006 base.

Summary. When the composite denominations set considered in chapter 1 of this volume was expanded to include 18 additional denominations, the number of church members in the giving analysis increased by 39%. The same patterns in giving as a percent of income were evident from 2006 to 2007 in both the composite denominations set and the expanded set of 44 denominations.

chapter 3

Church Member Giving in Denominations Defined by Organizational Affiliation, 1968, 1985, and 2007

Overview of Giving by Organizational Affiliation, 1968-2007

The communions included in the composite denominations data set considered in chapter 1 of this volume span the theological spectrum. Reviewing data for defined subsets within the composite group allows for additional analysis.

For example, the theory that evangelical Protestants donate more money to their churches than do members of mainline Protestant denominations can be tested by comparing giving patterns in two subgroups of communions within the composite denominations data set.

Of course, there is diversity of opinion within any denomination, as well as in multi-communion groupings. For purposes of the present analysis, however, two groups may serve as general standards for comparison, since they have been characterized as representing certain types of denominations. Specifically, the National Association of Evangelicals (NAE) has, by choice of its title, defined its denominational constituency. And traditionally, the National Council of the Churches of Christ in the U.S.A. (NCC) has counted mainline denominations among its members.

Recognizing that there are limitations in defining a denomination's theological perspectives merely by membership in one of these two organizations, a review of giving patterns of the two subsets of denominations may nevertheless provide some insight into how widely spread current giving patterns may be. Therefore, an analysis of 1968-2007 giving patterns was completed for the two subsets of those denominations that were affiliated with one of these two interdenominational organizations.

During the 1968-2007 period, members of evangelical Protestant denominations gave larger portions of income to their churches than did members of mainline Protestant denominations.

In spite of this fact, the 1968-2007 decline in giving as a portion of income to Total Contributions was greater among the members of the evangelical denominations

Figure 4: Per Member Giving as a Percent of Income to Total Contributions, Congregational Finances, and Benevolences, Eight NAE and Eight NCC Denominations, 1968, 1985, and 2007

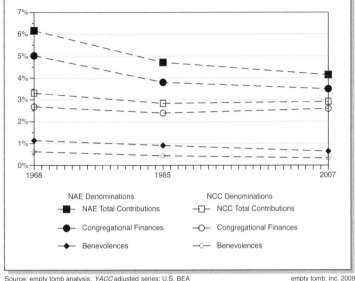

Source: empty tomb analysis; *YACC* adjusted series; U.S. BEA   empty tomb, inc. 2009

Figure 5: Per Member Giving to Total Contributions, Congregational Finances, and Benevolences, Eight NAE and Eight NCC Member Denominations, 1968, 1985, and 2007, Inflation-Adjusted 2000 Dollars

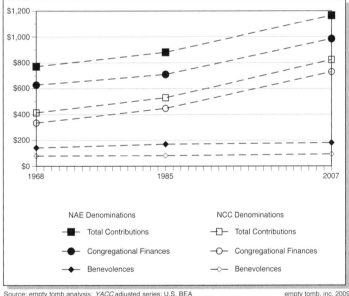

Source: empty tomb analysis; *YACC* adjusted series; U.S. BEA   empty tomb, inc. 2009

than it was among the members of the mainline denominations.

While giving as a portion of income to Congregational Finances declined among the NAE-affiliated denominations from 1968 to 1985, and again to 2007, the direction of change reversed in the NCC-affiliated denominations, increasing from 1985 to 2007.

Per member giving as a portion of income to Benevolences declined in both the evangelical and the mainline communions from 1968 to 1985, and again to 2007.

Figure 4 presents data for giving as a percent of income to Total Contributions, Congregational Finances, and Benevolences for both the NAE- and NCC-affiliated denominations in graphic form for the years 1968, 1985, and 2007.

In contrast to giving as a portion of income, per member giving in both current and inflation-adjusted dollars increased in both sets of denominations. Figure 5 presents the data for per member contributions in inflation-adjusted 2000 dollars in graphic form for the years 1968, 1985, and 2007 for both the NAE-affiliated denominations and the NCC-affiliated denominations.

Changes in membership were considered in combination with the giving patterns.

Membership in the evangelical denominations grew between 1968 and 2007, in contrast to the mainline denominations, which decreased in membership. Therefore, although evangelicals were receiving a smaller portion of income per member in 2007 than in 1968, aggregate donations in inflation-adjusted dollars were higher in 2007 than in 1968 for this group.

Among the mainline denominations, membership decreased from 1968 to 2007. This fact, in combination with the increase in inflation-adjusted dollars being directed to Congregational Finances, may account for the finding that aggregate Benevolences donations in inflation-adjusted dollars were 26% smaller in 2007 than in 1968 for these communions.

Details of Giving by Organizational Affiliation, 1968-2007

In the composite group, membership and financial data is available for 1968, 1985, and 2007 for eight communions affiliated with the National Association of Evangelicals (NAE).

Eight communions affiliated with the National Council of the Churches of Christ in the U.S.A. (NCC) also had membership and financial data available for 1968, 1985, and 2007.

Using 1985 data as the reference point, the eight denominations affiliated with the NAE in the present analysis represented 18% of the total number of NAE-member denominations listed in the *Yearbook of American and Canadian Churches* (*YACC*) series. These eight denominations represented 21% of the total number of NAE-member denominations with membership data listed in the *YACC*, and approximately 21% of the total membership of the NAE-member denominations that provided membership data in the *YACC*.[1]

Data for 2007 was also available for eight NCC-member denominations. In 1985, these eight denominations represented 27% of the total number of NCC constituent bodies listed in the *YACC*; 30% of the NCC constituent bodies with membership data listed in the *YACC*; and approximately 29% of the total membership of the NCC constituent bodies with membership data listed in the *YACC*.[2]

Per Member Giving to Total Contributions, 1968, 1985, and 2007.

As noted in Table 7, per member giving as a percent of income to Total Contributions for a composite of those eight NAE-member denominations was 6.16% in 1968. That year, per member giving as a percent of income to Total Contributions was 3.31% for a composite of these eight NCC-member denominations.

In 1985, the NAE denominations' per member giving as a percent of income level was 4.71%, while the NCC level was 2.83%.

Table 7: Per Member Giving as a Percent of Income to Total Contributions, Eight NAE and Eight NCC Denominations, 1968, 1985, and 2007

					Total Contributions					
	NAE Denominations					NCC Denominations				
Year	Number of Denom. Analyzed	Total Contrib. Per Member as % of Income	Diff. in Total Contrib. as % of Income from Previous Base	Change in Total Contrib. as % of Income Figured from Previous	Avg. Annual Percent Change in Total Contrib. as % of Income	Number of Denom. Analyzed	Total Contrib. Per Member as % of Income	Diff. in Total Contrib. as % of Income from Previous Base	Change in Total Contrib. as % of Income Figured from Previous	Avg. Annual Percent Change in Total Contrib. as % of Income
1968	8	6.16%				8	3.31%			
1985	8	4.71%	-1.46%	-23.63% from '68	-1.39%	8	2.83%	-0.48%	-14.51% from '68	-0.85%
2007	8	4.14%	-0.57%	-9.20% from '85	-0.42%	8	2.92%	0.10%	2.91% from '85	0.13%

Details in the above table may not compute to the numbers shown due to rounding.

The data shows the NAE-member denominations received a larger portion of their members' incomes than did NCC-affiliated denominations in both 1968 and 1985. This information supports the assumption that denominations identifying with an evangelical perspective received a higher level of support than denominations that may be termed mainline.

The analysis also indicates that the decline in levels of giving observed in the larger composite denominations set was evident among both the NAE-member denominations and the NCC-member denominations. While giving levels decreased for both sets of denominations between 1968 and 1985, the decrease in Total Contributions was more pronounced in the NAE-affiliated communions. The percent change in the percent of income donated in the NAE-member denominations, in comparison to the 1968 base, was -24% between 1968 and 1985, while the percent change in percent of income given to the NCC-member denominations was -15%.

A decline in giving as a percent of income continued among the eight NAE-member denominations during the 1985-2007 period. By 2007, per member giving as a percent of income to Total Contributions had declined from the 1985 level of 4.71% to 4.14%, a percentage change of -9% in the portion of members' incomes donated over that 22-year period.

In contrast, the eight NCC-affiliated denominations increased in giving as a percent of income to Total Contributions during 1985-2007, from the 1985 level of 2.83% to 2.92% in 2007, a percentage increase of 3% in the portion of income given to these churches.

Because of the decline in the portion of income given in the NAE-affiliated denominations and the increase among the NCC-affiliated denominations, in 2007 the difference in per member giving as a percent of income between the NAE-affiliated denominations and the NCC-affiliated denominations was not as large as it had been in 1968. Comparing the two rates in giving as a percent of income to Total Contributions between the NAE-member denominations and the NCC-member denominations in this analysis, the NCC-affiliated denominations received 54% as much of per member income as the NAE-member denominations did in 1968, 60% as much in 1985, and 71% in 2007.

For the NAE-affiliated denominations, during the 1985 to 2007 period, the rate of decrease in the average annual percent change in per member giving as a percent of income to Total Contributions slowed in comparison to the 1968-1985 annual percent change from the 1968 base. The 1968-1985 average annual percent change was -1.39%. The annual rate of change for 1985-2007 was -0.42%.

In the NCC-member denominations, the trend reversed. While the average annual percent change from the 1968 base in giving as a percent of income was -0.85% between 1968 and 1985, the average annual change from 1985 was an increase of 0.13% between 1985 and 2007.

Per Member Giving to Congregational Finances and Benevolences, 1968, 1985, and 2007. Were there any markedly different patterns between the two subsets of denominations defined by affiliation with the NAE and the NCC in regards to the distribution of Total Contributions between the subcategories of Congregational Finances and Benevolences?

While giving levels decreased for both sets of denominations between 1968 and 1985, the decrease in Total Contributions was more pronounced in the NAE-affiliated communions.

Table 8: Per Member Giving as a Percent of Income to Congregational Finances, Eight NAE and Eight NCC Denominations, 1968, 1985, and 2007

| | Congregational Finances | | | | | | | | | |
| | NAE Denominations | | | | | NCC Denominations | | | | |
Year	Number of Denom. Analyzed	Cong. Finances Per Member as % of Income	Diff. in Cong. Finances as % of Income from Previous Base	Change in Cong. Finances as % of Income Figured from Previous	Avg. Annual Percent Change in Cong. Finances as % of Income	Number of Denom. Analyzed	Cong. Finances Per Member as % of Income	Diff. in Cong. Finances as % of Income from Previous Base	Change in Cong. Finances as % of Income Figured from Previous	Avg. Annual Percent Change in Cong. Finances as % of Income
1968	8	5.02%				8	2.68%			
1985	8	3.80%	-1.22%	-24.40% from '68	-1.44%	8	2.39%	-0.29%	-10.87% from '68	-0.64%
2007	8	3.50%	-0.30%	-5.94% from '85	-0.27%	8	2.59%	0.20%	7.62% from '85	0.35%

Details in the above table may not compute to the numbers shown due to rounding.

Table 9: Per Member Giving as a Percent of Income to Benevolences, Eight NAE and Eight NCC Denominations, 1968, 1985, and 2007

| | Benevolences | | | | | | | | | |
| | NAE Denominations | | | | | NCC Denominations | | | | |
Year	Number of Denom. Analyzed	Benevol. Per Member as % of Income	Diff. in Benevol. as % of Income from Previous Base	Change in Benevol. as % of Income Figured from Previous	Avg. Annual Percent Change in Benevol. as % of Income	Number of Denom. Analyzed	Benevol. Per Member as % of Income	Diff. in Benevol. as % of Income from Previous Base	Change in Benevol. as % of Income Figured from Previous	Avg. Annual Percent Change in Benevol. as % of Income
1968	8	1.14%				8	0.63%			
1985	8	0.91%	-0.23%	-20.23% from '68	-1.19%	8	0.44%	-0.19%	-30.00% from '68	-1.76%
2007	8	0.64%	-0.27%	-23.48% from '85	-1.07%	8	0.33%	-0.11%	-17.16% from '85	-0.78%

Details in the above table may not compute to the numbers shown due to rounding.

In the subcategory of Congregational Finances, a difference was observable. The NCC-related denominations posted a decrease from 1968 to 1985, but an increase in 2007 from the 1985 level in the portion of income directed to this category. In the NAE-related denominations, the portion of income declined from 1968 to 1985, and again to 2007. Table 8 presents the Congregational Finances giving data for the NAE and NCC denominations in 1968, 1985, and 2007.

In the subcategory of Benevolences, both groups posted declines in the portion of income directed to that category. Table 9 presents the Benevolences giving data for the NAE and NCC denominations in 1968, 1985, and 2007.

In 1968, the NAE-affiliated members were giving 6.16% of their incomes to their churches. Of that, 5.02% went to Congregational Finances, while 1.14% went to Benevolences. In 1985, of the 4.71% of income donated to Total Contributions, 3.80% was directed to Congregational Finances. This represented a percent change in the portion of income going to Congregational Finances of -24% from the 1968 base. Per member contributions to Benevolences among these NAE-member denominations declined from 1.14% in 1968 to 0.91% in 1985, representing a percent change of -20% from the 1968 base in the portion of income donated to Benevolences.

In 2007, the 4.14% of income donated by the NAE-member denominations to their churches was divided between Congregational Finances and Benevolences at the 3.50% and 0.64% levels, respectively. The percent change between 1985 and 2007 in contributions to Congregational Finances as a percent of income was a decline of -6%. In contrast, the percent change in contributions to Benevolences as a percent of income was a decline of -23% in the same 22-year period. However, the annual rate in the percent change in giving as a percent of income to Benevolences slowed, from -1.19% from 1968 to 1985 to –1.07% from 1985 to 2007.

In 1968, the NCC-member denominations were giving 3.31% of their incomes to their churches. Of that, 2.68% went to Congregational Finances. In 1985, of the 2.83% of income donated to these communions, 2.39% went to Congregational Finances. This represented a percent change from the 1968 base in the portion of income going to Congregational Finances of -11%. In contrast, per member contributions as a percent of income to Benevolences among these same NCC-affiliated denominations had declined from 0.63% in 1968 to 0.44% in 1985, representing a percent change of -30% from the 1968 base in the portion of income donated to Benevolences.

In 2007, the 2.92% of income donated by the NCC-affiliated members to their churches was divided between Congregational Finances and Benevolences at the 2.59% and 0.33% levels, respectively. The 1985-2007 increase in per member Total Contributions as a percent of income was directed to Congregational Finances, which increased from 2.39% in 1985 to 2.59% in 2007. The 2007 percent change in contributions to Congregational Finances as a percent of income from 1985 was an increase of 8%.

The portion of income directed to Benevolences by these NCC-member denominations declined from 1968 to 1985, and continued to decline from 1985 to 2007. The percent change in contributions to Benevolences as a percent of income declined from 0.44% in 1985 to the 2007 level of 0.33%, a decline of 17% in this 22-year period. The annual percent change from the 1985 base in giving as a percent of income to Benevolences indicated a lower rate of decline at –0.78% between 1985 and 2007, compared to the 1968-1985 annual rate of –1.76%.

Changes in Per Member Giving, 1968 to 2007. For the NAE-affiliated denominations, per member giving as a percent of income to Congregational Finances declined from 5.02% in 1968 to 3.50% in 2007, a change of -30% from the 1968 base. In Benevolences, the -44% change reflected a decline from 1.14% in 1968 to 0.64% in 2007.

For the NCC-affiliated denominations, in the subcategory of Congregational Finances, per member giving as a percent of income was 2.68% in 1968, and 2.59% in 2007, a decline of 3%. In the subcategory of Benevolences, the level of giving decreased from 0.63% in 1968 to 0.33% in 2007, a 47% decline in the portion of income donated to this subcategory.

Table 10 presents the 1968-2007 percent change in per member giving as a percent of income to Total Contributions, Congregational Finances and Benevolences in both the NAE- and NCC-affiliated communions.

The portion of income directed to Benevolences by these NCC-member denominations declined from 1968 to 1985, and continued to decline from 1985 to 2007.

Table 10: Percent Change in Per Member Giving as a Percent of Income, Eight NAE and Eight NCC Denominations, 1968 to 2007

Year	NAE Denominations				NCC Denominations			
	Number of Denom. Analyzed	Total Contrib.	Cong. Finances	Benevol.	Number of Denom. Analyzed	Total Contrib.	Cong. Finances	Benevol.
1968	8	6.16%	5.02%	1.14%	8	3.31%	2.68%	0.63%
2007	8	4.14%	3.50%	0.64%	8	2.92%	2.59%	0.33%
% Chg. 1968-'07	8	-33%	-30%	-44%	8	-12%	-3%	-47%

Details in the above table may not compute to the numbers shown due to rounding.

Per Member Giving in Inflation-Adjusted 2000 Dollars. The NAE-affiliated group's level of per member support to Total Contributions in inflation-adjusted 2000 dollars was $771.00 in 1968. This increased to $880.52 in 1985, and by 2007 increased to $1,164.77.

For the NAE-affiliated denominations, per member contributions in inflation-adjusted 2000 dollars to the subcategory of Congregational Finances increased from 1968 to 1985, and again from 1985 to 2007. Per member contributions in inflation-adjusted 2000 dollars to Benevolences increased between 1968 and 1985, and, again between 1985 and 2007. Of the increased per member giving in inflation-adjusted dollars between 1968 and 2007, 90% went to Congregational Finances.

The NCC-affiliated group also experienced an increase in inflation-adjusted per member Total Contributions between 1968 and 2007. The 1968 NCC level of per member support in inflation-adjusted 2000 dollars was $413.69. In 1985, this had increased to $528.87, and in 2007 the figure was $822.44.

The NCC-member denominations experienced an increase in inflation-adjusted per member donations to Congregational Finances in both 1985 and 2007 as well. Although 96% of the increase between 1968 and 2007 was directed to Congregational Finances, gifts to Benevolences also increased in inflation-adjusted 2000 dollars between 1968 and 1985, and again between 1985 and 2007.

As a portion of Total Contributions, the NAE-member denominations directed 19% of their per member gifts to Benevolences in 1968, 19% in 1985, and 16% in 2007. The NCC-member denominations directed 19% of their per member gifts to Benevolences in 1968, 16% in 1985, and 11% in 2007.

Table 11 presents the levels of per member giving to Total Contributions, Congregational Finances and Benevolences, in inflation-adjusted 2000 dollars, and

Table 11: Per Member Giving, Eight NAE and Eight NCC Denominations, 1968, 1985, and 2007, Inflation-Adjusted 2000 Dollars

Year	NAE Denominations					NCC Denominations				
	Number of Denom. Analyzed	Total Contrib.	Cong. Finances	Benevol.	Benevol. as % of Total Contrib.	Number of Denom. Analyzed	Total Contrib.	Cong. Finances	Benevol.	Benevol. as % of Total Contrib.
1968	8	$771.00	$627.96	$143.04	19%	8	$413.69	$334.99	$78.69	19%
1985	8	$880.52	$709.91	$170.61	19%	8	$528.87	$446.49	$82.38	16%
2007	8	$1,164.77	$983.71	$181.07	16%	8	$822.44	$728.92	$93.52	11%
$ Diff. '68-'07		$393.77	$355.75	$38.03			$408.75	$393.92	$14.83	
% Chg. '68-'07		51%	57%	27%			99%	118%	19%	

Details in the above table may not compute to the numbers shown due to rounding.

the percentage of Total Contributions that went to Benevolences in 1968, 1985, and 2007, for both sets of denominations. In addition, the percent change from 1968 to 2007, from the 1968 base, in per member inflation-adjusted 2000 dollar contributions is noted.

Aggregate Dollar Donations, 1968 and 2007. The NCC-member denominations and the NAE-member denominations differed in terms of changes in membership. The impact of this difference was evident at the aggregate dollar level.

Table 12 considers aggregate giving data for the eight NAE-member denominations included in this analysis. Membership in these eight NAE-member denominations increased 58% from 1968-2007.

Table 12: Aggregate Giving, Eight NAE Denominations, 1968 and 2007, in Current and Inflation-Adjusted 2000 Dollars

Year	Number of Den. Analyzed	Member-ship	Current Dollars			Inflation-Adjusted 2000 Dollars		
			Total Contributions	Cong. Finances	Benevol.	Total Contributions	Cong. Finances	Benevol.
1968	8	535,865	$102,845,802	$83,765,677	$19,080,125	$413,151,496	$336,502,941	$76,648,556
2007	8	844,688	$1,178,804,897	$995,557,696	$183,247,201	$983,870,613	$830,926,273	$152,944,339
% Chg.		58%	1046%	1089%	860%	138%	147%	100%

Details in the above table may not compute to the numbers shown due to rounding.

As measured in current aggregate dollars, giving in each of the three categories of Total Contributions, Congregational Finances, and Benevolences was greater in 2007 than in 1968 for the NAE-member denominations. This was true even though per member giving as a portion of income declined to all three categories during this period.

The same can be said for the three aggregate categories when inflation was factored out by converting the current dollars to inflation-adjusted 2000 dollars. These denominations have been compensated for a decline in giving as a percent of income to all three categories by the increase in total membership. As long as these denominations continue to grow in membership, their national and regional programs may not be affected in the immediate future by the decline in the portion of income donated.

Table 13 below considers aggregate data for the eight NCC-member denominations. The NCC-related denominations experienced a membership decline of 38% between 1968 and 2007. The increase in current dollar donations was

Table 13: Aggregate Giving, Eight NCC Denominations, 1968 and 2007, in Current and Inflation-Adjusted 2000 Dollars

Year	Number of Den. Analyzed	Member-ship	Current Dollars			Inflation-Adjusted 2000 Dollars		
			Total Contributions	Cong. Finances	Benevol.	Total Contributions	Cong. Finances	Benevol.
1968	8	12,876,821	$1,326,045,714	$1,073,798,710	$252,247,004	$5,326,982,340	$4,313,657,293	$1,013,325,047
2007	8	7,986,865	$7,870,160,625	$6,975,219,163	$894,941,462	$6,568,703,417	$5,821,754,871	$746,948,546
% Chg.		-38%	494%	550%	255%	23%	35%	-26%

Details in the above table may not compute to the numbers shown due to rounding.

sufficient to result in an increase in aggregate current dollars in each of the three categories of Total Contributions, Congregational Finances and Benevolences.

However, the inflation-adjusted 2000 dollar figures account for the acknowledged financial difficulties in many of these communions, particularly in the category of Benevolences. The impact of the decline in membership was evident at the aggregate dollar level. The increase in giving to Congregational Finances as a portion of income noted above was tempered by a loss of members. Between 1968 and 2007, while the NCC-related communions experienced an increase of 99% in per member giving to Total Contributions in inflation-adjusted 2000 dollars—from $413.69 in 1968 to $822.44 in 2007—aggregate Total Contributions in 2007 to these eight denominations measured only 23% larger in inflation-adjusted 2000 dollars in 2007 than in 1968.

Further, Congregational Finances absorbed all of the increased giving at the aggregate level. The 26% decline in aggregate Benevolences receipts in inflation-adjusted 2000 dollars between 1968 and 2007 provides insight into the basis for any cutbacks at the denominational level.

Notes for Chapter 3

[1] The 1985 total church membership estimate of 3,388,414 represented by NAE denominations includes *YACC* 1985 membership data for each denomination where available or, if 1985 membership data was not available, membership data for the most recent year prior to 1985. Full or Confirmed membership data was used except in those instances where this figure was not available, in which case Inclusive Membership was used.

[2] The 1985 total church membership estimate of 39,621,950 represented by NCC denominations includes *YACC* 1985 membership data for each denomination where available or, if 1985 membership data was not available, membership data for the most recent year prior to 1985. Full or Confirmed membership data was used except in those instances where this figure was not available, in which case Inclusive Membership was used.

chapter 4

Church Member Giving and Membership in 11 Denominations, 1921-2007

Overview of Giving and Membership, 1921-2007

A continuing feature in this ongoing series on church member giving is an analysis of available giving data throughout this century. Because of the fixed nature of the data source, the analysis remains fairly static. However, the data can now be updated to include information through 2007. This data makes use of the U.S. Bureau of Economic Analysis (BEA) per capita Disposable (after-tax) Personal Income (DPI) series, with the benchmark year being 2000 to adjust current dollars for inflation.

For the period 1921 through 2007, the preferable approach would be to analyze the entire composite denominations data set considered in chapter 1 of this volume. Unfortunately, comparable data since 1921 is not readily available for these communions. However, data over an extended period of time is available in the *Yearbook of American and Canadian Churches* series for a group of 11 Protestant communions, or their historical antecedents. This set includes ten mainline Protestant communions and the Southern Baptist Convention.

The available data has been reported fairly consistently over the time span of 1921 to 2007.[1] The value of the multiyear comparison is that it provides a historical time line over which to observe giving patterns.

A review of per member giving as a portion of income during the 1921 through 2007 period found that the portion of income given was above three percent during two multiyear periods. From 1922 through 1933 and then again from 1958 through 1962, per member giving as a percent of income was at or above 3%. This relatively high level of giving is particularly interesting because per capita DPI was also increasing from 1922-1927 (with the exception of 1925) and from 1959 through 1962. However, unlike after 1933, when the country was experiencing the Great Depression followed by World War II, no major national catastrophes explain the drop below 3% after 1962.

Per member giving as a percent of income was at a low point during World War II, recovered during the 1950s, and then declined fairly steadily during the 1960s. The decline in giving as a percent of income that began after the peak in 1960 continued with little interruption until 1980. Giving as a portion of income then hit a low point of 2.30% in 1992, a level that had not occurred since 1948. An intermittent upward trend in giving was visible beginning in 1993. By 2007, the level of giving as a percent of income was at 2.50%, lower than 1999 through 2002. However, the 2007 level was higher than any year from 1971 through 1998, and measured the same as 2003 and 2005.

Figure 6: Per Member Giving as a Percent of Income in 11 Denominations, and U.S. Per Capita DPI, 1921-2007

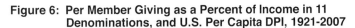

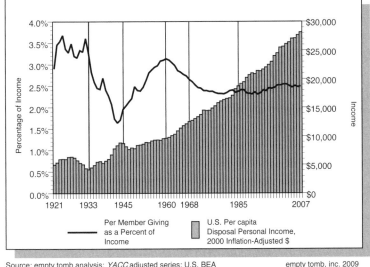

Figure 7: Per Member Giving as a Percent of DPI and Membership as a Percent of U.S. Population, 11 Denominations, 1921-2007

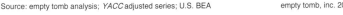

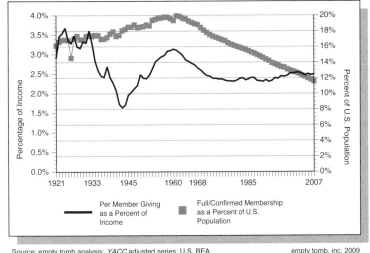

Figure 6 contrasts per member giving as a percentage of income for a group of eleven Protestant denominations, with U.S. per capita DPI in inflation-adjusted 2000 dollars, for the period 1921 through 2007.

By 2007, U.S. per capita DPI had increased 466% since 1921 in inflation-adjusted 2000 dollars, and 582% since 1933—the depth of the Great Depression.

Meanwhile, by 2007, per member giving in inflation-adjusted 2000 dollars had increased 387% since 1921, and 421% since the depth of the Great Depression.

Consequently, per member giving as a percentage of income was lower in 2007 than in either 1921 or 1933. In 1921, per member giving as a percentage of income was 2.9%. In 1933, it was 3.3%. In 2007, per member giving as a percent of income was 2.5% for the group of the eleven denominations considered in this section. The percent change in the per member portion of income donated to the church had declined by 14% from the 1921 base, from 2.9% in 1921 to 2.5% in 2007, and by 24% from the 1933 base, from 3.3% in 1933 to 2.5% in 2007.

Membership in absolute numbers increased for the group of 11 denominations on a fairly regular basis from 1921 until 1968, when it peaked. However, as a portion of U.S. population, the group's peak was earlier, in 1961, when membership in the 11 denominations represented 20% of the U.S. population. The decline in membership as a percent of U.S. population that began in 1962 continued through 2007.

It is of some interest to note that the first decline in membership as a percent of U.S. population in the set of 11 denominations occurred in 1962, one year after the decline in giving as a percent of income occurred in 1961. While giving as a portion of income displayed a pattern of increase in some years and decline in others, the decline in membership as a percent of U.S. population continued uninterrupted through the year 2007.

Figure 7 presents both per member giving as a percentage of income and membership as a percent of U.S. population, for the group of eleven Protestant denominations, from 1921 through 2007.

Details of Giving and Membership, 1921-2007

Giving as a Percent of Income. The period under consideration in this section of the report began in 1921. At that point, per member giving as a percentage of income was 2.9%. In current dollars, U.S. per capita Disposable (after-tax) Personal Income was $555, and per member giving was $16.10. When inflation was factored out by converting both income and giving to 2000 dollars, per capita income in 1921 measured $4,971 and per member giving was $144.29.

From 1922 through 1933, giving as a percent of income stayed above the 3% level. The high was 3.7% in 1924, followed closely by the amount in 1932, when per member giving measured 3.6% of per capita income. This trend is of particular interest inasmuch as per capita income was generally increasing between 1921 and 1927. Even as people were increasing in personal affluence, they also continued to maintain a giving level of more than 3% to their churches. Even after income began to decline, including the economic reverses in the early years of the Great Depression, giving measured above 3% from 1929 through 1933.

From 1922 through 1933, giving as a percent of income stayed above the 3% level.

The year 1933 was the depth of the Great Depression. Per capita income was at the lowest point it would reach between 1921 and 2007, whether measured in current or inflation-adjusted dollars. Yet per member giving as a percentage of income was 3.3%. Income had decreased by 17% between 1921 and 1933 in inflation-adjusted 2000 dollars, from $4,971 to $4,128. Meanwhile, per member giving had decreased 7%, from $144.29 in 1921 to $134.77 in 1933, in inflation-adjusted dollars. Therefore, giving as a percentage of income actually increased from 2.9% in 1921 to 3.3% in 1933, an increase of 12% in the portion of income contributed to the church.

Giving in inflation-adjusted 2000 dollars declined from 1933 to 1934, although income began to recover in 1934. Giving then began to increase again in 1935. In inflation-adjusted dollars, giving did not surpass the 1927 level of $221.45 until 1953, when giving grew from $212.70 in 1952 to $234.11 in 1953.

During World War II, incomes improved rapidly. Meanwhile, church member giving increased only modestly in current dollars. When inflation was factored out, per member giving was at $139.34 in 1941, the year the United States entered the war. It declined to $135.14 in 1942, increased in 1943 to $136.87 and then to $150.70 in 1944. However, income in inflation-adjusted dollars grew from $6,728 in 1941 to $7,805 in 1942, $8,344 in 1943, and reached a high for this period of $8,828 in 1944, an income level that would not be surpassed again until 1953. Thus, giving as a percentage of income reached a low point during the three full calendar years of formal U.S. involvement in World War II, at levels of 1.73% in 1942, 1.64% in 1943, and 1.71% in 1944.

In 1945, the last year of the war, U.S. per capita income was $8,726 in inflation-adjusted dollars. Giving in inflation-adjusted dollars increased from $150.70 in

1944, to $170.76 in 1945, the highest inflation-adjusted dollar amount it had been since 1930. Although per member giving increased 27% between 1933 and 1945, per capita income had increased 111%. Giving as a percentage of income therefore declined from the 3.3% level in 1933, to 2.0% in 1945.

The unusually high level of per capita income slumped after the war but had recovered to war levels by the early 1950s. By 1960, U.S. per capita income was 10% higher in inflation-adjusted 2000 dollars than it had been in 1945, increasing from $8,726 in 1945 to $9,620 in 1960. Meanwhile, per member giving in inflation-adjusted dollars had increased 77%, from $170.76 in 1945 to $301.43 in 1960. Giving as a portion of income recovered to the level it had been from 1922 through 1933, and stayed above 3% from 1958 through 1962. Giving as a percentage of income reached a postwar high of 3.13% in 1960, and then began to decline.

For the second time in the century, giving levels were growing to, or maintaining a level above, three percent of income even while incomes were also expanding. From 1921-1928, incomes expanded 24%. During this time giving grew to above 3% and stayed there. From 1950-1962, incomes grew 20%. Again, giving grew to above 3% in 1958 and stayed there through 1962. In both cases, church members increased or maintained their giving levels even as their incomes increased.

In the 1920s, the economic expansion was interrupted by the Great Depression, followed by World War II.

In contrast to the economic upheaval earlier in the century, however, the economy continued to expand through the 1960s. Yet the portion of income given was not sustained above 3%. By 1968, giving as a percentage of income had declined to 2.7% for this group of 11 communions. U.S. per capita income increased 30% in inflation-adjusted 2000 dollars between 1960 and 1968, from $9,620 in 1960 to $12,510 in 1968. In comparison, per member giving increased 10% in inflation-adjusted dollars, from the 1960 level of $301.43 to the 1968 level of $331.71.

By 1985, per member giving had increased 34% in inflation-adjusted 2000 dollars, from $331.71 in 1968 to $443.39 in 1985. U.S. per capita income measured $18,706, an increase of 50% over the 1968 level of $12,510. Giving as a percentage of income, therefore, measured 2.4% in 1985, representing an 11% decline from the 1968 level of 2.7%.

The year 2007 was the latest year for which data was available for the eleven denominations considered in this section. In that year, per member giving as a percentage of income was 2.5%, a 5% increase from the 1985 level. Per member giving increased 58% in inflation-adjusted 2000 dollars, from $443.39 in 1985 to $702.10 in 2007. U.S. per capita income increased 50% during this period, from the 1985 level of $18,706 to the 2007 level of $28,132. Since the numbers of dollars given increased at a faster rate than incomes, the percentage of income given increased.

Membership and Giving, 1921-2007. Membership was changing for this group of 11 denominations during the 1921-2007 period as well.

Between 1921 and 1961, the portion of U.S. population that this group of 11 denominations represented grew from 16.1% of the U.S. population to 20%, or one-fifth of the United States.

In that same year of 1961, the first decline in giving as a percentage of income occurred since 1951.

For the second time in the century, giving levels were growing to, or maintaining a level above, three percent of income even while incomes were also expanding.

The next year, in 1962, a decline in membership as a percent of U.S. population began for this group that would continue through the year 2007. Membership growth slowed and then the number of members declined between 1968 and 1969, from 37,785,048 to 37,382,659. Meanwhile, U.S. population continued to expand. Therefore, while this group represented 20% of U.S. population in 1961, by the year 2007, this group represented 11.6% of U.S. population.

During the 1961-2007 period, the Southern Baptist Convention grew from 9,978,139 to 16,266,920. Meanwhile, the other ten denominations, all of which might be termed mainline Protestant, declined in membership as a group, from 26,683,648 in 1961 to 18,619,252 in 2007.

The growth in the number of members in the Southern Baptist Convention offset the mainline Protestant membership loss to some degree. Nevertheless, the group's membership of the combined group of 11 denominations declined, measuring 36,661,788 in 1961 and 34,886,172 in 2007. U.S. population increased from 183,742,000 in 1961, when the group of 11 denominations represented 20% of the U.S. population, to 301,737,000 in 2007, when the 11 denominations represented 11.6% of the U.S. population.

Although the decrease in giving as a percent of income that began in 1961 resulted in giving levels varying between 2.34% and 2.31% during 1977 through 1981, the level of giving as a portion of income recovered to 2.40% by 1983 and was again at 2.41% in 1986 and 1987. It declined in the next few years until it reached 2.30% in 1992. An intermittent increase occurred through 2001 and 2002, when the percent given was 2.54%. The level of income declined by 2007 to 2.50%.

In contrast, membership as a percent of population for the 11 denominations as a group began a decline in 1962 that continued uninterrupted through the year 2007.

Change in Per Member Giving and Total Membership. In Table 14, giving as a percent of U.S. per capita DPI is presented for the first and last year in the period noted. The difference between giving in these two years was calculated and then divided by the number of annual intervals in the period to produce the Average Annual Change.

Table 14: **Average Annual Change in Per Member Giving as a Percent of U.S. DPI and in Membership as a Percent of U.S. Population, 11 Denominations, 1950-2007**

Time Period	Per Member Giving as % of Income			Membership as % of U.S. Population		
	First Year in Period	Last Year in Period	Average Annual Change	First Year in Period	Last Year in Period	Average Annual Change
1950-1955	2.39%	2.88%	0.10%	18.58%	19.64%	0.21%
1955-1960	2.88%	3.13%	0.05%	19.64%	19.34%	-0.06%
1960-1964 [2]	3.13%	2.86%	-0.07%	19.34%	19.53%	0.05%
1964-1970 [2]	2.86%	2.52%	-0.06%	19.53%	18.10%	-0.24%
1970-1975	2.52%	2.37%	-0.03%	18.10%	17.05%	-0.21%
1975-1980	2.37%	2.31%	-0.01%	17.05%	16.16%	-0.18%
1980-1985	2.31%	2.37%	0.01%	16.16%	15.48%	-0.14%
1985-1990	2.37%	2.31%	-0.01%	15.48%	14.59%	-0.18%
1990-1995	2.31%	2.38%	0.02%	14.59%	13.59%	-0.20%
1995-2000	2.38%	2.52%	0.03%	13.59%	12.81%	-0.16%
2000-2005	2.52%	2.50%	0.00%	12.81%	11.97%	-0.14%
2005-2007	2.50%	2.50%	0.00%	11.97%	11.56%	-0.20%

Details in the above table may not compute to the numbers shown due to rounding.

When considered as a portion of income in Table 14, the period of 1950-1955 posted the highest Average Annual Change in giving as a percent of income, followed by the 1955-1960 period. Giving grew to 3.1% in 1958, and a level above 3% was maintained through 1962. However, the 1960-1964 period also was the period within which giving as a portion of income began to decline. It is clear from the Average Annual Change column that giving as a portion of income began a downward trend in the 1960-1964 period that continued through the 1975-1980 period. Reversing in the 1980-1985 period, the average annual change was again negative in the 1985-1990 period. During the 1990-1995 and 1995-2000 periods, positive change was measured, but the increases did not recover to the 1950-1960 Average Annual Change levels. The Average Annual Change for the 2000-2005 and 2005-2007 periods both rounded to 0.00%. However, in both periods, the unrounded number at the third decimal indicated a slight decline.

Meanwhile, during the 1950-2007 period, the group of 11 denominations shrank as a portion of U.S. population. The 1950-1955 period posted an average annual increase of 0.21% in the portion of U.S. population that these denominations represented. The 1955-1960 period posted a decline. The group of 11 denominations nevertheless peaked in 1961 at 20% of U.S. population. Although the 1960-1964 period posted an increase, the average annual level was less than the previous five years' rate of decline. In 1964-1970, a period of decline began that continued through 2007.

The longest sustained period of average annual increases in per member giving in inflation-adjusted dollars during the 1921-2007 period occurred during the 26-year interval of 1976 to 2002.

Change in Per Member Giving and U.S. Per Capita Disposable Personal Income, in Inflation-adjusted 2000 Dollars.

For this group of 11 communions, per member giving in inflation-adjusted 2000 dollars increased half the time during the 1921-1947 period. Per member giving in inflation-adjusted dollars decreased from 1924 to 1925. While it increased from 1925 to 1926 and again in 1927, giving began a seven-year decline in 1928. This seven-year period, from 1928 to 1934, included some of the worst years of the Great Depression. Giving increased again in 1935. Declines in 1939, 1940, 1942, 1946, and 1947 alternated with increases in the other years.

Then, from 1948 through 1968,[3] the members in these 11 communions increased per member giving in inflation-adjusted 2000 dollars each year. During the first 12 years of this period, 1948-1960, per member giving averaged an increase of $10.51 a year. Although giving continued to increase for the next few years, it was at the slower rate of $3.78 per year. Overall, in inflation-adjusted 2000 dollars, income grew 57% from 1948 to 1968, while per member giving increased 89%, resulting in the recovery of giving levels to 3% or more in the late 1950s and early 1960s.

Per member giving in inflation-adjusted dollars declined in 1969, 1970, and 1971, followed by two years of increase and two of decline.

The longest sustained period of average annual increases in per member giving in inflation-adjusted dollars during the 1921-2007 period occurred during the 26-year interval of 1976 to 2002. During this time, income increased an average of $431.24 annually in inflation-adjusted 2000 dollars. Meanwhile, per member giving increased $11.93 on average each year, a higher overall rate than during the 20-year interval of 1948-1968, when the annual increase was $7.82. However, while giving increased 88% from 1976 to 2002, it increased 89% from 1948-1968. U.S. per capita income increased 76% from 1976 to 2002. Because giving increased at a faster rate

Table 15: Average Annual Change in U.S. Per Capita DPI and Per Member Giving, 11 Denominations, 1950-2007, Inflation-Adjusted 2000 Dollars

Time Period	U.S. Per Capita Income			Per Member Giving			Avg. Ann. Chg. Giv. as % Avg. Annual Chg. in Income
	First Year in Period	Last Year in Period	Average Annual Change	First Year in Period	Last Year in Period	Average Annual Change	
1950-1955	$8,388	$9,155	$153.43	$200.90	$263.37	$12.49	8.14%
1955-1960	$9,155	$9,620	$92.97	$263.37	$301.43	$7.61	8.19%
1960-1964 [2]	$9,620	$10,900	$319.81	$301.43	$311.56	$2.53	0.79%
1964-1970 [2]	$10,900	$13,038	$356.40	$311.56	$328.83	$2.88	0.81%
1970-1975	$13,038	$14,478	$287.92	$328.83	$343.00	$2.83	0.98%
1975-1980	$14,478	$16,333	$370.99	$343.00	$377.66	$6.93	1.87%
1980-1985	$16,333	$18,706	$474.66	$377.66	$443.39	$13.15	2.77%
1985-1990	$18,706	$20,997	$458.18	$443.39	$484.43	$8.21	1.79%
1990-1995	$20,997	$22,024	$205.42	$484.43	$525.02	$8.12	3.95%
1995-2000	$22,024	$25,473	$689.84	$525.02	$640.94	$23.18	3.36%
2000-2005	$25,473	$27,082	$321.79	$640.94	$677.88	$7.39	2.30%
2005-2007	$27,082	$28,132	$525.11	$677.88	$702.10	$12.11	2.31%

Details in the above table may not compute to the numbers shown due to rounding.

than income during the 1976 to 2002 period, giving as a percentage of income was 2.37% in 1976 and 2.54% in 2002.

By reviewing this data in smaller increments of years from 1950 to 2007, the time period in which giving began to decline markedly can be identified. In Table 15, data for the first and last year in each period is presented. The difference between these two years was calculated and then divided by the number of annual intervals in the period. The Average Annual Change in Giving as a Percent of the Average Annual Change in Income column presents the Per Member Giving Average Annual Change divided by the U.S. Per Capita Income Average Annual Change.

As indicated in Table 15, during the 1950 to 2007 period, the highest increase in the average annual change in per member giving measured in inflation-adjusted 2000 dollars occurred from 1995-2000. However, when the average annual change in per member giving was considered as a portion of the average annual change in per capita income, the largest increase occurred in the 1955-1960 period, followed by the 1950-1955 period. In 1995-2000, the annual dollar increase in giving of $23.18 represented 3% of the average annual increase in U.S. per capita income, compared to the 8% represented by the increased dollars given during 1950-1955 and 1955-1960.

Between 1960 and 1964 in these communions, the average annual change in per member giving declined markedly from the previous five years. While income was increasing at an annual rate of $319.81 in this four-year period, 244% greater than in the 1955-1960 period, the average annual increase in per member contributions in inflation-adjusted 2000 dollars was $2.53 in 1960-1964, only a third of the $7.61 annual rate of increase in the 1955-1960 period.

The 1960-1964 period predates many of the controversial issues often cited as reasons for declining giving as a percent of income. Also, it was in the 1960-1964 period when membership as a percent of population began to decrease in mainline denominations, ten of which are included in this group. Therefore, additional exploration of that period of time might be merited.

Increases in per member giving were consistently low from 1960-1975. The annual rates of increase of $2.53 per year from 1960 to 1964, $2.88 from 1964 to 1970, and $2.83 from 1970 to 1975, were the lowest in the 1950 to 2007 period. From 1960 to 1975, the increase in dollars given represented less than 1% of the average annual increase in per capita income.

In the 1975-1980 period, the average annual increase in giving grew to $6.93, representing 1.87% of the average annual increase in per capita income.

From 1980 to 1985, the average annual increase in giving of $13.15 represented 2.77% of the average annual increase in income during this period. As a portion of the increase in per capita income, the 2.77% of the 1980 to 1985 period ranked fifth among the twelve periods from 1950 to 2007.

The annual average change in giving as a percent of the average annual income increase during 1985 to 1990 fell from the 1980 to 1985 period. The 1990-1995 Average Annual Change in Giving as a Percent of the Average Annual Change in Income represented about double the 1985-1990 figure, although the Average Annual Change in Per Member Giving was comparable in the two periods. The slower growth in income during the 1990-1995 period resulted in the increase in dollars given representing a larger portion of the increase in income.

In the 1995-2000, the average annual change in giving as a percentage of the average annual change in income decreased from the 1990-1995 period. This was the case even though the average annual change in the number of dollars given on a per member basis was almost triple that of the previous period. During the 1995-2000 segment, income was increasing at the fastest rate in the 1950-2007 period, in terms of per capita inflation-adjusted dollars. Thus the larger average number of dollars given was nevertheless a smaller portion of the average income increases during the same period. This rate of growth in giving was less than half the rate during the 1950-1960 period, when considered as a portion of the income increases.

For the period 2000-2005, the average annual change in dollars given as a percent of the annual change in income was 2.30%. In the 2005-2007 period, although the average number of dollars given, $12.11, was at a level almost as high as the 1950-1955 period, U.S. per capita income was also increasing at a high rate. Therefore, the average annual change in giving as a percent of the average annual change in income was 2.31%, similar to the 2000-2005 period.

Appendix A contains a listing of the denominations contained in this analysis.

Notes for Chapter 4

[1] Data for the period 1965-1967 was not available in a form that could be readily analyzed for the present purposes, and therefore data for these three years was estimated by dividing the change in per member current dollar contributions from 1964 to 1968 by four, the number of years in this interval, and cumulatively adding the result to the base year of 1964 data and subsequently to the calculated data for the succeeding years of 1965 and 1966 in order to obtain estimates for the years 1965-1967.

[2] Use of the intervals 1960-1964 and 1964-1970 allows for the use of years for which there is known data, avoiding the use of the 1965 through 1967 years for which estimated data is used in this chapter.

[3] For the years 1965 through 1967, estimated data is used. See first footnote in this chapter.

chapter 5

Church Member Giving
and Membership Trends
Based on 1968-2007 Data

Overview of Church Member Giving and Membership Trends

Information as a Tool. The rich historical data series in the *Yearbook of American and Canadian Churches* has, in this volume, been supplemented with and revised by additional denominational data for the 1968-2007 period.

Analysis of this data has been presented in the *State of Church Giving* series since the early 1990s. When first published, the finding that giving as a portion of income was shrinking was received with some surprise and intense interest in many quarters.

Now the series has continued for a number of years. The trends identified in earlier analyses impact current activities. Various denominations continue to face decisions about staff cuts and, in some cases, whether to decrease missionary forces. The emphasis on local internal operations indicated by the trend in giving to Congregational Finances has, in fact, resulted in changed dynamics between local congregations and national church offices. The numbers did not cause such changes to occur. The numbers only described symptoms of priorities. These priorities produced behaviors resulting in the changed relationships.

It is generally acknowledged that most individuals do not decide how much to give based on academic information such as that contained in these analyses. However, it is possible for institutional leaders at all levels of the church, local as well as national, to make use of trend information to formulate strategies in response to the findings. For example, the data indicated that giving to Congregational Finances began to increase as a portion of income in 1993. It is possible that local church leadership recognized a negative general trend and took steps to address it. The fact that the upturn in giving that began in 1993 has essentially benefited local expenses, with only a slowing of the decline to Benevolences, indicates that church leadership may yet be operating with a limited vision of whole-life stewardship. However, it also indicates that the direction of trends can change.

Facts and figures may be useful to those responsible for promoting the health of the church. The analyses in this chapter are presented in an effort to expand the available information base.

The Meaning of Trends. Statistical regression models are a tool to help leaders plan in response to reported data. Experts evaluate trends in weather to plan strategies that will safeguard agriculture. Demographers map out population change trends to help government at local, national, and international levels plan for needs in education, aging, and trade.

Statistical techniques can also be used to suggest both consequences and possibilities regarding church giving and membership patterns. Of course, trend data only indicates future directions. Data does not dictate what will happen. Available information, including trend analysis, can help formulate intelligent responses to identified factors. Church leaders and members can help decide, through action or inaction, what the future will look like.

Trend analysis was first included in this series partly in response to developments in national church offices. After talking with a number of denominational officials who were making painful decisions about which programs to cut, in light of decreased Benevolences dollars being received, it seemed useful to see where the present patterns of giving might lead if effective means were not found to alter present behavior. Were current patterns likely to prove a temporary setback, or did the data suggest longer-term implications?

The data for both Benevolences and Congregational Finances can be projected using linear and exponential regression analysis. Linear regression is sometimes called a "straight-line" projection. An exponential regression is also labeled a "decay" model. To determine which type of analysis more accurately describes the data in a category's giving pattern, the data for 1968-1985 was projected using both techniques. Then, the actual data for 1986 through 2007 was plotted. The more accurate projection was judged to be the procedure that produced the trend line most closely resembling the actual 1986-2007 data.

General Trends in Church Member Giving. As noted in earlier chapters, Total Contributions from church members are divided into the two general categories of Congregational Finances and Benevolences. In the category of Congregational Finances, giving as a portion of income declined overall between 1968 and 2007 for the composite denominations. Yet a trend toward increase in the level of giving to this category was observed beginning in 1993. These intermittent increases from one year to the next were in contrast to the decline indicated by an exponential projection through 2007, based on 1968-1985 giving data. However, since 2002, the percent of income given to this category decreased in more years than it increased. Long-term projections for this category may be of limited use. Certainly, monitoring of future years' data is merited.

The continued decline in actual data for giving to Benevolences as a portion of income throughout the 1968-2007 period in the composite denominations initially followed the linear trend. In 1993, the rate of decline began to slow, although the level of giving remained closer to the linear trend. In 1997, the decline moved above the exponential trend. Although Benevolences may be expected to be above either trend line, if the pattern of decline observed in the 1968-2007 period continues,

Although Benevolences may be expected to be above either trend line, if the pattern of decline observed in the 1968-2007 period continues, Benevolences may represent a substantially reduced portion of income throughout the current century.

Benevolences may represent a substantially reduced portion of income throughout the current century.

Membership trends across the theological spectrum point to a decline when membership was considered as a percent of U.S. population.

Eleven mainline Protestant denominations represented 13.2% of the population in 1968, and 6.2% in 2007, a decline of 53% from the 1968 base.

The composite data set communions analyzed in earlier chapters of this volume measured 14.1% of U.S. population in 1968 and 10.0% in 2007, down 29% as a portion of U.S. population from the 1968 base.

A set of fifteen evangelical denominations grew 48% in the number of members between 1968 and 2007, but posted a 1% decline as a portion of U.S. population, since U.S. population expanded at a faster rate. The growth as a percent of population for this group peaked in the mid-1980s, and then began a slow decline, reaching its lowest point of the period in 2007.

Membership in a set of 37 Protestant denominations, including some of the fastest growing denominations in the U.S., and the Roman Catholic Church represented 45% of U.S. population in 1968, and 37% in 2007, a decline of 19% from the 1968 base. A trend line for this set of denominations suggests that the group will represent only one-quarter or less of the U.S. population by 2100, and 16 % in 2200, if current patterns continue.

When considered as a portion of income, spending on new construction of religious buildings was higher in 1965 than in 2007, although, in inflation-adjusted dollars, the aggregate billions spent in 2001 was the highest annual amount spent in the 1964-2007 period.

Membership in a set of 37 Protestant denominations, including some of the fastest growing denominations in the U.S., and the Roman Catholic Church represented 45% of U.S. population in 1968, and 37% in 2007...

Details of Church Giving and Membership Trends

The Current Trend in Church Giving. The first chapter in this report indicates that per member giving as a percentage of income decreased between 1968 and 2007. Further, contributions to the category of Benevolences were declining proportionately faster than those to Congregational Finances between 1968 and 2007.

The data for the composite denominations analyzed for 1968 through 2007 has been projected in *The State of Church Giving* series, beginning with the edition that included 1991 data.[1] The most recent projection is based on data from 1968 through 2007.

The Trend in Congregational Finances. The 1968-2007 church giving data contained in this report indicates that giving as a percentage of income for Congregational Finances declined from 2.45% in 1968, to 2.20% in 2007, a decline of 10%.

Both linear and exponential regression were used to analyze the data for giving as a percentage of income to Congregational Finances for the 17-year interval of 1968 through 1985. Then the actual data for 1986 through 2007 was plotted. The actual data for 1986-1992 followed the exponential curve more closely than the linear regression. In 1993, giving as a percent of income to Congregational Finances began to increase rather than decrease to this category, unlike either projection. However starting in 2003, an intermittent decline in the giving level began again.

Nevertheless, the actual data remained above the decline pattern of the exponential curve. The results are shown in Figure 8.

The upturn between 1993 and 2002 differed markedly from the previous trend through 1992. The pattern of increase beginning in 2003 still posted an overall decline by 2007. These variations suggest that long-term projections may be difficult in this category. However, the importance of the activity in local church support suggests the trend merits continuing observation and evaluation.

The Trend in Benevolences. Per member contributions to Benevolences as a percent of income decreased from 0.66% in 1968 to 0.37% in 2007, a percent decrease in giving as a percent of income of 44% from the 1968 base, the lowest point in the 1968-2007 period.

Figure 8: Projected Trends for Composite Denominations, Giving as a Percent of Income to Congregational Finances, Using Linear and Exponential Regression Based on Data for 1968-1985, with Actual Data for 1986-2007

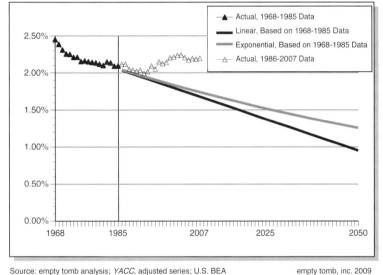

Source: empty tomb analysis; *YACC,* adjusted series; U.S. BEA   empty tomb, inc. 2009

Figure 9: Projected Trends for Composite Denominations, Giving as a Percent of Income to Benevolences, Using Linear and Exponential Regression Based on Data for 1968-1985, with Actual Data for 1986-2007

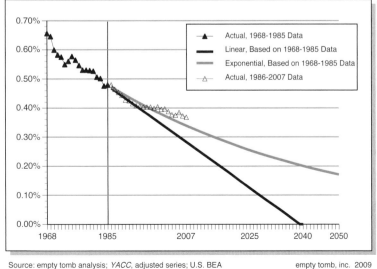

Source: empty tomb analysis; *YACC,* adjusted series; U.S. BEA   empty tomb, inc. 2009

The data for giving as a percentage of income to Benevolences for the 17-year interval of 1968 through 1985 was also projected using both linear and exponential regression. The actual data for 1986 through 2007 was then plotted. The results are shown in Figure 9.

Reported per member giving as a percentage of income to Benevolences was near or below the projected value of the linear regression for 1989 through 1992. In 1993, the rate of decline slowed to the point that the actual data was above, but still closer to, the linear trend line. However, from 1997-2007, giving as a percent of income to Benevolences moved above the exponential line, suggesting that, although the decline continued, the rate slowed even further. In 2007, per member giving as a portion of income to Benevolences reached its lowest point in the 1968-2007 period. As discussed in chapter 1, it appears that the external factors of tsunami and hurricane relief efforts contributed to the increase observed in this category in 2005, since data for both 2006 and 2007 again posted declines.

Although giving to Benevolences as a portion of income between 1968 and 2007 continued to decline, the rate slowed toward the end of that period.

A second analysis was done on the entire period from 1968-2007. A linear trend based on the entire period of 1968-2007 data indicated that per member giving as a portion of income to the category of Benevolences will reach 0.05% of income in the year A.D. 2050. The exponential curve based on 1968-2007 data indicated that giving in 2050 would be 0.19%, down 48% from the 0.37% level in 2007.[2] Extending the exponential trend to 2100, Benevolences would represent 0.09% of income in that year.

These trend lines may be more useful to predict the general level of giving, rather than precise numbers. However, the overall direction suggests that by 2050 the amount of income going to support Benevolences, including denominational structures, would be severely reduced, if the overall pattern of the last 40 years continues.

Trends in Church Membership as a Percentage of U.S. Population, 1968-2007.[3] Membership data for various church groupings is available for review for the years 1968 through 2007. When the reported data is considered as a percent of U.S. population, the membership data is placed in the larger context of the changing environment in which the church exists. This measurement is similar to giving as a percent of income, which reflects how much a financial donation represents of the resources available to the donor. In a similar way, measuring membership as a percent of U.S. population takes into account the fact that the potential population for church membership also changed.

The State of Church Giving through 1993 included a chapter entitled, "A Unified Theory of Giving and Membership."[4] The hypothesis explored in that discussion is that there is a relationship between a decline in church member giving and membership patterns. One proposal considered in that chapter is that a denomination that is able to involve its members in a larger vision, such as mission outreach, as evidenced in levels of giving to support that idea, will also be attracting additional members.

In the present chapter, discussion will focus on patterns and trends in membership as a percentage of U.S. population.

Membership in the Composite Denominations, 1968-2007. The

composite denominations, which span the theological spectrum, included 28,255,960 Full or Confirmed Members in 1968. By 2007, these communions included 29,985,626 members, an increase of 6%.[5] However, during the same 39-year interval, U.S. population increased from 200,745,000 to 301,737,000, an increase of 50%. Therefore, while this church member grouping represented 14.1% of the U.S. population in 1968, it included 9.9% in 2007, a decline of 29% from the 1968 base. Figure 10 presents membership as a percent of U.S. population, and giving as a percentage of income, for the composite denominations, 1968-2007.

Figure 10: Membership as a Percent of U.S. Population and Giving as a Percent of U.S. Per Capita Disposable Personal Income, Composite Denominations, 1968-2007

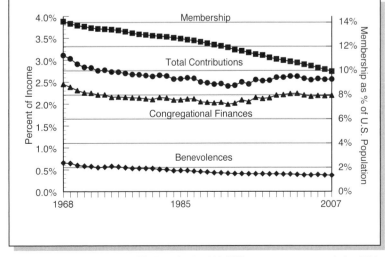

Source: empty tomb analysis; *YACC* adjusted series; U.S. BEA　　　empty tomb, inc. 2009

Membership Trends in Three Church Groups. Membership data for

three subgroups within the historically Christian church in the U.S. is available. Data was analyzed for 11 mainline denominations, 15 evangelical denominations, and the Roman Catholic Church.

The declining membership trends have been noticed most markedly in the mainline Protestant communions. Full or Confirmed Membership in 11 mainline Protestant denominations affiliated with the National Council of the Churches of Christ in the U.S.A.[6] decreased as a percentage of U.S. population between 1968 and 2007. In 1968, this group included 26,508,288, or 13.2% of U. S. population. In 2007, the 11 denominations included 18,662,899, or 6.2% of U.S. population, a decline of 53% from the 1968 base.

Data is also available for a group of 15 denominations that might be classified on the evangelical end of the theological spectrum.[7] Although one or more of the communions in this grouping might prefer the term "conservative" to "evangelical" as a description, the latter term in its current sociological usage may be useful.

Figure 11: Membership as a Percent of U.S. Population, 15 Evangelical Denominations, 11 Mainline Denominations, and the Roman Catholic Church, 1968-2007

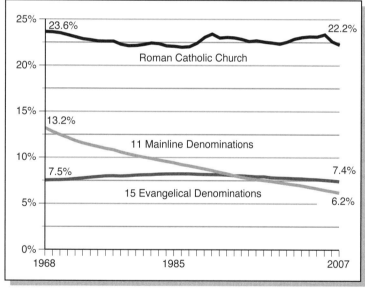

Source: empty tomb analysis; *YACC* Adjusted series; US BEA   empty tomb, inc. 2009

These communions included some of the fastest growing denominations in the United States. This group grew 48% in membership, from 15,101,542 in 1968 to 22,397,258, in 2007, while U.S. population grew 50%. As a result, this group measured 7.52% of U.S. population in 1968, and 7.42% in 2007. In the mid-1980s, the group peaked at 8.23% as a portion of U.S. population, and then declined to 7.42% by 2007, a decline of 10% as a portion of U.S. population from the 1986 peak. In 1993, these 15 evangelical communions surpassed the 11 mainline communions in the portion of U.S. population that they represented.

The Roman Catholic Church included 47,468,333 members in 1968, or 24% of U.S. population. Although the church's membership grew 41%, to 67,117,016 in 2007, it decreased to 22% as a portion of the faster-growing U.S. population, a decline of 6%.

Figure 11 presents the membership data for these groups of communions.

Projected Membership Trends in 11 Mainline Denominations. As with

giving as a percentage of income to Congregational Finances and Benevolences, trend lines using both linear and exponential regression were developed for the 11 mainline Protestant communions discussed above, using their 1968-1985 membership data. The actual 1986 through 2007 data was also plotted. As shown in Figure 12, the actual 1986-2007 data was slightly above the exponential curve for these denominations in the early 2000s, but has been on the curve in the last few years.

An exponential curve based on the entire 1968-2007 reported data series suggested that these denominations would represent 2.7% of the U.S. population in 2050, if the present rate of decline continues.

Projected Membership Trends in the Composite Denominations.

Nine of the 11 mainline Protestant denominations discussed above are included in the composite set of denominations that have been considered in earlier chapters of this report. Regression analysis was carried out on the 1968-1985 membership data for the composite denominations to determine if the trends in the larger grouping differed from the mainline denomination subset. The results were then compared to the actual 1986 through 2007 membership data for the composite data set.

The composite denominations represented 14.1% of the U.S. population in 1968, and 12.6% in 1985. Linear trend analysis of the 1968-1985 data suggested that this grouping would have represented 10.9% of U.S. population in 2007, while exponential regression suggested it would have included 11.1%. In fact, this composite grouping of communions represented 9.9% of the U.S. population in 2007, a smaller figure than that indicated by linear regression, suggesting the trend is closer to that predicted by linear regression than the exponential curve. By 2050, these composite denominations would represent 5.9% of the U.S. population if a linear trend remains the more accurate analysis. Figure 13 presents this information in graphic form.

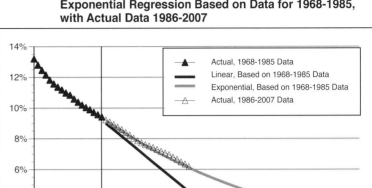

Figure 12: Trend in Membership as a Percent of U.S. Population, 11 Mainline Protestant Denominations, Linear and Exponential Regression Based on Data for 1968-1985, with Actual Data 1986-2007

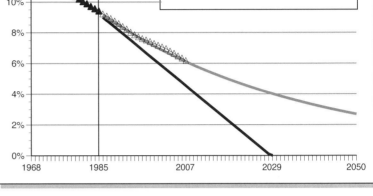

Figure 13: Trend in Membership as a Percent of U.S. Population, Composite Denominations, Linear and Exponential Regression Based on Data for 1968-1985, with Actual Data 1986-2007

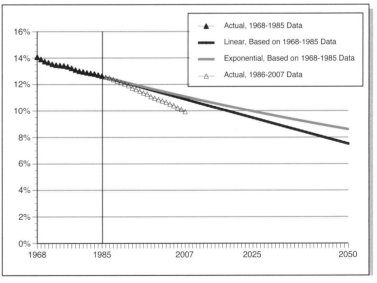

Membership and Projected Membership Trends in 38 Communions.

In 1968, a set of 37 Protestant denominations and the Roman Catholic Church included a total of 90,252,228 members. The Protestant churches included a broad representation of the theological spectrum, and also included some of the fastest growing denominations in the U.S. With the U.S. population at 200,745,000, these Christians constituted 45% of the 1968 U.S. population. By 2007, the group had grown to 110,173,258 members. However, with U.S. population having grown to

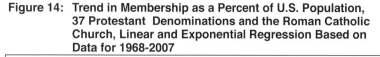

Figure 14: Trend in Membership as a Percent of U.S. Population, 37 Protestant Denominations and the Roman Catholic Church, Linear and Exponential Regression Based on Data for 1968-2007

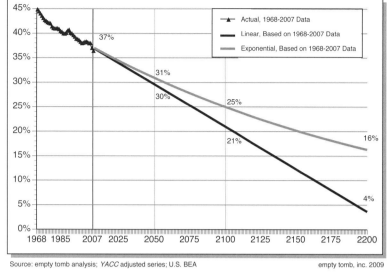

Source: empty tomb analysis; *YACC* adjusted series; U.S. BEA   empty tomb, inc. 2009

301,737,000 in 2007, these Christians comprised 36.5% of the American population, a percent change of -19% from the 1968 base.

Because of the broad nature of the sampling of these historically Christian communions, a projection was extended to 2200, based on membership data for the entire period of 1968 through 2007. The purpose was to forecast, based on past patterns, the role this group of denominations would play at the end of the current century. By 2050, the linear projection suggested the group will have declined from representing 37% of the U.S. population in 2007 to include 30%. The exponential projection forecasted 31% in 2050. By the year 2100, the linear trend projected 21% while the exponential trend projected 25% of the U.S. population will be affiliated with these 38 communions. If the trends continue long term, in 2200 this group of communions will represent 16.3% of U.S. population, according to the exponential curve, or 3.6%, if the linear trend proves more accurate. Figure 14 presents these findings in graphic form.

Trends in One Denomination. The quality of trend data will be affected by the measurements taken. An example from one denomination may illustrate the point.

The United Methodist Church resulted from the merger of The Methodist Church and The Evangelical United Brethren in 1968. In 2007, The United Methodist Church was the second largest Protestant denomination, and third largest communion overall in the U.S. While The Methodist Church reported data for 1968 in the 1970 *YACC* edition, the Evangelical United Brethren did not. Therefore, data for The United Methodist Church, including both The Methodist Church and the Evangelical United Brethren, was not available in 1968, and as a result this communion was not included in the composite denominations.

Two years after the merger, in 1971, The United Methodist Church changed its reporting methodology for its information published in the *YACC* series. Specifically, the category of "Connectional Clergy Support" was switched from Congregational Finances to Benevolences. UMC Connectional Clergy Support includes district superintendents and Episcopal salaries, which would standardly be included in Benevolences for other communions as well. However, UMC Connectional Clergy Support also includes pastor pension and benefits, including health insurance, and a category of Equitable Salary Funds, which would be included in Congregational Finances in most denominations.

UMC Connectional Clergy Support increased fairly rapidly between 1969 and 2007. When UMC Connectional Clergy Support was included in per member giving as a percentage of income to the UMC Benevolences series, Benevolences increased from 0.40% in 1969 to 0.46% in 2007, a 15% increase from the 1969 base.

However, when UMC Connectional Clergy Support was taken out of the UMC Benevolences series for 1971 to 2007, giving as a portion of income to Benevolences in the United Methodist Church declined from 0.40% in 1969 to 0.28% in 2007, a decrease of 30%.

Per member giving as a portion of income to the single category of UMC Connectional Clergy Support increased 44% from 1969 to 2007.

Figure 15 illustrates the two trends in Benevolences giving, based on whether the category includes Connectional Clergy Support or not.

The two different trends in UMC Benevolences illustrate the point that definitions of the categories being measured are important.

If the traditional definition of Benevolences is used, which would place pastor health insurance and other benefits in Congregational Finances, then Benevolences giving in The United Methodist Church declined as a portion of income in a noticeable fashion between 1969 and 2007. If, however, a category that was initially included in Congregational Finances is transferred to Benevolences, the UMC Benevolences giving as a portion of income increased between 1969-2007.

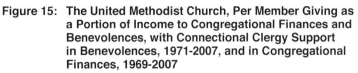

Figure 15: The United Methodist Church, Per Member Giving as a Portion of Income to Congregational Finances and Benevolences, with Connectional Clergy Support in Benevolences, 1971-2007, and in Congregational Finances, 1969-2007

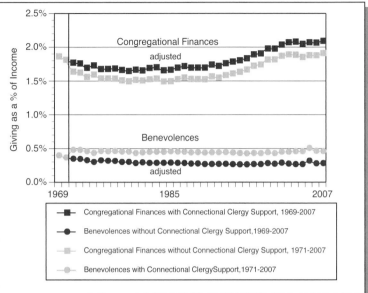

Source: empty tomb analysis; *YACC* adjusted series; U.S. BEA   empty tomb, inc. 2009

The former definition of Benevolences, that excludes those congregationally-based expenses, provides a more specific measurement of member support for the larger mission of the church. The latter definition, which includes pastor health insurance and other benefits with broader church activities, weights the measurement toward the funding of institutional operations.

The denominational leadership needs to be clear about its primary goal, whether it is focused on maintaining an institution or mobilizing church members to increased mission outreach through denominational channels. When that priority has been identified, the denomination can choose the most accurate definition to measure progress toward the goal.

Church Member Giving in Recessions. The current report contains available church member giving data through 2007. As of the writing of this report, experts concluded that a peak in December 2007[8] was the beginning of a recession, with the economic contraction beginning in January 2008. Therefore, the next edition in *The State of Church Giving* series should have access to church member giving data for 2008, and can therefore analyze giving patterns in the 12 months of 2008. A previous analysis of church member giving patterns in recession years covered the period of 1968-2005, and was presented in the previous edition in *The State of Church Giving* series. That document is available at <http://www.emptytomb.org/recessions68-05.pdf>.

Buildings. How does 2007 construction activity among churches in the U.S. compare to other years?

Census Bureau data provides information on the new construction of religious buildings.[9] According to the data, current dollar aggregate construction of religious buildings was $1.04 billion dollars in 1964, compared to $7.43 billion in 2007. On a current-dollar aggregate level, more building was going on in 2007 than in the mid-1960s.

However, as has been emphasized in previous chapters of this volume, aggregate numbers considered apart from inflation, or that do not take into account changes in population and income, do not give a complete picture.

When inflation was factored out, the data indicated that the total aggregate $35.2 billion cost of new religious building construction, summed for the 2003-2007 period, was higher than the 1964-1968 period cost of $24.8 billion. The highest single year inflation-adjusted amount in the 1964-2007 period was the 2001 level of $8.2 billion. The 1965 level of $5.6 billion had been the highest amount of aggregate, inflation-adjusted dollars spent on the construction of new religious buildings from 1964 through 1996. In 1997, aggregate inflation-adjusted spending passed the 1965 level, and religious building expenditures continued to increase through 2001. Expenditures were at or above $8 billion a year in inflation-adjusted dollars from 2000 through 2003, and decreased to $6.2 billion in 2007.

...as a portion of income, Americans spent 0.25% on the construction of new religious buildings in 1965, compared to 0.07% in 2007.

Yet, to obtain the most realistic picture about building patterns, changes in population and income also need to be factored into the evaluation. For example, taking population changes into account, in 1965 the per capita expenditure in the U.S. on religious buildings was $29 dollars per person in inflation-adjusted 2000 dollars. In 2007, it was $21 dollars.

The period 1964 through 1968 posted an average per capita expenditure on new religious buildings of $25. The period 2002-2007 was $24, suggesting that construction of new religious buildings was on a par in the two periods, when changes in population were taken into account.

Of course, a smaller portion of the entire U.S. population may have been investing in religious buildings in the late 1990s through 2007 than in the mid-1960s. To have the most meaningful comparison, changes in membership as a portion of population would have to be taken into account. Data considered above suggests that membership in historically Christian churches declined as a portion of the U.S. population between 1964 and 2007. However, other religions were added to the religious milieu of the United States during this period. The Census data includes all religious construction, not just Christian churches. So the rough estimate may be fairly useful as a first approximation.

Even comparing per capita inflation-adjusted dollars spent is of limited use because it does not account for the difference in incomes in the two periods. To review, the $29 per capita spent on religious buildings in 1965 represented a different portion of income than the $21 spent in 2007. In fact, as a portion of income, Americans spent 0.25% on the construction of new religious buildings in 1965, compared to 0.07% in 2007.

Figure 16:   Construction of Religious Buildings in the U.S., 1964-2007, Aggregate Millions of Inflation-Adjusted 2000 Dollars, and Per Capita Spending as a Percent of U.S. Per Capita DPI

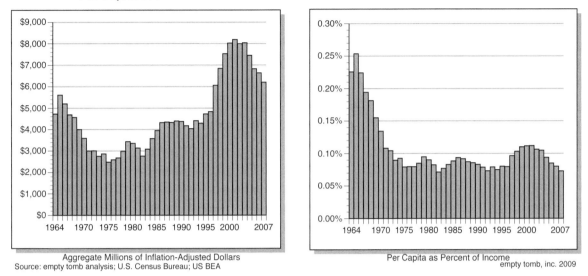

Aggregate Millions of Inflation-Adjusted Dollars
Source: empty tomb analysis; U.S. Census Bureau; US BEA

Per Capita as Percent of Income
empty tomb, inc. 2009

One must conclude, therefore, that the population was investing a higher portion of available resources in religious buildings in the mid-1960s than at the beginning of this century. The building activity occurring in the late 1990s through 2007 has to be evaluated in the context of the general affluence produced by decades of economic expansion in the U.S. in order to make an intelligent evaluation of whether religious construction has in fact increased over the mid-1960s level. This fact is clear from the two charts in Figure 16. These charts contrast the annual aggregate inflation-adjusted dollar value of new religious building construction with the per capita expenditure as a portion of U.S. per capita income for the 1964-2007 period. One can observe that the picture is very different when the per person cost of the building is set in the context of the income available to the people paying for the building.

The Response to the Trends.   As in other sectors, trend lines in church giving and membership are designed to provide an additional source of information. Planning, evaluation and creative thinking are some of the types of constructive responses that can be made in light of projections. The information on church member giving and membership trends is offered as a possible planning tool.[10] The trend lines are not considered to be dictating what must happen, but rather are seen as providing important indicators of what might happen if present conditions continue in an uninterrupted fashion. Trends in church giving and membership, if used wisely, may be of assistance in addressing conditions present in the body of Christ in the United States.

Notes for Chapter 5

[1] John Ronsvalle and Sylvia Ronsvalle, *The State of Church Giving through 1991* (Champaign, IL: empty tomb, inc., 1993), and subsequent editions in the series. The edition with data through 1991 provides a discussion of the choice to use giving as a percentage of income as a basis for considering future giving patterns.

[2] In the linear regression for the 1968-2007 data, the value for the correlation coefficient, or r_{XY}, for the Benevolences data is -.97. The strength of the linear relationship in the present set of 1968-

2007 data, that is, the proportion of variance accounted for by linear regression, is represented by the coefficient of determination, or r^2_{XY}, of .94 for Benevolences. In the exponential regression, the value for r_{XY}, for the Benevolences data is -.98, while the strength of the exponential relationship is .97. The Benevolences F-observed values of 651.74 for the linear, and 1,053.55 for the curvilinear, regression are substantially greater than the F-critical value of 7.35 for 1 and 38 degrees of freedom for a single-tailed test with an Alpha value of 0.01. Therefore, the regression equation is useful at the level suggested by the r^2_{XY} figure in predicting giving as a percentage of income.

[3] The denominations analyzed in this section include the composite data set whose financial patterns were analyzed in earlier chapters. The data for the composite communions is supplemented by the data of eight denominations included in an analysis of church membership and U.S. population by Roozen and Hadaway in David A. Roozen and Kirk C. Hadaway, eds., *Church and Denominational Growth* (Nashville: Abingdon Press, 1993), 393-395.

[4] This article is available on the Internet at: <http://www.emptytomb.org/UnifiedTheory.pdf>.

[5] See Appendix B-1 for details of the composite denomination data included in these analyses. Consult Appendix B-4 for the total Full or Confirmed Membership numbers used for the American Baptist Churches in the U.S.A. See Appendix B-3.3 and Appendix B-4 for the membership data of the other denominations included in subsequent analyses in this chapter that are not one of the composite denominations.

[6] These 11 denominations include nine of the communions in the composite set of denominations as well as The Episcopal Church and The United Methodist Church.

[7] A list of the communions in this set is presented in Appendix A.

[8] Business Cycle Dating Committee, National Bureau of Economic Research; "Determination of the December 2007 Peak in Economic Activity"; December 2008; <http://www.nber.org/cycles/dec2008.html>; p. 1 of 8/19/2009 10:32 AM printout.

[9] For a series beginning in 1964 titled "Annual Value of Construction Put in Place," the Census Bureau defined its Religious category as follows: "*Religious* includes houses of worship and other religious buildings. Certain buildings, although owned by religious organizations, are not included in this category. These include education or charitable institutions, hospitals, and publishing houses." (U.S. Census Bureau, Current Construction Reports, C30/01-5, *Value of Construction Put in Place*: May 2001, U.S. Government Printing Office, Washington, DC 20402, Appendix A, "Definitions," p. A-2). A 2003 revision of this series presented the definitions as follows: "Religious: Certain buildings, although owned by religious organizations, are not included in this category. These include educational or charitable institutions, hospitals, and publishing houses; House of worship: Includes churches, chapels, mosques, synagogues, tabernacles, and temples; Other religious: In addition to the types of facilities listed below, it also includes sanctuaries, abbeys, convents, novitiates, rectories, monasteries, missions, seminaries, and parish houses; Auxiliary building—includes fellowship halls, life centers, camps and retreats, and Sunday schools." (U.S. Census Bureau; "Definitions of Construction"; July 30, 2003; <http://www.census.gov/const/C30/definitions.pdf>; 8/17/2003 PM printout.) Although documentation for the revised series stated that the 1993 through 2001 data was not comparable to the earlier 1964-2000 data, a comparison of the two series found that there was an average of 0.1% difference between the estimated millions of dollars spent on construction of religious buildings from 1993-2000. For the purposes of the present discussion, the difference in the two series was not deemed sufficient to impact the multi-decade review to the degree that discussion would not be useful. The source for the religious construction data is:

• U.S. Census Bureau; Table 1: Annual Value of Construction Put in Place in the U.S.: [Year-Year], p. 1: Current $s & Constant (1996) $s; last revised July 1, 2002;

1964: 1964-1968; <http://www.census.gov/pub/const/C30/tab168.txt>

1965-1969: 1965-1969; <http://www.census.gov/pub/const/C30/tab169.txt>

1970-1974: 1970-1974; <http://www.census.gov/pub/const/C30/tab174.txt>

1975-1979: 1975-1979; <http://www.census.gov/pub/const/C30/tab179.txt>

1980-1984: 1980-1984; <http://www.census.gov/pub/const/C30/tab184.txt>

1985-1989: 1985-1989; <http://www.census.gov/pub/const/C30/tab189.txt>

1990: 1990; <http://www.census.gov/pub/const/C30/tab190.txt>

1991-1992: 1991-1995; <http://www.census.gov/pub/const/C30/tab195.txt>

• 1993-2001: U.S. Census Bureau; Annual: Annual Value of Construction Put in Place in the U.S.: 1993-2002, p. 1: Current $s & Constant (1996) $s; July 29, 2003; <http://www.census.gov/const/C30/Private.pdf>

• 2002-2008: U.S. Census Bureau; Annual: Annual Value of Construction Put in Place in the U.S.: 1993-2008, p. 1 Current $s; February 27, 2009; <http://www.census.gov/const/C30/total.pdf>

[10] For additional discussion of the implications of the trends, see Ronsvalle and Ronsvalle, *The State of Church Giving through 1991*, pp. 61-67.

chapter 6

The Potential of the Church

There are two ways to evaluate whether individual church members in the United States, and the church as a whole, have been faithful with "worldly wealth" as a precursor to more responsibility with "true riches."

The first is to consider what Christians in the U.S. have done with the resources available to them.

The second is to explore what Christians could have done with the resources available to them.

In this chapter, the focus will be on the potential of the church to impact, in Jesus' name, the needs of both global and local neighbors. The implications of the facts will be discussed in more detail in chapter 8.

Overview of the Potential of the Church

The analyses in this chapter consider present levels of church member giving in light of several potential standards.

One such standard is the classic tithe, or giving ten percent of income.[1] Calculating that difference between current giving levels and a congregationwide average of 10%, the result suggests that there would have been an additional $161 billion available for the work of the church in 2007, if historically Christian church members had given 10% of income, instead of the 2.56% that was donated. If church members had chosen to allocate 60% of this additional giving to global word and deed need, there would have been an additional $96 billion available, an amount substantially greater than estimates of the most urgent global word and deed need costs. If 20% had been directed to domestic need in the U.S., an additional $32 billion would have been available to address domestic needs including poverty, with an equal amount available for costs related to the increased international and domestic activity.

Jesus Christ assigned the church the task of the Great Commission—Jesus telling his followers to go into all the world, baptizing and teaching new converts to obey the tenets of the faith (see Matthew 28:18-20 and Acts 1:8). This assignment sits in the context of the Great Commandment—to love God and therefore love the neighbor (see Mark 12:28-31). The role of mission in relationship to the differential indicated by potential church giving levels is therefore a subject worth exploring.

One measure of the church's commitment to mission is the level of spending on international missions. In response to a survey sent out by empty tomb, inc., a set of denominations, for which 2003 through 2007 Total Contributions data was available, also provided Overseas Missions Income data for the years 2003 through 2007. The weighted average in 2007 for the group was 2.0% of Total Contributions being directed to denominational overseas ministries. Stated another way, of every dollar donated to a congregation, 2¢ was spent on denominational overseas missions. In 2007, two communions within the group of 34 gave 12¢ of each dollar to missions, while nine denominations each gave about 1¢ or less.

In general, the level of support for denominational overseas missions was lower in 2007 than in the 1920s.

The potential of the church can also be evaluated from the point of view of the need. For example, one denomination developed an estimate for the number of missionaries needed to engage the remaining unreached people groups. This information, combined with other estimates as well, allowed calculations to be made of the cost to complete this task.

An analysis built on the evangelism cost estimates yielded the finding that the cost would be only cents per day for groups of various church members.

If the goal were expanded to include not only evangelization, but also the cost of helping to stop, in Jesus' name, global child-deaths, providing primary education for all children around the world, and providing a budget for addressing poverty in the U.S., then the bottom line would increase and yet still only require less than a quarter per day per church member.

A potential giving number was calculated for each of the Roman Catholic archdioceses in the U.S. that has, or has traditionally had, a cardinal. The total additional level of giving among these nine archdioceses combined would have resulted in billions of dollars that could be applied to Catholic schools domestically and international need.

A 2009 report highlighted an estimate for the amount of money that flowed out of the U.S. to other countries. A review of the data suggested that foreign-born residents of the U.S. were about one-fourth the number of the native-born church member population in the U.S., and yet sent seven times the amount of money internationally than did the native-born church members.

A model of one organization's approach to its global evangelization task is introduced at the end of chapter 6, and discussed further in chapter 8.

Details of the Potential of the Church

Potential Giving at 10% of Income in 2007. If members of historically Christian churches had chosen to give 10% to their congregations in 2007, rather than the 2.56% given that year, there would have been an additional $161 billion available for work through the church. [2]

> If members of historically Christian churches had chosen to give 10% to their congregations in 2007, rather than the 2.56% given that year, there would have been an additional $161 billion available for work through the church.

Further, if those members had specified that 60% of their increased giving were to be given to international missions, there would have been an additional $96 billion available for the international work of the church. That would have left an additional $32 billion for domestic missions, including poverty conditions in the U.S., and an equal amount for costs related to the increased missions activity.[3]

This level of giving could have made a major impact on global need.

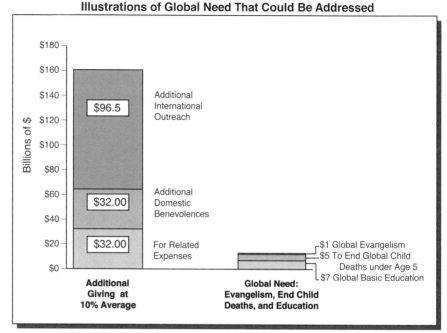

Figure 17: Potential Additional Church Giving at a 2007 Average of 10%, and Illustrations of Global Need That Could Be Addressed

Source: empty tomb analysis; UNICEF

empty tomb, inc., 2009

One estimate is that an additional $70 to $80 billion a year could address the basic needs of the poorest people around the world.[4] Basic primary education for all children around the globe would cost $7 billion a year.[5] Of the estimated 9.2 million children under five dying around the globe each year,[6] about two-thirds are dying from causes that could be addressed through low-cost solutions, according to one international study. The report stated: "Our findings show that about two-thirds of child deaths could be prevented by interventions that are available today and are feasible for implementation in low-income countries at high levels of population coverage."[7] The cost for these interventions might be about $5 billion a year for the portion focused specifically on the children.[8] An annual estimate of $1 billion to cover the costs of global evangelization is discussed below.

Figure 17 displays the potential giving levels, and issues of global need that could be addressed by the increased giving.

Per Capita Giving to International Missions. A survey of a group of 34 Protestant denominations found that, on average, two cents of each dollar donated to their affiliated congregations in 2007 funded international missions through the denominations.

The goal of the empty tomb, inc. research survey form was to discern how much of Overseas Missions Income came from living member giving. "Overseas Missions Income" was used in the title of the survey form, and "overseas ministries income" was used in the text of the questions on the survey form. In this volume, the two terms, "overseas missions" and "overseas ministry," are used interchangeably. The following questions were asked on the denominational Overseas Missions Income survey form for those denominations that had reported 2003, 2004, 2005, and 2006 data in previous years.

1. What was the amount of income raised in the U.S. during the calendar or fiscal year 2007 for overseas ministries?

2. How many dollars of the total amount on Line 1 came from endowment, foundation, and other investment income?

3. Of the total amount on Line 1, what is the dollar value of government grants, either in dollars or in-kind goods for distribution?

4. Balance of overseas ministries income: Line 1 minus Lines 2 and 3.

The form sent to denominations that had provided data in previous years included four columns labeled "Reported 2003," "Reported 2004," "Reported 2005," and "Reported 2006." These columns presented on each line the data previously reported by that denomination. A column to the right of these four columns was labeled "Newly Requested 2007" and included blank cells for each of the four lines.

A total of 34 denominations had complete data available for 2007.[9] The 34 denominations included a combined total of 39.8 million Full or Confirmed members in 2007.

...for each dollar of Total Contributions donated to a congregation, the denomination used 2¢ for overseas missions.

Data for 34 denominations, including Overseas Missions Income and Total Contributions, is presented in Tables 16 through 20, for the years 2003, 2004, 2005, 2006, and 2007, respectively.

The following observations can be drawn from the data in Tables 16-20.

The overall weighted average of Overseas Missions Income as a percent of Total Contributions to the denominations in 2007 was 2.0%. That is, for each dollar of Total Contributions donated to a congregation, the denomination used 2¢ for overseas missions.

Information in the endnotes to Tables 16 through 20 indicates that several of the denominations noted in survey correspondence that the dollar figure for international mission activity provided was only for activities funded through the national denominational office, and did not include overseas missions funded directly by the congregations. That is, some of the national denominational offices were of the opinion that congregations may be doing international mission activity in addition to any contributions sent to their offices. In at least two instances, dialogue with the denominational offices resulted in the finding that the national office sends a congregation statistics report form to affiliated congregations, and that this report form does not ask the congregation to distinguish that portion of Benevolences that was spent for international mission activity other than through the national denominational office. One denomination indicated that the national office obtains information from the congregations about missions done both directly by the congregation, and also through the denomination.

Congregational forms, sent by denominations to their congregations to obtain annual reports, could routinely, but apparently often do not, include details of congregational global missions expenditures that are not conducted through the denomination. The denominational structures presumably monitor other congregational expenditures, such as staff compensation and payments for pastor health insurance and pension benefits, as well as the general unified budget assessments requested from the congregations.

Table 16: Overseas Missions Income, Excluding Any Investment or Government Income, as a Percent of Total Contributions to Congregations, 34 Denominations, 2003

Denomination	2003 Overseas Missions Income (Line 4)	2003 Total Contributions	Overseas Missions Income as % of Total Contributions	Cents of Each Dollar for Overseas Ministries
Allegheny Wesleyan Methodist Connection	$262,260	$5,216,941	5.0%	5¢
American Baptist Churches in the U.S.A.	$8,513,838	$452,422,019	1.9%	2¢
Associate Reformed Presbyterian Church (General Synod)	$3,332,992	$44,279,992	7.5%	8¢
Brethren in Christ Church	$1,606,911	$36,309,353	4.4%	4¢
Christian Church (Disciples of Christ)	$4,079,019	$501,756,492	0.8%	1¢
Christian and Missionary Alliance [10]	$43,160,960	$381,439,326	11.3%	11¢
Church of the Brethren [11]	$1,563,623	$93,876,819	1.7%	2¢
Church of God General Conference (Oregon, Ill., and Morrow, Ga.)	$67,193	$4,297,394	1.6%	2¢
Church of the Lutheran Confession	$155,156	$5,855,961	2.6%	3¢
Church of the Nazarene	$45,640,480	$728,931,987	6.3%	6¢
Churches of God General Conference	$899,679	$27,444,027	3.3%	3¢
Conservative Congregational Christian Conference [12]	$147,805	$52,572,753	0.3%	0.3¢
Cumberland Presbyterian Church	$290,764	$49,168,885	0.6%	1¢
The Episcopal Church [13]	$13,193,855	$2,133,772,253	0.6%	1¢
Evangelical Congregational Church	$1,045,237	$19,628,647	5.3%	5¢
Evangelical Covenant Church	$7,913,682	$247,440,270	3.2%	3¢
Evangelical Lutheran Church in America	$19,637,381	$2,517,027,671	0.8%	1¢
Evangelical Lutheran Synod	$246,587	$13,013,890	1.9%	2¢
Fellowship of Evangelical Churches	$912,689	$14,138,539	6.5%	6¢
Free Methodist Church of North America	$9,121,599	$137,005,736	6.7%	7¢
General Association of General Baptists	$1,858,866	$35,428,127	5.2%	5¢
Lutheran Church-Missouri Synod [14]	$13,079,041	$1,256,382,217	1.0%	1¢
Moravian Church in America, Northern Province [15]	$467,570	$17,864,570	2.6%	3¢
The Orthodox Presbyterian Church	$1,214,449	$36,644,100	3.3%	3¢
Presbyterian Church in America	$24,070,885	$529,220,570	4.5%	5¢
Presbyterian Church (U.S.A.) [16]	$23,255,000	$2,743,637,755	0.8%	1¢
Primitive Methodist Church in the U.S.A.	$536,903	$4,771,104	11.3%	11¢
Reformed Church in America [17]	$7,852,464	$275,354,238	2.9%	3¢
Seventh-day Adventists, North Am. Div. [18]	$48,225,234	$1,088,682,947	4.4%	4¢
Southern Baptist Convention	$239,663,000	$9,648,530,640	2.5%	2¢
United Church of Christ	$8,373,084	$878,974,911	1.0%	1¢
The United Methodist Church [19]	$82,000,000	$5,376,057,236	1.5%	2¢
The Wesleyan Church	$8,507,914	$260,315,979	3.3%	3¢
Wisconsin Evangelical Lutheran Synod	$10,779,164	$278,209,035	3.9%	4¢
Total/Average for 34 Denominations	$631,675,283	$29,895,672,384	2.1%	2¢

Source: empty tomb, inc. analysis, 2009. See data notes at the end of the chapter. See Appendix B-5 for detail.

Table 17:   Overseas Missions Income, Excluding Any Investment or Government Income, as a Percent of Total Contributions to Congregations, 34 Denominations, 2004

Denomination	2004 Overseas Missions Income (Line 4)	2004 Total Contributions	Overseas Missions Income as % of Total Contributions	Cents of Each Dollar for Overseas Ministries
Allegheny Wesleyan Methodist Connection	$266,299	$5,638,852	4.7%	5¢
American Baptist Churches in the U.S.A.	$9,491,848	$432,734,941	2.2%	2¢
Associate Reformed Presbyterian Church (General Synod)	$3,954,575	$49,290,082	8.0%	8¢
Brethren in Christ Church	$1,800,963	$32,235,440	5.6%	6¢
Christian Church (Disciples of Christ)	$3,832,092	$493,377,355	0.8%	1¢
Christian and Missionary Alliance [10]	$43,534,066	$401,702,995	10.8%	11¢
Church of the Brethren [11]	$1,558,320	$90,440,250	1.7%	2¢
Church of God General Conference (Oregon, Ill., and Morrow, Ga.)	$113,497	$4,445,000	2.6%	3¢
Church of the Lutheran Confession	$206,896	$6,187,297	3.3%	3¢
Church of the Nazarene	$48,173,085	$743,526,726	6.5%	6¢
Churches of God General Conference	$1,047,148	$28,360,228	3.7%	4¢
Conservative Congregational Christian Conference [12]	$149,299	$59,795,058	0.2%	0.2¢
Cumberland Presbyterian Church	$323,340	$49,800,171	0.6%	1¢
The Episcopal Church [13]	$14,781,000	$2,132,774,534	0.7%	1¢
Evangelical Congregational Church	$941,409	$22,831,988	4.1%	4¢
Evangelical Covenant Church	$8,591,574	$267,267,027	3.2%	3¢
Evangelical Lutheran Church in America	$23,431,081	$2,568,013,806	0.9%	1¢
Evangelical Lutheran Synod	$266,241	$12,926,484	2.1%	2¢
Fellowship of Evangelical Churches	$847,526	$16,525,789	5.1%	5¢
Free Methodist Church of North America	$10,186,619	$147,016,945	6.9%	7¢
General Association of General Baptists	$1,768,537	$33,771,637	5.2%	5¢
Lutheran Church-Missouri Synod [14]	$13,177,379	$1,307,764,010	1.0%	1¢
Moravian Church in America, Northern Province [15]	$528,733	$18,514,925	2.9%	3¢
The Orthodox Presbyterian Church	$1,374,254	$38,660,300	3.6%	4¢
Presbyterian Church in America	$24,319,185	$544,857,944	4.5%	4¢
Presbyterian Church (U.S.A.) [16]	$24,588,000	$2,774,907,848	0.9%	1¢
Primitive Methodist Church in the U.S.A.	$526,640	$5,565,638	9.5%	9¢
Reformed Church in America [17]	$7,284,560	$296,856,834	2.5%	2¢
Seventh-day Adventists, North Am. Div. [18]	$46,752,585	$1,121,549,712	4.2%	4¢
Southern Baptist Convention	$242,140,000	$10,171,197,048	2.4%	2¢
United Church of Christ	$7,935,678	$895,654,110	0.9%	1¢
The United Methodist Church [19]	$91,200,000	$5,541,540,536	1.6%	2¢
The Wesleyan Church	$8,881,386	$259,011,346	3.4%	3¢
Wisconsin Evangelical Lutheran Synod	$10,304,863	$296,791,013	3.5%	3¢
Total/Average for 34 Denominations	$654,278,678	$30,871,533,869	2.1%	2¢

Source: empty tomb, inc. analysis, 2009. See data notes at the end of the chapter. See Appendix B-5 for detail.

Table 18:   Overseas Missions Income, Excluding Any Investment or Government Income, as a Percent of Total Contributions to Congregations, 34 Denominations, 2005

Denomination	2005 Overseas Missions Income (Line 4)	2005 Total Contributions	Overseas Missions Income as % of Total Contributions	Cents of Each Dollar for Overseas Ministries
Allegheny Wesleyan Methodist Connection	$399,514	$5,383,333	7.4%	7¢
American Baptist Churches in the U.S.A.	$11,096,481	$336,894,843	3.3%	3¢
Associate Reformed Presbyterian Church (General Synod)	$4,516,302	$50,921,233	8.9%	9¢
Brethren in Christ Church	$1,920,000	$39,800,056	4.8%	5¢
Christian Church (Disciples of Christ)	$4,222,777	$503,045,398	0.8%	1¢
Christian and Missionary Alliance [10]	$54,267,422	$442,917,566	12.3%	12¢
Church of the Brethren [11]	$2,270,134	$97,940,974	2.3%	2¢
Church of God General Conference (Oregon, Ill., and Morrow, Ga.)	$80,000	$4,496,822	1.8%	2¢
Church of the Lutheran Confession	$309,823	$6,551,799	4.7%	5¢
Church of the Nazarene	$52,753,682	$765,434,742	6.9%	7¢
Churches of God General Conference	$1,130,100	$32,249,551	3.5%	4¢
Conservative Congregational Christian Conference [12]	$166,875	$59,346,227	0.3%	0.3¢
Cumberland Presbyterian Church	$293,346	$54,148,837	0.5%	1¢
The Episcopal Church [13]	$15,371,967	$2,180,974,503	0.7%	1¢
Evangelical Congregational Church	$725,089	$21,408,687	3.4%	3¢
Evangelical Covenant Church	$9,008,719	$291,847,011	3.1%	3¢
Evangelical Lutheran Church in America	$26,084,001	$2,604,798,005	1.0%	1¢
Evangelical Lutheran Synod	$222,204	$13,831,771	1.6%	2¢
Fellowship of Evangelical Churches	$785,676	$18,426,832	4.3%	4¢
Free Methodist Church of North America	$10,720,240	$154,525,029	6.9%	7¢
General Association of General Baptists	$1,924,508	$40,146,583	4.8%	5¢
Lutheran Church-Missouri Synod [14]	$17,175,578	$1,296,818,738	1.3%	1¢
Moravian Church in America, Northern Province [15]	$482,157	$17,835,255	2.7%	3¢
The Orthodox Presbyterian Church	$1,856,529	$40,736,400	4.6%	5¢
Presbyterian Church in America	$25,890,591	$586,824,356	4.4%	4¢
Presbyterian Church (U.S.A.) [16]	$31,618,000	$2,814,271,023	1.1%	1¢
Primitive Methodist Church in the U.S.A.	$497,845	$5,541,336	9.0%	9¢
Reformed Church in America [17]	$10,727,347	$310,909,691	3.5%	3¢
Seventh-day Adventists, North Am. Div. [18]	$52,130,967	$1,273,399,341	4.1%	4¢
Southern Baptist Convention	$259,394,000	$10,721,544,568	2.4%	2¢
United Church of Christ	$7,652,371	$908,726,794	0.8%	1¢
The United Methodist Church [19]	$127,600,000	$5,861,722,397	2.2%	2¢
The Wesleyan Church	$9,769,938	$280,214,570	3.5%	3¢
Wisconsin Evangelical Lutheran Synod	$8,794,293	$299,324,485	2.9%	3¢
Total/Average for 34 Denominations	$751,858,476	$32,142,958,756	2.3%	2¢

Source: empty tomb, inc. analysis, 2009. See data notes at the end of the chapter. See Appendix B-5 for detail.

Table 19: **Overseas Missions Income, Excluding Any Investment or Government Income, as a Percent of Total Contributions to Congregations, 34 Denominations, 2006**

Denomination	2006 Overseas Missions Income (Line 4)	2006 Total Contributions	Overseas Missions Income as % of Total Contributions	Cents of Each Dollar for Overseas Ministries
Allegheny Wesleyan Methodist Connection	$286,781	$4,891,827	5.9%	6¢
American Baptist Churches in the U.S.A.	$8,779,170	$312,485,013	2.8%	3¢
Associate Reformed Presbyterian Church (General Synod)	$3,821,297	$48,592,174	7.9%	8¢
Brethren in Christ Church	$2,117,594	$41,396,500	5.1%	5¢
Christian Church (Disciples of Christ)	$4,421,669	$539,112,457	0.8%	1¢
Christian and Missionary Alliance [10]	$52,505,044	$458,063,183	11.5%	11¢
Church of the Brethren [11]	$1,887,202	$92,834,308	2.0%	2¢
Church of God General Conference (Oregon, Ill., and Morrow, Ga.)	$63,355	$4,421,793	1.4%	1¢
Church of the Lutheran Confession	$188,817	$6,965,144	2.7%	3¢
Church of the Nazarene	$50,969,965	$792,831,191	6.4%	6¢
Churches of God General Conference	$1,233,843	$33,061,351	3.7%	4¢
Conservative Congregational Christian Conference [12]	$123,509	$65,417,224	0.2%	0.2¢
Cumberland Presbyterian Church	$290,307	$54,727,911	0.5%	1¢
The Episcopal Church [13]	$14,806,793	$2,187,308,798	0.7%	1¢
Evangelical Congregational Church	$1,326,393	$22,174,004	6.0%	6¢
Evangelical Covenant Church	$8,530,245	$313,771,228	2.7%	3¢
Evangelical Lutheran Church in America	$21,541,809	$2,664,147,210	0.8%	1¢
Evangelical Lutheran Synod	$330,651	$16,412,280	2.0%	2¢
Fellowship of Evangelical Churches	$700,159	$19,031,219	3.7%	4¢
Free Methodist Church of North America	$11,878,875	$158,820,542	7.5%	7¢
General Association of General Baptists	$2,048,570	$35,905,960	5.7%	6¢
Lutheran Church-Missouri Synod [14]	$13,432,946	$1,355,458,558	1.0%	1¢
Moravian Church in America, Northern Province [15]	$512,828	$17,780,604	2.9%	3¢
The Orthodox Presbyterian Church	$1,706,292	$45,883,300	3.7%	4¢
Presbyterian Church in America	$27,627,770	$650,091,428	4.2%	4¢
Presbyterian Church (U.S.A.) [16]	$20,964,000	$2,854,719,850	0.7%	1¢
Primitive Methodist Church in the U.S.A.	$566,116	$5,080,485	11.1%	11¢
Reformed Church in America [17]	$7,486,527	$328,793,517	2.3%	2¢
Seventh-day Adventists, North Am. Div. [18]	$48,905,616	$1,290,321,473	3.8%	4¢
Southern Baptist Convention	$275,747,000	$11,372,608,393	2.4%	2¢
United Church of Christ	$7,539,124	$920,094,107	0.8%	1¢
The United Methodist Church [19]	$83,100,000	$6,012,378,898	1.4%	1¢
The Wesleyan Church	$13,105,882	$292,826,250	4.5%	4¢
Wisconsin Evangelical Lutheran Synod	$10,468,560	$314,016,686	3.3%	3¢
Total/Average for 34 Denominations	$699,014,709	$33,332,424,866	2.1%	2¢

Source: empty tomb, inc. analysis, 2009. See data notes at the end of the chapter. See Appendix B-5 for detail.

Table 20: Overseas Missions Income, Excluding Any Investment or Government Income, as a Percent of Total Contributions to Congregations, 34 Denominations, 2007

Denomination	2007 Overseas Missions Income (Line 4)	2007 Total Contributions	Overseas Missions Income as % of Total Contributions	Cents of Each Dollar for Overseas Ministries
Allegheny Wesleyan Methodist Connection	$332,511	$4,973,589	6.7%	7¢
American Baptist Churches in the U.S.A.	$9,866,010	$325,941,205	3.0%	3¢
Associate Reformed Presbyterian Church (General Synod)	$4,819,622	$49,424,200	9.8%	10¢
Brethren in Christ Church	$2,171,822	$46,806,908	4.6%	5¢
Christian Church (Disciples of Christ)	$4,774,004	$519,082,964	0.9%	1¢
Christian and Missionary Alliance [10]	$55,964,407	$467,812,148	12.0%	12¢
Church of the Brethren [11]	$1,736,654	$88,668,503	2.0%	2¢
Church of God General Conference (Oregon, Ill., and Morrow, Ga.)	$103,495	$4,378,745	2.4%	2¢
Church of the Lutheran Confession	$277,600	$7,207,712	3.9%	4¢
Church of the Nazarene	$50,591,155	$817,722,230	6.2%	6¢
Churches of God General Conference	$1,118,921	$35,106,856	3.2%	3¢
Conservative Congregational Christian Conference [12]	$169,508	$74,467,155	0.2%	0.2¢
Cumberland Presbyterian Church	$352,644	$57,766,770	0.6%	1¢
The Episcopal Church [13]	$15,028,559	$2,221,167,438	0.7%	1¢
Evangelical Congregational Church	$1,464,523	$17,180,755	8.5%	9¢
Evangelical Covenant Church	$7,954,834	$323,916,976	2.5%	2¢
Evangelical Lutheran Church in America	$21,747,378	$2,725,349,028	0.8%	1¢
Evangelical Lutheran Synod	$504,018	$16,104,636	3.1%	3¢
Fellowship of Evangelical Churches	$700,590	$19,031,219	3.7%	4¢
Free Methodist Church of North America	$12,478,468	$158,820,542	7.9%	8¢
General Association of General Baptists	$2,179,048	$31,385,133	6.9%	7¢
Lutheran Church-Missouri Synod [14]	$13,186,920	$1,399,774,702	0.9%	1¢
Moravian Church in America, Northern Province [15]	$524,149	$19,021,572	2.8%	3¢
The Orthodox Presbyterian Church	$1,824,389	$45,730,400	4.0%	4¢
Presbyterian Church in America	$28,456,453	$686,331,677	4.1%	4¢
Presbyterian Church (U.S.A.) [16]	$8,908,000	$2,916,788,414	0.3%	0.3¢
Primitive Methodist Church in the U.S.A.	$566,810	$4,632,031	12.2%	12¢
Reformed Church in America [17]	$7,611,613	$338,446,877	2.2%	2¢
Seventh-day Adventists, North Am. Div. [18]	$52,038,112	$1,259,280,736	4.1%	4¢
Southern Baptist Convention	$278,313,000	$12,107,096,858	2.3%	2¢
United Church of Christ	$7,107,090	$936,862,062	0.8%	1¢
The United Methodist Church [19]	$79,500,000	$6,295,942,455	1.3%	1¢
The Wesleyan Church	$13,554,996	$321,461,982	4.2%	4¢
Wisconsin Evangelical Lutheran Synod	$10,672,195	$323,082,651	3.3%	3¢
Total/Average for 34 Denominations	$696,599,498	$34,666,767,129	2.0%	2¢

Source: empty tomb, inc. analysis, 2009. See data notes at the end of the chapter. See Appendix B-5 for detail.

Table 21: **Overseas Missions Income, Excluding Any Investment or Government Income, as a Percent of Total Contributions to Congregations, 34 Denominations, Ranked by Cents per Dollar, 2007**

Rank	Denomination	Cents of Each Dollar for Overseas Ministries	Number of Members
1	Primitive Methodist Church in the U.S.A.	12¢	3,635
2	Christian and Missionary Alliance [20]	12¢	195,481
3	Associate Reformed Presbyterian Church (General Synod)	10¢	34,954
4	Evangelical Congregational Church	9¢	19,339
5	Free Methodist Church of North America	8¢	67,259
6	General Association of General Baptists	7¢	46,242
7	Allegheny Wesleyan Methodist Connection	7¢	1,414
8	Church of the Nazarene	6¢	635,526
9	Brethren in Christ Church	5¢	26,468
10	The Wesleyan Church	4¢	116,985
11	Presbyterian Church in America	4¢	270,605
12	Seventh-day Adventists, North Am. Div. [20]	4¢	1,000,472
13	The Orthodox Presbyterian Church	4¢	21,031
14	Church of the Lutheran Confession	4¢	6,262
15	Fellowship of Evangelical Churches	4¢	6,834
16	Wisconsin Evangelical Lutheran Synod	3¢	309,658
17	Churches of God General Conference	3¢	33,083
18	Evangelical Lutheran Synod	3¢	15,734
19	American Baptist Churches in the U.S.A.	3¢	1,358,351
20	Moravian Church in America, Northern Province [20]	3¢	17,554
21	Evangelical Covenant Church	2¢	123,150
22	Church of God General Conference (Oregon, Ill., and Morrow, Ga.)	2¢	3,039
23	Southern Baptist Convention	2¢	16,266,920
24	Reformed Church in America [20]	2¢	162,182
25	Church of the Brethren [20]	2¢	125,418
26	The United Methodist Church [20]	1¢	7,899,147
27	Lutheran Church-Missouri Synod [20]	1¢	1,835,064
28	Christian Church (Disciples of Christ)	1¢	447,340
29	Evangelical Lutheran Church in America	1¢	3,533,956
30	United Church of Christ	1¢	1,145,281
31	The Episcopal Church [20]	1¢	1,720,477
32	Cumberland Presbyterian Church	1¢	78,451
33	Presbyterian Church (U.S.A.) [20]	0.3¢	2,209,546
34	Conservative Congregational Christian Conference [20]	0.2¢	41,772

Source: empty tomb, inc. analysis, 2009. See data notes at the end of the chapter. See Appendix B-5 for detail.

Table 21 lists the 34 denominations with complete 2007 data in order of the level of unrounded cents per dollar donated to the congregation that was directed to denominational overseas missions. The membership for each denomination is also listed.

Figure 18 presents, in graphic form, the 2007 cents per dollar donated to the congregation that were directed to denominational overseas missions in 34 denominations in the U.S., and includes, for comparison, the 2005 giving level of the Antioch Presbyterian Church, Chonju, South Korea, a church that has set a global standard for missions support.

Appendix B-5 lists the four lines of data for the 34 denominations for 2003 through 2007.

A Comparison of Per Member Giving to Overseas Missions in Three Denominations. In the discussion immediately above, aggregate overseas missions income is set in the context of Total Contributions for each denomination.

One can also consider contributions to overseas missions income on a per member basis. A review of three denominations provided the following results.

The three denominations were selected as follows. The Church of the Nazarene, with 635,526 Full or Confirmed Members in 2007 was the largest denomination with membership in the National Association of Evangelicals that provided data. The Southern Baptist Convention, with 16,266,920 Full or Confirmed Members in 2007, was the largest Protestant denomination in the U.S. The United Methodist Church, with 7,899,147 Full or Confirmed Members in 2007, was the largest denomination with membership in the National Council of the Churches of Christ in the U.S.A. that provided data.

Dividing the amount of overseas missions income by the number of reported members resulted in a per member dollar giving level for each denomination. Since

Figure 18: Cents Directed to Denominational Overseas Missions, Per Dollar Donated to the Congregation, 34 Denominations in the U.S., 2007, and Antioch Presbyterian Church, Chonju, South Korea, 2005

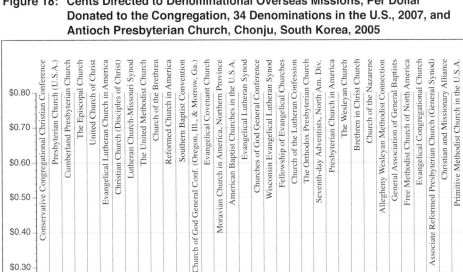

Source: empty tomb, inc. Analysis   empty tomb, inc., 2009

the data is for the year 2007 for all three denominations, current dollars can be effectively used in the comparison.

The dollar figure for per member giving to denominational overseas missions for the Church of the Nazarene was $80 in 2007.

The dollar figure for per member giving to denominational overseas missions for the Southern Baptist Convention was $17 in 2007.

The dollar figure for per member giving to denominational overseas missions for The United Methodist Church was $10 in 2007.

Further analysis of factors that might have contributed to the difference in the level of support for denominational overseas missions may yield insight about how denominational structures and priorities affect the level of overseas missions support.

Denominational Overseas Missions Income, 1916-1927. *The Yearbook of American and Canadian Churches* series began with the 1916 *Federal Council Year Book.* The second edition, published in 1917, and continuing through the 1927 edition, presented detailed denominational "foreign missions" information. Income as well as geographical placement and type of missionaries were presented on multi-page tables.

Changes in the level of mission support also led a group of denominations to commission a report, published in 1929, about levels of missions giving. As found in Table 22, the 1929 study provided per capita giving to Foreign Missions, Benevolences, and Total Contributions for 11 denominations.[21] With this information, it was possible to calculate per capita Foreign Missions as a percent of per capita Benevolences, and per capita Foreign Missions as a percent of per capita Total Contributions.

**Table 22: Foreign Missions, Benevolences, and Total Contributions,
11 Denominations, 1916-1927, Current Dollars**

Year	Per Capita Foreign Missions Income from Living Donors	Per Capita Benevolences	Per Capita Foreign Missions as a Percent of Per Capita Benevolences (Calculated)	Per Capita Total Contributions	Per Capita Foreign Missions as a Percent of Per Capita Total Contributions (Calculated)
1916	$0.73	$2.24	32.59%	$10.11	7.22%
1917	$0.74	$2.52	29.37%	$10.75	6.88%
1918	$0.86	$2.89	29.76%	$11.44	7.52%
1919	$1.18	$3.89	30.33%	$12.90	9.15%
1920	$1.66	$5.75	28.87%	$16.45	10.09%
1921	$1.70	$5.51	30.85%	$17.20	9.88%
1922	$1.46	$5.18	28.19%	$17.19	8.49%
1923	$1.44	$5.12	28.13%	$17.69	8.14%
1924	$1.32	$4.97	26.56%	$18.44	7.16%
1925	$1.27	$4.59	27.67%	$18.74	6.78%
1926	$1.32	$4.49	29.40%	$18.94	6.97%
1927	$1.24	$4.17	29.74%	$18.95	6.54%

Source: empty tomb analysis; Charles H. Fahs, *Trends in Protestant Giving* (1929), Tables XVIII and XXIX

During the 1916-1927 period, for the group of 11 denominations, Foreign Missions Income represented about 30% of all Benevolences. The 1929 study was commissioned in response to the concern of members of the Foreign Missions Conference of North America that giving to foreign missions was declining. As seen in Table 22, per capita Foreign Missions Income had decreased to 6.54% of Total Contributions in 1927.

By 2007, some 80 years later, per capita Foreign Missions Income had decreased further, to 2.0% of Total Contributions for a set of 34 Protestant denominations.

The overall average of per capita Foreign Missions Income as a percent of Total Contributions for 11 denominations for the 1916 through 1927 period was 7.9%, compared to 2.0% for 34 denominations in 2007. The average U.S. per capita Disposable Personal Income (DPI) during the 1916-1927 period was $5,614, in inflation-adjusted 2000 dollars. That average income figure compares to the inflation-adjusted U.S. per capita DPI figure of $28,132 in 2007. Since per capita income was five times the average in the 1916-1927 period, Americans had 401% more after-tax income in 2007 than in the earlier period. The data indicates that overseas missions support was not as high a priority in 2007 as it was in the 1920s, in spite of improved communication about global needs and a higher level of member income in 2007 compared to the 1916-1927 period.

Calculating the Cost of Missions: Word Mission. One area that is exclusively within the realm of the church is the cost of global evangelization. Interestingly, there have been few if any firm cost estimates for insuring that people around the globe have the opportunity to make an informed choice about responding to the Christian message. This has been true even though the accessibility to information about Christianity can be regarded as a justice issue. As a report from one international organization observed:

> There is also a tragic coincidence that most of the world's poor have
> not heard the Good News of the Gospel of Jesus Christ; or they

could not receive it, because it was not recognized as Good News in the way in which it was brought. This is a double injustice: they are victims of oppression of an unjust economic order or an unjust political distribution of power, and at the same time they are deprived of the knowledge of God's special care for them. To announce the Good News to the poor is to begin to render the justice due to them.[22]

One term that is often used to describe the population most excluded from accessibility to the Christian message is "unreached people group" although the term "least-reached" may also be used. Wikipedia footnotes the Joshua Project for the definition that reads:

A people group among which there is no indigenous community of believing Christians with adequate numbers and resources to evangelize this people group.[23]

Estimates of the number of unreached people groups vary among those concerned with the topic.[24] The difference in estimates may have to do with defining the size of the people group or other factors.

One denomination that is on record as having a particular concern about unreached people groups is the Southern Baptist Convention. The Southern Baptist Convention (SBC) is the second largest communion, and the largest Protestant denomination, in the United States. As noted on the Web site of the SBC Executive Committee Director, Dr. Morris Chapman, "In 1845, a network of churches was organized into the Southern Baptist Convention for the purpose of evangelizing the world...."[25] The SBC International Mission Board (IMB) is the group within the Convention that is currently charged with supervising the continuing task of global evangelization.

"To announce the Good News to the poor is to begin to render the justice due to them."

Information from the IMB can assist in developing a cost model for making contact with unreached people groups.

An IMB figure for the number of unreached people groups was 5,903 in April 2008.[26]

An advertisement in a denominational magazine announced that the "number of additional IMB missionaries needed to engage the unreached people groups around the world with the gospel" was 2,800.[27]

A working estimate of $65,000[28] per missionary was applied to the figure of 2,800 additional missionaries to calculate a total cost figure of $182,000,000 to field these additional missionaries.

While the above model is built on information from the Southern Baptist Convention, another model can be developed for mission costs that could be pursued by the broad spectrum of the church.

For example, other communions are also actively pursuing the engagement of unreached people groups. Some groups opt to send cross-cultural missionaries, and others choose to work through missionaries born in the region in which the unreached people groups are located.

Two groups that build their outreach through native-born missionaries are Christian Aid Mission and Gospel for Asia.

Table 23: **Great Commandment and Great Commission Outreach Estimated Costs, Calculated Per Member for Selected Church Populations, 2007**

	A. Engage Unreached People Estimate (SBC) $182,000,000	B. Combined Estimate for Global Evangelization $544,240,000	C. High Estimate for Global Evangelization $1,000,000,000	D. Stopping, in Jesus' Name Global Under-5 Child Deaths $5,000,000,000	C. + D. + Global Elementary Education + Domestic Poverty $15,000,000,000
Love Expressed in Great Commission Outreach					
Engage Unreached People Estimate (So. Baptist Conv.)	$182,000,000				
Combined Estimate for Global Evangelization		$544,240,000			
High Estimate for Global Evangelization			$1,000,000,000		$1,000,000,000
Stopping in Jesus' Name Under-Five Child Deaths				$5,000,000,000	$5,000,000,000
Global Elementary Education					$7,000,000,000
Domestic U.S. Poverty Need					$2,000,000,000
Total Per Year	$182,000,000	$544,240,000	$1,000,000,000	$5,000,000,000	$15,000,000,000
Historically Christian Church Members (59.45% US Pop. = 179,657,900)					
Annual Amount per Historically Christian Ch. Member	$1	$3	$6	$28	$83
Daily Amount per Historically Christian Church Member	Less than $0.01	$0.01	$0.02	$0.08	$0.23
Evangelical Christians (7% US Pop. = 21,154,000)					
Annual Amount per Evangelical Christian	$9	$26	$47	$236	$709
Daily Amount per Evangelical Christian	$0.02	$0.07	$0.13	$0.65	$1.94
Born Again Christians (40% US Pop. = 120,880,000)					
Annual Amount per Born Again Christian	$2	$5	$8	$41	$124
Daily Amount per Born Again Christian	Less than $0.01	$0.01	$0.02	$0.11	$0.34
National Council of the Churches of Christ in the U.S.A. **Inclusive Members** (= 42,557,867)					
Annual Amount per NCCC Member	$4	$13	$23	$117	$352
Daily Amount per NCCC Member	$0.01	$0.04	$0.06	$0.32	$0.97
Roman Catholic Members (= 67,117,016)					
Annual Amount per Roman Catholic Member	$3	$8	$15	$74	$223
Daily Amount per Roman Catholic Member	$0.01	$0.02	$0.04	$0.20	$0.61
Southern Baptist Members (= 16,266,920)					
Annual Amount per Southern Baptist Member	$11	$33	$61	$307	$922
Daily Amount per Southern Baptist Member	$0.03	$0.09	$0.17	$0.84	$2.53
United Methodist Members (= 7,899,147)					
Annual Amount per United Methodist Member	$23	$69	$127	$633	$1,899
Daily Amount per United Methodist Member	$0.06	$0.19	$0.35	$1.73	$5.20

Note: The annual and daily numbers in the above table would be divided by two if wealthy Christians in that grouping provided half in the form of matching funds.

Source: empty tomb, inc. analysis, 2009.

Christian Aid Mission coordinates with native workers in various countries to "establish a witness for Christ in every unreached nation." Its Web site states, "Approximately 100,000 of these [native missionaries] have no regular support..." The average monthly support number cited is $50 a month.[29] At $600 a year per missionary, the cost to fund the 100,000 missionaries would be $60,000,000 a year.

Gospel for Asia also trains and coordinates a network of native missionaries through Asian countries. To reach a goal of supporting 100,000 missionaries,[30] Gospel for Asia would need to support an additional 83,500 missionaries over the current number of 16,500.[31] The costs for Gospel for Asia missionaries range from

$90 to $150 a month.[32] Taking an average cost of $120 a month, the annual cost of $1,440 was multiplied by the 83,500 figure for the number of additional missionaries needed, yielding a total need of $120,240,000 a year.

The estimate for Christian Aid Mission and Gospel for Asia additional missionaries would total $180,240,000 a year.

Other communions and para-denominational groups in the U.S. are also focused on the goal of engaging the unreached. If the cost of those efforts were on a par with the estimate for the Southern Baptist Convention, the cost would be $182,000,000.

Combining these amounts, the four sets of numbers equal $544,420,000.

If the total cost of evangelization were to be estimated, including not only expanded but also ongoing work, the increased total might not exceed $1 billion a year.[33]

Various groups could accept the challenge of funding the cost of this expanded budget for global evangelization. Table 23 indicates the daily and annual costs based on the population of each group.[34]

Of course, the Great Commission, in the context of the Great Commandment, would present the good news of Jesus Christ in both word and deed. Christians generally agree about God's concern for the children of the world. About 26,600 children under the age of five die each day around the globe. With about 17,700 of these children dying from preventable poverty conditions for which there are low-cost immediate solutions, the church should recognize both the possibility and the responsibility inherent in this challenge. Table 23 considers the annual and daily costs for various groups if members should choose to prevent more deaths among children under five around the globe.

However, the choice need not be between global evangelization *or* helping to stop, in Jesus' name, global child deaths, *or* primary education, *or* addressing poverty within the United States. When Jesus Christ came to announce God's love for the world in a physical body, he combined the power of the spoken word with healing, feeding, clothing, and freeing those he encountered. Given the resources and the broad base of the church, the current body of Jesus Christ, Christians in the early 21st century have the power to follow Jesus' example of loving the whole person in need. The higher cost for combining evangelization, addressing global child deaths, providing primary education, and having $2 billion a year additional to address domestic poverty needs within the U.S. in Jesus' name was estimated at $15 billion a year. Table 23 also displays the annual and daily costs for various groupings of Christians to engage all of these needs simultaneously.

If creative church leadership were displayed, wealthy Christians might be found who would provide matching funds for donations from the general church population for these needs. In that case, the annual and daily costs presented in Table 23 would be divided by two.

Table 24 considers the same word and deed needs from a slightly different perspective. In this table, the size of the population with varying degrees of wealth was calculated for four sets of church groups. Annual and daily costs to meet the outlined needs are presented for households with $5 million net worth, $1 million

However, the choice need not be between global evangelization *or* helping to stop, in Jesus' name, global child deaths, *or* primary education, *or* addressing poverty within the United States.

Table 24: **Great Commandment and Great Commission Outreach Estimated Costs, Calculated Per Household for Populations with Selected Levels of Net Worth apart from Primary Residence, 2007**

	A. Engage Unreached People Estimate (SBC) $182,000,000	B. Combined Estimate for Global Evangelization $544,240,000	C. High Estimate for Global Evangelization $1,000,000,000	D. Stopping, in Jesus' Name Global Under-5 Child Deaths $5,000,000,000	C. + D. + Global Elementary Education + Domestic Poverty $15,000,000,000
Love Expressed in Great Commission Outreach					
Engage Unreached People Estimate (So. Baptist Conv.)	$182,000,000				
Combined Estimate for Global Evangelization		$544,240,000			
High Estimate for Global Evangelization			$1,000,000,000		$1,000,000,000
Stopping in Jesus' Name Under-Five Child Deaths				$5,000,000,000	$5,000,000,000
Global Elementary Education					$7,000,000,000
Domestic U.S. Poverty Need					$2,000,000,000
Total Per Year	$182,000,000	$544,240,000	$1,000,000,000	$5,000,000,000	$15,000,000,000
Historically Christian Church Households					
Greater than or Equal to $5 million (= 689,620)					
Annual Amount per Historically Christian Ch. Household	$264	$789	$1,450	$7,250	$21,751
Daily Amount per Historically Christian Church Hshld.	$0.72	$2.16	$3.97	$19.86	$59.59
Greater than or Equal to $1 million = 5,469,400)					
Annual Amount per Historically Christian Ch. Household	$33	$100	$183	$914	$2,743
Daily Amount per Historically Christian Church Hshld.	$0.09	$0.27	$0.50	$2.50	$7.51
Greater than or Equal to $500,000 (= 9,333,650)					
Annual Amount per Historically Christian Ch. Household	$19	$58	$107	$536	$1,607
Daily Amount per Historically Christian Church Hshld.	$0.05	$0.16	$0.29	$1.47	$4.40
Evangelical Christian Households					
Greater than or Equal to $5 million (= 81,200)					
Annual Amount per Evangelical Christian Household	$2,241	$6,702	$12,315	$61,576	$184,729
Daily Amount per Evangelical Christian Household	$6.14	$18.36	$33.74	$168.70	$506.11
Greater than or Equal to $1 million (= 644,000)					
Annual Amount per Evangelical Christian Household	$283	$845	$1,553	$7,764	$23,292
Daily Amount per Evangelical Christian Household	$0.77	$2.32	$4.25	$21.27	$63.81
Greater than or Equal to $500,000 (= 1,099,000)					
Annual Amount per Evangelical Christian Household	$166	$495	$910	$4,550	$13,649
Daily Amount per Evangelical Christian Household	$0.45	$1.36	$2.49	$12.46	$37.39
Born Again Christian Households					
Greater than or Equal to $5 million (= 464,000)					
Annual Amount per Born Again Christian Household	$392	$1,173	$2,155	$10,776	$32,328
Daily Amount per Born Again Christian Household	$1.07	$3.21	$5.90	$29.52	$88.57
Greater than or Equal to $1 million (= 3,680,000)					
Annual Amount per Born Again Christian Household	$49	$148	$272	$1,359	$4,076
Daily Amount per Born Again Christian Household	$0.14	$0.41	$0.74	$3.72	$11.17
Greater than or Equal to $500,000 (= 6,280,000)					
Annual Amount per Born Again Christian Household	$29	$87	$159	$796	$2,389
Daily Amount per Born Again Christian Household	$0.08	$0.24	$0.44	$2.18	$6.54
NCCCUSA Households					
Greater than or Equal to $5 million (= 163,359)					
Annual Amount per NCCC Household	$1,114	$3,332	$6,121	$30,607	$91,822
Daily Amount per NCCC Household	$3.05	$9.13	$16.77	$83.86	$251.57
Greater than or Equal to $1 million (= 1,295,607)					
Annual Amount per NCCC Household	$140	$420	$772	$3,859	$11,578
Daily Amount per NCCC Household	$0.38	$1.15	$2.11	$10.57	$31.72
Greater than or Equal to $500,000 (= 2,210,981)					
Annual Amount per NCCC Household	$82	$246	$452	$2,261	$6,784
Daily Amount per NCCC Household	$0.23	$0.67	$1.24	$6.20	$18.59

Note: The annual and daily numbers in the above table would be divided by two if the general church population provided half the money in response to matching funds offered by wealthy church members.

Source: empty tomb, inc. analysis, 2009.

net worth, and $500,000 net worth, apart from primary residence.[35] Again, if the general church population were to provide half the funds needed to address these needs, the numbers in the table would be divided by two.

A discussion of the role that church members with considerable wealth at their disposal could play in mobilizing all church members is discussed in chapter 8.

Potential Roman Catholic Giving. The Roman Catholic Church is the largest single religious body in the United States. Unfortunately, that communion has opted not to publish financial giving data on a regular basis. Therefore, any estimates of giving among this major part of the body of Christ must be only approximations. Given the size of the Catholic Church, however, such an approximation is worth exploring.

There has been some discussion in Catholic circles about the practice of the tithe in recent years.[36]

To explore that idea further, a review of potential giving levels at an average of 10% per member was done for the nine archdioceses that have, or traditionally have had, a cardinal. Each archdiocese comprises certain U.S. counties. As a result, the total population[37] and the U.S. per capita Disposable Personal Income could be obtained for each archdiocese.[38] A general estimate of 1.2% of income was used as the current level of Catholic giving.[39]

The nine archdioceses combined had a present estimated giving level of $9.3 billion dollars. If Catholics in these archdioceses increased from the current 1.2% of income given to 10% of income, the additional total would have been $67.9 billion in 2007. The increased amounts varied from $2 billion in the Archdiocese of Baltimore, to $15 billion in the Archdiocese of New York.

The results of the calculations are shown in Table 25.

The application of this potential giving could make an impact on domestic as well as international Catholic missions. For example, Catholic schools are closing across the U.S. Many of these schools have focused on the inner cities. The

Table 25: Potential Additional Giving at 10% of Income, Nine Roman Catholic Archdioceses in the U.S., 2007

Area Name	Total U.S. BEA Personal Income for Counties in Archdioceses ($s)	% Catholic of Total Population in Area	Calculated U.S. BEA Personal Income Available to Catholics ($s)	Estimated Current Catholic Giving at 1.2% of Income ($s)	Estimated Potential Additional Catholic Giving at 10% Income ($s)
Archdiocese of Baltimore	$137,716,642,000	16.36%	$22,531,294,260	$270,375,531	$1,982,753,895
Archdiocese of Boston	$220,244,416,103	46.14%	$101,630,112,091	$1,219,561,345	$8,943,449,864
Archdiocese of Chicago	$278,305,807,000	39.00%	$108,549,465,876	$1,302,593,591	$9,552,352,997
Archdiocese of Detroit	$171,845,178,000	32.79%	$56,346,300,856	$676,155,610	$4,958,474,475
Archdiocese of Galveston-Houston	$258,724,417,000	19.54%	$50,566,365,245	$606,796,383	$4,449,840,142
Archdiocese of Los Angeles	$445,526,122,000	36.20%	$161,289,547,445	$1,935,474,569	$14,193,480,175
Archdiocese of New York	$378,601,529,000	45.00%	$170,370,681,410	$2,044,448,177	$14,992,619,964
Archdiocese of Philadelphia	$184,342,322,000	37.60%	$69,305,571,660	$831,666,860	$6,098,890,306
Archdiocese of Washington	$144,184,693,000	21.96%	$31,656,199,279	$379,874,391	$2,785,745,537
Total: 9 Archdioceses with Cardinals	$2,219,491,126,103		$772,245,538,122	$9,266,946,457	$67,957,607,355

Source: empty tomb, inc. analysis, 2009.

schools provided an educational alternative to low-income families. As Sister Dale McDonald, the National Catholic Education Association director, commented, "The church has always had a strong sense of mission, particularly to the poor… As it becomes more and more difficult, not only on the poor but on middle-income people, we're not really fulfilling the mission of the church to serve all if we only can afford to serve the people who can afford the big bucks."[40]

As proposed above, increased giving at the 10% level could be allocated so that 60% is directed to international ministries and 20% to domestic needs. That distribution could direct as much as $3.2 billion to inner-city Catholic schools in these nine archdioceses, even while providing critical resources for missions that address international need.

However, as shown earlier in Table 23, Catholics, as well as all other Christians, could make a dramatic impact on global word and deed need for much less than the cost of increasing giving to the classic tithe.

Putting Potential into Perspective. A 2009 report introduced an additional estimate on the amount of money being sent from the United States to other countries. *The Index of Global Philanthropy and Remittances 2009* is the fourth in a series from the Hudson Institute.[41]

> …Catholics, as well as all other Christians, could make a dramatic impact on global word and deed need for much less than the cost of increasing giving to the classic tithe.

The ambitious project seeks to bring a broad and fresh perspective to the growing area of global philanthropy. The report is not limited to the traditional boundaries of the area, instead including, for example, "private capital flows," representing investment on market terms by for-profit businesses in developing countries, and remittances by foreign-born residents to their home countries into the mix.

The focus of the discussion in the current chapter is on the potential of religious giving. Some preliminary calculations, based on the text descriptions that are presented, suggest that the *Index*'s $8.6 billion may be a somewhat low estimate for religious philanthropy directed to other countries. That is, in order not to double-count $2.3 billion in congregational donations to U.S.-based relief and development organizations, the *Index* included that $2.3 billion in the Private Voluntary Organization category, and subtracted that amount from its estimate of international assistance provided by Religion. However, in the present discussion of Religion giving to international ministry, there is no basis for excluding that $2.3 billion. When that amount is added to the *Index*'s Religion figure of $8.6 billion, a revised total of $10.9 billion given internationally by people in the U.S. can be described as given as a function of Religion.[42]

Two observations about the *Index*'s numbers as they are presented can be made. One observation considers the potential to stop child deaths in light of total assistance to developing countries, and the second compares religious philanthropy to remittances.

Total Assistance to Developing Countries and Child Deaths. In 2007, the "Total U.S. Economic Engagement with Developing Countries, 2007" was estimated to be $235.2 billion.[43]

As noted earlier in this chapter, a figure of $5 billion a year has been calculated as the amount needed to stop the deaths of two-thirds of the 9.2 million children under five being killed each year by preventable causes that could be addressed with available, low-cost solutions.

A comparison of the $235.2 billion economic engagement with developing countries, and the $5 billion needed to stop most of the child deaths in those countries, leads to a question of priorities. Why have the leaders responsible for the billions of dollars transmitted to developing countries not focused 2% of that total on the strategies available to prevent these child deaths? Or alternatively, why have the leaders not organized to increase the total slightly, with the targeted goal of applying the increase to addressing these child deaths?

Church Giving to Global Need Compared to Immigrant Remittances. The *Index of Global Philanthropy*'s estimate of private religious philanthropy to developing countries figure was $8.6 billion in 2007. As noted above, this figure of $8.6 billion has been adjusted to $10.9 billion, to compare a maximum estimate of religious giving in the U.S. to international causes for the present analysis. An estimate of 156,687,291 native-born members in historically Christian churches in the U.S. in 2007 was used in the comparison.[44] For purposes of the present discussion, one may attribute all of the $10.9 billion in private religious assistance to these native-born church members.

That figure of $10.9 billion from native-born church members in the U.S. can be compared to the $79 billion figure of "U.S. Remittances."[45] The category is defined as assistance "sent home by migrants working abroad."[46] The developing countries that received the largest amount of these remittances were Mexico, other countries in Latin America and the Caribbean, the Philippines, India, and China.[47]

A comparison of these numbers leads to questions of both potential and priorities. There were an estimated 156,687,291 native-born church members, which was more than four times the 38,059,694 foreign-born people living in the U.S.[48] Yet, those foreign-born inhabitants sent seven times the amount of assistance to developing countries than did the native-born church members. Given the list of recipient countries, one might hypothesize that the foreign-born people living in the U.S. and sending remittances to developing countries are from varying economic backgrounds, and not necessarily wealthier than native-born church members. These foreign-born inhabitants have to obtain housing, food, and clothing to maintain themselves while living in the U.S., as do the native-born church members.

If the total remittances sent by foreign-born people in the United States figure is divided by the foreign-born population in the U.S., the amount is calculated to be $2,076. Following a similar procedure for the native-born church members, it is estimated that the per member contribution to international ministries in 2007 was $70. If native-born church members in the U.S. were to donate to international ministries on the same level as foreign-born people in the U.S., the additional donations would total $314 billion more.

The numbers are another demonstration of the potential of church members in the U.S. to increase contributions to approach the level of foreign-born people's remittances, in order to impact global needs. The numbers also point out the disparity of priorities between the foreign-born inhabitants and the church members. The first is presumably sending assistance to family. The second is directed by Jesus Christ to send assistance to him via "the least of these" (see Matthew 25:31-46). Will native-born church members honor Jesus' wishes to the same degree that foreign-born people living in the U.S. honor their families?

If native-born church members in the U.S. were to donate to international ministries on the same level as foreign-born people in the U.S., the additional donations would total $314 billion more.

A Model for Increased Mission Funding. If the potential for increased missions funding remains only theoretical, the analysis in this chapter will do little to assist those in desperate physical and spiritual need around the globe. That is why it is important to identify models that actually increase funding for missions.

In chapter 8, a campaign undertaken by Wycliffe Bible Translators is reviewed. The specific goal of the organization is to have begun, by the year 2025, Bible translations for all remaining languages. The approach that the Wycliffe organization has taken in pursuing this goal may provide a useful model for furthering mission work in denominations as well.

Making Missions Giving a Priority in Order to Act on the Potential. The numbers in this chapter document the potential for church members in the U.S. to increase giving, and outline some of the impact on global word and deed need, as well as domestic need, that could be made as a result.

Various comparisons in this chapter demonstrate that the issue of meeting global and domestic need is not one of resources, but of priorities and intentions. The Biblical mandate, as well as various methodologies, are in place to lay the groundwork for impacting global word and deed need in Jesus' name. Chapter 8 explores how more of the potential might be translated into a greater reality.

Notes for Chapter 6

[1] See Jesus' statement in Matthew 23:23. For a discussion of various views of the tithe, see John and Sylvia Ronsvalle, *Behind the Stained Glass Windows: Money Dynamics in the Church* (Grand Rapids, MI: Baker Book House, 1996), pp. 187-193.

[2] The basis for the calculations of potential giving by historically Christian churches in the U.S. in 2007 is as follows. In chapter seven of this volume titled "Why and How Much Do Americans Give?" a 2007 figure of total giving to religion was presented in the "Denomination-Based Series Keyed to 1974 Filer Estimate." That figure was $75.1 billion. A figure of 73.8% was multiplied by the 2007 figure for giving to religion of $75.1 billion to determine what amount was given by those who identify with the historically Christian church. The result was $55.4 billion. In 2007, if giving had increased to an average of 10% from the actual level of 2.56% given, instead of $55.4 billion, an amount of $216 billion would have been donated to historically Christian churches. The difference between the $55.4 billion given and the potential of $216 billion is $161 billion, the additional money that would have been available at an average of 10% giving. The above figure of 73.8% was based on an empty tomb, inc. analysis of data published in Barry A. Kosmin and Ariela Keysar; *American Religious Identification Survey [ARIS 2008] Summary Report*; Hartford, Conn.: Trinity College, March 2009; p. 5 of 7/4/2009 printout, and referred to that portion of the U.S. population that identifies with the historically Christian church—those communions and traditions, such as Roman Catholic, Orthodox, evangelical and mainline Protestant, Pentecostal, and Anabaptist, that profess a commitment to the historic tenets of the faith.

[3] It may be noted that the estimate of an additional $161 billion that would be available if average giving were at 10% is at the lower end. Rather than using the calculation detailed in the previous endnote, two other estimates of $549 billion and $695 billion for 2007 were obtained based on alternate assumptions. An alternative estimate of $549 billion was derived based on the assumption that: (1) 59.45% of Americans are members of historically Christian churches, with aggregate after-tax income of $6.0 trillion; (2) religious giving was $75.1 billion in 2007; and (3) 73.8% of religious giving was from self-identifying Christians (estimate based on ARIS 2008). The results indicated that the giving level among self-identifying Christians was 0.92% of historically Christian church member after-tax income in 2007, rather than the 2.56% noted in the previous endnote. In that case, the difference between 2007 giving at 0.92% and 10% would

have been $549 billion. Alternatively, one could base the potential giving level calculation on the assumptions that: (1) 73.8% of Americans identify with the historically Christian church, whether or not they are members (estimate based on ARIS 2008); (2) this portion of Americans had an aggregate after-tax income of $7.5 trillion; and (3) the calculation considered contributions as possibly available from this 73.8% of U.S. population. In that case, giving levels would have been at the 0.74% of income level. In that case, the difference between self-identified Christian giving in 2007 at the 0.74% level and a potential 10% level would have yielded an additional $695 billion in 2007. The estimate of 59.45% church member figure was an empty tomb, inc. calculation based on Gallup, *Religion in America 2002*, pp. 28, 40. The 2007 aggregate Disposable Personal Income figure of $10.1705 trillion that was multiplied by the church member population figures in the two alternative calculations contained in this endnote above was obtained from U.S. Bureau of Economic Analysis National Income and Product Accounts, Table 2.1, Personal Income and Its Disposition, line 26, data published 3/26/2009.

[4] Carol Bellamy, *The State of the World's Children 2000* (New York: UNICEF, 2000), p. 37.

[5] Carol Bellamy, *The State of the World's Children 1999* (New York: UNICEF, 1999), p. 85.

[6] Ann M. Veneman, *The State of the World's Children 2009* (New York: UNICEF, 2008), p. 121.

[7] Gareth Jones et al.; "How Many Child Deaths Can We Prevent This Year?"; *The Lancet*, vol. 362; 7/5/2003; <http://www.thelancet.com/journal/vol1362/iss9377/full/llan.362.9377.child_survival.26292.1>; p. 6 of 7/7/03 2:06 PM printout.

[8] James Grant, *The State of the World's Children 1990* (New York: Oxford University Press, 1990), p. 16, estimated that $2.5 billion a year would be needed by the late 1990s to stop preventable child deaths. An updated figure of $5.1 billion was cited in Jennifer Bryce et al.; "Can the World Afford to Save the Lives of 6 Million Children Each Year?"; *The Lancet*, vol. 365; 6/25/2005; p. 2193; <http://www.thelancet.com/journals/lancet/article/PIIS014065667773/fulltext>; p. 1 of 1/11/2006 printout.

[9] Three additional denominations provided Overseas Missions Income for some or all years of 2003 through 2007. Two indicated that they were not able to provide Total Contributions for those years. Those denominations and their data are listed in a table in Appendix B-5. It should be noted that in 2004, Friends United Meeting changed fiscal years to end June 30, 2004, and so only six months of data was available for 2004. The North American Baptist Conference provided all data for 2003, 2004, and 2006. However, that communion changed fiscal years in 2005, and was able to provide only eight months data for 2005. Therefore, the 2005 data for that denomination was not comparable to the 2003, 2004, and 2006. The North American Baptist Conference did not provide data for 2007. Data for Tables 16-20, and the three denominations, is presented in Appendix B-5.

[10] Christian and Missionary Alliance: "Since both domestic and overseas works are budgeted through the same source (our 'Great Commission Fund'), the amount on lines 1 and 4 are actual amounts spent on overseas missions."

[11] Church of the Brethren: "This amount is national denominational mission and service, i.e., direct staffing and mission support, and does not include other projects funded directly by congregations or districts, or independent missionaries sponsored by congregations and individuals that would not be part of the denominational effort."

[12] Conservative Congregational Christian Conference: The structure of this communion limits the national office coordination of overseas ministries activity. By design, congregations are to conduct missions directly, through agencies of their choice. The national office does not survey congregations about these activities. The one common emphasis of affiliated congregations is a focus on Micronesia, represented by the reported numbers.

[13] The Episcopal Church: "The Episcopal Church USA Domestic and Foreign Missionary Society does not specifically raise money to support our non-domestic ministries. Many of the activities included in our budget are, however, involved, directly or indirectly with providing worldwide mission...Many other expenditures (e.g., for ecumenical and interfaith relations; for military chaplaincies; for management's participation in activities of the worldwide Anglican Communion)

contain an overseas component; but we do not separately track or report domestic vs. overseas expenses in those categories."

[14] Lutheran Church-Missouri Synod: "Since 1968, many of the Lutheran Church-Missouri Synod (LCMS) 35 geographic districts now sponsor mission fields directly. The money does not flow through LCMS World Mission and LCMS World Relief, but through various mission societies. In 1996, the LCMS also established the Association of Lutheran Mission Agencies which includes 'recognized service agencies' of LCMS World Mission. They work in places where LCMS World Mission used to work (or might work today), but they direct and fund the work on their own. Millions of dollars of support from LCMS members is raised and spent by these 75+ mission societies. The Congregation Statistics Reports do not include information about missions spending other than that sent to LCMS World Mission and LCMS World Relief. The dollars that support the mission societies and the Lutheran Mission Agencies would not be included in the Congregation Statistics Reports. Nothing outside of the money that flows through the mission accounting department is verifiable, and no central accounting is made of mission societies spending. District support is only a small portion of the World Mission Support figure, with most of the budget coming from direct gifts from individuals."

[15] Moravian Church, Northern Province: The Overseas Missions Income figure was estimated for the Northern Province by the Board of World Mission of the Moravian Church. The Northern Province is the one of the three Moravian Provinces that reports Total Contributions to the *Yearbook of American and Canadian Churches* series.

[16] Presbyterian Church (U.S.A.): For Data Year 2005, Nos. 1 & 4: "Higher for Asian Tsunami Relief."

[17] Reformed Church in America: "We do not know how much money was given to missions outside the RCA structure." Also, the staff submitting the 2005 data wrote: "The Reported 2003 and Reported 2004 totals listed could not be substantiated."

[18] Seventh-Day Adventist, North American Division: This estimate, prepared by the General Conference Treasury Department, is for the U.S. portion of the total donated by congregations in both Canada and the U.S.

[19] The United Methodist Church: "The above represents total income received by the General Board of Global Ministries, The United Methodist Church." For 2005 data: "Increase due to funding received for Tsunami."

[20] See notes for Tables 16 through 20.

[21] Charles H. Fahs, *Trends in Protestant Giving* (New York: Institute of Social and Religious Research, 1929), pp. 26, 29, 53. The eleven denominations included in the 1916-1927 figures are: Congregational; Methodist Episcopal; Methodist Episcopal, South; Northern Baptist Convention; Presbyterian Church in the U.S.; Presbyterian Church in the U.S.A.; Reformed Church in the United States; Reformed Church in America; Southern Baptist Convention; United Brethren; and United Presbyterian. For a more detailed discussion of the Fahs study, and a comparison of church member giving in the 1920s and 2003, see John and Sylvia Ronsvalle, *The State of Church Giving through 2003* (Champaign, IL: empty tomb, inc., 2005), pp. 55-60. The chapter is also available at <http://www.emptytomb.org/scg03missions.pdf>.

[22] Commission on World Mission and Evangelism of the World Council of Churches, "Mission and Evangelism—An Ecumenical Affirmation, *International Review of Mission*, vol. LXXI, no. 284 (October, 1982), p. 440.

[23] "Unreached People Group"; Wikipedia; modified 07/20/2008; <http://en.wikipedia.org/wiki/Unreached_peop...>; p. 1 of 8/16/2008 6:00 PM printout.

[24] The Joshua Project posted a number 6,750 (<http://www.jsohuaproject.net>; p. 1 of 8/16/2008 5:51 PM printout. Caleb Resources posted "3,000+" (<http://www.calebresources.org>; p. 1 of 8/16/2008 6:07 PM.

[25] Morris Chapman; "The Conversation is Changing"; published July 1, 2006; <http://www.morrischapman.com/article.asp?is=57>; p. 1 of 8/6/06 4:48 PM printout.

[26] Mark Kelly; "WRAP-UP: Churches Filling Missions Gaps"; Baptist Press; posted 4/11/2008; <http://www.bpnews.net/printerfriendly.asp?ID=27821>; page 1 of 4/12/2008 11:53 AM printout.

[27] Full-page advertisement, *SBC Life*, September 2007, p. 9, and April 2008, p. 5.

[28] John Ronsvalle and Sylvia Ronsvalle, *The State of Church Giving through 2004: Will We Will?* (Champaign, IL: empty tomb, inc., 2006), p. 63 and footnote 22 on p. 77, calculated the cost based on information contained in the Minutes of the International Mission Board Meeting, Richmond, Virginia, January 9-11, 2006, pp. 25-26.

[29] "Frequently Asked Questions"; Christian Aid Mission; n.d.; <http://www.christianaid.org/About/FAQ.aspx>; pp. 1-2 of 6/10/2008 1:58 PM printout.

[30] "F.A.Q.'s"; Gospel for Asia; <http://www.gfa.org/gfa/faqs>; p. 2 of 8/23/2005 8:48 AM printout.

[31] "Frequently Asked Questions"; Gospel for Asia; 2008; <http://www.gfa.org/faqs#q13>; p. 1 of 6/10/2008 2:42 PM printout.

[32] "Sponsorship FAQ's"; Gospel for Asia; 2008; <http://www.gfa.org/sponsore-faqs>; p. 1 of 6/10/2008 3:36 PM printout.

[33] John Ronsvalle and Sylvia Ronsvalle, *The State of Church Giving through 2005: Abolition of the Institutional Enslavement of Overseas Missions* (Champaign, IL: empty tomb, inc., 2007), pp. 66-67.

[34] Membership data for specific denominations is provided in Appendix B. The Evangelical and Born Again population percents are taken from "The Barna Update: Barna Survey Reveals Significant growth in Born Again Population"; The Barna Group; <http://www.barna.org/FlexPage/aspx?Page=BarnaUpdate&BarnaUpdateID=271>; p. 2 of 7/9/2007 9:22 AM printout. The National Council of the Churches of Christ in the U.S.A. inclusive membership figure was obtained from Eileen W. Lindner, ed., *Yearbook of American and Canadian Churches 2009* (Nashville: Abingdon, 2009); pp. 374-75.

[35] Spectrem Group; "Affluent Market Insights 2009.pdf"; Spectrem Group; created 3/24/2009, downloaded 5/5/2009; p. 5 of 5/6/2009 printout.

[36] For a brief review of this topic, see John Ronsvalle and Sylvia Ronsvalle, *The State of Church Giving through 2002* (Champaign, IL: empty tomb, inc., 2004), pp. 65-66. Also available at <http://www.emptytomb.org/scg036Potential.php>.

[37] The percent Catholic for each diocese was derived by dividing "Total Catholic Population" by "Total Population" as found in *The Official Catholic Directory*, P.J. Kenedy & Sons, New Providence, NJ, 2008, subtitled, "Giving Status of the Catholic Church as of January 1, 2008." The population data for the Archdioceses under consideration was found in the *OCD* as follows: Baltimore (p. 74), Boston (p. 130), Chicago (p. 246), Detroit (p. 381), Galveston-Houston (p. 481), Los Angeles (p. 697-98), New York (pp. 863-64: corrected data from Sr. Eileen Clifford, Vice Chancellor, Roman Catholic Archdiocese of New York, email correspondence to author, June 16, 2009), Philadelphia (p. 1011), and Washington (p. 1462). The percent Catholic calculated for each diocese was used to obtain an estimate of U.S. BEA Personal Income for Catholics in each Archdiocesan county. An alternative approach would have been to employ data from Dale E. Jones et al., *Religious Congregations & Membership in the United States, 2000* (Nashville: Glenmary Research Center, 2002). The RCMUS provided "Total Adherents" as a "% of Total Pop." data for Catholics as well as other denominations and religions for each county. A cursory review in 2005 of this data for selected counties suggested that this latter approach using somewhat older data would have resulted in marginal differences.

NOTE: In *The State of Church Giving through 2006*, Table 24, p. 72, the "Calculated U.S. BEA Personal Income Available to Catholics," "Estimated Current Catholic Giving at 1.2% of Income," and "Estimated Potential Additional Catholic Giving at 10% of Income" were incorrectly calculated for the Archdiocese of Boston. The "% Catholic of Total Population in Area" used for the Archdiocese of Boston was 46.4% percent. The figure should have been 48.8%. Thus, the potential increased giving for the Archdiocese of Boston was understated. The error also affected the Total. The correct figures for the 2006 table are below.

The State of Church Giving through 2006, Corrected Table 24 (p. 72): Potential Additional Giving at 10% of Income, Nine Roman Catholic Archdioceses in the U.S., 2006

Area Name	Total U.S. BEA Personal Income for Counties in Archdioceses ($s)	% Catholic of Total Population in Area	Calculated U.S. BEA Personal Income Available to Catholics ($s)	Estimated Current Catholic Giving at 1.2% of Income ($s)	Estimated Potential Additional Catholic Giving at 10% Income ($s)
Archdiocese of Baltimore	$129,050,551,000	16.59%	$21,404,127,511	$256,849,530	$1,883,563,221
Archdiocese of Boston	$206,756,259,442	48.83%	*$100,954,652,148*	*$1,211,455,826*	*$8,884,009,389*
Archdiocese of Chicago	$259,500,542,000	38.99%	$101,190,521,040	$1,214,286,252	$8,904,765,851
Archdiocese of Detroit	$169,472,095,000	33.28%	$56,403,473,576	$676,841,683	$4,963,505,675
Archdiocese of Galveston-Houston	$236,523,026,000	24.20%	$57,237,195,958	$686,846,351	$5,036,873,244
Archdiocese of Los Angeles	$420,604,329,000	36.74%	$154,509,782,241	$1,854,117,387	$13,596,860,837
Archdiocese of New York	$350,021,245,000	45.00%	$157,509,517,087	$1,890,114,205	$13,860,837,504
Archdiocese of Philadelphia	$174,120,302,000	37.50%	$65,287,241,275	$783,446,895	$5,745,277,232
Archdiocese of Washington	$135,119,357,000	22.00%	$29,726,246,291	$356,714,955	$2,615,909,674
Total: 9 Archdioceses with Cardinals	$2,081,167,706,442		*$744,222,757,126*	*$8,930,673,086*	*$65,491,602,627*

[38] Total 2007 U.S. BEA Personal Income for Counties in Archdioceses ($s) County level U.S. BEA Personal Income data for 2007, the latest year listed, was accessed on 5/1/2009 via <http://www.bea.gov/regional/reis/drill.cfm>. The Archdiocese of Boston was adjusted for Archdiocesan "excepting the towns of Marion, Mattapoisetts and Wareham" from Plymouth County, MA. This involved using the 2007 population of the five Archdiocesan counties and the aforementioned three excepted towns. Population for these entities were derived from <http://www.bea.gov/bea/regional/bearfacts/> and <www.city-data.com> or cached versions thereof, respectively.

[39] The source for the estimate employed for current Catholic giving as 1.2% of income is as follows: " '…[W]e know that the national statistics are that Catholics give to the church about 1.2 percent of their income…' [Tim Dockery, director of development services for the Chicago archdiocese] said" (Cathleen Falsani, Religion Reporter, "Archdiocese May Ask for 10%: Cardinal George Considers Program That Includes Tithing," *Chicago Sun-Times*, Sunday, February 1, 2004, pp. 1A, and 6A).

[40] Matt Sedensky, Associated Press writer; "More Catholic Schools Closing Across U.S."; Christian Post; posted 4/14/2008; <http://www.christianpost.com/pages/rint.htm?aid=31934>; p. 2 of 4/14/2008 10:10 AM printout.

[41] *The Index of Global Philanthropy and Remittances 2009*; Hudson Institute Center for Global Prosperity; created 4/21/2009, modified 4/22/2009: downloaded 5/18/2009; <http://www.Hudson/org/files/documents/Indec%20of%20Global%20Philanthropy%20 and%20Remittances%202009.pdf>; p. 16 of 5/18/2009 printout.

[42] *The Index of Global Philanthropy and Remittances 2009*, p. 80.

[43] *The Index of Global Philanthropy and Remittances 2009*, p. 16.

[44] The native-born church member figure was calculated by multiplying the native-born population figure of 263,561,465 by 59.45%, the estimated percent of the U.S. population that has membership in historically Christian churches. The result was 156,687,291. The 263,561,465 figure for the native-born population was from U.S. Census Bureau; 2007 American Community Survey, Data Set: 2007 American Community Survey 1-Year Estimates: Selected Social Characteristics in the United States: 2007; Accessed 7/28/2009; <http://factfinder.census.gov/servlet/ADPTable?_bm=y&-geo_id=01000US&-ds_name=ACS_2007_1YR_G00_&-_lang=en&-_caller=geoselect&-format=>; p. 3 of 7/28/2009 10:55 AM printout. The figure of 59.45% is an empty tomb analysis of data in George H. Gallup, Jr., *Religion in America 2002*, pp. 28, 40.

[45] *The Index of Global Philanthropy and Remittances 2009*, p. 16.

[46] *The Index of Global Philanthropy and Remittances 2009*, p. 69.

[47] *The Index of Global Philanthropy and Remittances 2009*, p. 71.

[48] U.S. Census Bureau; 2007 American Community Survey; p. 3 of 7/28/09 10:55 AM printout.

chapter 7

Why and How Much Do Americans Give?

Overview of Why and How Much Americans Give

Why Do Americans Give? The reasons for donating money vary by individual, and for the individual, may vary by circumstance.

Even so, some evidence exists regarding the broad motivation for the active participation among Americans in the practice of donating to charity.

A key source of information is the United States Government Department of Labor Bureau of Labor Statistics (BLS) that takes a regular survey of Americans' spending patterns. In the Consumer Expenditure Survey (CE), the respondents are asked to categorize their charitable donations among four categories: (1) "charities and other organizations"; (2) "church, religious organizations"; (3) "educational institutions"; (4) "gifts to non-CU [consumer unit] members of stocks, bonds, and mutual funds."

In 2007, the category of gifts to "church, religious organizations" represented 64 percent of the charitable donations reported by Americans.

This percentage differs from other sources that report a lower percent directed to the category of "religion." The difference may be due to the fact that, in other surveys, the frame of reference is the structure imposed upon the recipient categories by the survey instrument, rather than either the perception of the donors, or the self-understanding and governance of the recipient organizations themselves.

One suggestion for improving this categorization process is a revision of the nonprofit Form 990 reporting document. Before selecting one of the ten core definition categories, the reporting nonprofit organization could first indicate its form of governance as either "faith-based" or "secular."

How Much Do Americans Give? Various surveys provide different answers to the question of how much Americans give. The source that serves as a benchmark is the Consumer Expenditure Survey.

The Consumer Expenditure Survey. The U.S. Government Bureau of Labor Statistics Consumer Expenditure Survey (CE) is a sophisticated research instrument that affects many aspects of American life through the Consumer Price Index.

The Consumer Expenditure Survey serves as a benchmark for understanding charitable giving patterns. The data series provides information about Americans' giving patterns by age, region of residence, and income levels.

In 2007, the CE figure for charitable giving by living individuals was $1,074.05 per consumer unit. Given that there were 120.171 million consumer units in the U.S. in 2007, the aggregate amount of charitable giving from living individuals in 2007 was calculated to be $129.1 billion.

Other Sources of Giving Estimates. Another source of information about charitable giving is found in the U.S. Internal Revenue Service Form 990. The Form 990 series must be filled out by charitable organizations with at least $25,000 in income, and by foundations. Data for the Form 990 series was obtained for the period 1989 through 2005, the latest year for which data for Form 990 was listed on the IRS Web site.

A third major source of philanthropic information is the *Giving USA* series. A major component of this series is based on deductions claimed on IRS Individual Tax returns. The series is "researched and written" on behalf of professional fundraisers by a university-based philanthropy center.

By adjusting both the Form 990 and the *Giving USA* series to yield cash contributions by living donors, the CE, the Form 990, and the *Giving USA* series were compared for 1989 through 2005. The resulting estimates of these three sources differed by as much as $61 billion.

Details of How Much Americans Give

Details of the Consumer Expenditure Survey, 2007. The U.S. Department of Labor, Bureau of Labor Statistics, Consumer Expenditure Survey (CE) provides a benchmark measure of Americans' charitable cash contributions. The CE provides the U.S. Government data designed to measure Americans' charitable contributions.

The CE presents data per "consumer unit." The definition reads:

> A consumer unit consists of any of the following: (1) All members of a particular household who are related by blood, marriage, adoption, or other legal arrangements; (2) a person living alone or sharing a household with others or living as a roomer in a private home or lodging house or in permanent living quarters in a hotel or motel, but who is financially independent; or (3) two or more persons living together who use their incomes to make joint expenditure decisions. Financial independence is determined by spending behavior with regard to the three major expense categories: Housing, food, and other living expenses. To be considered financially independent, the respondent must provide at least two of the three major expenditure categories, either entirely or in part.

> The terms consumer unit, family, and household are often used interchangeably for convenience. However, the proper technical term for purposes of the Consumer Expenditure Survey is consumer unit. [1]

The Consumer Expenditure Survey serves as a benchmark for understanding charitable giving patterns.

The CE data for 2007 was aggregated, conflated, and analyzed by empty tomb, inc. The result found that Americans gave $129.07 billion in cash contributions to charitable causes in 2007, the latest year for which data was available.

The CE categories include "Cash contributions to: charities and other organizations; church, religious organizations; and educational institutions" as well as "Gifts to non-CU [Consumer Unit] members of stocks, bonds, and mutual funds."[2] An analysis of the CE data resulted in the finding that Americans contributed 64% of their charitable contributions to "church, religious organizations" in 2007.

Further detail regarding this analysis of U.S. Department of Labor, Bureau of Labor Statistics, Consumer Expenditure Survey charitable giving data is presented in Table 26.[3]

Table 26:   U.S. Bureau of Labor Statistics, Consumer Expenditure Survey, 2007 Cash Contributions: Americans' Charitable Giving (Aggregated)

Item	Average Annual Expenditures Multiplied by 120.171 million Consumer Units: Aggregated (billions $)	Item as % of Total
Annual Expenditures		
Cash Contributions for Charitable Giving		
Cash contributions to:		
charities and other organizations	$33.16	25.7%
church, religious organizations	82.29	63.7%
educational institutions	6.14	4.8%
Gifts to non-CU members of stocks, bonds, and mutual funds	7.48	5.8%
Total	$129.07	100.0%

Details in the above table may not compute to the numbers shown due to rounding.
Source: empty tomb, inc. 2009 analysis of U.S. Bureau of Labor Statistics Consumer Expenditure Survey, 2007

Cash Contributions by Income Level, 2007

The CE measured Americans' cash contributions to charitable causes by income levels.[4]

An analysis was conducted for 12 income levels, ranging from "$5,000 to $9,999" up to both "$120,000 to $149,999" and the highest category of "$150,000 and more," with the average "Income after taxes" for the income levels ranging from $8,128 to $126,792, and $230,849, respectively.[5]

A comparison of cash contributions among different income brackets may be of interest.

However, it should be noted that CE lower income brackets, which for purposes of this analysis ranged from $5,000 through $19,999, reported higher expenses than income before taxes. The CE observes:

Data users may notice that average annual expenditures presented in the income tables sometimes exceed income before taxes for the lower income groups. The primary reason for that is believed to be the underreporting of income by respondents, a problem common to most household surveys…

There are other reasons why expenditures exceed income for the lower income groups. Consumer units whose members experience a spell of unemployment may draw on their savings to maintain their expenditures. Self-employed consumers may experience

Table 27: **U.S. Bureau of Labor Statistics, Consumer Expenditure Survey, 2007 Cash Contributions for Charitable Giving by Income Level**

Item	All consumer units	$5,000 to $9,999	$10,000 to $14,999	$15,000 to $19,999	$20,000 to $29,999	$30,000 to $39,999	$40,000 to $49,999	$50,000 to $69,999
Number of consumer units (in thousands)	120,171	5,406	7,552	7,562	14,720	13,211	11,824	18,390
Consumer unit characteristics:								
Income after taxes	$60,858	$8,128	$12,762	$17,327	$24,709	$34,325	$43,628	$57,835
Average Annual Expenditures								
Cash Contributions for Charitable Giving								
Cash contributions to:								
charities and other organizations	$275.94	$35.75	$52.60	$58.94	$49.76	$83.50	$87.44	$109.25
church, religious organizations	684.76	192.22	230.79	355.28	330.42	446.80	769.83	597.95
educational institutions	51.10	0.94	1.66	3.77	5.79	11.68	11.30	18.06
Gifts to non-CU members of stocks, bonds, and mutual funds	62.25	0.24	"No data reported."	3.91	1.41	3.15	148.35	7.39
Total (calculated)	$1,074.05	$229.15	$285.05	$421.90	$387.38	$545.13	$1,016.92	$732.65
Calculated:								
% of Income after Taxes								
Cash contributions to:								
charities and other organizations	0.45%	0.44%	0.41%	0.34%	0.20%	0.24%	0.20%	0.19%
church, religious organizations	1.13%	2.36%	1.81%	2.05%	1.34%	1.30%	1.76%	1.03%
educational institutions	0.08%	0.01%	0.01%	0.02%	0.02%	0.03%	0.03%	0.03%
Gifts to non-CU members of stocks, bonds, and mutual funds	0.10%	0.00%	"No data reported."	0.02%	0.01%	0.01%	0.34%	0.01%
Total	1.8%	2.8%	2.2%	2.4%	1.6%	1.6%	2.3%	1.3%

Details in the above table may not compute to the numbers shown due to rounding.
Source: empty tomb, inc. 2009 analysis of U.S. Bureau of Labor Statistics Consumer Expenditure Survey, 2007

Table 28: **U.S. Bureau of Labor Statistics, Consumer Expenditure Survey, 2007 Cash Contributions for Charitable Giving by Higher Income Level**

Item	All consumer units	$70,000 to $79,999	$80,000 to $99,999	$100,000 to $119,999	$120,000 to $149,999	$150,000 and more
Number of consumer units (in thousands)	120,171	6,957	9,777	6,651	5,708	8,229
Consumer unit characteristics:						
Income after taxes	$60,858	$72,129	$85,638	$103,496	$126,792	$230,849
Average Annual Expenditures						
Cash Contributions for Charitable Giving						
Cash contributions to:						
charities and other organizations	$275.94	$294.49	$173.44	$224.69	$505.45	$2,290.64
church, religious organizations	684.76	874.73	877.35	1,281.55	1,259.41	1,828.09
educational institutions	51.10	30.88	27.03	48.39	70.48	507.36
Gifts to non-CU members of stocks, bonds, and mutual funds	62.25	2.76	5.46	122.89	16.79	548.23
Total (calculated)	$1,074.05	$1,202.86	$1,083.28	$1,677.52	$1,852.13	$5,174.32
Calculated						
% of Income after Taxes						
Cash contributions to:						
charities and other organizations	0.45%	0.41%	0.20%	0.22%	0.40%	0.99%
church, religious organizations	1.13%	1.21%	1.02%	1.24%	0.99%	0.79%
educational institutions	0.08%	0.04%	0.03%	0.05%	0.06%	0.22%
Gifts to non-CU members of stocks, bonds, and mutual funds	0.10%	0.00%	0.01%	0.12%	0.01%	0.24%
Total	1.8%	1.7%	1.3%	1.6%	1.5%	2.2%

Details in the above table may not compute to the numbers shown due to rounding.
Source: empty tomb, inc. 2009 analysis of U.S. Bureau of Labor Statistics Consumer Expenditure Survey, 2007

business losses that result in low or even negative incomes, but are able to maintain their expenditures by borrowing or relying on savings. Students may get by on loans while they are in school, and retirees may rely on savings and investments.[6]

Tables 27 and 28 display the data from the CE Survey of cash contributions by income level.

Similar reasons may contribute to the fact that although income before taxes is slightly higher than average expenditures for the $30,000 to $39,999 bracket, income after taxes was slightly lower than average annual expenditures.

To the extent that income is proportionately underreported across all income levels, but is more evident in lower income brackets, then comparisons across income brackets may be informative on an exploratory basis.

Having noted this caveat, it is still of interest to observe that consumer units in the "$5,000 to $9,999" through the "$15,000 to $19,999" income brackets reported a higher portion of after-tax income, charitable cash contributions than in the $20,000 to $39,999 and the $50,000 to $149,999 brackets. The $150,000 and more bracket was equivalent to the $10,000 to $14,999 bracket. The $40,000 to $49,999 bracket was the exception among the middle-income categories, contributing more than 2% of after-tax income.

It may be observed that 2007 giving as a percent of income after taxes to "church, religious organizations" was higher in eleven of the twelve income levels, than to either "charities and other organizations," "educational institutions," or "Gifts to non-CU members of stocks, bonds, and mutual funds." Among those in the $150,000 and more bracket, contributions to "charities and other organizations" exceeded gifts to "church, religious organizations."

In the other eleven brackets, "charities and other organizations" received the second largest dollar donation per consumer unit, after "church, religious organizations" and before "educational institutions." In the $150,000 and more bracket, the dollars donated to the "charities and other organizations" category were at least four times as high as in other brackets.

> In each income bracket, with the exception of the $150,000 and more category, the dollars given to "church, religious organizations" was greater than the sum of the dollars given to "charities and other organizations" and "educational institutions."

Gifts to "education institutions" uniformly represented a smaller portion of income than that given to either "church, religious organizations" or "charities and other organizations" in each of the brackets. In the $150,000 and more bracket, such gifts were 10 percent of the portion of income donated.

In each income bracket, with the exception of the $150,000 and more category, the dollars given to "church, religious organizations" was greater than the sum of the dollars given to "charities and other organizations" and "educational institutions."

Cash Contributions by Age, 2007

The CE also measured Americans' cash contributions to charitable causes by age of contributor.[7]

The seven age categories under consideration started with the "Under 25 years" grouping, proceeded with "25-34 years" as the first of five 10-year periods, and culminated with the "75 years and older" cohort.

In 2007, giving as a percent of income after taxes to "church, religious organizations" grew as a portion of income in each bracket as age advanced. It may be noted that the 65-74 years bracket showed a decline in dollars given to this category, but also posted a decline in income, so the portion of income increased from the previous bracket. Although the 75 years and older cohort had the second

Table 29: U.S. Bureau of Labor Statistics, Consumer Expenditure Survey,
2007 Cash Contributions for Charitable Giving by Age

Item	All consumer units	Under 25 years	25-34 years	35-44 years	45-54 years	55-64 years	65-74 years	75 years and older
Number of consumer units (in thousands)	120,171	8,150	20,499	23,416	25,245	19,462	12,011	11,390
Consumer unit characteristics: Income after taxes	$60,858	$30,802	$55,765	$74,051	$77,075	$67,965	$46,334	$31,634
Average Annual Expenditures **Cash Contributions for Charitable Giving** Cash contributions to:								
charities and other organizations	$275.94	$16.35	$59.30	$192.42	$283.51	$652.47	$217.05	$425.26
church, religious organizations	684.76	210.16	393.74	567.33	807.50	863.94	839.29	1,048.34
educational institutions	51.10	1.38	11.52	24.32	85.28	113.04	24.40	59.54
Gifts to non-CU members of stocks, bonds, and mutual funds	62.25	"No data reported."	3.48	1.94	9.78	256.77	25.33	159.39
Total (calculated)	$1,074.05	$227.89	$468.04	$786.01	$1,186.07	$1,886.22	$1,106.07	$1,692.53
Calculated **% of Income after Taxes** Cash contributions to:								
charities and other organizations	0.45%	0.05%	0.11%	0.26%	0.37%	0.96%	0.47%	1.34%
church, religious organizations	1.13%	0.68%	0.71%	0.77%	1.05%	1.27%	1.81%	3.31%
educational institutions	0.08%	0.00%	0.02%	0.03%	0.11%	0.17%	0.05%	0.19%
Gifts to non-CU members of stocks, bonds, and mutual funds	0.10%	"No data reported."	0.01%	0.00%	0.01%	0.38%	0.05%	0.50%
Total	1.8%	0.7%	0.8%	1.1%	1.5%	2.8%	2.4%	5.4%

Details in the above table may not compute to the numbers shown due to rounding.
Source: empty tomb, inc. 2009 analysis of U.S. Bureau of Labor Statistics Consumer Expenditure Survey, 2007

lowest dollar income, giving to the category of church, religious organizations was highest in this bracket, both in dollars and as a portion of income.

Contributions to "educational institutions" as a portion of income were highest in the 75 years and older age bracket, followed by the 55-64 bracket.

Contributions to "charities, and other organizations" as a portion of income increased up through the 55-64 years cohort and were highest in the 75 years and older bracket.

Table 29 presents the data from the CE Survey on cash contributions by age.

The fact that members of the "Under 25 years" directed 92% of their giving as a percent of after-tax income to the "church, religious organizations" category provides support for the view that religion serves as the seedbed of philanthropic giving in America. Giving to that category among this group was considerably higher at 0.68% than to "charities and other organizations" at 0.05%. There was no measurable contribution to "educational institutions" in this age bracket.

The age bracket in which total charitable giving as a portion of income was highest was the 75 years and older cohort.

One factor that all age brackets had in common was that giving as a portion of income to "church, religious organizations" was the largest category. Further, in all cohorts, giving to "church, religious organizations" as a portion of income was greater than the sum of the two categories of "charities and other organizations" plus "educational institutions."

Cash Contributions by Region, 2007

In addition, as shown in Table 30, the CE also measured Americans' cash contributions to charitable causes by region.[8]

The four region categories for which information was presented in the CE data were Northeast, Midwest, South, and West. Regional charitable giving data and regional income figures were available for the comparison.

Analysis of the 2007 data showed that contributions to charitable causes were highest in the West at 2.3% of income after taxes, followed by the Midwest at 1.9%, the South at 1.8%, and the Northeast at 1.0%.

In each of the four regions, contributions to "church, religious organizations" were higher than the sum of contributions to "charities and other organizations" and "educational institutions."

The marked difference between the Northeast and the other three regions in 2007 was significant at the 0.05 level in each case for the categories of "total giving" and "church, religious organizations."

Records were available back to 1987 from the Bureau of Labor Statistics Consumer Expenditure Survey. The specific category of "Gifts to non-CU members

Table 30: U.S. Bureau of Labor Statistics, Consumer Expenditure Survey, Cash Contributions for Charitable Giving by Region of Residence, 2007

Item	All consumer units	Northeast	Midwest	South	West
Number of consumer units (in thousands)	120,171	22,382	27,462	43,152	27,176
Consumer unit characteristics: Income after taxes	$60,858	$67,440	$57,514	$56,177	$66,250
Average Annual Expenditures Cash Contributions for Charitable Giving Cash contributions to:					
charities and other organizations	$275.94	$223.93	$173.10	$161.23	$604.84
church, religious organizations	684.76	426.42	707.42	738.49	789.30
educational institutions	51.10	34.59	41.05	38.59	94.74
Gifts to non-CU members of stocks, bonds, and mutual funds	62.25	15.31	152.18	49.85	29.72
Total (calculated)	$1,074.05	$700.25	$1,073.75	$988.16	$1,518.60
Calculated % of Income after Taxes Cash contributions to:					
charities and other organizations	0.45%	0.33%	0.30%	0.29%	0.91%
church, religious organizations	1.13%	0.63%	1.23%	1.31%	1.19%
educational institutions	0.08%	0.05%	0.07%	0.07%	0.14%
Gifts to non-CU members of stocks, bonds, and mutual funds	0.10%	0.02%	0.26%	0.09%	0.04%
Total	1.8%	1.0%	1.9%	1.8%	2.3%

Details in the above table may not compute to the numbers shown due to rounding.
Source: empty tomb, inc. 2009 analysis of U.S. BLS CE, 2007

of stocks, bonds, and mutual funds," however, was not available before the second quarter of 2001. Therefore, in the historical series for 1987-2007, comparing Charitable Giving as a portion of after-tax income, Charitable Giving included the three categories of "charities and other organizations," "church, religious organizations," and "educational institutions." Consequently, the 2007 numbers in Table 31, which does not include the category of "Gifts to non-CU members of stocks, bonds, and mutual funds," differ slightly from the figures in Table 30, which does include that category.

As can be seen in Table 31, the regional pattern indicates the South had the highest average percent of after-tax income in the "cash contributions for charitable giving" category in the 1987-2007 period. The Midwest and the West were next, and then the Northeast.

The South's overall average was 1.7% of income given to charity during the 1987-2007 period. The Northeast posted the lowest portion of income donated for charitable purposes consistently throughout the 1987 through 2007 period, with the exception of 1994, when the Northeast was third and the West was the lowest in the comparison. In unrounded numbers, the Midwest's 1987-2007 average of 1.63% was slightly greater than the West's average of 1.59%.

The question may be asked whether regional differences in spending on other expenditures categories influence or limit charitable giving levels in the four regions. Table 32 presents expenditure data by region of residence for 2007. The category of "Cash Contributions for Charitable Giving" was subtracted from the expenditures total. The reason for this adjustment was to calculate the portion of income remaining after expenditures, other than those for charitable giving. The adjusted total expenditures figure was then divided by the region's after-tax income. The resulting percentage is shown in Table 32.

It was instructive to note that variations in giving to charity by region did not seem to be a function of regional expenditures in comparison to regional income differentials. The West had the highest expenditures as a percent of after-tax income. The Northeast had both the highest income and the second highest level of expenditures. However, the Northeast spent the lowest portion of after-tax income on expenditures, apart from charitable contributions.

Table 31: U.S. Bureau of Labor Statistics, Consumer Expenditure Survey, 2007 Expenditures for Charitable Giving by Region of Residence, 1987-2007

Year	All consumer units	Northeast	Midwest	South	West
1987	1.46%	0.86%	1.53%	1.76%	1.56%
1988	1.40%	0.83%	1.43%	1.68%	1.52%
1989	1.56%	1.04%	1.55%	2.01%	1.47%
1990	1.43%	1.03%	1.40%	1.69%	1.50%
1991	1.58%	1.11%	1.69%	1.74%	1.72%
1992	1.58%	1.26%	1.78%	1.78%	1.42%
1993	1.46%	0.98%	1.57%	1.57%	1.68%
1994	1.44%	1.30%	1.42%	1.73%	1.20%
1995	1.50%	1.06%	1.41%	1.66%	1.79%
1996	1.42%	0.93%	1.57%	1.75%	1.23%
1997	1.39%	0.88%	1.41%	1.70%	1.41%
1998	1.41%	0.89%	1.42%	1.68%	1.50%
1999	1.58%	1.03%	1.59%	1.83%	1.75%
2000	1.46%	0.95%	1.93%	1.42%	1.50%
2001	1.53%	1.14%	1.66%	1.72%	1.48%
2002	1.55%	1.14%	1.69%	1.64%	1.65%
2003	1.57%	0.99%	1.75%	1.82%	1.57%
2004	1.47%	0.84%	1.93%	1.53%	1.52%
2005	1.68%	1.13%	1.94%	1.99%	1.49%
2006	1.82%	1.19%	1.91%	1.81%	2.28%
2007	1.66%	1.02%	1.60%	1.67%	2.25%
Average for the 1987-2007 Period	1.5%	1.0%	1.6%	1.7%	1.6%

Source: empty tomb, inc. 2009 analysis of U.S. Bureau of Labor Statistics Consumer Expenditure Survey, 1987-2007

Table 32: **U.S. Bureau of Labor Statistics, Consumer Expenditure Survey, Expenditures as a Percent of Income after Taxes, by Region of Residence, 2007**

Item	All consumer units	Northeast	Midwest	South	West
Number of consumer units (in thousands)	120,171	22,382	27,462	43,152	27,176
Consumer unit characteristics:					
Income after taxes	$60,858	$67,440	$57,514	$56,177	$66,250
Average Annual Expenditures Seven Major Categories					
Food	$6,133.40	$6,419.41	$5,792.78	$5,780.50	$6,810.60
Housing	16,919.99	19,085.18	15,379.70	14,910.67	19,885.34
Apparel and services	1,880.72	2,068.47	1,865.91	1,692.20	2,041.75
Transportation	8,757.65	8,014.27	8,683.66	8,484.67	9,882.10
Health care	2,852.77	2,645.32	3,097.40	2,800.23	2,860.17
Entertainment	2,697.99	2,811.17	2,585.11	2,320.44	3,319.35
Personal insurance and pensions	5,336.15	5,558.19	5,315.16	4,948.12	5,790.63
Other Expenses*	5,059.28	5,021.74	5,293.84	4,526.66	5,700.62
Total Expenditures (calculated)	$49,637.95	$51,623.75	$48,013.56	$45,463.49	$56,290.56
Charitable Giving	$1,074.05	$700.25	$1,073.75	$988.16	$1,518.60
Total Expenditures Less Charitable Giving	$48,563.90	$50,923.50	$46,939.80	$44,475.36	$54,771.95
Calculated: Average Annual Expenditures Less Charitable Giving as % Income after Taxes	80%	76%	82%	79%	83%

Details in the above table may not compute to the numbers shown due to rounding.

*Other expenses include: "Alcoholic beverages; Personal care products and services; Reading; Education; Tobacco products and smoking supplies; Miscellaneous; Cash contributions."

"Cash contributions" includes: "Support for college students; Alimony expenditures; Child support expenditures; 'Charitable giving' (Cash contributions to charities and other organizations; Cash contributions to church, religious organizations; Cash contributions to educational institutions; Gift to non-CU members of stocks, bonds, and mutual funds); Cash contribution to political organizations."

Source: empty tomb, inc. 2009 analysis of U.S. Bureau of Labor Statistics Consumer Expenditure Survey, 2007

The ratio of expenditures (excluding charitable giving) as a percent of after-tax income reflected the same order of levels of charitable giving noted in Table 32. That is, the West had the highest level of expenditures as a portion of income, and the highest level of charitable giving as a percent of income. The Midwest ranked second in both, the South third, and the Northeast fourth.

General Information regarding the Consumer Expenditure Survey

One benefit of the CE is its unbiased data. The Mission Statement of the U.S. Department of Labor, Bureau of Labor Statistics reads:

The **Bureau of Labor Statistics (BLS)** is the principal fact-finding agency for the Federal Government in the broad field of labor economics and statistics. The BLS is an independent national statistical agency that collects, processes, analyzes, and disseminates essential statistical data to the American public, the U.S. Congress, other Federal agencies, State and local governments, business, and labor. The BLS also serves as a statistical resource to the Department of Labor.

BLS data must satisfy a number of criteria, including relevance to current social and economic issues, timeliness in reflecting today's rapidly changing economic conditions, accuracy and consistently high statistical quality, and impartiality in both subject matter and presentation.[9]

The BLS, among its various activities, is the source for the following indexes:

Producer price index (PPI)—This index, dating from 1890, is the oldest continuous statistical series published by BLS. It is designed to measure average changes in prices received by producers of all commodities, at all stages of processing, produced in the United States...

Consumer price indexes (CPI)—The CPI is a measure of the average change in prices over time in a "market basket" of goods and services purchased either by urban wage earners and clerical workers or by all urban consumers. In 1919, BLS began to publish complete indexes at semiannual intervals, using a weighting structure based on data collected in the expenditure survey of wage-earner and clerical-worker families in 1917-19 (BLS Bulletin 357, 1924)...

International price indexes—The BLS International Price Program produces export and import price indexes for nonmilitary goods traded between the United States and the rest of the world.[10]

Among the numerous applications of the BLS Consumer Expenditure Survey, the Survey is used for periodic revision of the Consumer Price Index (CPI). Following are excerpted comments from a "Brief Description of the Consumer Expenditure Survey."

Among the numerous applications of the BLS Consumer Expenditure Survey, the Survey is used for periodic revision of the Consumer Price Index (CPI).

The current CE program was begun in 1980. Its principal objective is to collect information on the buying habits of U.S. consumers. Consumer expenditure data are used in a variety of research endeavors by government, business, labor, and academic analysts. In addition, the data are required for periodic revision of the CPI.

The survey, which is conducted by the U.S. Census Bureau for the Bureau of Labor Statistics, consists of two components: A diary or recordkeeping, survey... and an interview survey, in which expenditures of consumer units are obtained in five interviews conducted at 3-month intervals...

Each component of the survey queries an independent sample of consumer units that is representative of the U.S. population...The Interview sample, selected on a rotating panel basis, surveys about 7,500 consumer units each quarter. Each consumer unit is interviewed once per quarter, for 5 consecutive quarters. Data are collected on an ongoing basis in 105 areas of the United States.[11]

The BLS, in commenting on the various functions of the Consumer Expenditure Survey, observed that, "Researchers use the data in a variety of studies, including those that focus on the spending behavior of different family types, trends in expenditures on various expenditure components including new types of goods and services, gift-giving behavior, consumption studies, and historical spending trends."[12]

Writing in the mid-1980s with reference to the then forthcoming Consumer Expenditure Survey-based revisions in the CPI, eminent business columnist, Sylvia Porter, remarked that the CPI is "the most closely watched, widely publicized and influential government statistic we have..."[13]

In addition to the fact that the "CPI is used to adjust federal tax brackets for inflation,"[14] a glimpse into the wide-ranging, Consumer Expenditure Survey-based network of CPI usage in American culture is gained from the following information:

The CPI is the most widely used measure of inflation and is sometimes viewed as an indicator of the effectiveness of government economic policy. It provides information about price changes in the Nation's economy to government, business, labor, and private citizens and is used by them as a guide to making economic decisions. In addition, the President, Congress, and the Federal Reserve Board use trends in the CPI to aid in formulating fiscal and monetary policies.

The CPI and its components are used to adjust other economic series for price changes and to translate these series into inflation-free dollars. Examples of series adjusted by the CPI include retail sales, hourly and weekly earnings, and components of the National Income and Product Accounts...

The CPI is often used to adjust consumers' income payments (for example, Social Security) to adjust income eligibility levels for government assistance and to automatically provide cost-of-living wage adjustments to millions of American workers. As a result of statutory action the CPI affects the income of about 80 million persons: the 51.6 million Social Security beneficiaries, about 21.3 million food stamp recipients, and about 4.6 million military and Federal Civil Service retirees and survivors. Changes in the CPI also affect the cost of lunches for 28.4 million children who eat lunch at school, while collective bargaining agreements that tie wages to the CPI cover over 2 million workers. Another example of how dollar values may be adjusted is the use of the CPI to adjust the Federal income tax structure. These adjustments prevent inflation-induced increases in tax rates, an effect called *bracket creep*...

Data from the Consumer Expenditure Survey conducted in 2001 and 2002, involving a national sample of more than 30,000 information families, provided detailed information on respondents' spending habits. This enabled BLS to construct the CPI market basket of goods and services and to assign each item in the market basket a weight, or importance, based on total family expenditures...[15]

How Much Do Americans Give? An Estimate of Aggregate Giving to Religion, 1968-2007.

An estimate of Americans' giving to religion has been calculated for the 1968 to 2007 period. This estimate employed a 1974 benchmark estimate of $11.7 billion for giving to religion provided by the watershed Commission on Private Philanthropy and Public Needs of the 1970s, commonly referred to as the Filer Commission.[16]

The amount of change from year to year, calculated for 1968 to 1973 and also 1975 to 2007, was the annual percent change in the composite denomination set analyzed in other chapters of this report.[17] This calculation yielded a total of $8.04 billion given to religion in 1968, and $75.08 billion in 2007. Table 33 presents this data both in aggregate form, and as adjusted for population and income.

Table 33: Giving to Religion, Based on the Commission on Private Philanthropy and Public Needs (Filer Commission) Benchmark Data for the Year of 1974, and Annual Changes in the Composite Denomination-Based Series, 1968-2007, Aggregate Billions of Dollars and Per Capita Dollars as Percent of DPI

Year	Denomination-Based Series Keyed to 1974 Filer Estimate	
	Billions Dollars	Per Capita Dollars as % of Disposable Personal Income
1968	8.04	1.29%
1969	8.35	1.24%
1970	8.69	1.18%
1971	9.15	1.14%
1972	9.79	1.13%
1973	10.72	1.10%
1974	11.70	1.09%
1975	12.75	1.07%
1976	13.86	1.06%
1977	15.01	1.05%
1978	16.39	1.02%
1979	18.12	1.01%
1980	20.06	1.00%
1981	22.12	0.98%
1982	23.97	0.99%
1983	25.63	0.98%
1984	27.75	0.95%
1985	29.44	0.95%
1986	31.15	0.95%
1987	32.38	0.94%
1988	33.61	0.90%
1989	35.40	0.88%
1990	36.88	0.86%
1991	38.28	0.86%
1992	39.34	0.83%
1993	40.40	0.82%
1994	43.33	0.84%
1995	44.16	0.82%
1996	47.65	0.84%
1997	49.38	0.82%
1998	52.24	0.82%
1999	55.04	0.82%
2000	59.29	0.82%
2001	61.79	0.83%
2002	63.84	0.82%
2003	64.53	0.79%
2004	66.90	0.77%
2005	69.32	0.76%
2006	72.18	0.75%
2007	75.08	0.74%

Source: empty tomb, inc. analysis 2009; Commission on Private Philanthropy and Public Needs; *YACC*, adjusted series; U.S. BEA

A Comparison of Three Sources

Estimates of charitable giving vary by substantial margins. Three sources of information can be described and compared in an attempt to develop an overview of aggregate charitable giving patterns among Americans.

Consumer Expenditure Survey, 2007. The U.S. Government Bureau of Labor Statistics Consumer Expenditure Survey (CE) is a sophisticated research instrument that affects many aspects of American life. The CE is used to inform the Consumer Price Index which, in turn, is used, among other purposes, to adjust federal tax brackets, Social Security benefits, and military retirement benefits for inflation. The CE's figure for charitable giving serves as a benchmark for the level of philanthropy in the U.S.

Table 34: Living Individual Charitable Giving in the United States, Consumer Expenditure Survey, 2007

Item	Average Annual Expenditure: All Consumer Units	Average Annual Expenditures Multiplied by 120,171 Consumer Units in 000's: Aggregated 000's of $	Item as Percent of Total
"Cash contributions to charities and other organizations"	$275.94	$33,159,986	25.69%
"Cash contributions to church, religious organizations"	$684.76	$82,288,294	63.75%
"Cash contributions to educational institutions"	$51.10	$6,140,738	4.76%
"Gifts to non-CU members of stocks, bonds, and mutual funds"	$62.25	$7,480,645	5.80%
Total	$1,074.05	$129,069,663	100%

Details in the above table may not compute to the numbers shown due to rounding.
Source: empty tomb, inc. 2009 analysis of U.S. BLS CE, 2007.

Table 34 presents CE data for the year 2007 in both "consumer unit" and aggregate values.[18] The CE data included the categories of: "Cash contributions to charities and other organizations"; "Cash contributions to church, religious organizations"; "Cash contributions to educational institutions"; and "Gifts to non-CU [Consumer Unit] members of stocks, bonds, and mutual funds." The annual average expenditure for the four categories in 2007 was $1,074.05 per consumer unit. In 2007, there were 120.171 million consumer units in the United States. The average annual expenditure amount of $1,074.05 multiplied by the number of consumer units, resulted in a 2007 estimate of total charitable giving of $129.07 billion.

Form 990 Series. A second source of information about charitable giving is found in the U.S. Internal Revenue Service Form 990 series. The Form 990 series must be filled out by charitable organizations with at least $25,000 in income, and by foundations. Form 990 data was obtained for the years 1989-2005, the latest year listed on the IRS Web site.[19]

Table 35 presents Form 990 data for the year 2005. As can be seen in that table, nonprofit charitable organizations in the United States reported on Form 990 that they received $140.3 billion in Direct Public Support in 2005, and another $21.6 billion from Indirect Public Support. The category of Indirect Public Support includes receipts from parent charitable organizations or groups like the United Way. These two sources of support totaled $162 billion. Organizations with at least $25,000 but less than $100,000 in gross receipts were able to use Form 990-EZ to report receipts of $1.5 billion in 2005, for a Form 990 and Form 990-EZ contributions total of $163 billion.

A figure of $27.5 billion was added to the Public Support figure to account for giving in 2005 to private foundations.[20] Private foundations are required to file the IRS Form 990-PF. An adjusted total for giving to foundations was published in *Giving USA 2009*.

Based on the Form 990 series data, the combined total of $190.9 billion is the amount that charitable organizations received in 2005.

Form 990 could, but does not, request data for cash contributions by living individuals. One recommendation to improve the usefulness of information in the Form 990 is that charitable organizations be required to report cash contributions from living individuals on a separate line of the form.

In order to compare the Form 990 series data with the CE data for cash contributions from living individuals for a 1989 to 2005 series, the Form 990 series information was adjusted. To obtain a figure for contributions from living individuals, estimates for giving by corporations and foundations, and receipts from bequests,[21] were subtracted from the "Gifts to charities and foundations" figure in Table 35. Giving by Living Individuals was thus estimated to be $118 billion in 2005.

The Form 990 data also includes "Other than cash contributions." Therefore, the value of "Other than cash contributions" was subtracted from the Form 990 data to allow a comparison of charitable cash contributions. As shown in Table 35, the IRS estimated that Americans deducted $48 billion in "Other than cash contributions" in 2005.[22] This amount was subtracted from the Giving by Living Individuals figure of $118 billion, resulting in a subtotal of $70.4 billion in 2005.

Table 35: Living Individual Charitable Giving in the United States, Form 990 Series, 2005

	000's of $
Form 990	
Direct Public Support	$140,348,374
Indirect Public Support	+ $21,624,408
Total Public Support	$161,972,782
Form 990-EZ contributions	+ $1,469,440
Form 990 and 990-EZ contributions	$163,442,222
Gifts to foundations	+ $27,460,000
Gifts to charities and foundations	$190,902,222
Less gifts from other than Living Individuals	
Giving by Corporations	- $16,590,000
Giving by Foundations	- $32,410,000
Giving by Bequests	- $23,450,000
Giving by Living Individuals	$118,452,222
Less Individual "Other than cash contributions"	- $48,056,520
Living Individuals Giving in cash, not including giving to church	$70,395,702
Church: Individual Giving to church, adjusted for religious organizations included in Form 990	+ $74,653,555
Total Cash Giving by Living Donors	$145,049,257

Data may not compute to the numbers shown due to rounding.

Suorce: empty tomb, inc. 2009 analysis, IRS Form 990 series data, 2005, U.S. BLS CE 2007, *Giving USA 2009*

To develop an estimate of Form 990 organizational receipts that could be compared with the CE figure of what people gave required one additional step. Churches are not required to file Form 990. The CE estimate, however, included a measure for charitable contributions to churches and religious organizations. The following procedure was used to develop an estimate for church giving to be added to the Form 990 Living Individuals contributions figure. The CE figure for 2005 "Cash contributions to church, religious organizations" was $74.65 billion. The present analysis employs a working estimate that giving to church represents about 90% of giving to religion, based in part on the work of two publications in this area.[23] Charitable organizations that combine religion with international or human services activities would be expected to file Form 990, and therefore these figures would already be included in the 2005 Form 990 Living Individual figure of $70.4 billion. Subtracting 10% from the 2005 CE figure for "church, religious organizations" of $82.9 billion resulted in an estimate of $74.65 billion given to churches in 2005. When this "giving to church" estimate was added to the estimated 2005 Form 990 "Living Individual Giving in cash, not including giving to church" figure of $70.4 billion, Total Cash Giving by Living Donors was calculated to be $145 billion in 2005, based on the Form 990 series information.

Table 35 presents the procedure and results in tabular form for 2005. A similar procedure was followed to calculate the Form 990 series figures for 1989-2004,[24] to compare with the CE series for those years.

Giving USA *Series.* A third source of charitable giving information, which is the most widely reported in the popular media, is from *Giving USA*, a series begun in the 1950s as an industry information compilation by a former vice president for public relations of a major professional fundraising firm.[25] The series has continued, and is currently prepared by a university-based philanthropy program, with active oversight by professional fundraisers. A major component of this series is based on deductions claimed on the IRS Individual Tax Returns. The *Giving USA 2009* Editorial Review Board was comprised of 16 principals or representatives of fundraising firms, 13 of whom are affiliated with "member firms" of the 34 companies that make up the "Giving Institute: Leading Consultants to Non-Profits."[26] This report is acknowledged as a fundraising tool for those in the profession,[27] and the publication's most recent estimates of philanthropy are built on the pre-academic measurements in the historical series.

In order to compare a *Giving USA* estimate for individual giving with the CE data for the 1989-2005 period, the category of "Other than cash contributions" was subtracted from the *Giving USA* numbers. For the 2005 data, for example, the IRS $48 billion figure for "Other than cash contributions" that was subtracted from the Form 990 series data in the analysis above also was subtracted from the *Giving USA* figure. The *Giving USA* estimate for individual giving in 2005 was $220.75

Table 36: **Living Individual Charitable Giving in the United States,** *Giving USA*, **2005**

Data Year 2005	000's of $
Giving by Individuals	$220,750,000
Less Individual "Other than cash contributions"	- $48,056,520
Total Individual Cash Giving	$172,693,480

Source: *Giving USA*, IRS, empty tomb, inc. analysis 2009

billion.[28] When the $48 billion figure for "Other than cash contributions" was subtracted from that number, the result was a Total Individual Cash Giving figure of $172.7 billion.

Table 36 presents the development of the *Giving USA* figure for 2005 to be used in a comparison with the CE and Form 990 series data. A similar procedure was used to calculate comparable *Giving USA* figures for 1989 through 2004.

A Comparison of Three Charitable Giving Estimates, 1989-2005.

The CE charitable giving series is also available for the 1989-2005 period. However, the CE category of "Gifts to non-CU members of stocks, bonds, and mutual funds" was not available before the year 2000. Also, both the Form 990 series and the *Giving USA* series were adjusted to remove noncash donations; that category includes gifts of stocks, bonds and mutual funds. Therefore, the CE series for 1989-2005 used in Table 37 does not include the category of "Gifts to non-CU members of stocks, bonds, and mutual funds." The category of "Gifts to non-CU members of stocks, bonds, and mutual funds" is included in the discussion of 2007 CE charitable giving data elsewhere in this chapter.

As can be observed in Table 37, the three sources of information on Total Charitable Giving in the U.S. differed by up to $61 billion in 2005. For example, the CE measurement for Total Individual Contributions in 2005 was calculated to be $110.8 billion dollars. Data from the Form 990 series reports filed by recipient organizations, with an estimate of giving to religion added and other-than-cash contributions subtracted, resulted in a calculation of $145 billion received by nonprofits and foundations in 2005. Meanwhile, a *Giving USA* number for financial giving by living individuals in 2005, with other-than-cash contributions subtracted, was $172.7 billion, exceeding the benchmark CE figure by 56 percent.

The CE is a detailed U.S. BLS survey carried out on a quarterly basis.

The Form 990 series reports are completed by charitable organizations and foundations, based on their accounting records. Because the Form 990 does not presently ask

Table 37: Living Individual Charitable Giving in the United States, A Comparison of the Consumer Expenditure Survey, Form 990 Series, and *Giving USA*, 1989-2005

Year	U.S. Bureau of Labor Statistics, Consumer Expenditure Survey (Calculated) 000's of $	Form 990 Series (Adjusted) 000's of $	*Giving USA* (Adjusted) 000's of $
1989	$42,631	$49,875	$71,899
1990	$40,052	$52,558	$73,546
1991	$47,601	$55,614	$74,588
1992	$48,721	$56,842	$78,067
1993	$46,695	$57,680	$79,721
1994	$48,593	$56,032	$77,781
1995	$52,239	$77,101	$81,838
1996	$51,674	$75,578	$86,261
1997	$53,747	$70,895	$96,239
1998	$57,864	$89,687	$109,094
1999	$69,861	$92,783	$116,343
2000	$66,217	$85,833	$127,254
2001	$75,330	$104,296	$135,352
2002	$81,652	$101,547	$140,147
2003	$88,159	$116,413	$143,919
2004	$89,384	$120,779	$157,987
2005	$110,846	$145,049	$172,693

Source: empty tomb, inc. 2009 analysis

for cash contributions from living individuals, only a calculated estimate for cash contributions by living individuals can be developed. If for any reason the estimates for giving by corporations, foundations, or bequests—the categories that are used to calculate a Form 990 cash donations from living individuals figure—are not sound, that degree of error will impact the calculation. In this regard, it may be of interest to note that in 2007 the *Akron Beacon Journal* posted a short item with the lead sentence: "Warning: Analyzing trends in corporate philanthropy is far from a perfect science." Citing The Foundation Center, the Committee Encouraging Corporate Philanthropy, and *Giving USA*, the article noted corporate philanthropy in 2007 either increased 2.7% or 4.7%, or decreased 7.6%.[29]

The *Giving USA* series is based largely on deductions taken by Americans on their IRS Individual Income Tax Returns.

A discussion of problems of noncash contributions estimates was presented in some detail in a previous edition in the *State of Church Giving* series.[30] Two comments may be relevant in the present review of the widely different estimates of individual giving presented in Table 37.

The results of this comparison of three estimates of individual giving suggest that the area of philanthropy measurement needs quality attention.

When he was Internal Revenue Service Commissioner, Mark W. Everson, in written testimony submitted to a Congressional hearing, in a section titled "Over-stated Deductions" wrote that, "A common problem occurs when a taxpayer takes an improper or overstated charitable contribution deduction. This happens most frequently when the donation is of something other than cash or readily marketable securities."[31] In a *Chronicle of Philanthropy* article, Mr. Everson was quoted as suggesting that noncash deductions may be overstated by as much as $15 to $18 billion a year.[32]

The problems observed by Mark Everson apparently have not been resolved. A 2008 *Chronicle of Philanthropy* item reported:

> The misuse of nonprofit organizations to shield income or provide fake tax breaks has once again appeared on the Internal Revenue service's "dirty dozen," the agency's annual list of the top 12 tax scams in the United States. Most of the abuse stems from people giving money or property to charities but retaining too much control over the donations, or from people overestimating the value of donated property. In addition, the IRS says that an old scam—claiming private tuition payments as charitable donations—continues to grow.[33]

Scott Burns, business writer for *The Dallas Morning News* and Universal Press Syndicate columnist, considered the topic of "over-statement" of deductions in a 2007 column. A reader wrote in to say that a consultant had told the reader how he "can claim up to 10 percent of the total income as a write-off without proof or receipts." The reader wrote that he was pleased to be getting money back from the IRS, instead of paying taxes. He went on, "Our total income for 2005 was $101,083. My consultant has entered $9,224 for charities, $12,253 for job expenses and certain miscellaneous deductions, and $3,825 for meals and entertainment. I can tell you, those figures are exaggerated. But is it legal?"

Scott Burns began his reply with the comment, "Excuse me if I sound like a close relative of Goody Two Shoes, but do you really want to be a lying freeloader just because others are?" Burns also noted that, "The IRS has estimated unpaid taxes exceed $290 billion a year. The Treasury inspector general for tax administration thinks the IRS is low-balling the number." Burns advised the man to keep good records and deduct appropriately.[34]

The exchange in Scott Burns' column highlights some of the difficulties with using deductions from IRS Individual Income Tax Returns as a basis for calculating charitable giving in the U.S.

The results of this comparison of three estimates of individual giving suggest that the area of philanthropy measurement needs quality attention.

Recommendations for Improving the Measurements. Past editions in *The State of Church Giving* series have presented recommendations for improving the measurement of philanthropy in the United States.[35] Presently, the CE data has become an important source of information on the giving patterns of Americans. The CE, by reporting only cash contributions, avoids the problems inherent in using tax records, including cash and noncash deductions. It is recommended that the U.S. Department of Labor, Bureau of Labor Statistics, Consumer Expenditure Survey be utilized as the unbiased, broad-gauge benchmark of living Americans' aggregate cash giving to charity, until such time as the U.S. Internal Revenue Service makes summary Form 990 living individual giving data available on an annual basis.

With some adjustments, the Form 990 information could also provide a sound basis on which to answer the question of how much Americans give. This source would be improved by obtaining a measure of giving by living donors, providing information about contributions by source, and allow charitable groups to provide a self-definition of purpose and governance type.

One recommendation deserves further attention. An important refinement would provide a more complete picture of philanthropy in America. Before selecting one of the ten core definition categories, the nonprofit organization could first indicate its form of governance as either "faith-based" or "secular." This identification could provide valuable information to help clarify the role of religion in the area of giving. Form 990 could also require that the organization define itself, first by selecting either faith-based or secular as the category of governance, and then the specific activity described by one or more of the National Taxonomy of Exempt Organizations core codes.

The importance of being able to classify giving by both faith-based or secular categories, as well as by specific activity codes can be seen from an observation in *Giving USA 1990*'s discussion of "Giving to Religion." That issue of *Giving USA*, edited by Nathan Weber, noted, "Further, among many religious groups, giving to religion is considered identical with giving to human services, health care, etc., when such services are administered by organizations founded by the religious groups" (p. 187). An analysis of the CE data for 2007 found that donors identified 64% of their charitable donations as given to churches and religious organizations. That figure compares to the *Giving USA 2009* estimate for 2007 of 32%.[36] The extent of this variation suggests that the definitions of what constitutes a religious organization differ broadly among the charitable giving estimate sources.

In their book on the Unified Chart of Accounts, Russy D. Sumariwalla and Wilson C. Levis reproduced a graphic originally prepared by United Way of America that depicts how the account classification would appear in practical application.[37] For purposes of the present discussion, that graphic was adapted to include a statement

Before selecting one of the ten core definition categories, the nonprofit organization could first indicate its form of governance as either "faith-based" or "secular." This identification could provide valuable information to help clarify the role of religion in the area of giving.

Figure 19: Account Classification Application with Faith-based/Secular Governance Option Included

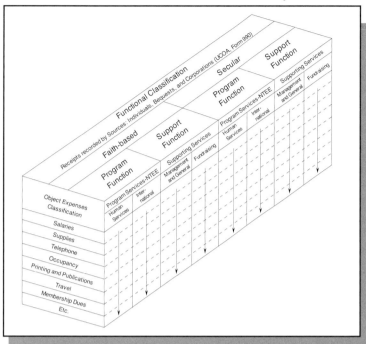

Source: Adaptation of graphic in Sumariwalla and Levis   empty tomb graphic 2001

about receipts classification, and to describe at what point the choice of faith-based or secular governance would be included in the accounting hierarchy (see Figure 19).

Associated Press Reports on Philanthropy Inconsistent with General Reporting Standards.
Here's a story problem.

In a town of 1,000 people, each person gave $10 to support a local cause. Those donations resulted in $10,000 for the cause.

The next year, the town's population swelled to 2,000. Now each person gave $5 to support the same cause. The donations totaled $10,000.

Should the newspaper report that giving stayed the same? Or does the newspaper have a responsibility to report on the 50% decline in the rate of individual giving? Is it truthful to say that people are just as generous in one year as the next, because a total of $10,000 was raised each year? Or does the public need to know about an important trend toward declining individual giving?

Rarely does the media provide numbers to the public without placing those numbers in a larger context. Consider that the press routinely reports the crime rate, the unemployment rate, the savings rate, the poverty rate, the on-time flight rate, the unpaid mortgage rate, and the Consumer Confidence Index. In each case, numbers are put into context of the larger population so that the reader has some basis to evaluate the meaning. For example, what does it mean that 14.5 million people were unemployed in July 2009? That number is put into context by a 9.4 percent unemployment rate.[38]

Researchers considering the status of religion in the world offered another example of the importance of changes in population:

> An interesting overall comment is that virtually all activities of Christian churches, missions, denominations, and communions are growing numerically and expanding. This is usually interpreted as showing the success of church programs. In fact, however, everybody's programs are all expanding fast because since AD 1800 populations everywhere have been expanding rapidly and now stand at 372,000 births a day.

> In fact, the key to understanding religious trends is the ability to compare growth rates of religious variables with secular ones. This is the only way to know if a religion is growing faster or slower than the general population.[39]

Good reporting seems to include the responsibility of placing numbers in the larger context so the reader will understand the importance of the figures being quoted.

The exception seems to be in the area of reporting philanthropy.

The media has consistently reported the *Giving USA* figure to the American public as the definitive estimate of charitable giving. Once again in 2009, the Associated Press article that appeared on the release of the new *Giving USA* report reflected the *Giving USA* press release focus on the aggregate billions of dollars raised. The lead emphasized the percent change in those aggregate billions of dollars from the previous year. With the exception of coverage in 2008, different Associated Press reporters' lead focus did not adjust the announced aggregate data for population and economy changes. As a result, the articles announce, in most years, an increase in aggregate current dollars, even though a decrease has occurred when population and the economy are taken into account.

Two years in the 2000 to 2008 period displayed somewhat different patterns. The change from 2004-2005 in Total Contributions was reported as an increase of 6.1 percent. When those billions of dollars were adjusted to a percent of Gross Domestic Product (GDP), there was actually a decline of 0.3%. Individual giving that year, as a percent of Disposable (after-tax) Personal Income (DPI), increased 2%. The change in Total Contributions aggregate billions of dollars from 2007-2008 was reported as -2%. When those billions were adjusted to a percent of GDP, the decline was -5.2%. Individual giving that year, adjusted to a percent of DPI, was -7%.

According to the Urban Institute, the nonprofit sector accounts for "5 percent of GDP, 8 percent of the economy's wages, and nearly 10 percent of jobs."[40]

Yet reporting about philanthropy in the U.S. is not put into context of the giving rate, but rather is left as the total amount of aggregate dollars.

Returning to the story problem, is $10,000 given by 1,000 people the same as $10,000 given by 2,000? Suppose the giving supported the zoo. Both years, the zoo had $10,000 to spend. However, the cost of meat that the lions eat and the special medicine the elephants need had doubled. The $10,000 did not buy the same amount in the current year that it did the last. Therefore, the dollars should be adjusted for inflation to indicate whether the $10,000 had the same buying power from one year to the next.

Also, consider the change in population. In the first year, the zoo had $10,000 to serve 1,000 people. Now, 2,000 people are expecting the same level of services for the same $10,000. Even with economy of scale, the $10,000 needed to be adjusted for the change in population and the resulting increased demand on services.

Finally, it may be important to note that people in the story problem were giving at a rate that was only half of what it was the previous year. Although the zoo had $10,000 to spend both years, the decline in per person donations could be a trend that might lead to an absolute decline in aggregate dollars the next year.

The American people have a right to know how their charitable giving rates are changing from year to year. The measure that validly conveys that information is the category of individual giving as a percent of income, which adjusts the aggregate numbers for changes in both population and income. As illustrated in earlier chapters in this volume, church giving appears different when considered in aggregate form, and when giving is considered per member and as a portion of an after-tax income.

The American people have a right to know how their charitable giving rates are changing from year to year.

97

Table 38:   **Associated Press Reported Aggregate Changes, Americans' Individual Giving Changes as Percent of Disposable Personal Income, and Total Giving Changes as Percent of Gross Domestic Product, 2000-2008, from Prior Year's Base: Giving Data from** *Giving USA* **2002, 2003, 2004, 2005, 2006, 2007, 2008, and 2009 Editions**

Giving USA Edition	*Giving USA* Data Year Interval	AP: First Percent Change from Previous Year Listed in AP Story: Aggregate Bil. $[41]	Per Capita Individual Giving as % of Per Capita DPI: % Change from Base Year[42]	Total Giving as % of Gross Domestic Product: % Change from Base Year[43]	AP Headline and AP First Mention of Percent Change	AP Byline and AP Dateline
2002	2000-01	0.5%	-2.6%	-2.8%	"2001 Charitable Giving Same As 2000" "Total giving by individuals, corporations and other groups amounted to $212 billion, up 0.5 percent from 2000 before inflation is figured in…"	Helena Payne, Associated Press Writer, New York
2003	2001-02	1.0%	-4.7%	-2.5%	"Donations Held Steady in 2002" "Giving rose 1 percent last year to $240.92 billion from $238.46 billion in 2001…"	Mark Jewell, The Associated Press, Indianapolis
2004	2002-03	2.8%	-2.0%	-1.9%	"Charitable Giving Rises in 2003" "…the survey showed a 2.8 percent increase over 2002, when giving amounted to $234.1 billion"	Kendra Locke, The Associated Press, New York
2005	2003-04	5.0%	-1.6%	-1.6%	"Charitable Giving Among Americans Rises" "Americans increased donations to charity by 5 percent in 2004…"	Adam Geller, AP Business Writer, New York
2006	2004-05	6.1%	2.0%	-0.3%	"Charitable Giving in U.S. Nears Record Set at End of Tech Boom" "The report released Monday by the Giving USA foundation estimates that in 2005 Americans gave $260.28 billion, a rise of 6.1 percent…"	Vinnee Tong, AP Business Writer, New York
2007	2005-06	1.0%	-0.9%	-2.0%	"Americans Give Nearly $300 Billion to Charities in 2006, Set a New Record" "Donors contributed an estimated $295.02 billion in 2006, a 1 percent increase when adjusted for inflation, up from $283.05 billion in 2005."	Vinnee Tong, AP Business Writer, New York
2008	2006-07	"remained at…" [0.0% implied]	-2.8%	-1.0%	"Americans Are Steady in Donations to Charity" "Donations by Americans to charities remained at 2.2 percent of gross domestic product in 2007…"	Vinnee Tong, AP Business Writer, New York
2009	2007-08	-2.0%	-7.0%	-5.2%	"Amid Meltdown, Charitable Gifts in US Fell in 2008" "Charitable giving by Americans fell by 2 percent in 2008 as the recession took root…"	David Crary, AP National Writer [AP National Reporting Team: Family and Relatioinships], New York

Source: Associated Press, USBEA, Giving USA, empty tomb, inc. analysis 2009

Tables and Chart regarding the Disparity between Associated Press Reports on Aggregate Charitable Giving Levels, and Giving Adjusted for Population and Income. As pointed out above, the Associated Press charitable giving articles' lead

Table 39: *Giving USA* **Executive Statement or Foreword First Mention of Percent Change and** *Giving USA* **Attribution**

Giving USA Executive Statement or Foreword First Mention of Percent Change	Giving USA Attribution
"The 0.5 percent increase in giving for 2001 is more attributable to the economy than to crisis."	(Indianapolis, Ind.: AAFRC Trust for Philanthropy, 2002), p. 1 Executive Statements: Statement of Chair, AAFRC Trust for Philanthropy: Leo P. Arnoult, CFRE, Chair, AAFRC Trust for Philanthropy
"Giving in 2002 is estimated to be $240.92 billion, growing one percent over the new estimate for 2001 of $238.46 billion."	(Indianapolis, Ind.: AAFRC Trust for Philanthropy, 2003), p. ii Foreword: Leo P. Arnoult, CFRE, Chair, AAFRC Trust for Philanthropy John J. Glier, Chair, AAFRC Eugene R. Tempel, Ed.D., CFRE, Executive Director, The Center on Philanthropy at Indiana University
"Giving in 2003 grew 2.8 percent over the revised estimate for 2002 of $234.09 billion."	(Glenview, Ill.: AAFRC Trust for Philanthropy, 2004), p. ii Foreword: Henry (Hank) Goldstein, CFRE, Chair, *Giving USA* Foundation John J. Glier, Chair, AAFRC Eugene R. Tempel, Ed.D., CFRE, Executive Director, The Center on Philanthropy at Indiana University
"Giving grew at the highest rate since 2000, 5.0 percent over a revised estimate of $236.73 billion for 2003 (2.3 percent adjusted for inflation)."	(Glenview, Ill.: AAFRC Trust for Philanthropy, 2005), p. ii Foreword: Henry (Hank) Goldstein, CFRE, Chair, *Giving USA* Foundation™, President, The Oram Group, Inc., New York, New York C. Ray Clements, Chair, American Association of Fundraising Counsel, CEO and Managing Member, Clements Group, Salt Lake City, Utah Eugene R. Tempel, Ed.D., CFRE, Executive Director, The Center on Philanthropy at Indiana University, Indianapolis, Indiana
"The combined result is that charitable giving rose to $260.28 billion, showing growth of 6.1 percent (2.7 percent adjusted for inflation)."	(Glenview, Ill.: Giving USA Foundation, 2006), p. ii Foreword: Richard T. Jolly, Chair, *Giving USA* Foundation™, George C. Ruotolo, Jr., CFRE, Acting Chair, Giving Institute: Leading Consultants to Non-Profits Eugene R. Tempel, Ed.D., CFRE, Executive Director, The Center on Philanthropy at Indiana University
"In constant [*sic*] dollars, the increase was 4.2 percent over 2005; in inflation-adjusted numbers, the increase was 1.0 percent."	(Glenview, Ill.: Giving USA Foundation, 2007), p. ii Foreword: Richard T. Jolly, Chair, Giving USA Foundation™, George C. Ruotolo, Jr., CFRE, Chair, Giving Institute: Leading Consultants to Non-Profits Eugene R. Tempel, Ed.D., CFRE, Executive Director, The Center on Philanthropy at Indiana University
"The estimates for 2007 indicate that giving rose by 3.9 percent over the previous year (1 percent adjusted for inflation), to reach a record $306.39 billion."	(Glenview, Ill.: Giving USA Foundation, 2008), p. ii Foreword: Del Martin, CFRE, Chair, Giving USA Foundation™, George C. Ruotolo, Jr., CFRE, Chair, Giving Institute: Leading Consultants to Non-Profits Eugene R. Tempel, Ed.D., CFRE, Executive Director, The Center on Philanthropy at Indiana University
"This is a drop of 2 percent in current dollars (-5.7 percent adjusted for inflation), compared to 2007."	(Glenview, Ill.: Giving USA Foundation, 2009), p. ii Foreword: Del Martin, CFRE, Chair, Giving USA Foundation™, publisher of *Giving USA* Nancy L. Raybin, Chair, Giving Institute: Leading Consultants to Non-Profits Patrick M. Rooney, Ph.D., Executive Director, The Center on Philanthropy at Indiana University

Source: Associated Press, USBEA, Giving USA, empty tomb, inc. analysis 2009

routinely with an emphasis on the upbeat tone of the *Giving USA* press releases in terms of aggregate billions of dollars raised, unadjusted for population and income.

An analysis of AP reporting of *Giving USA* releases for the past eight years found the following. In 2002, 2003, 2004, 2005, and 2007, the AP article released nationally and internationally led with a percent change that indicated an increase in total charitable giving from the previous year. Yet, when a basic adjustment for changes in U.S. population and economic growth was made to the *Giving USA* aggregate numbers, individual giving as a percent of DPI declined rather than increased in seven of the eight years, and total giving as a percent of U.S. GDP declined in all eight years.

This pattern of disparity between AP reports on aggregate billions of dollars raised, and the complete picture of changes in charitable giving patterns, can be observed in Table 38, which also includes the text from the related AP release. This AP text can be compared with the first mention of percent change included in the related editions in the *Giving USA* series presented in Table 39.

Figure 20 illustrates the disparity in the category of percent changes in aggregate total charitable giving reported by the AP and the same Total Contributions aggregate billions adjusted to a percent of GDP. In addition, the percent change from one year to the next for each *Giving USA* edition's Individual giving figure is presented as a portion of DPI.

The observation may be made that the Associated Press apparently chooses to highlight an industry's interpretation of its own work in a relatively uncritical fashion that de-emphasizes essential elements of the whole truth.

Total current dollar philanthropy as presented by *Giving USA*, unadjusted by population and income, has increased, that is, "set a new record" each year for 53 years from the first edition in 1955 through 2008, with qualifications obtaining only for the years 1987 and 2008.[44] This consistent pattern of growth is not surprising in light of the fact that both U.S. population and U.S. per capita DPI in current dollars have increased each year during the period under consideration.[45]

When correspondence was sent to then-Associated Press Vice President and Senior Managing Editor Mike Silverman, describing this topic, he responded in a May 8, 2008, letter: "You make some interesting points about how we might put these reports into better perspective for our readers." Note in Table 38 that Associated Press business writer Vinee Tong led in the 2008 article on the release of *Giving USA 2008* with the aggregate billions of charitable dollars as a percent of GDP, which accounted for changes in population. This perspective was an improvement in the reported information provided to the public, even though the percent change in Total Giving as a percent of GDP between 2006 and 2007 was actually -1.0%.

However, the 2009 Associated Press article on the release of *Giving USA 2009* was written by someone listed on the AP Web site as reporting on Family and Relationships, and the lead returned to the standard aggregate current dollar change. It may be reasonable that the writer focused on the decrease in aggregate current dollars of -2% as newsworthy, given that only in 1987 did such a decline also occur. In the fifteenth paragraph of a 16-paragraph story, the AP writer did note that when adjusted for inflation, aggregate total charitable giving was down 5.7%. However, in the sixteenth paragraph, when discussing individual giving, the writer again referred to aggregate dollars declining 2.7%, and did not present individual giving as a percent of DPI, which measure was down 7%. Also, there was no discussion of the fact that total charitable giving, as a percent of GDP, was down 5.2% from 2007 to 2008. Both of the latter measures would have placed the charitable giving numbers into the broader context of the economy, including changes in population, and helped the reader understand rates of giving rather than only gross amounts.

The nonprofit area constitutes a large enough sector of the American economy that the philanthropy practices supporting it deserve the quality of reporting applied to other economic sectors, including adjustment for population and income to provide information about changes in the rate of giving.

Figure 20: Associated Press Reported Aggregate Changes, Americans' Individual Giving Changes as a Percent of Disposable Personal Income, and Total Giving Changes as a Percent of Gross Domestic Product, 2000-2008, from Previous Year's Base: Data from *Giving USA* 2002, 2003, 2004, 2005, 2006, 2007, 2008, and 2009 Editions

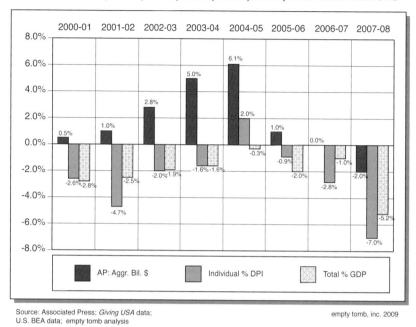

Source: Associated Press; *Giving USA* data; U.S. BEA data; empty tomb analysis

empty tomb, inc. 2009

Summary

Individuals give to charity for a variety of reasons. When given the opportunity to categorize their own donations in 2007, Americans indicated that 64% of their giving is to "churches, religious organizations." This finding suggests that the role of religion plays a vital role in the practice of philanthropy in the United States.

Three estimates of aggregate individual giving in the U.S. vary by as much as $61 billion. Of three available giving estimate sources, the U.S. Bureau of Labor Statistics Consumer Expenditure Survey serves as a benchmark in providing unbiased information about giving levels in the United States.

Notes for Chapter 7

[1] U.S. Department of Labor Bureau of Labor Statistics; "Frequently Asked Questions"; n.d.; <http://www.bls.gov/cex/csxfaqs.htm>; p. 2 of 5/28/2005 10:32 AM printout.

[2] The above estimate of $129.07 billion is likely a high measure of charitable giving insofar as it includes all of the $7.48 billion in the category, "Gift[s] to non-CU members of stocks, bonds, and mutual funds." This attribution thus assumes that all of the $7.48 billion given in this category went to charitable organizations, although the CE does not allocate the funds of this category between charitable and non-charitable recipients.

[3] Americans' charitable giving was calculated by multiplying the 120,171,000 "Number of consumer units" by each of the average annual consumer unit contributions for 2007, the components of which were $275.94 ("charities and other organizations"), $684.76 ("church, religious organizations"), $51.10 ("educational institutions"), and $62.25 ("Gifts to non-CU members of stocks, bonds, and mutual funds"). The resultant sum of the aggregated components

yielded a total giving amount of $129.07 billion. The "Cash contributions to church, religious organizations" amount, therefore, was calculated by multiplying the number of consumer units by $684.76 yielding an amount of $82.29 billion for 2006. Religion as a percent of the total was calculated by dividing $82.29 billion by $129.07 billion, yielding 64%. "Cash contributions" items not included in the above calculations for charitable contributions were "Support for college students (Sec.19); Alimony expenditures (Sec. 19); Child support expenditures (Sec. 19); Cash contribution to political organizations; Other cash gifts." Data source: U.S. Department of Labor, U.S. Bureau of Labor Statistics, "Table 1800. Region of residence: Average annual expenditures and characteristics, Consumer Expenditure Survey, 2007" [Item detail]; StTable1800Region2007.pdf; Created 11/13/2008 9:12 AM; unnumbered pp. 1, 17 & 29 of 3/25/3009 printout.

[4] Data sources: U.S. Department of Labor, U.S. Bureau of Labor Statistics, "Table 1202. Income before taxes: Average annual expenditures and characteristics, Consumer Expenditure Survey, 2007" [Item detail]; StTable1200Income2007.pdf; Created 11/13/2008 9:06 AM; unnumbered pp. 1, 18, & 30 of 3/25/2009 printout; and "Table 2301. Higher Income before taxes: Average annual expenditures and characteristics, Consumer Expenditure Survey, 2007" [Item detail]; StTable2301HiInc2007.pdf; Created 11/13/2008 9:19 AM; unnumbered pp. 1, 18, & 30 of 3/25/2009 printout.

[5] Information from the outlier "Less than $5,000" bracket, while part of the "All consumer units" data, was not otherwise included in the present analysis.

[6] Consumer Expenditure Survey "Frequently Asked Questions"; U.S. Department of Labor, U.S. Bureau of Labor Statistics, Consumer Expenditure Surveys, Branch of Information and Analysis; Last Modified Date: March 17, 2005; <http://www.bls.gov/cex/csxfaqs.htm>; p. 7 of 5/28/05 10:32 AM printout.

[7] Data source: U.S. Department of Labor, U.S. Bureau of Labor Statistics, "Table 1300. Age of reference person: Average annual expenditures and characteristics, Consumer Expenditure Survey, 2007" [Item detail]; StTable1300Age2007.pdf; Created 11/13/2008 9:06 AM; unnumbered pp. 1, 18 & 30 of 3/25/2009 printout.

[8] Data source: U.S. Department of Labor, U.S. Bureau of Labor Statistics , "Table 1800. Region of residence: Average annual expenditures and characteristics, Consumer Expenditure Survey, 2007"; unnumbered pp. 1, 17 & 29.

[9] "Mission Statement"; U.S. Department of Labor, Bureau of Labor Statistics; Last Modified Date: October 16, 2001; <http://www.bls.gov/bls/blsmissn.htm>; p. 1 of 8/15/05 4:59 PM printout.

[10] U.S. Census Bureau, *Statistical Abstract of the United States: 2006*, 125th edition; published 2005; <http://www.census.gov/prod/2005pubs/06statab/prices.pdf>; pp. 479, 481 of 5/31/06 printout.

[11] "Consumer Expenditures in 2004"; Report 992; U.S. Department of Labor, U.S. Bureau of Labor Statistics; April 2006; <http://www.bls.gov/cex/csxann04.pdf>; pp. 4-5 of 5/30/06 printout.

[12] Consumer Expenditure Survey "Frequently Asked Questions"; U.S. Department of Labor, U.S. Bureau of Labor Statistics, Consumer Expenditure Surveys, Branch of Information and Analysis; Last Modified Date: March 17, 2005; <http://www.bls.gov/cex/csxfaqs.htm>; p. 2 of 5/28/05 10:32 AM printout.

[13] Sylvia Porter, "Out-of-Date Consumer Price Index to Be Revised in '87," a "Money's Worth" column appearing in *Champaign (Ill.) News-Gazette,* January 9, 1985, sec. D, p. 3.

[14] "Price Index Undergoes Statistical Adjustment," an Associated Press (Washington) article appearing in the *Champaign (Ill.) News-Gazette,* April 19, 1998, sec. C, p. 1.

[15] Consumer Price Indexes "Addendum to Frequently Asked Questions"; U.S. Department of Labor, Bureau of Labor Statistics, Division of Consumer Prices and Price Indexes; Last Modified Date: March 28, 2005; <http://www.bls.gov/cpi/cpiadd.htm#2_1>; pp. 1-2 of 5/31/06 10:54 AM printout.

[16] Gabriel Rudney, "The Scope of the Private Voluntary Charitable Sector," Research Papers Sponsored by The Commission on Private Philanthropy and Public Needs, Vol. 1, History, Trends, and Current Magnitudes, (Washington, DC: Department of the Treasury, 1977), p. 136. The nature

of these numbers, specifically whether they are for giving to church only or combine giving to church and religious organizations, would benefit from a review in light of the relatively recent CE introduction of the "church, religious organizations" category.

[17] For this comparison, the composite data set of denominations was adjusted for missing data.

[18] U.S. Department of Labor, Bureau of Labor Statistics; "Table 1800.Region of Residence: Average annual expenditures and characteristics, Consumer Expenditure Survey, 2007"; unnumbered pp. 1, 17 & 29.

[19] See Appendix B-6 for sources of Form 990 series detail.

[20] *Giving USA 2009* (Glenview, IL: Giving USA Foundation, 2009), pp. 213.

[21] *Giving USA 2009*, p. 210.

[22] "Charitable contributions deduction: Other than cash contributions": "Table 3.—Returns with Itemized Deductions: Sources of Income, Adjustments, Itemized Deductions by Type, Exemptions, and Tax Items, by Size of Adjusted Gross Income, Tax Year 2005"; IRS; <http://www.irs.gov/pub/irs-soi/05in03id.xls>; p. 3 of 4/10/2008 7:07 PM printout.

[23] Dean R. Hoge, Charles Zech, Patrick McNamara, Michael J. Donahue, *Money Matters: Personal Giving in American Churches* (Louisville: Westminster John Knox Press, 1996), p.49; Jerry White, *The Church & the Parachurch* (Portland, OR: Multnomah Press, 1983), p.104.

[24] See Appendix B-6 for the data used and sources.

[25] *Giving USA 1980 Annual Report* (New York: American Association of Fund-Raising Counsel, Inc., 1980), p. 9.

[26] *Giving USA 2009*, pp. 233, 236.

[27] The Association of Fundraising Professionals Golden Gate Chapter June 30, 2006 "Fundraising Morning 2006" program listed a session titled "Giving USA 2006: Changing Data Into Action," to be presented by the vice president of a fundraising firm: "Ms. McGuire will present an incisive summary of the newly-released Giving USA report, followed by a lively panel discussion on strategic insights to transform the data into winning funding strategies to help your organization stay ahead of the curve." <http://www.afp-ggc.org/frm/program.html>; pp. 1, 4 of 6/15/2006 8:14 AM printout. The Alford Group (motto: "Strengthening the not-for-profit community") offered free sessions scheduled in different U.S. cities: "The Alford Group helps you make sense of Giving USA 2006! Take part in one of our informational sessions, illuminating who gave last year, to whom, how much, what the historical trends tell us, and what that means for your organization." <http://www.alford.com/site/pp.asp?c=9fLNGWOrH1E&b=293745>; p. 2 of 7/7/2006 8:13 AM printout.

[28] *Giving USA 2008*, p. 210.

[29] Paula Schleis; "Ups and Downs"; Akron Beacon Journal; posted 8/13/07; <http://www.ohio.com/business/9119806.html>; p. 1 of 8/15/07 11?45 AM printout.

[30] John Ronsvalle and Sylvia Ronsvalle, *The State of Church Giving through 2003* (Champaign, IL: empty tomb, inc., 2005), pp. 91-93. The chapter is also available at: <http://www.emptytomb.org/scg03chap7.pdf>.

[31] Mark W. Everson; "Written Statement of Mark W. Everson, Commissioner of Internal Revenue, Before The Committee on Finance, United States Senate, Hearing On Exempt Organizations: Enforcement Problems, Accomplishments, and Future Direction"; April 5, 2005; <http://finance.senate.gov/hearings/testimony/2005test/metest040505.pdf>; p. 9 of 4/27/05 printout.

[32] Brad Wolverton (Washington), "Taking Aim at Charity," *Chronicle of Philanthropy*, published by The Chronicle of Higher Education, Inc., Washington, D.C., April 14, 2005, p. 27.

[33] Sam Kean, Peter Panepento, and Grant Williams, "Tax Watch: Write-Offs," *The Chronicle of Philanthropy*, April 3, 2008, p. 42.

[34] Scott Burns, "No, It's Not OK to Lie on Return," (*The Champaign (Ill.) News-Gazette,* May 10, 2006, p. B-8.

[35] For the complete discussion of these recommendations, see Ronsvalle and Ronsvalle, *The*

State of Church Giving through 2003, pp. 93-100. The chapter is also available at: <http://www. emptytomb.org/scg03chap7.pdf>.

[36] *Giving USA 2009*, p. 212.

[37] Russy D. Sumariwalla and Wilson C. Levis, Unified *Financial Reporting System for Not-for-Profit Organizations: A Comprehensive Guide to Unifying GAAP, IRS Form 990, and Other Financial Reports Using a Unified Chart of Accounts* (San Francisco: Jossey-Bass, 2000), p. 41.

[38] U.S. Bureau of Labor Statistics; "Economic News Release: Employment Situation Summary: The Employment Situation – July 2009"; August 7, 2009; <http://www.bls.gov/news.release/ empsit.nr0.htm>; p. 1 of 8/16/2009.

[39] David B. Barrett, Todd M. Johnson, and Peter F. Crossing, "Missiometrics 2008: Reality checks for Christian World Communions," *International Bulletin of Missionary Research*, Vol. 32, No. 1, January 2008, p. 27.

[40] The Urban Institute; "Nonprofits"; 2009; <http://www.urban.org/nonprofits/index.cfm>; p. 1 of 8/16/2009 12:56 PM printout.

[41] The references for the Associated Press stories listed are as follows:

• Helena Payne, Associated Press Writer; "2001 Charitable Giving Same As 2000"; published June 20, 2002, 12:20 PM; <http://www.washingtonpost.com/ac2/wp-dyn/A17534-2002Jun20?language=printer>; p. 1 of 6/27/02 9:09 PM printout.

• Mark Jewell; "Donations Held Steady in 2002"; published June 23, 2003, 4:23 PM; <http:// www.washingtonpost.com/ wp-dyn/A23604-2003Jun23.html>; p. 1 of 6/26/03 8:49 AM printout.

• Kendra Locke; "Charitable Giving Rises in 2003"; published June 21, 2004, 12:24 AM; <http:// www.washingtonpost.com/wp-dyn/articles/A56830-2004Jun21.html>; p. 1 of 6/25/04 4:56 PM printout.

• Adam Geller, AP Business Writer; "Charitable Giving Among Americans Rises"; published June 14, 2005 10:16 AM; <http://www.guardian.co.uk/worldlateststory/0,1280,-5073041,00.html>; p. 1 of 6/15/2005 9:42 AM printout.

• Vinnee Tong, AP Business Writer; "Charitable Giving in U.S. Nears Record Set at End of Tech Boom"; The Associated Press, New York, published June 18, 2006 11:10 PM GMT; <http://web. lexis.com[…extended URL]>; p. 1 of 6/20/2006 8:51 AM printout.

• Vinnee Tong, AP Business Writer; "Americans Give Nearly $300 Billion to Charities in 2006, Set a New Record"; published June 25, 2007 4:58 GMT; <http://web.lexis.com…>; p. 1 of 6/25/07 5:01 PM printout.

• Vinee Tong, AP Business Write; {Americans Are Steady in Donations to Charity"; published June 23, 2008; 11:43 AM GMT; <http://web.lexis.com…>; p. 1 of 6/23/2008 5:23 PM printout.

• David Crary, AP National Writer; "Amid Meltdown, Charitable Gifts in US Fell in 2008"; published June 10, 2009; 04:01 AM GMT; <http://web.lexis.com…>; p. 1 of 6/10/2009 5:11 PM printout.

[42] See Appendix C for the source of data on which the calculation of "Per Capita Individual Giving as % of Per Capita Disposable Personal Income: % Change from Base Year" figures by empty tomb, inc. was based.

[43] The calculation of "Total Giving as % of Gross Domestic Product: % Change from Base Year" figures by empty tomb, inc. was based on the following data. The aggregate Total giving sources for the 2000-01, 2001-02, 2002-03, 2003-04, 2004-05, 2005-06, 2006-2007, and 2008-2009 intervals were the 2002 (p. 169), 2003 (p. 194), 2004 (p. 218), 2005 (p. 194), 2006 (p. 204), 2007 (p. 212), 2008 (p. 210), and 2009 (p. 210) *Giving USA* editions, respectively. The source of Gross Domestic Product (GDP) data in current dollars for the 2000-01 interval was the 2002 edition of *Giving USA* (p. 177). The source of GDP for the 2002-2008 data was the U.S. Bureau of Economic Analysis; "Table 1.1.5. Gross Domestic Product"; Line 1: "Gross Domestic Product"; National Income and Product Accounts Tables;

• <http://www.bea.gov/bea/dn/nipaweb/GetCSV.asp?GetWhat=SS_Data/Secton1All_xls. xls&Section=2>; for 2002, last revised May 27, 2004 and downloaded June 30, 2004; for 2003, last revised April 28, 2005 and downloaded May 25, 2005; for 2004, last revised April 28, 2006 and downloaded May 16, 2006.

• <http://www.bea.gov/bea/dn/nipaweb/SS_Data/Section1All_xls.xls>; for 2005, published April 27, 2007 and downloaded April 27, 2007.

• <http://www.bea.gov/national/nipaweb/SS_Data/Section1All_xls.xls>; for 2006, published March 27, 2008 and downloaded March 27, 2008; for 2007 and 2008, published March 26, 2009 and downloaded on March 26, 2009.

[44] For the years 1955 through 1979, see *Giving USA, 1980 Annual Report, 25th Anniversary Issue* (New York: American Association of Fund-Raising Counsel, Inc., 1980), p. 22. For a revised, overlapping series covering the years 1966 through 2008, see *Giving USA 2009* (p. 212).

In the 1988 edition of *Giving USA: The Annual Report for the Year 1987* (New York: American Association of Fund-Raising Counsel Trust for Philanthropy, 1988), Total Contributions increased from 1986 to 1987 (p. 11). Although the 1987 figure was later revised to show a decrease from 1986 (see *Giving USA 1998: The Annual Report on Philanthropy for the Year 1997,* p. 156), any media reports at the time of the release of the 1988 *Giving USA* edition would have had access only to the information that giving increased in 1987.

The 1988 edition of *Giving USA* Foreword, coauthored by Maurice G. Gurin, Chairman, AAFRC Trust for Philanthropy, and George A. Brakeley III, Chairman, American Association of Fund-Raising Counsel, opened with the following paragraph. "The stock market crash of October 19 and the loss of the charitable deduction gave rise to predictions that philanthropic giving last year would suffer significantly. Quite the opposite occurred: total giving increased significantly. Indeed it achieved an impressive new high" (p. 5).

The "State of the Philanthropic Sector, 1987" section, located a number of pages further in the same volume, opens with the heading in bold type and closing punctuation of "$93.68 Billion!" The complete first two paragraphs of that section including the ellipsis follow. "Stock market crash. End of the charitable tax deduction for non-itemizers. Decline in the economy's competitiveness. Well-publicized hijinks of televangelists using much of the money donated for 'religion' to create their own heavens on earth…. In the face of it all, estimated giving in the United States reached an all-time high in 1987—$93.68 billion.

"That amount represents an increase of 6.45 percent over the estimated amount donated a year earlier. The yearly increase marks the continuation of a decades-long trend" (p. 16). Yet, as noted above, subsequent corrections to the initial estimate so enthusiastically announced and reported on found that giving actually declined rather than increased from 1986 to 1987.

[45] U.S Bureau of Economic Analysis; "Table 7.1. Selected Per Capita Product and Income Series in Current and Chained Dollars"; Line 16: "Population (midperiod, thousands)"; National Income and Product Accounts Tables; <http://www.bea.gov/national/nipaweb/SS_Data/Section7All_xls. xls>; published March 26, 2009.

What Are Our Christian Billionaires Thinking– Or Are They?

"The master commended the dishonest manager because he had acted shrewdly. For the people of this world are more shrewd in dealing with their own kind than are the people of the light. I tell you, use worldly wealth to gain friends for yourselves, so that when it is gone, you will be welcomed into eternal dwellings…

"So if you have not been trustworthy in handling worldly wealth, who will trust you with true riches?"
    — Jesus Christ, quoted in Luke 16:8-9, 11 (NIV)

Money and the church.

Judging by how many times the topic is addressed by Jesus, one might reasonably assume it is important to the life of the church.

Certainly, the issue is raised regularly in local congregations and denominational publications regarding the costs of operations.

However, as in the parable Luke records in his sixteenth chapter, Jesus' focus does not seem to be paying the bills. In fact, it seems that Jesus goes out of his way to make a distinction between "worldly wealth" and "true riches." Further, Jesus does not criticize those who handle money "shrewdly." Rather Jesus holds them up as an example to be emulated.

Christians in the U.S., by living in the largest economy the world has ever seen, have access to great resources. It behooves them, therefore, to be sure they understand Jesus' views on this matter. However, the giving patterns discussed in earlier chapters suggest that the great potential that Jesus hints at in Luke 16 is not being realized.

This chapter will explore several topics that relate to the handling of money and what might constitute the "true riches" that can benefit from the application of "worldly wealth."

The first section of this chapter explores the perspective that there are "wholesale billionaire philanthropists" (large-capacity donors) and "retail billionaire philanthropists" (donors of lesser amounts that combine to support multibillion dollar institutions). In this section, a role for leadership from the wholesale billionaire philanthropists to mobilize more of the potential of the retail billionaire philanthropists is discussed. Also considered are some of the dynamics that the wholesale billionaire philanthropist should understand before venturing into the realm of church mobilization.

The second section of this chapter presents a "Model to Calculate Country-Specific Costs for Preventing Child Deaths."

Under-5 child deaths is one of two issues identified through the construct of "global triage" as meriting the immediate attention and intervention of the church in the U.S. The approach of global triage for helping to set the church's mission agenda was explored in the previous edition of *The State of Church Giving* series.[1] As a result, preventable under-5 child deaths around the globe is one of two issues proposed as the focus of the wholesale billionaire philanthropists' mobilizing activities.

The third section of the chapter considers the other issue identified using the global triage construct, that is, completing the church's task of global evangelization. This task is often termed the Great Commission, which was given to the church as a responsibility just before Jesus ascended to Heaven. In this third section, the Wycliffe Bible Translators campaign, to have begun the translation of the Bible into all languages by the year 2025, is explored as a possible model for use by denominations. Also in the third section, a case study of the Southern Baptist Convention's efforts to pursue their stated goal of global evangelization is presented. Finally, the third section considers a strategy for wholesale billionaires who want to apply "worldly wealth" in a "shrewd" way to pursue "true riches."

> There are two kinds of billionaire philanthropists.

Wholesale and Retail Billionaire Philanthropists

There are two kinds of billionaire philanthropists.

The first sort is the "wholesale" billionaire philanthropist. Names immediately come to mind of individuals who have made their mark in industry and the charitable sector: Rockefeller, Carnegie, Gates, Buffett, Turner. A wholesale billionaire philanthropist is a "high capacity" donor, one who personally controls vast wealth and can write or authorize a check for a phenomenal amount of money.

The second is the "retail" billionaire philanthropist. Separately, these people do not have access to extraordinary individual amounts of resources. However, as a group, they support a vast network of multibillion-dollar churches and nonprofits that accomplish much of the good done in society. Each church member who attends Sunday service and deposits a sum, no matter how small, becomes part of a network of philanthropists who enable a multibillion-dollar system of services. Although the "retail" billionaire philanthropist cannot access this wealth for personal expenses, to the degree the member is a full partner in what might be termed the Kingdom of God, on a practical level he or she joins together with others as combined billionaire philanthropists.

The potential and need for "wholesale" billionaires to mobilize "retail" billionaires to increase the latter's investment in the charitable works of the church will be explored on the following pages.

How Many "Wholesale" Billionaires Are in the Church? A review of the largest philanthropic gifts in two recent years suggests that wealthy people do not focus on religion when making their mega-gifts. A review of "The 2007 *Slate* 60: The 60 Largest American Charitable Contributions of the Year," found that only five of the sixty gifts given had any reference to religious organizations in the gift descriptions. Two were to Jewish organizations, one to Oral Roberts University, one to the Archdiocese of New York for scholarships to area Catholic schools, and one to Baylor College of Medicine for medical research. A number of gifts were to the donors' foundations, with the balance mostly to hospitals and higher education.[2]

A list of "The Philanthropy 50: America's Most-Generous Donors in 2008" included a summary of the types of organizations that received gifts. On that list were 42 colleges and universities, 16 foundations, 16 museums and libraries, 15 environmental and animal-related groups, and then 11 "religious groups," although a review of the list seemed to indicate that most of the gifts to "religious groups" may have come from one donor.[3]

Based on the giving patterns in these two lists, one might wonder if there are many extraordinarily wealthy people among those who confess Jesus Christ and are church members.

One may calculate a theoretical number, based on the Forbes 400 list, to estimate the presence of church members on the roster.[4] Such a calculation would assume that the 400 individuals represented on the Forbes list in 2008 reflect a similar percent of church membership as is present in the U.S. as a whole. In that case, as noted in the calculations in chapter 6, 59.45% of those on the list would claim membership in a historically Christian church. Applying that percent to the 400 on the Forbes list results in an estimate of 238 billionaires who are members of historically Christian churches. Given that the total worth of the 400 was estimated by Forbes to be $1.57 trillion dollars, this subset of church members might be worth $933.4 billion dollars (59.45% of $1.57 trillion). Assuming that these individuals earned eight percent a year from their money, the group would have $74.7 billion dollars a year available to spend. A tithe of the spending amount would therefore be $7.5 billion for the group. With 238 individuals in the church member subset, each individual would have a potential tithe of $31.4 million dollars a year ($7.5 billion divided by 238).

An interesting point can be observed about the calculation of the tithe for the estimated number of historically Christian church members on the Forbes 400 list. That is, the calculated tithe of $7.5 billion, from current income, for the estimated 238 historically Christian church members on the list is less than one-twentieth of what would be available if the retail billionaires, the general church population in the U.S., chose to increase their giving to the classic tithe. That is, in chapter 6, the difference between present giving levels and potential additional giving at 10% of income was conservatively estimated to be $161 billion. This potential moves from the theoretical to the practical when one considers the discussion in chapter 6 about the $79 billion in remittances sent internationally by non-native born residents in the U.S. Given that there are four times the number of native-born church members, compared to foreign-born people, in the U.S., native-born church members giving at the same level as remittances are sent out of the country would yield an additional $314 billion more a year for missions. The great potential of retail billionaire philanthropists becomes evident.

A review of the largest philanthropic gifts in two recent years suggests that wealthy people do not focus on religion when making their mega-gifts.

Wholesale Billionaires and Retail Billionaires Combined Could Accomplish Additional Significant Goals. As noted above, the potential giving from current income by wholesale billionaires is considerably less than the combined potential of the many church members with much lower incomes who support multibillion-dollar institutions.

At least three of the currently highly visible wholesale billionaires appear to be well aware of the limits confronting their individual efforts. Bill and Melinda Gates, co-trustees of the largest foundation, have said on more than one occasion that the tasks that need to be done are larger than they can handle. On a panel, Melinda Gates called the resources at her disposal "a drop in the bucket" compared to the challenges of global need.[5]

In their book *Philanthrocapitalism*, Matthew Bishop and Michael Green quote Bill Gates:

> "Are we big enough to play our role in AIDS? Are we big enough to play our role in malaria? No, we are not big enough," says Bill Gates. "We're a tiny, tiny little organization...
>
> "How many people work on, say, brownie mix? How many people work on a soft drink? Is it possible that there should be a foundation that has a fifth as many people working on saving lives as there are working on Diet Pepsi?"[6]

Bishop and Green also quote Warren Buffett, the third co-trustee of the Gates Foundation and the first or second richest man in the world, depending on what year it is. Describing his thoughts about the large gift he made to the Gates Foundation, they write: "Buffett admits that his gift amounts to only 'one dollar each per year for the poorest half of the world population' and describes philanthropy as a 'tougher game' than business."[7]

The humility with which Bill and Melinda Gates and Warren Buffett approach their desire to impact global need is not only refreshing; it is also practical. From within their business backgrounds, they would know that the smartest approach to a problem is to have an honest evaluation of currently available resources, and then figure out how to leverage those to make the biggest possible impact on the solution.

Wholesale Billionaires' Role in Mobilizing Retail Billionaires' Increased Missions Giving. Presently, based on the review of major gifts, extraordinarily wealthy individuals do not focus on religious activities when making major gifts. There could be a variety of reasons for this pattern.

As discussed in previous editions in this series, a significant problem may be the lack of vision in church circles that would attract single mega-gifts. As one businessman commented, "I've never been given a vision big enough to challenge my entrepreneurial skills, so I've always been an usher."[8] If the agenda is institutional maintenance, then the level of gifts will be limited to maintenance levels as well, whether from wholesale or retail billionaire philanthropists.

This lack of vision at a scale to address major global problems could be a factor in a lack of major gifts to the category of religion. Apparently, this is not a new problem. The Commission on Private Philanthropy and Public Needs produced reports and papers in the early 1970s for the U.S. Treasury Department. One such paper observed:

"Are we big enough to play our role in AIDS? Are we big enough to play our role in malaria? No, we are not big enough," says Bill Gates. "We're a tiny, tiny little organization..."

There is the added reality, omitted by the Commission's report, that patterns of support reflect what *donees seek*, as well as what donors select. Churches do not seek large individual gifts as a pattern, especially for their operating purposes. Universities do seek very large individual gifts, not only for current operations, but for capital and endowment purposes. Donee influence likewise affects bequests. It is too simplistic to attribute the patterns of objects of gifts only to the wishes of the donors[9] [italics in original].

In any event, currently there is no movement to mobilize the potential billions of dollars in increased giving to help eliminate the problems facing either the unevangelized, or the millions of children dying from preventable conditions around the globe. In contrast, denominations spent great energy on "getting out the vote" for the 2008 election. Voter guides provided either the communion's teachings as a reference point (Roman Catholic)[10] or raised selected issues, comparing the two main political parties' positions on fliers distributed in congregations (The United Methodist Church).[11] The second largest of the "big three" denominations in the U.S. organized a 40-day prayer and study guide to build up to Election Day (the Southern Baptist Convention).[12]

All these political activities may be within the realm of church leadership encouraging members to be good citizens in a democracy. However, it may be asked, where is the same level of goal setting to impact the lack of Bibles or the child deaths that occur not every four years but on a daily basis? Where are the intentional organizational and mobilization efforts on the part of church leadership at any level to solve some of the problems that threaten the spiritual and physical lives of so many around the globe?

On a practical rather than rhetorical level, leadership has been lacking on the part of congregations, and regional and national denominational offices. Crisis response and maintenance of ongoing activities continue to be the focus of church efforts. And this maintenance approach may not be attractive to wholesale billionaire philanthropists who are used to money being effective in achieving specific large goals.

It is in this realm that church members who are wholesale billionaires could bring their entrepreneurial insight and expertise to bear. In the next section in this chapter, for example, a model is presented that calculates cost estimates to address various causes of death in children under five who live in 68 nations in the world, representing 95% of those deaths. The last section in this chapter is a case study of a denomination's approach to a global evangelization goal. Energetic and creative leadership on the part of some subset of wealthy church members to mobilize additional resources among the general church population could make a vital impact on these specific needs.

However, there may well be dynamics that will resist the efforts of wholesale billionaires to move the church beyond a maintenance level. A brief review of some of those issues might prepare any brave leader who feels led to engage church members and denominational leaders in a quest for fulfilling their potential to love others in word and deed, and in Jesus' name. Following the discussion of those issues are some reasons why wholesale billionaires might want to venture forth in this area in spite of the accompanying challenges before them. At the end of the chapter is a proposal that takes some of these dynamics into account.

...this maintenance approach may not be attractive to wholesale billionaire philanthropists who are used to money being effective in achieving specific large goals.

Denominational Dynamics. As noted above, denominations spent a great deal of effort to organize and educate church members in the 2008 Presidential election. In contrast, the efforts of the international mission departments in most communions are restricted to a maintenance level of activity.

The economic downturn has only accelerated trends of decline in many denominations. The membership figures in chapter 5 of this volume note the general decrease in membership as a percent of U.S. population, not only in mainline denominations, but also in a broad spectrum of denominations. Membership impacts donations in the collection plates. Further, denominations that have become dependent on investments as an income stream were seriously affected by the economic downturn. For example, two mainline denominations announced personnel and program cutbacks, and a conservative denomination announced a hiring freeze and pension-contribution decrease in recent months.[13]

Whatever the economy is doing, denominations have seen international missions as a marketing tool to encourage general giving that supports the entire denominational structure. As a rule, denominational leaders wanting to balance various departments have effectively enforced the "institutional enslavement of overseas missions," putting caps on that category lest it receive a disproportionate amount of support.[14] Therefore, the wholesale billionaire should be aware that any effort to mobilize general church giving on behalf of global needs, including the international missions department that supervises it, may meet a surprising level of resistance from other denominational leaders within the structure. Both creativity and diplomacy will be required to create a consensus that increased dedicated funding for international mission outreach is even necessary.

Another factor is that denominations often find it more attractive to lobby government than to do the hard work of engaging their congregation members or regional officials in individual transformation. There are a variety of efforts to lobby government officials in which denominational officials are visible leaders, such as the Micah Challenge and the Mobilization to End Poverty. Denominational officials may envision a large effect as a result of talking to a limited number of government officials, an approach that is understandably more attractive than undertaking the formidable task of convincing each one of the millions of church members to actively cooperate on a single goal. Yet, not to expend the effort necessary to communicate and build an expansive consensus with congregation members as well as regional officials within the denominations has contributed to the extended trends of decline, in both giving and membership, that have been considered in previous chapters. Again, part of the entrepreneurial challenge for interested wholesale billionaires will be to create either a market among denominational officials for mobilizing their own members to increase giving for international missions, or to figure out ways to initiate a movement at the congregational level that will pick up the denominations in the backwash.

Finally, current denominational relationships with their congregations may actually hinder the initiation of a movement. Many denominations have lost ground with their local churches. For example, when asked in a magazine interview about the shift from denominational to congregational missions, Princeton sociologist Robert Wuthnow replied, "First, there's a history in some congregations of feeling a bit separated from the denomination, if they are part of a denomination. And a

> Both creativity and diplomacy will be required to create a consensus that increased dedicated funding for international mission outreach is even necessary.

growing number of congregations are independent or are part of denominations that are only loosely coordinated. But in our conversations with pastors, there was the feeling that they wanted a direct role in supervising, overseeing, and participating in relationship with another church or ministry overseas so that they didn't have to rely on some bureaucrat saying, 'This is what you should do.' "[15] Thus, it cannot be taken for granted that the communication systems needed to foster a movement among the general church population are readily available within denominational structures. However, that should not be a justification to abandon these national organizational systems. On the contrary, many of the denominations have frameworks in place now that would only have to be rebuilt, with great loss of time and service to others, were the denominations to be dismantled.

Preventative action now could strengthen the denominations' relationship with their congregations and result in increased mission activity. The challenge will be to help denominational officials, distracted by the energy of lobbying efforts and preoccupation with maintenance concerns, to take the broader view of the potential mobilization of congregation members to help others in Jesus' name.

General Resistance. Denominational leaders may have good reason to find lobbying government preferable to engaging church members to solve global and domestic problems. Church members come to worship services for a variety of reasons, and are at various stages of spiritual development, or in some cases atrophy. As noted above, the wholesale billionaire who feels led to use his or her skills and knowledge to help activate the body of Christ should be prepared for a variety of resistance strategies that are evident in the church.

There appears to be a strong consensus that the church in the U.S. is struggling with what can be termed a "lukewarm" attitude. Such a condition is not healthy for the church, as Jesus' intention to "spit out" lukewarm church members in Rev. 3:15-16 is not an attractive prospect. Table 40 presents a variety of comments from national church leaders and other sources that suggest the problem is far-reaching in the church in the U.S.

In addition, human beings have a natural tendency to resist change. The Apostle Paul often referred to this struggle as one of the "old self" (e.g., Romans 6:5, 2 Corinthians 5:17, Ephesians 4:22, Colossians 3:9).

Controversial Princeton ethicist Peter Singer, who promotes "preference utilitarianism,"[27] wrote a book titled *The Life You Can Save: Acting Now to End World Poverty*. He wrote the book to urge wealthy people in the West to acknowledge the preferences of millions around the globe, not to die of starvation or live with physical damage inflicted during war. Singer explores why people resist helping others who obviously need the help. His efforts begin to appear almost as though he is trying to create a Christian ethic of "love your neighbor as yourself" without the Christian part. Among the studies Singer cites in his book is one in which people were offered the opportunity to help refugees at risk in a Rwandan camp. Each time, the study subjects were told, the donation would help 1,500 refugees. Donations were much higher from the group that understood the total number of refugees to be 3,000 than the group told there were 10,000 refugees at risk. Paul Slovic, who coauthored this study, concludes that 'the *proportion* of lives saved often carries more weight than the *number* of lives saved."[28] The implication seems to be that people don't want to act unless they know it will make a significant difference.

There appears to be a strong consensus that the church in the U.S. is struggling with what can be termed a "lukewarm" attitude.

113

Table 40:   Church Leaders Comment on the Lukewarm Church in the U.S.

"…the godless spirit that takes away our freedom and liberty to be God's salt in this culture is not so much 'out there' as it is right within us…Even those of us in the church—we may be the godless people we ought most to fear. We are the people who wear God's name but have so little of Him within us. And that is precisely our slavery. That is the ultimate loss of freedom…   "We've got a culture to confront…and I don't want to diminish that a bit, but I also want us to remember we don't do it with empty gas tanks." Joel Belz, *World* magazine founder [16]
According to a Gallup Poll, the percent of the U.S. population that thinks religion is losing its influence on American life has increased from 48% in 2005 to 67% in 2008. [17]
"Citing the 13-year-old who won the National Spelling Bee when given the word 'Laodicean,' Hunt said much of America could not define a word drawn from the biblical context of Revelation 3:15 to describe someone who is lukewarm and indifferent. 'America has not heard of the word Laodicean, but I'm afraid the church has not perceived [its relevance]. There's a vision problem.' " [18]   "Hunt implied that many pastors and laypeople are modern-day Laodiceans. 'We challenge the people, go home and forget what we preach just as quickly as they do.' " [19] Southern Baptist Convention President Johnny Hunt
"America has a spiritual depth problem partly because the faith community does not have a robust definition of its spiritual goals." David Kinnaman, president, The Barna Group [20]
"Evangelical leaders are very bullish on the future growth of Christianity, except in America." National Association of Evangelicals president Leith Anderson, commenting on an Evangelical Leaders Survey that found expectations for growth to be outside the United States, unless there is a national spiritual awakening within the U.S. [21]
"Here's the fourth and final thing to remember, and there's no easy way to say it. The Church in the United States has done a poor job of forming the faith and conscience of Catholics for more than 40 years. And now we're harvesting the results - in the public square, in our families and in the confusion of our personal lives. I could name many good people and programs that seem to disprove what I just said. But I could name many more that do prove it…" Archbishop Charles J. Chaput, Archdiocese of Denver, CO [22]
"We need a reformation. America can no longer afford a powerless religion that promotes a powerless God…Religion becomes absurd when it loses its ability to diagnose its own problems. We need new leaders with bigger goals than cloning dead religion or becoming the next mega big shot." Steve Gray, host of an Emmy® award winning television show and author of *My Absurd Religion* [23]
"If you get outside the Christian bubble…you find a lot of people who want to believe, and perhaps even did believe, but who are disillusioned. What they read in the Gospels is not what they see in the church….Would seeing Christians give sacrificially make a difference with me? I'm not sure. Would it make a difference with those disillusioned? I think it might." William Lobdell, author of *Losing My Religion*, describing his conversion to, and then rejection of, Christianity [24]
"Much is at stake. I am convinced that things must change…At present I believe that too many of us are settling for easy goals. It is one thing to grow a church numerically. It is quite another to seek the transformation of heart, mind, and character." Brad Waggoner, author of *The Shape of Faith to Come: Spiritual Formation and the Future of Discipleship*, in which he reports that "only 17 percent of Protestant churchgoers in America demonstrated a 'decent' level of discipleship or spiritual maturity" [25]
"A colleague who teaches international finance challenged me to explain why the churches have been so silent on issues of greed, especially over the past decade when the effects of greed were becoming more prevalent culturally." L. Gregory Jones, Dean of Duke University Divinity School [26]

A somewhat related stumbling block to moving the church from crisis-response to making plans to solve global problems is what the Rev. Val J. Peter refers to as "learned helplessness." Considering seven secular challenges confronting Catholics, and, one might add indeed all Christians, he finds learned helplessness keeps people from even trying. "No one can grow spiritually or renew the church if they have learned to be helpless. Deepening of spirituality cannot take root in our lives if one believes, *This is the way things are and there is nothing I can do about it*'"[29] [emphasis in the original].

The result is a group of people who resemble the Ents in J.R.R. Tolkein's Trilogy of the Rings. These tree shepherds had lost the "Entwives" and so there were no "Entings." Now, the trees were slipping more and more into a deep sleep while the Ents rambled the forest, avoiding the increasingly hostile events beyond their borders. Of course, those events invaded their forest and in a slow deliberative way the Ents consider whether to remain uninvolved, even though the choice is no longer theirs to make.

Another character in the trilogy that sounds too painfully familiar is King Theoden. When he is first introduced in the story, Theoden is feeble and helpless on his throne, disconnected even from the fact that his own son has been killed. Under the drug-like influence of the wizard Saruman, the king does not feel his own power for good or even care about how to pursue his own best interest.

Tragedy and imminent disaster are the factors that move the Ents and release King Theoden. To the degree that church members in the U.S. are like the isolated Ents or the drugged king, one hopes another method will be found for waking them to their potential for good.

A side effect of this learned helplessness has been an acceptance of happiness being defined as life's goal. Churches often preach how to be happy as the goal in and of itself, rather than as a byproduct of sometimes uncomfortable transformation. Today, much of American culture, and too many in the church in the U.S., sound alarmingly like Aldous Huxley's *Brave New World*, where the Controller saw the danger of waking people from their stupor of instant self-gratification that kept them within their defined roles. Deciding to ban a book, the Controller reflects, "It was the sort of idea that might easily decondition the more unsettled minds among the higher castes—make them lose their faith in happiness as the Sovereign Good and take to believing, instead, that the goal was somewhere beyond, somewhere outside the present human sphere…"[30]

> Churches often preach how to be happy as the goal in and of itself, rather than as a byproduct of sometimes uncomfortable transformation.

The wholesale billionaire who wants to mobilize the general church population cannot assume that church members are anxiously waiting for a leader to point the way. Those church members may, in fact, be content with a lethargic ignorance of the bigger world and their own potential to help others. Church members have been trained for crisis response, and consider that level of involvement adequate. It will take the best efforts of the most creative wholesale billionaires to counter these forces, and the help of any allies available will be needed. Although pastors could be of assistance with this goal, the clergy bring their own set of issues.

Pastor Dynamics. Pastors at the congregational level may be no more excited than denominational officials about the prospect of enthusiastic efforts to increase church member giving beyond the local congregation. Pastors who preach visionary sermons have very practical matters to contend with on a daily basis.

Pastors have long served in the role of the small businessman. Although there is a distaste among some for the analogy, on a practical level the institution of the local congregation or parish rises or falls on the pastor's ability to run it successfully. In years past, the pastor, through denominational contacts, was one of the most nationally and globally informed people in the congregation, and probably with the largest private library. Now, Duke Endowment's rural church program director W. Joseph Mann was quoted as observing, "…church members are often as well educated as their pastor, and look at the church through a more consumer-oriented lens. They demand more programs for their families, such as child care and support groups, and they expect the pastor to operate as efficiently as the chief executives they see at their own jobs."[31]

In addition to the building and general operations of the congregation, the pastor faces the task of justifying and securing benefits such as family health insurance, increasingly a challenge as national offices pull back support for this traditional perk.[32] For pastors of independent congregations or in denominations that do not offer those support structures, the pastor needs to either get a second job that has the benefits or depend on a working spouse's job for health insurance.[33]

The tension between meeting the needs of the congregation, and thus providing for the pastor's family, and funding the larger missions vision of the church can collide in a very personal way for the pastor. The fact that money follows vision may sound as theoretical and impractical to the pastor as to the national denominational official. The risk involved in "stepping out in faith" to increase missions giving at the congregational level is not only important on a theoretical basis, but potentially also has intensely personal consequences for the pastor of a congregation. A survey of clergy in a region of one denomination found, "Making their churches stronger financially, they indicated, would lead to increased incomes and less financial stress for themselves."[34] So efforts to increase missions giving may be perceived by the pastor as in direct competition with the internal operations of the congregation, and therefore even with providing for the pastor's family.

Then there is the challenge of balancing the various interest groups in the congregation. Perhaps it is similar to the challenge faced by former French president Charles de Gaulle (b.1890-d.1970) who lamented, "How do you govern a country that has 246 varieties of cheese?" Given that the local congregation is as close to pure democracy—one person, one vote voiced through attendance or contributions to the offering plate—as exists in the present-day United States, the pastor is highly aware of the tensions that exist in keeping the choir, the Sunday school teachers, the finance committee, and the missions committee functioning to achieve their respective tasks without upsetting the others. Although an overarching vision of mission support could bind these disparate groups together, the pastor will be keenly aware of the communication challenge to get these groups to the point of recognizing that possibility.

A final challenge for the well-meaning wholesale billionaire philanthropist who wants to leverage the possibilities for impacting global and domestic need in Jesus' name, by mobilizing more resources of the retail billionaire philanthropists, is the question of "turf." Priest and novelist Andrew Greeley once noted, "Each priest is pope in his own parish." A Presbyterian pastor observed, "A pastor cannot do anything single-handedly in a congregation, but a pastor can stop anything single-handedly in

The tension between meeting the needs of the congregation, and thus providing for the pastor's family, and funding the larger missions vision of the church can collide in a very personal way for the pastor.

a congregation."[35] And Frank Page, when he was president of the Southern Baptist Convention, wrote in a denominational magazine, "I heard it said once that preachers are unique human beings in that they can strut while sitting down."[36]

It would be in the interest of any wholesale philanthropist to recognize that these ordained shepherds of the flock who fill the pulpits throughout America are not yet done being human.

The 2007 film, *There Will Be Blood*,[37] won two Academy Awards® for its portrayal of a protracted struggle between a businessman and a preacher. Publicity for the film announced that it was "inspired" by Upton Sinclair's 1927 novel, *Oil!* The relationship between the book and the movie is a nodding acquaintance at best. Sinclair's 548-page tome is an in-depth look at the emerging labor movement in the U.S., with its socialist and communist roots. The oil-obsessed and viciously greedy J. Arnold Ross character that won Daniel Day Lewis a Best Actor award in the film is, in the novel, one of the kinder individuals, supportive of his workers and protecting his wealthy biological (as opposed to the film-version adopted) son, who is drawn toward the active support of the laborers.

Thus, one must conclude that the film abandoned Sinclair's treatment of the labor movement, which seems rather quaint from the distance of eight decades in a post-Berlin wall world, and instead chose to explore with twenty-first century sensibilities the power dynamics on the topic of mammon and greed. The R-rated movie uses physical violence to augment the depiction of the psychic damage human beings can inflict on each other. Suffice it to say that neither the businessman nor the preacher come off as heroes. Both are ravaged by their commitment to mammon by the end of the film.

> In any discussion of mobilizing increased church giving, it is necessary to confront these forces, and even confess their reality.

Yet, the film in its extreme portrayals addresses a topic that is often actively ignored in church circles. Pastors do want to influence their congregants, hopefully for good. However, some find it difficult to avoid crossing the line to the point that a pastor identifies so closely with the congregation that an undeclared conflict of interest shades the pastor's perceptions of what is "best" for the congregation. Alone, independent to varying degrees, responsible for his or her family, with no visionary guidance from the national office but rather another responsibility and pressure to meet denominational financial askings, the pastor may not view a well-intentioned effort to increase missions giving as a positive development, but rather a disruptive threat affecting the pastor both professionally and personally.

Certainly, as is the case with any group of professionals, the number of servant-hearted and nurturing pastors, albeit often at a maintenance level, is probably far greater than the pastors who do more harm than good. Still, harrowing stories can be told of the use made by some pastors (and, for that matter, denominational officials) of their ecclesiastical authority for spiritual intimidation. The stereotype of ruthless businessmen who pursue their individual goals, regardless of the collateral damage they cause in the lives around them, is also not uncommon. The point is that those who choose a ministerial career are not totally immune to the same influences that tempt the businessman.

In any discussion of mobilizing increased church giving, it is necessary to confront these forces, and even confess their reality. It is necessary because when these dynamics are ignored, the church members who could be doing so much more good are prey to the individual power struggles of their leaders, both lay and clergy.

And while the church is internally preoccupied with these matters, around the globe children are dying needlessly, and some who want the life-giving information in the Bible cannot receive one, because the church is not using more of its power for good.

It is only when those with power are willing, mutually, to submit to an Arbitrator who is recognized as having more power, and whose opinion carries more weight, than the forces of mammon, that the power dynamics, both financial and interpersonal, that are currently immobilizing the church at a maintenance level can be neutralized. The process is costly and can be dangerous. That's why an effort by wholesale billionaires to mobilize the general church population for increased mission outreach is not to be undertaken lightly or without awareness of what it will involve. However, there are compelling reasons why undertaking the task of encouraging such a movement would be worth the difficulties that may await.

Reasons to Confront the Challenges and Encourage Increased Missions Giving. Denominational leaders may not be primed for a movement among their members. Church members may be committed to learned helplessness. Pastors may have agendas that limit their openness to increased missions giving.

"The truth is that faith and obedience are two sides of the same coin and are always found together in the Scriptures."

Why should wholesale billionaire philanthropists pursue an effort to mobilize and expand the involvement of retail billionaire philanthropists in meeting global word and deed need in Jesus' name?

God's Preference. There are several reasons, not the least of which being the issue is very close to God's heart. Choosing to communicate through Scripture, God expresses the goal of the Great Commission (Matt. 28:19-20 as well as Mark 16:15-16, Luke 24:45-48, Acts 1:8) in the context of the Great Commandment to love God and love others (Matthew 22:37-40, Mark 12:29-31, Luke 10:25-28). To be faithful to Jesus Christ requires not only belief but also obedience by showing God's love to others in both word and deed (1 John 3:16-18). As A. W. Tozer has written:

> The truth is that faith and obedience are two sides of the same coin and are always found together in the Scriptures. As well try to pry apart the two sides of a half-dollar as to separate obedience from faith. The two sides, while they remain together and are taken as one, represent good sound currency and constitute legal tender everywhere in the United States. Separate them and they are valueless. Insistence upon honoring but one side of the faith-obedience coin has wrought frightful harm in religious circles. Faith has been made everything and obedience nothing. The result among religious persons is moral weakness, spiritual blindness and a slow but constant drift away from New Testament Christianity. [38]

Encouraging the entire church to greater obedience is no less the responsibility for wholesale billionaire philanthropists than it is for any concerned Christian.

Possibility. Another reason to foster a movement for increased missions giving is that wholesale billionaires may be in a unique position to do so. In the book in the Bible that bears her name, Esther is resisting the idea of going to the king to plead for the lives of the Jewish people who are scheduled to be slaughtered. She offers reasons as to why she's probably not the person to take on the task. Her uncle Mordecai finally sends her this message:

> Do not think that because you are in the king's house you alone of all the Jews will escape. For if you remain silent at this time, relief and deliverance for the

Jews will arise from another place, but you and your father's family will perish. And who knows but that you have come to royal position for such a time as this. Esther 4:12b-14 (NIV)

Who knows if the incredible accumulated resources that are now in the hands of some individuals do not also have some long-planned purpose. The wholesale billionaire who confesses Christ has to acknowledge at some level that the resources under his or her control are as much a function of God's larger purpose as being solely due to "chance" or one's abilities (which, it may be noted, were also provided by God). If there is a larger purpose, could it not have to do with the visibility and ability of the wholesale philanthropist to influence those around him or her?

In *Philanthrocapitalism*, Bishop and Green write that Paul Schervish of the Center on Wealth and Philanthropy "calls the superrich who engage in philanthropy 'hyperagents: individuals who can do what it would otherwise take a social movement to do.' "[39]

Perhaps God has put these great resources at the disposal of some Christian wholesale billionaires at a time when even large global tasks are doable. The next section in this chapter outlines a country-specific cost analysis for specific diseases that could be addressed. The final section provides a case study of a denomination, the Southern Baptist Convention, and its response and its potential response to its stated goal of completing the task of global evangelization. The information about the needs and what can be done is available now when it was not so for previous millennia. Is it possible that God has also provided the creative leadership necessary to mobilize the church, God's answer to the world's problems, to make use of this information about potential solutions?

Integrity. A third reason is that moving the church to greater obedience is a simple matter of integrity.

Gary Haugen, previously a senior trial attorney in the U.S. Department of Justice Civil Rights Division, is now the CEO of International Justice Mission, helping to rescue victims and prosecute perpetrators of sexual exploitation, slavery and other abuses in 12 countries. In an interview in *World* magazine, he was asked about a "subtle but deep discontent that you see among many Christians." He responded:

> They feel this way because they thought that the Christian life would offer them something that was somehow bigger, more glorious — but at the end of the day, they find themselves wondering, *Is this all there is?* Christians seem to be yearning to be liberated from a life of accumulated triviality and small fears, and I see in Scripture a clear pathway to freedom — namely, in answering Christ's call to join Him in His struggle for justice in the world.[40]

In a teleconference panel discussion about global need, Lynn Hybels of Willow Creek Church in South Barrington, IL, stated, "I think part of that advocacy, in what we want the government to do, is we also have to call ourselves to do it and our congregation members to do it. We have to change the way we live. We have to change our own lifestyle, so that we can have more money, so that we can be more generous. I think only then we have the integrity to call our government to do the same."[41] Moving beyond the "seeker-friendly" environment that Willow Creek helped to popularize nationally, the congregation is challenging members to take on a more personal involvement in global need. In early 2009, Willow Creek attenders

Is it possible that God has also provided the creative leadership necessary to mobilize the church, God's answer to the world's problems?

were challenged to participate in a "Hunger+Thirst" campaign for five days. The recommended food choices and portion sizes were limited to the amount eaten by most people around the globe. Tap water, rather than bottled water, was the drink of choice. Participants were urged to donate the difference in the cost of a standard diet and the challenge diet to global hunger needs.[42]

Another major "megachurch" that has changed focus from a growth model to an obedience model is Saddleback Church in Orange County, California. Kay Warren, wife of pastor and author Rick Warren, was instrumental in expanding her husband's awareness of global need. Writing in *Christianity Today*, she described the "miraculous," successful and harrowing delivery of her premature grandson, and then went on:

> Health-care access isn't initially as riveting a cause as rescuing children from the sex trade or finding a vaccine for HIV. But when someone you love needs medical help fast, your perspective changes. Suddenly your world is reduced to one objective: Help her survive. Let him live. Americans are used to hospitals minutes away, doctors and nurses on duty, lifesaving procedures, and the latest technology and medication available. When you live in a developing country, all bets are off.

> When will this unconscionable disparity touch our hearts? When will it begin to dawn on us that the widening gap between the haves and the have-nots is a subject worthy of our passion? When will North American Christians decide that what they consider essential for their families is essential for all?

> Our miracle baby is nearly a month old. Another miracle baby was born 2,000 years ago—a different situation certainly. But the baby born in the manger grew up and showed us how much he values children, each one a precious miracle deserving a chance to live.[43]

Haugen claims that many church members are actually anxious about not meeting the expectations that Christianity seems to advertise. Hybels asserts that the authority to confront government must be rooted in personal obedience. Warren challenges that the disparities that exist between what North American Christians expect for themselves and what they will tolerate for the rest of the world are unacceptable. All three national leaders are pointing out that helping those in need is a basic matter of integrity for those who claim to know Jesus Christ.

Youth. It is possible that if the church increased its level of integrity by expanding its global outreach, it would have a greater influence on youth. Right now, there are signs that the youth in the U.S. are in need of a positive influence.

A study by Junior Achievement found that 46% of the youth surveyed admitted lying to their parents. Forty-five percent had a friend who cheated on a test, apparently with the survey respondent's knowledge. Unaddressed in the survey was to what extent these youth informed their teachers about their friends' cheating, and yet 75% of the youth surveyed said they were likely or very likely to "reveal your knowledge of unethical activities in your workplace" in the future. In terms of role models, 54% chose "Your parents" while only 3% chose "Your clergyman, pastor, rabbi, or imam," and 11% claimed no role model.[44]

A study by the Josephson Institute Center on Youth Ethics 2008 found that 30% of the almost 30,000 teens surveyed had stolen from a store in the past year,

A third reason is that moving the church to greater obedience is a simple matter of integrity.

and 64% (up from 60% in 2006) had cheated on a test in the past year. Again, the disconnect between these findings and the fact that 93% of the students expressed satisfaction with their personal ethics suggests that America's youth are in need of credible moral guidance. [45]

Some suggest that fewer youth are turning to the church as the place to seek such guidance.[46] To the extent this trend is accurately identified, it would have implications not only for the youth but also society in general. The Consumer Expenditure Survey data in chapter 7 suggested that youth were learning their charitable giving habits in the church. However, if fewer youth are in church, they will not be exposed to these values as they form their life approaches. In his 2008 book, *unChristian*, Gabe Lyons wrote about a survey of 16 to 29 year olds exploring their attitudes toward the Christian religion. The majority of the young people surveyed numbered at least five self-identified "Christians" among their friends and/or had attended church for at least six months. Of those surveyed, 87% viewed Christians as judgmental, 85% viewed Christians as hypocritical, and 78% viewed Christians as "sheltered."[47]

A report on a forthcoming book from Harvard University political scientist Robert Putnam, coauthored with David Campbell of Notre Dame and titled *American Grace: How Religion Is Reshaping Our Civic and Political Lives*, describes the finding that active church members are more engaged in society and civic responsibilities, and are even measurably "nicer," but that young people are not joining the faith communities that produce these behaviors. [48]

Self Interest. The findings about youth suggest that there is a present and future social cost to a declining church. Therefore, one element of self-interest in mobilizing the church is that a more active church could strengthen society as a whole. Certainly, there is something wrong with the social fabric when, according to a Reuters article on a Pew research study, Department of Justice figures indicate the United States "has the highest incarceration rate and biggest prison population of any country in the world." According to the article, "One in every 31 U.S. adults is in the corrections system" up from one in 77 in 1982. The article also says the Pew research found that prison and jail populations have grown 273 percent in 25 years, to 2.3 million in 2008.[49]

During the past 40 years, as discussed in chapter 1 of this volume, churches have increasingly turned inward, as shown by the increasing percent of donations spent on their internal programs and the shrinking percent spent on the larger mission of the church. There may or may not be a relationship between ethics-challenged youth and increasing prison populations and these giving patterns, but then there's the question raised by Jesus in Matthew 5:13 about the future of the salt meant to flavor society (to be thrown out when it has lost its flavor).

There's a more positive aspect of self-interest in terms of philanthropy in general, and mobilizing the general church population for increased missions in specific. The fact is that pursuing a larger purpose feels good. For example, "happiness expert" and Gallup Organization senior scientist Ed Diener wrote a book with his son, Robert Biswas-Diener, titled *Happiness: Unlocking the Mysteries of Psychological Wealth*. Ed Diener acknowledges that money helps a person to be happier—under certain circumstances. He asserts that, "rich people tend to be happier than poor people, and rich countries tend to be happier than poor countries." But there is a point at which

The findings about youth suggest that there is a present and future social cost to a declining church.

more money can produce diminishing returns and even prove "toxic" to happiness. Other factors contributing to happiness need to be taken into account. Those factors include: "good health, a positive attitude, positive relationships, a sense of spirituality and meaning, engaging activities and life satisfaction."[50] Having a larger purpose for money, beyond personal gratification, appears to enhance the value of money. Within the Christian construct, pursuing God's larger purpose for one's money enhances the level of happiness to the greatest degree possible.

Benedict XVI, in his recent encyclical *Caritas In Veritate*, emphasizes the importance of integrating one's meaning with other life pursuits:

> Without the perspective of eternal life, human progress in this world is denied breathing-space. Enclosed within history, it runs the risk of being reduced to the mere accumulation of wealth; humanity thus loses the courage to be at the service of higher goods, at the service of the great and disinterested initiatives called forth by universal charity. Man does not develop through his own powers, nor can development simply be handed to him. In the course of history, it was often maintained that the creation of institutions was sufficient to guarantee the fulfillment of humanity's right to development. Unfortunately, too much confidence was placed in those institutions, as if they were able to deliver the desired objective automatically. In reality, institutions by themselves are not enough, because integral human development is primarily a vocation, and therefore it involves a free assumption of responsibility in solidarity on the part of everyone. Moreover, such development requires a transcendent vision of the person, it needs God: without him, development is either denied, or entrusted exclusively to man, who falls into the trap of thinking he can bring about his own salvation, and ends up promoting a dehumanized form of development. Only through an encounter with God are we able to see in the other something more than just another creature, to recognize the divine image in the other, thus truly coming to discover him or her and to mature in a love that 'becomes concern and care for the other.'[51]

"Without the perspective of eternal life, human progress in this world is denied breathing-space."

So it appears that using both money and skills to mobilize church members to greater faithfulness in expanding missions outreach will not only increase the church's integrity, but also provide a good model, thereby perhaps challenging youth and strengthening the social fabric within the United States, meanwhile pleasing God and providing personal satisfaction.

Those reasons would seem to outweigh the resistance that such efforts might engender in the short run. The Apostle Paul had to choose to face resistance as he pursued his calling. Having done so, he advises us, "I consider that our present sufferings are not worth comparing with the glory that will be revealed in us" (Romans 8:18, NIV).

Once the challenge is accepted to mobilize general church giving to increase missions outreach, the next step is to set the goals. Two major global challenges are ending the preventable deaths of children under five, and the completion of the 2,000 year old mandate to offer the good news of Jesus Christ to everyone on earth.

The next section provides a country-specific cost analysis of addressing child deaths in 68 countries that account for 95% of the under-5 child deaths in the world.

The last section in this chapter presents a case study of the Southern Baptist Convention and the task of global evangelization.

A Model to Calculate Country-Specific Costs for Preventing Child Deaths

Where does one start to address world need? How can the most sincere individual venture into an area that talks about physical and spiritual death faced by millions from both man-made and natural disasters? The most courageous can still feel so overwhelmed as to wonder if ignorance is not truly bliss.

In *The State of Church Giving through 2006*,[52] the concept of "global triage" was introduced. Using the same strategy applied in field medical units and emergency rooms, global needs can be rated and treated in order of severity. It was proposed in that edition of the series that the preventable deaths of children under five and unreached people groups are two emergencies for which the church has a clear Biblical mandate, and which command immediate attention.

The clarity from the triage model does not undervalue the importance of many other needs in the world. However, the drastic and urgent consequences of these two challenges recommend them for the church's special organizing attention.

The issue of unreached people groups will be considered in the third section of this chapter. In the present section, a model will be presented that is designed to make the tragedy of children under five dying from preventable causes more accessible to the possibility of a solution.

Child mortality is the focus of Millennium Development Goal 4. The Millennium Development Goals are a set of objectives adopted by many governments in the world, to improve the conditions of the world's poorest citizens by the year 2015.[53] MDG 4 is to reduce by two-thirds, between 1990 and 2015, the mortality rate of children under the age of five.

The world is seriously behind on meeting this goal. As can be seen in Figure 21, there is a large gap between where the world should be in reducing these child deaths, and where it was in the year 2007. As indicated in the figure, although the goal for 2007 was a reduction to 44 under-5 child deaths per 1,000 live births, the actual 2007 number was 68, well behind the goal.

The church has learned from Scripture that God cares for the children. When Jesus was on earth, he repeatedly talked about the importance of children in the Kingdom of God (e.g., Matthew 18:10 and

Figure 21: Exponential Interpolation of MDG 4 Under-5 Child Deaths Per 1,000 Live Births, Based on Actual 1990 and Goal 2015 Data, with Actual Data, 1995, 2000, 2005, and 2006, and 2007 Noted

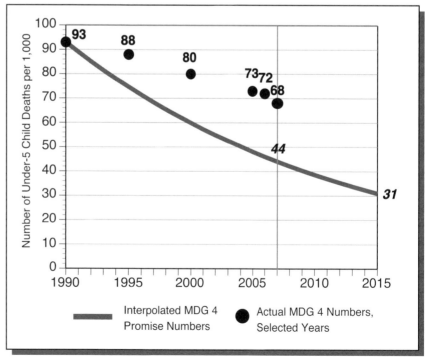

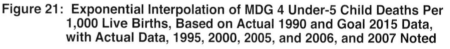

Source: empty tomb, inc. analysis, UNICEF data

empty tomb, inc., 2009

123

Figure 22: Propotional Cartogram of the Social and Economic World: Gross Domestic Product

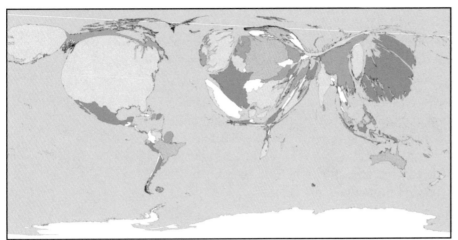

Mark Newman, 2006. Used with permission.

Figure 23: Propotional Cartogram of the Social and Economic World: Chlid Mortality

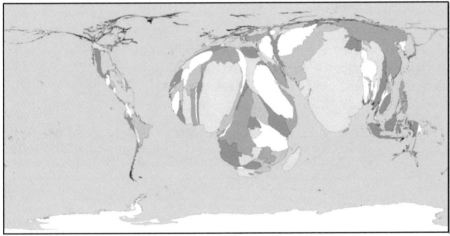

Mark Newman, 2006. Used with permission.

Matt. 19:14, Mark 9:37, Mark 10:14, Luke 18:16). We also know from the Bible that we as the church are to help the weak and helpless (e.g., Psalm 41:1, Psalm 82:3-4, James 1:27).

So the church has the stated charge of helping children. The lack of progress in meeting MDG 4 suggests a need for special intervention.

Two maps prepared by Mark Newman, Professor of Physics at the University of Michigan,[54] are as convincing as any other arguments for urging creative intervention on the part of wholesale billionaires in addressing the issue of child mortality.

The first is a map of the world's nations, proportioned to reflect the Gross Domestic Product of each. The second is proportioned to reflect the number of under-5 child deaths in each. Compare not only the United States and Europe but also the continent of Africa in the two maps.

Perhaps not surprisingly, there is an inverse relationship between Gross Domestic Product and the rate of under-5 child deaths. Further, later in this chapter is a map

124

that depicts the location of "unreached people groups." Comparing the maps, one finds a noteworthy overlap within some nations of low GDP, high child mortality, and the presence of unreached people groups. While there may be a causal relationship between GDP and child mortality, it is not clear that such a causal relationship exists between those factors and unreached people groups. What is clear is that the church has a responsibility to assist those people who live in the multiple-need areas.

As noted earlier in this chapter, "preferences utilitarianism" ethicist Peter Singer highlighted the fact that many people want to feel an action will have a significant impact before being willing to take action. That attitude does not justify inaction in the face of great need. As a counter to that view, Singer describes an interaction that occurred when Bill Gates was sitting on a panel at the 2007 World Economic Forum. Another panel member made the point, "….that all the aid given to Africa over the years has failed to stimulate economic growth there. Gates responded sharply: 'I don't promise that when a kid lives it will cause a GNP increase. I think life has value.' "[55] Still, the foundation Gates oversees brings expectations of "specific milestones and time frames" to the review of grant applications to be approved.[56]

It is reasonable that the smartest approach be taken to solve a problem, even if the task is undertaken for spiritual reasons. In the case of Christian wholesale billionaire philanthropists, one of the strengths these individuals can bring to the task is an expectation of results. When many church members have become accustomed to "learned helplessness," those who bring gifts of entrepreneurship can analyze the problem of mission and break it down into accessible segments.

In the case of Christian wholesale billionaire philanthropists, one of the strengths these individuals can bring to the task is an expectation of results.

The thinking behind breaking down a problem into accessible segments inspired an effort to combine available information into a cost analysis of stopping child deaths. If church members were to be challenged to solve, rather than cope with, the killing of children by preventable diseases and other factors, it seems reasonable that those church members would expect to know how much it would cost to accomplish the task. In the same way, it seems likely that any wholesale philanthropist would expect some clear cost estimates before venturing into an effort to involve millions of church members in an effort to help stop, in Jesus' name, under-5 child deaths.

The initial cost-estimate model is limited to currently available data. Nevertheless, the results presented in the tables below provide a dollar-cost estimate for the causes of under-5 deaths in each of the countries included in the tables. The model suggests the type of information that can be developed to foster initiatives to eliminate conditions that result in needless child deaths.

Two valuable sources of information served as the basis of the analysis. The United Nations International Children's Fund (UNICEF) annual *State of the World's Children* report provides detailed information on quality of life factors, including the number of under-5 child deaths by country.[57]

Second, *Countdown to 2015: Maternal, Newborn & Child Survival; Tracking Progress in Maternal, Newborn & Child Survival: the 2008 Report* was available on the UNICEF web site, <childinfo.org>.[58] This report provided, for 68 countries, a percentage enumeration for eight "Causes of under-5 deaths," one of which was the summary category, "Neonatal." Additionally, detail data for seven "Causes of neonatal deaths" was provided. The number of under-5 child deaths in these 68 countries accounted for 95% of the under-5 child deaths in the world.

The information was analyzed as follows. The annual number of under-5 child deaths for each country was entered on that country's row of a spreadsheet. The sum of the under-5 child deaths in these 68 countries totaled 8,776,000 in 2007. With a UNICEF figure of 9,217,000 under-5 deaths in 2007, it was calculated that these 68 countries accounted for 95% of the under-5 child deaths in 2007.

Next, the percent of the under-5 deaths due to each cause was entered in the spreadsheet row for each of the 68 nations.

Each country's percent of the total number of child deaths was then calculated.

Having calculated a percent of the total under-5 child deaths for each country, that individual percent was used as a multiplier for $5 billion, which served as a base cost figure for preventing the 9.217 million annual under-5 child deaths. The result was the cost-per-country dollar figure that would be needed to address causes of under-5 mortality in that country. The total calculated cost for the 68 countries was $4.76 billion, or 95% of the $5 billion total.

The cost estimate of $5 billion is the same figure used to develop a cost-per-child death figure in chapter 6. The *Bulletin of the World Health Organization* cited a figure of $52.4 billion that will be needed over the ten years, from 2006 through 2015, to "address the major causes of mortality among children aged < 5 years."[59] The annual average for that estimate was $5.2 billion a year, thus providing support for the use of $5 billion for the present purpose.

Once a dollar figure was developed for each country, that dollar figure was multiplied by the percent of each cause of under-5 child deaths within that country. The result was a dollar-cost estimate by country per cause of death for each of the measured categories. Those categories included: Pneumonia; Diarrhoea; Measles; Malaria; HIV/AIDS; Injuries; Other; and Neonatal.

Similarly, a dollar-cost estimate was calculated for each of the seven "Causes of neonatal deaths." The "Neonatal" categories included: Diarrhoea; Other; Congenital; Tetanus; Asphyxia; Preterm; and Infection.

This model, a first approximation for estimating country-specific costs to prevent child deaths, was based on the assumption that the cost of the disease remedies was equal for each disease. A second working assumption was that the cost of a package of disease remedies per child was the same across the different countries. While this model can be refined by disease-specific and country-specific pricing factors, this first approximation may be useful for exploring how to address, and mobilize for meeting, specific country goals.

In Table 41, a summed dollar figure for all Neonatal causes is presented.

In Table 43, the summed Neonatal dollar figure is broken out for each country for which there was country-specific percentage data provided for the various causes of neonatal deaths.

Two Totals are provided for the causes of Neonatal death.

The "Total for 57 Nations (Actual Sum Seven Neonatal Causes of Death Data)" of $918,428,285 (italicized in Table 43) adds together the column totals of each neonatal cause of death for the 57 countries that provided data for these categories.

... it seems reasonable that those church members would expect to know how much it would cost to accomplish the task.

The "Total for 68 Nations (Adjusted Seven Neonatal Causes of Death Data)" of $1,640,002,170 is the sum of the "Country Total Neonatal Need ($s)" column. The $1.6 billion figure was used to provide an estimate of the cost for each of the seven "Causes of Neonatal Deaths" categories, for all 68 countries, based on the assumption that the "Causes of Neonatal Deaths" in the 11 countries for which there was "No data" were distributed in the same way as the "Causes of Neonatal Deaths" were distributed in the 57 countries for which data was available. The "Total for 57 Nations (Actual Sum of Seven Neonatal Causes of Death Data)" percent for each "Cause of Neonatal Deaths" was multiplied by the $1,640,002,170 figure, in order to obtain the estimate of an adjusted cost for each of the seven "Causes of Neonatal Deaths" categories, for all 68 countries.

It was observed that the 57 nations, for which there was neonatal cause of death data, represented 56% of the total neonatal deaths, and 68% of under-5 child deaths. The balance of the neonatal deaths, or 44% of the total, was attributable to the 11 countries with no neonatal cause of death detail. These 11 countries accounted for 32% of the total under-5 deaths, according to the UNICEF data.

The information in these tables could be put to a variety of uses. A single "high-capacity" donor might become engaged in a plan to eradicate a particular disease. Former president Jimmy Carter has taken such a moderating role in eliminating Guinea worm disease, attracting large grants from other funders, for example.[60]

A creative wholesale philanthropist could recognize the potential use to be made of the information in these tables in a broader effort, to help mobilize the vast millions of church members to increase missions giving. Targeting specific causes of child deaths in specific countries, and urging specific actions and timetables, could empower church members to impact the lives of children who are in desperate need.

At the end of this chapter, a strategy will be discussed that might be useful for wholesale billionaire philanthropists who want to leverage their giving by multiplying their efforts through mobilizing church members.

In the meantime, a review of the tables should dispel the myth that the number of child deaths that exist in the world needs to be tolerated. Although only a rough estimate, the fact that it would take a limited number of dollars to tackle measles and malaria, two causes of death long under control in the U.S., ought to motivate the many church members of all ages who sing about how Jesus loves the little children of the world. The figures in the above tables begin to provide handles for concerned church members to recognize specific tasks to be accomplished, a happy alternative to confronting a hopeless mass of impossibility.

Earlier in this chapter, several reasons why wholesale billionaire philanthropists should provide creative intervention to mobilize the potential of the retail billionaire philanthropists were discussed. One reason considered was that such positive initiative could have an impact on currently disaffected youth. A constructive agenda might counter a trend identified by sociologist Michael Kimmel as "Guyland," a state being inhabited by more and more young American men who prefer not to grow toward manhood. It apparently is not a purely American phenomenon, as "Laddism" has been identified in Britain and Australia, and "mammonis" (Mama's boys) in Italy continue to live at home at the amazing rate of 82% of young men aged 18-30.[61]

In the meantime, a review of the tables should dispel the myth that the number of child deaths that exist in the world needs to be tolerated.

Table 41: Country-Specific Dollar-Cost Estimates for Causes of Under-5 Child Deaths, 68 Countries

Nation	Under-5 Mortality Rank	Annual no. of Under-5 Deaths (000s) 2007	Country Total as % of Total Annual No. of Under-5 Deaths (000s) 2007	Country Total $s Need, Based on $5 Billion Total Estimate
Africa: 44 Nations		4,701	51.00%	$2,550,179,017
1 Angola	16	128	1.39%	69,436,910
2 Benin	25	45	0.49%	24,411,414
3 Botswana	69	2	0.02%	1,084,952
4 Burkina Faso	7	125	1.36%	67,809,482
5 Burundi	10	72	0.78%	39,058,262
6 Cameroon	18	96	1.04%	52,077,683
7 Central African Republic	12	27	0.29%	14,646,848
8 Chad	3	103	1.12%	55,875,014
9 Congo	24	17	0.18%	9,222,090
10 Côte d'Ivoire	22	87	0.94%	47,195,400
11 Democratic Rep. of the Congo	15	502	5.45%	272,322,882
12 Djibouti	22	3	0.03%	1,627,428
13 Egypt	77	66	0.72%	35,803,407
14 Equatorial Guinea	4	4	0.04%	2,169,903
15 Eritrea	50	13	0.14%	7,052,186
16 Ethiopia	27	381	4.13%	206,683,303
17 Gabon	40	3	0.03%	1,627,428
18 Gambia	34	7	0.08%	3,797,331
19 Ghana	30	81	0.88%	43,940,545
20 Guinea	17	57	0.62%	30,921,124
21 Guinea-Bissau	5	17	0.18%	9,222,090
22 Kenya	26	179	1.94%	97,103,179
23 Lesotho	45	5	0.05%	2,712,379
24 Liberia	20	25	0.27%	13,561,896
25 Madagascar	32	81	0.88%	43,940,545
26 Malawi	33	64	0.69%	34,718,455
27 Mali	6	117	1.27%	63,469,676
28 Mauritania	27	12	0.13%	6,509,710
29 Morocco	81	22	0.24%	11,934,469
30 Mozambique	14	144	1.56%	78,116,524
31 Niger	11	123	1.33%	66,724,531
32 Nigeria	8	1,126	12.22%	610,827,818
33 Rwanda	9	79	0.86%	42,855,593
34 Senegal	31	50	0.54%	27,123,793
35 Sierra Leone	1	70	0.76%	37,973,310
36 Somalia	19	54	0.59%	29,293,696
37 South Africa	60	64	0.69%	34,718,455
38 Sudan	34	134	1.45%	72,691,765
39 Swaziland	40	3	0.03%	1,627,428
40 Togo	37	25	0.27%	13,561,896
41 Uganda	21	188	2.04%	101,985,462
42 United Republic of Tanzania	29	186	2.02%	100,900,510
43 Zambia	13	80	0.87%	43,398,069
44 Zimbabwe	43	34	0.37%	18,444,179

Details in the above table may not compute to the numbers shown due to rounding
Sources: empty tomb, inc. 2009 analysis of UNICEF data.

	Pneumonia	Diarrhoea	Measles	Malaria	HIV/AIDS	Injuries	Other	Neonatal (Total)
Africa	$531,729,413	$423,055,224	$110,719,323	$455,636,324	$166,057,285	$52,679,831	$143,094,282	$671,275,903
1	17,359,228	13,193,013	3,471,846	5,554,953	1,388,738	694,369	11,804,275	15,276,120
2	5,126,397	4,149,940	1,220,571	6,591,082	488,228	488,228	0	6,102,853
3	10,850	10,850	0	0	585,874	32,549	0	433,981
4	15,596,181	12,883,802	2,034,284	13,561,896	2,712,379	1,356,190	6,780,948	12,205,707
5	8,983,400	7,030,487	1,171,748	3,124,661	3,124,661	781,165	5,858,739	8,983,400
6	11,457,090	8,853,206	2,083,107	11,977,867	3,645,438	1,041,554	0	13,019,421
7	2,782,901	2,197,027	1,025,279	2,782,901	1,757,622	292,937	0	3,954,649
8	12,851,253	10,057,502	3,911,251	12,292,503	2,235,001	1,117,500	0	13,410,003
9	1,291,093	1,014,430	645,546	2,397,743	829,988	276,663	0	2,858,848
10	9,439,080	7,079,310	1,415,862	9,911,034	2,831,724	943,908	0	16,518,390
11	62,634,263	49,018,119	13,616,144	46,294,890	10,892,915	5,446,458	16,339,373	70,803,949
12	325,486	276,663	65,097	16,274	48,823	32,549	423,131	439,405
13	5,370,511	4,654,443	0	0	0	716,068	9,308,886	15,753,499
14	368,884	303,786	151,893	520,777	151,893	65,097	0	607,573
15	1,339,915	1,128,350	211,566	987,306	423,131	211,566	916,784	1,904,090
16	45,470,327	35,136,161	8,267,332	12,400,998	8,267,332	4,133,666	28,935,662	62,004,991
17	179,017	146,468	65,097	455,680	162,743	48,823	0	569,600
18	607,573	455,680	113,920	1,101,226	37,973	113,920	0	1,405,012
19	6,591,082	5,272,865	1,318,216	14,500,380	2,636,433	1,318,216	0	12,742,758
20	6,493,436	5,256,591	1,855,267	7,730,281	618,422	309,211	0	8,967,126
21	2,121,081	1,752,197	276,663	1,936,639	276,663	92,221	553,325	2,213,302
22	19,420,636	16,507,540	2,913,095	13,594,445	14,565,477	2,913,095	4,855,159	23,304,763
23	135,619	108,495	0	0	1,518,932	54,248	0	895,085
24	3,119,236	2,305,522	813,714	2,576,760	542,476	271,238	0	3,932,950
25	9,227,514	7,469,893	2,197,027	8,788,109	439,405	878,811	3,515,244	11,424,542
26	7,985,245	6,249,322	0	4,860,584	4,860,584	694,369	2,777,476	7,638,060
27	15,232,722	11,424,542	3,808,181	10,789,845	1,269,394	634,697	3,808,181	16,502,116
28	1,432,136	1,041,554	130,194	781,165	0	130,194	390,583	2,538,787
29	1,670,826	1,432,136	0	0	0	477,379	2,864,273	5,370,511
30	16,404,470	13,279,809	0	14,842,140	10,155,148	781,165	0	22,653,792
31	16,681,133	13,344,906	4,670,717	9,341,434	667,245	667,245	10,008,680	11,343,170
32	122,165,564	97,732,451	36,649,669	146,598,676	30,541,391	12,216,556	6,108,278	158,815,233
33	9,856,786	8,142,563	857,112	2,142,780	2,142,780	857,112	10,285,342	9,428,230
34	5,695,997	4,611,045	2,169,903	7,594,662	271,238	813,714	0	6,238,472
35	9,873,061	7,594,662	1,898,666	4,556,797	379,733	379,733	4,936,530	8,354,128
36	7,030,487	5,565,802	2,050,559	1,464,685	292,937	878,811	5,858,739	6,737,550
37	347,185	347,185	0	0	19,789,519	1,735,923	347,185	12,151,459
38	11,630,682	9,449,929	3,634,588	15,265,271	2,180,753	3,634,588	4,361,506	22,534,447
39	195,291	162,743	0	0	764,891	65,097	16,274	439,405
40	2,305,522	1,898,666	949,333	3,390,474	813,714	406,857	0	3,932,950
41	21,416,947	17,337,528	3,059,564	23,456,656	8,158,837	2,039,709	2,039,709	24,476,511
42	21,189,107	17,153,087	1,009,005	23,207,117	9,081,046	2,018,010	0	27,243,138
43	9,547,575	7,811,652	433,981	8,245,633	6,943,691	433,981	0	9,981,556
44	2,766,627	2,213,302	553,325	0	7,562,113	184,442	0	5,164,370

**Table 42: Country-Specific Dollar-Cost Estimates for Causes of
Under-5 Child Deaths, 68 Countries, continued**

Nation	Under-5 Mortality Rank	Annual no. of under-5 deaths (000s) 2007	Country Total as % of Total Annual No. of Under-5 Deaths (000s) 2007	Country Total $s Need, Based on $5 Billion Total Estimate
Asia: 17 Nations		3,842	41.68%	$2,084,192,253
1 Afghanistan	2	338	3.67%	183,356,841
2 Azerbaijan	71	5	0.05%	2,712,379
3 Bangladesh	58	244	2.65%	132,364,110
4 Cambodia	40	35	0.38%	18,986,655
5 China	107	382	4.14%	207,225,778
6 Dem. People's Rep. of Korea	62	17	0.18%	9,222,090
7 India	49	1,953	21.19%	1,059,455,354
8 Indonesia	86	136	1.48%	73,776,717
9 Iraq	66	41	0.44%	22,241,510
10 Lao People's Dem. Republic	50	11	0.12%	5,967,234
11 Myanmar	36	92	1.00%	49,907,779
12 Nepal	62	44	0.48%	23,868,938
13 Pakistan	43	400	4.34%	216,990,344
14 Philippines	94	64	0.69%	34,718,455
15 Tajikistan	54	12	0.13%	6,509,710
16 Turkmenistan	65	5	0.05%	2,712,379
17 Yemen	48	63	0.68%	34,175,979
Latin America/Caribbean: 6 Nations		221	2.40%	$119,887,165
1 Bolivia	61	15	0.16%	8,137,138
2 Brazil	107	82	0.89%	44,483,021
3 Guatemala	71	18	0.20%	9,764,565
4 Haiti	47	21	0.23%	11,391,993
5 Mexico	78	73	0.79%	39,600,738
6 Peru	112	12	0.13%	6,509,710
Oceania: 1 Nation				
1 Papua New Guinea	56	12	0.13%	$6,509,710
Total for 68 Nations		8,776	95.22%	$4,760,768,146

Details in the above table may not compute to the numbers shown due to rounding
Sources: empty tomb, inc. 2009 analysis of UNICEF data.

In considering what could be causing young men's "failure to launch," one might reflect on what has engendered manhood in the past. The hunters and gatherers were responsible for providing for families in primitive cultures. The role of breadwinner and the inevitability of children within marriage have been replaced by two-family incomes and family planning in a society that supports personal gratification above childrearing as a major social good. The trend to seek perpetual adolescence might be particularly evident among young men, but the question may be asked: What is the purpose of anyone working hard when basic needs are so easily met? If one is content to consume television and play video games, then there is no call to self-discipline—unless it is for some recognized greater good.

The image of perpetually self-indulgent youth can be contrasted with a movement that will be celebrated in 2010 in Edinburgh, Scotland. The centennial plans are a commemoration of the first World Missionary Conference in 1910, the movement that had as its motto, "the evangelization of the world in this generation."[62] The late nineteenth and early twentieth century missionary efforts being lauded included a

	Pneumonia	Diarrhoea	Measles	Malaria	HIV/AIDS	Injuries	Other	Neonatal (Total)
Asia	$387,636,975	$377,563,198	$67,852,881	$24,807,421	$11,565,585	$56,477,162	$249,669,090	$916,350,222
1	45,839,210	34,837,800	11,001,410	1,833,568	0	1,833,568	40,338,505	47,672,779
2	488,228	406,857	0	27,124	0	27,124	542,476	1,193,447
3	23,825,540	26,472,822	2,647,282	1,323,641	0	3,970,923	14,560,052	59,563,849
4	3,987,198	3,227,731	379,733	189,867	379,733	379,733	4,936,530	5,695,997
5	26,939,351	24,867,093	0	0	0	16,578,062	33,156,125	101,540,631
6	1,383,313	1,752,197	92,221	92,221	92,221	276,663	1,752,197	3,873,278
7	201,296,517	211,891,071	42,378,214	10,594,554	10,594,554	21,189,107	95,350,982	476,754,909
8	10,328,740	13,279,809	3,688,836	737,767	0	2,213,302	16,230,878	28,035,152
9	4,003,472	2,891,396	222,415	222,415	0	1,334,491	2,446,566	11,343,170
10	1,133,775	954,758	358,034	59,672	0	119,345	1,312,792	2,088,532
11	9,482,478	10,480,634	998,156	4,491,700	499,078	998,156	2,994,467	19,464,034
12	4,535,098	5,012,477	716,068	238,689	0	477,379	2,864,273	10,502,333
13	41,228,165	30,378,648	4,339,807	2,169,903	0	4,339,807	13,019,421	121,514,593
14	4,513,399	4,166,215	347,185	0	0	1,041,554	11,804,275	12,845,828
15	1,301,942	1,041,554	0	65,097	0	195,291	1,952,913	1,952,913
16	515,352	433,981	0	27,124	0	135,619	596,723	1,030,704
17	6,835,196	5,468,157	683,520	2,734,078	0	1,367,039	5,809,916	11,278,073
LA/C	$15,384,615	$12,444,396	$113,920	$640,122	$1,269,394	$5,359,661	$35,038,516	$50,097,646
1	1,383,313	1,139,199	0	81,371	0	406,857	2,034,284	3,092,112
2	5,782,793	5,337,962	0	444,830	0	1,334,491	14,679,397	16,903,548
3	1,464,685	1,269,394	0	0	292,937	195,291	2,929,370	3,612,889
4	2,278,399	1,936,639	113,920	113,920	911,359	0	3,075,838	2,961,918
5	3,564,066	1,980,037	0	0	0	2,772,052	10,692,199	20,988,391
6	911,359	781,165	0	0	65,097	650,971	1,627,428	2,538,787
Ocen.								
1	$1,236,845	$976,457	$130,194	$65,097	$0	$130,194	$1,627,428	$2,278,399
Total	$935,987,849	$814,039,275	$178,816,318	$481,148,964	$178,892,264	$114,646,848	$429,429,315	$1,640,002,170

strong component of youth, such as the "…Student Volunteer Movement for Foreign Missions, which had begun at a summer student conference under [Dwight L.] Moody's leadership in 1886 and had swept with great power through the colleges, universities, and theological seminaries of the United States."[63]

There is a contrast between the original conference, which coordinated a vital movement interrupted by two world wars and the Great Depression, and the conference one hundred years later, coming after decades of unprecedented economic expansion, communications and travel improvements, which will have to face the fact that the original goal has still not been met. This contrast raises a question. Is it possible that youth are having difficulty entering adulthood—where they would, in fact, join adults no less adrift—because no one is asking anyone to do anything great? The artful cynicism that permeates American culture is not countered in a church that has largely turned inward, a conclusion drawn on the basis of the giving patterns outlined in chapter 1.

Is another compelling reason for intervening in child deaths, or launching efforts to reach the final unreached people groups, that such efforts would actually help church members in America out of a malaise? Perhaps Christians in the wealthiest

Table 43: Country-Specific Dollar-Cost Estimates Detail for Causes of Neonatal Deaths, 68 Countries

Nation	Country Total Neonatal Need ($s)	Neonatal Diarrhoea ($s)	Neonatal Other ($s)	Neonatal Congential ($s)	Neonatal Tetanus ($s)	Neonatal Asphyxia ($s)	Neonatal Preterm ($s)	Neonatal Infection ($s)
Africa: 44 Nations	$671,275,903	$20,914,397	$46,537,431	$44,132,635	$39,927,742	$162,093,740	$174,612,835	$184,037,214
1 Angola	15,276,120	763,806	1,069,328	763,806	916,567	3,666,269	3,819,030	4,430,075
2 Benin	6,102,853	122,057	305,143	488,228	244,114	1,159,542	1,708,799	2,074,970
3 Botswana	433,981	13,019	26,039	30,379	13,019	91,136	156,233	104,155
4 Burkina Faso	12,205,707	244,114	732,342	610,285	610,285	2,441,141	2,807,313	4,760,226
5 Burundi	8,983,400	269,502	628,838	449,170	449,170	2,245,850	2,066,182	2,784,854
6 Cameroon	13,019,421	260,388	911,359	1,041,554	390,583	3,254,855	3,905,826	3,254,855
7 Central African Republic	3,954,649	158,186	237,279	237,279	395,465	870,023	909,569	1,146,848
8 Chad	13,410,003	402,300	1,072,800	670,500	1,341,000	3,620,701	2,413,801	3,754,801
9 Congo	2,858,848	57,177	200,119	228,708	57,177	743,300	886,243	657,535
10 Côte d'Ivoire	16,518,390	991,103	991,103	825,919	1,982,207	3,138,494	4,790,333	3,799,230
11 Democratic Rep. of the Congo	70,803,949	2,124,118	4,956,276	4,956,276	3,540,197	16,284,908	19,825,106	19,117,066
12 Djibouti	439,405	13,182	26,364	65,911	26,364	87,881	105,457	118,639
13 Egypt	15,753,499	157,535	945,210	2,205,490	315,070	3,465,770	4,726,050	4,095,910
14 Equatorial Guinea	607,573	24,303	42,530	24,303	30,379	151,893	200,499	139,742
15 Eritrea	1,904,090	19,041	133,286	95,205	57,123	495,063	514,104	571,227
16 Ethiopia	62,004,991	2,480,200	4,340,349	2,480,200	5,580,449	14,881,198	9,920,799	22,321,797
17 Gabon	569,600	11,392	34,176	51,264	17,088	119,616	210,752	125,312
18 Gambia	1,405,012	42,150	84,301	70,251	56,200	281,002	379,353	491,754
19 Ghana	12,742,758	382,283	764,565	764,565	509,710	2,930,834	3,313,117	4,077,683
20 Guinea	8,967,126	179,343	627,699	448,356	358,685	2,062,439	2,600,467	2,600,467
21 Guinea-Bissau	2,213,302	66,399	132,798	132,798	199,197	442,660	531,192	730,389
22 Kenya	23,304,763	466,095	1,864,381	1,631,333	466,095	6,292,286	5,826,191	6,292,286
23 Lesotho	895,085	17,902	71,607	71,607	17,902	241,673	304,329	179,017
24 Liberia	3,932,950	235,977	196,647	157,318	550,613	747,260	1,061,896	983,237
25 Madagascar	11,424,542	342,736	799,718	685,472	456,982	2,856,135	3,541,608	2,741,890
26 Malawi	7,638,060	152,761	458,284	534,664	229,142	1,756,754	2,291,418	2,215,037
27 Mali	16,502,116	660,085	825,106	660,085	1,650,212	3,135,402	3,960,508	5,610,719
28 Mauritania	2,538,787	76,164	152,327	177,715	152,327	583,921	660,085	761,636
29 Morocco	5,370,511	53,705	322,231	644,461	107,410	1,181,512	1,450,038	1,557,448
30 Mozambique	22,653,792	453,076	1,359,228	1,359,228	1,132,690	5,210,372	5,889,986	7,249,213
31 Niger	11,343,170	340,295	794,022	567,159	1,134,317	2,608,929	1,928,339	4,083,541
32 Nigeria	158,815,233	6,352,609	12,705,219	11,117,066	12,705,219	42,880,113	39,703,808	34,939,351
33 Rwanda	9,428,230	377,129	659,976	565,694	377,129	2,451,340	1,885,646	3,017,034
34 Senegal	6,238,472	124,769	374,308	374,308	249,539	1,247,694	1,746,772	2,058,696
35 Sierra Leone	8,354,128	334,165	417,706	334,165	668,330	1,587,284	2,088,532	2,923,945
36 Somalia	6,737,550	269,502	471,629	539,004	539,004	1,684,388	1,482,261	1,751,763
37 South Africa	12,151,459	121,515	729,088	1,215,146	121,515	2,794,836	4,739,069	2,308,777
38 Sudan	22,534,447	225,344	1,126,722	1,802,756	676,033	4,281,545	11,267,224	3,154,823
39 Swaziland	439,405	13,182	30,758	35,152	8,788	109,851	140,610	101,063
40 Togo	3,932,950	78,659	235,977	235,977	157,318	825,919	1,179,885	1,179,885
41 Uganda	24,476,511	489,530	1,713,356	1,713,356	489,530	6,363,893	6,119,128	7,587,718
42 United Republic of Tanzania	27,243,138	544,863	1,907,020	1,907,020	544,863	7,083,216	7,355,647	7,900,510
43 Zambia	9,981,556	299,447	698,709	698,709	299,447	2,495,389	2,495,389	3,094,282
44 Zimbabwe	5,164,370	103,287	361,506	464,793	103,287	1,239,449	1,704,242	1,187,805

Details in the above table may not compute to the numbers shown due to rounding
Sources: empty tomb, inc. 2009 analysis of UNICEF data.

country in history have a special challenge to find out the difference between "worldly wealth" and "true riches" described by Jesus in Luke 16:11. To be trustworthy with

Nation	Country Total Neonatal Need ($s)	Neonatal Diarrhoea ($s)	Neonatal Other ($s)	Neonatal Congential ($s)	Neonatal Tetanus ($s)	Neonatal Asphyxia ($s)	Neonatal Preterm ($s)	Neonatal Infection ($s)
Asia: 17 Nations	$916,350,222	$8,233,265	$11,645,709	$15,440,870	$14,856,786	$41,502,984	$40,069,600	$64,319,898
1 Afghanistan	47,672,779	2,383,639	2,860,367	3,337,094	4,767,278	9,534,556	8,104,372	17,162,200
2 Azerbaijan	1,193,447	23,869	71,607	131,279	NA	262,558	417,706	238,689
3 Bangladesh	59,563,849	No data	No data	No data	No data	No data	No data	No data
4 Cambodia	5,695,997	No data	No data	No data	No data	No data	No data	No data
5 China	101,540,631	No data	No data	No data	No data	No data	No data	No data
6 Dem. People's Rep. of Korea	3,873,278	No data	No data	No data	No data	No data	No data	No data
7 India	476,754,909	No data	No data	No data	No data	No data	No data	No data
8 Indonesia	28,035,152	No data	No data	No data	No data	No data	No data	No data
9 Iraq	11,343,170	567,159	567,159	1,020,885	794,022	1,928,339	2,949,224	3,402,951
10 Lao People's Dem. Republic	2,088,532	No data	No data	No data	No data	No data	No data	No data
11 Myanmar	19,464,034	No data	No data	No data	No data	No data	No data	No data
12 Nepal	10,502,333	No data	No data	No data	No data	No data	No data	No data
13 Pakistan	121,514,593	4,860,584	7,290,876	9,721,167	8,506,021	26,733,210	24,302,919	40,099,816
14 Philippines	12,845,828	No data	No data	No data	No data	No data	No data	No data
15 Tajikistan	1,952,913	39,058	117,175	214,820	NA	449,170	663,990	390,583
16 Turkmenistan	1,030,704	20,614	61,842	113,377	NA	226,755	360,746	206,141
17 Yemen	11,278,073	338,342	676,684	902,246	789,465	2,368,395	3,270,641	2,819,518
Latin America/Caribbean: 6 Nations	$50,097,646	$182,597	$3,459,857	$6,948,899	$332,972	$7,893,349	$20,193,718	$11,091,787
1 Bolivia	3,092,112	61,842	247,369	278,290	61,842	803,949	958,555	711,186
2 Brazil	16,903,548		1,014,213	2,197,461		1,690,355	7,268,526	4,732,993
3 Guatemala	3,612,889	36,129	289,031	289,031	72,258	975,480	939,351	1,011,609
4 Haiti	2,961,918	59,238	236,953	177,715	148,096	799,718	770,099	770,099
5 Mexico	20,988,391		1,469,187	3,777,910		2,938,375	9,444,776	3,358,143
6 Peru	2,538,787	25,388	203,103	228,491	50,776	685,472	812,412	507,757
Oceania: 1 Nation								
1 Papua New Guinea	$2,278,399	No data	No data	No data	No data	No data	No data	No data
Total	$1,640,002,170							
Total for 57 Nations (Actual Sum of Seven Neonatal Causes of Death Data)	*$918,428,285*	$29,330,259	$61,642,997	$66,522,404	$55,117,500	$211,490,073	$234,876,153	$259,448,899
Percent of Total for Causes of Neonatal Deaths	*100%*	3%	7%	7%	6%	23%	26%	28%
Total for 68 Nations (Adjusted Seven Neonatal Causes of Death Data)	*$1,640,002,170*	*$52,373,919*	*$110,073,535*	*$118,786,506*	*$98,421,207*	*$377,649,713*	*$419,409,339*	*$463,287,950*

worldly wealthy may not mean to accumulate it, or to satisfy ourselves with it. Rather the Biblical view of worldly wealth may well be: Do something great with it. As Hugh Magers, then director of stewardship for The Episcopal Church once observed,

> *We* human beings are the treasure. We can use our resources to nurture folk into Heaven. We have an opportunity to establish a deep appropriation of the faith. Instead of being in a world with starving babies, we have the opportunity to help there be well babies, and to support a friend for eternity.[64]

A movement of helping others in Jesus' name, in word and deed, might not only help those who receive the assistance, but may be as healing for those who are able to provide the help.

Stopping, in Jesus' name, child deaths, country by country, could be a vision large enough to attract broad support among the millions of unorganized retail billionaires. A unique, servanthood role could be played by wholesale billionaires in launching such a direction. In addition to the physical need, many in the areas where the children are dying do not have access to information that would allow them to know more about Jesus, if they wanted to do so. In the next section of this chapter, both a model to achieve the goal of global evangelization, and a case study of one denomination's approach to that goal, may point the way to other great things that the church could do.

A Model and a Case Study of Completing the Task of Global Evangelization

The intersection of word and deed ministry can be seen in rural Afghanistan, where a grandfather justified addicting a toddler to opium by explaining the medical clinic that could treat the boy's pain was many miles away: "If there is no medicine here, what should we do? The only way to make him feel better is to give him opium."[65]

The tragedy of this circumstance should be especially felt by those in the church in the U.S., with its long history of medical missions. The first annuals in the *Yearbook of American and Canadian Churches* series, during the 1920s, included tables outlining the number of each denomination's missionaries, and even the number of male and female physicians deployed throughout the world.[66] Further, the goodwill value of medical outreach is recognized beyond church circles. The retiring director of the U.S. Department of Health and Human Services, Mark Leavitt, recalled traveling the world and interacting with people grateful for U.S. Government efforts to distribute medicine for AIDS, malaria, and other diseases. He summed up people's reactions with the comment, "The language of health is heard by the heart."[67]

Christians have long recognized that the Good News of Jesus Christ can be presented through both word and deed mission. As the apostle John pointed out in 1 John 3:16-18, the transition from recognizing the sacrifice Jesus made by laying down His life to loving others in both word and deed is vital to the faith of the believer.

As noted earlier, there is a convergence in some areas of the world where many people are in physical need and can also be described as "unreached people," or people without a viable church present to share the Christian message. The Joshua Project is actively involved in documenting the location of those people without access to the Gospel. The organization has a full-color map on its Web site that outlines the current status of the task of global evangelization by geographical area. The black and white copy in Figure 24, reproduced with permission, does not provide as clear a distinction between some levels of Gospel exposure as the color map, but does give a general idea of the location of those without access to the Gospel.

Comparing this map with the earlier proportional cartogram that presents child mortality, it is clear that some areas of the world have active churches and yet also experience a high level of child deaths. As various verses in the Bible indicate, Christians with resources have a responsibility to help other Christians in need (e.g., James 2:14-17, Galatians 6:10).

As the apostle John pointed out in 1 John 3:16-18, the transition from recognizing the sacrifice Jesus made by laying down His life to loving others in both word and deed is vital to the faith of the believer.

Figure 24: Map of Progress of the Gospel by People Group

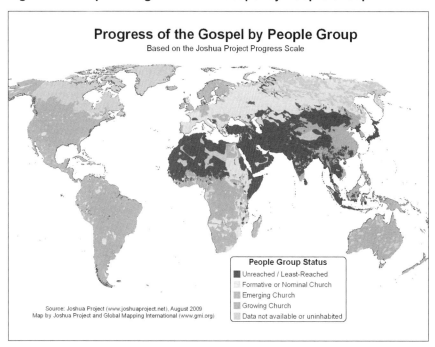

Source: Joshua Project, reprinted with permission

However, those who experience desperate physical and spiritual needs also have a compelling claim on the attention of those who identify themselves as followers of Jesus Christ.

The Wycliffe Model. One group that is combining both word and deed witness is the Wycliffe Bible Translators. Bob Creson, president of Wycliffe Bible Translators, put the ministry's work into accessible terms. In one statement he explained, "Helping a mother become literate can make a more lasting impact on a community than providing a doctor…While a doctor can fight disease and sickness with medicine, mothers—and ultimately communities—are better served through literacy programs that help mothers read prescriptions, medicine bottles, and educate themselves on healthcare." Some Wycliffe Bible translation teams are also involved in such activities as translating an AIDS education program into the local language, to promote health education.[68] In some areas, the ministry distributes malaria repellant not only to protect the translators, but also the communities in which the missionaries serve.[69] Those involved in translation sometimes also become involved in water purification and other community development efforts as well. [70]

However, the primary task for the organization remains the translation of the Bible. In the last decade, the organization took stock and decided that it needed to proceed with more urgency. As its Web site explains:

> In 1999, Wycliffe and SIL (Summer Institute of Linguistics) leadership recognized that the rate of Bible translation was too slow. At the 1999 pace, the Bible would not be available to the last language community until sometime around 2150. So Wycliffe decided to work differently and with a renewed sense of urgency.

> Vision 2025 was adopted as Wycliffe's mission. It is our resolve to achieve a dramatic increase in new Bible translations—to start the last translation by the year 2025.[71]

Having a clear goal, Wycliffe calculated the amount of money to accomplish the task. The specific goal is $1.15 billion dollars. The Wycliffe Web site explains that this amount will not only support the new projects, but also insure ongoing work. A table on the Web site breaks out the total goal by "Goal Area," "Description," and "Financial Opportunity," with a specific dollar amount for each category.[72]

The response to the campaign has been encouraging. Before it was officially launched in November 2008, an anonymous gift of $50 million was given to the campaign. That amount was the largest gift in the organization's 75-year history.[73] By April 2009, donors had given, pledged, or made other commitments that increased the total raised to $117 million.[74]

At least three factors seem key to the success of the campaign. First, Wycliffe set a clearly stated financial goal and explained the purpose for which the money was needed.

Second, Wycliffe was apparently effective in communicating the specific needs that will be met by donors. Although wishing to remain anonymous, the $50 million donor nevertheless issued a statement that indicated a heartfelt understanding of Wycliffe's goal: "Literacy is key to helping people work their way out of poverty and resist oppression by others…Children who first learn to read in their own language are more likely to become literate and to stay in school than those who first learn in a different language."[75]

The energy and strategy the organization has taken to complete a 2,000-year-old task could serve as a model for others wanting to make a difference in the world.

Third, Wycliffe showed a strong commitment to reach the goal by adapting its methods as necessary to use the latest technology. A brief description on the Wycliffe Web site quickly informs the reader about the organization's challenges and the strategies it is taking to meet them. Referring to the 1999 leadership decision to "work differently and with a renewed sense of urgency," the Web site explains the improvements enabled by new approaches:

> Working differently has taken many forms. Training national translators to take up the task has made a major contribution in starting new languages. As members of the local community are trained in translation skills, they bring a ready passion for their culture and an urgency to reach and teach their children and their neighbors.
>
> Where untranslated languages share a similarity with a translated language, computer tools can now provide a first draft of a rough translation, based on "predicting" key terms and phrases. Where several languages can be started at the same time, a "cluster approach" to translation begins all languages simultaneously, rather than sequentially. Where a community has no written language, a start can be made by first translating Bible stories or the Gospel of Luke, and then partnering with other ministries to reach these oral communities with the gospel. In most cases these partnership strategies rapidly lead to a translation.[76]

The energy and strategy the organization has taken to complete a 2,000-year-old task could serve as a model for others wanting to make a difference in the world.

Indeed, it would not be surprising if leaders at Wycliffe were familiar with successful entrepreneurial strategies, adapting those to help reach their goal. For example, in their book, *Philanthrocapitalism*, authors Matthew Bishop and Michael Green quote Bill Gates when Gates returned to Harvard to speak to students there: "Cutting through complexity to find a solution runs through four predictable stages: determine a goal, find the highest-leverage approach, discover the ideal technology for that approach, and in the meantime, make the smartest application of the technology you already have." For the Gates Foundation, leveraging involves strategic alliances with government, organizations, and other foundations.[77]

The Wycliffe model to solve the problem of Bible translation reflected several of these steps. The goal to start Bible translations in all people groups by 2025 was clearly articulated, and the supporting reasons were made accessible to those who might have an interest in the goal. The leveraging involved a campaign to raise the money to fund the goal by having a good cost estimate and explaining why each part was needed. The organization then engendered trust that it was serious about reaching the goal by evaluating current technology available and adapting its methods as necessary.

The success of the Wycliffe model raises a question highly pertinent to the present discussion. That is, can one or more denominations evidence similar progress toward success in achieving a large, globally-significant, at-scale-with-the-need stated goal? The question is important in a discussion of the role of wholesale billionaire philanthropists mobilizing the vast but currently dissipated potential of the millions of retail philanthropists. A large number of these retail philanthropists attend churches that are affiliated with denominations. The denominations, therefore, could be effective leaders in assisting efforts to mobilize coordinated campaigns to impact global need in Jesus' name.

The difficulty is that very few of these national church offices have a large, clearly articulated goal around which their members could actively organize. Even when attempts are made, they lack the clarity evident in the Wycliffe model. An exception is the Southern Baptist Convention.

A Case Study: The Southern Baptist Convention. The Southern Baptist Convention has stated clearly the focus of its activity as taking the Gospel to the world. The 1845 founding of the Southern Baptist Convention was for "the purpose of 'organizing a plan for eliciting, combining, and directing the energies of the whole denomination in one sacred effort, for the propagation of the Gospel.' "[78] In recent years, this initial impetus has taken the more focused goal of engaging all the unreached people groups by increasing the missions force from its present level of 5,300 to about 8,000, with a tentative goal of 2010.[79]

The Southern Baptist Convention is the second largest communion in the United States, and the largest Protestant grouping. With its clearly stated goal of engaging all unreached people groups, it lends itself to a case study of whether a denomination can be a leading force in mobilizing many retail billionaires to apply their potential to a clear goal.

The Plan: Additional Missionaries to Engage Unreached People Groups. The Southern Baptist Convention (SBC) International Mission Board (IMB) began publicizing the need for 2,800 more missionaries in 2007. A full-page ad in the September 2007 issue of the denominational magazine, *SBC Life* (p. 9) announced: "2,800, The number of additional IMB missionaries needed to engage the unreached people groups around the world with the gospel." A similar ad was published in the April 2008 magazine (p. 5), and there may have been others as well. Further, the 2008 Convention annual meeting was to contain an exploration of the need for additional missionaries to engage the remaining people groups that presently had no one "advancing the Gospel" among them.[80]

The Southern Baptist Convention International Mission Board began publicizing the need for 2,800 more missionaries in 2007.

In contrast to the Wycliffe model, no clear cost estimate for the 2,800 additional missionaries was made available to those who might be interested in the need. None of the publicity provided such a dollar figure. Information on the SBC Web site can be found that lists an annual cost per missionary of $40,931.64.[81] Using a calculator, the industrious inquirer can calculate that 2,800 additional missionaries at that rate would cost an additional $114,608,592 a year, or about $7 per Southern Baptist member.[82] However, this number was never publicized as a stated goal.

The IMB, which would be supervising the missionaries, is funded through two methods. From 2007 through at least the first eight months of 2009, neither income stream advertised the need for the additional $114 million.

Each year, 100% of the Lottie Moon Christmas Offering® is directed to the International Mission Board. According to the denominational Web site, "After considering IMB leadership's recommendation, the Woman's Missionary Union sets the Lottie Moon Christmas Offering goal at its annual meeting."[83] Although the announcement of the IMB's need for 2,800 more missionaries was announced in 2007, the next year's Lottie Moon offering goal, to be taken in December 2008, did not integrate that stated need. It would have been possible for the estimated cost of the additional missionaries to be added to the previous year's goal, for a total of $279 million. Instead, the goal was increased from $165 million in 2007 to $170 million in 2008, with no reference made to the cost of expanding the mission force.[84]

The other source of IMB funding is via a percent of the SBC Cooperative Program income that comes from the congregations, a portion of which is passed on by the state conventions. The Cooperative Program (CP) is the unified budget of the SBC. It would appear that the denomination wanted the money for the additional missionaries to come through the CP based on the two *SBC Life* ads noted above. In both cases, the top half of the full-page ad announced the goal of 2,800 additional missionaries, and the bottom half was devoted to promotion of the CP. Since the IMB receives only a half of the income to the SBC CP, the ad could not have stated the cost of the additional 2,800 missionaries as $114 million, since the amount needed for the IMB to receive $114 million more through the CP would actually be $228 million to the SBC CP, with the IMB receiving half. Further, the SBC CP funding is only a portion of what comes to the state conventions. State conventions forward anywhere from 14 to 57% of the money sent from the congregations.[85]

The Result of the Present Approach. The stated goal—the need for 2,800 additional individuals to serve as missionaries—was effective. There was a reported increase in qualified missions applications. Unfortunately, the funding to send the missionaries was not received.

The Lottie Moon annual offering did not meet its 2008 goal of $170 million, but rather totaled $141 million, $9 million less than the final 2007 amount. As a consequence, one IMB official wrote on the denominational publication Web site, "We've had to take drastic measures. We're not sending the number of missionaries to the field we normally do. It means that some who are called, gifted and ready cannot go. We have canceled or scaled back short-term missionary programs knowing the results from some present work will not be realized."[86]

One IMB board member outlined the probable consequences of the restriction on missionaries, based on the last time it happened in 2001: "First, we learned

The stated goal— the need for 2,800 additional individuals to serve as missionaries— was effective. There was a reported increase in qualified missions applications. Unfortunately, the funding to send the missionaries was not received.

138

that restricting missionary appointments is not a temporary move with temporary consequences. It takes a long time to regain lost ground—years. The seriousness of the decision to restrict appointments cannot be overstated."[87]

The personal consequences were articulated in a denominational publication article about one missionary family that was put on standby. The couple, two of the 69 long-term missionaries who were told there would be a delay, had sold their house, quit their jobs, and given away their dog in preparation for the planned deployment date. When those plans were changed, no firm date was promised for the future. Meanwhile, the couple already on the field who had been planning on the additional help, expressed great discouragement at having to continue to be over-extended, responsible for the extensive mission outreach that could not be managed well without additional workers. [88]

Proposal for Increased Giving. One proposal to remedy the underfunding of the IMB suggested strengthening the CP through a change in percentage allocations. The traditional standards have been 10% from the congregation forwarded to the states,[89] and 50% of the money that comes into the state conventions being forwarded to the national SBC CP. [90]

Table 44 demonstrates the distribution of the current levels of CP funds provided by the congregations. If the percentage of the CP distribution changed to the traditional 10%-50% model, the congregations would need to direct $330 million more to the CP. States would then direct 50%, rather than the current average of 38%, to the SBC CP. With the revised allocations, the congregations would be giving the state conventions an additional $101 million more for their operations.

Table 44: **A Comparison of Actual 2007, and Calculated Traditional 10% & 50% Model, Funding Levels of the Southern Baptist Convention Cooperative Program, with the Goal of Raising $114.6 Million Additional to Support 2,800 More Missionaries through the International Mission Board to Engage the Unreached People Groups Around the World**

		A	B	C	D
		Actual Congregation Contribution to CP at 6.2%, State to SBC CP at 38%, 2007	Traditional Model Goal: Congregation Contribution to CP at 10%, State to SBC CP at 50% (Calculated)	Additional Receipts Using Traditional Model CP Support, Compared to Actual (Col. B - Col. A)	Non-IMB Funding Increase in Traditional Model (Row 5-8, Row 8-11)
1	Total Receipts to SBC congregations	$10,845,108,310	$10,845,108,310		
2	Undesignated Receipts as % of Total	80%	80%		
3	Undesignated Receipts	$8,699,869,367	$8,699,869,367		
4	CP % of Undesignated Receipts	6.20%	**10%**		
5	Donation to Cooperative Program: Total	$539,608,678	$869,986,937	$330,378,259	
6	Add'l for States after 50% to SBC CP				$101,101,624
7	% of CP to Southern Baptist Convention	38%	**50%**		
8	CP Total Donation to SBC	$205,716,834	$434,993,468	$229,276,634	
9	Add'l for SBC Entities with 50% to IMB				$114,638,318
10	SBC CP % to International Mission Board	50%	50%		
11	SBC CP Donation to IMB	$102,858,418	$217,496,734	$114,638,316	
	Add'l Non-IMB $ to Be Raised in Order to Fund Add'l 2,800 Missionaries through CP				$215,739,943

Source: empty tomb, inc. Analysis; Southern Baptist Convention Data

Details in the above table may not compute to the numbers shown due to rounding.

The SBC CP would continue to direct 50% of receipts to the IMB. The increase for the non-IMB entities would be $114.6 million, the same amount as the increase to the IMB for the support of the additional 2,800 missionaries needed to engage all unreached people groups.

The effect of working through the CP to raise the additional $115 million needed for the 2,800 missionaries is that the congregations would have to give the non-IMB entities at the state and national levels an additional $215 million, in order to get $115 million more to the IMB for the 2,800 missionaries.

Stated another way, in order to fund the $114.6 million cost for the 2,800 additional missionaries to complete the global mission task, congregations would need to raise an additional $330 million, with two-thirds directed to non-IMB activities. Were the traditional model in place and more money needed for IMB support services beyond the direct support for missionaries, for every $10 million needed to expand the work of the IMB through the CP, a total of $400 million in undesignated receipts would have to be given at the congregational level.[91]

A difficulty is that when a standard of 10% to the CP was proposed as a guideline at the 2007 Convention annual meeting, the idea engendered strong debate.[92] The trend has been for a smaller percentage of congregational undesignated gifts to be directed to the Cooperative Program, In the 1980s, the average percent of congregational undesignated funds directed to the Cooperative Program was 10.5%. In fiscal year 2006-2007, it was 6.2%.[93]

R. Albert Mohler, Jr., president of the Southern Baptist Theological Seminary, addressed a forum on the future of the SBC in August 2009. He posed ten choices before the SBC that will impact whether the denomination grows or declines in the future. He also commented on the CP structure:

"We have problems in terms of the fact that we say we are sold out to missions and yet the closer you look at the actual infrastructure of the Southern Baptist Convention at every level and all the rest of you trace the dollars, only a small portion of that offering plate ever gets close to the International Mission Board."

Having noted that the Cooperative Program may reflect more of a business efficiency model that is not actually helping Southern Baptists achieve their stated goals, he went on to observe that, "…as it's presented it sounds like our greatest goal is to cooperate. Well, the United States Army can have a Cooperative Program….Do we cooperate? Yes, and in 1925 [when the Cooperative Program was founded] the big question is whether Southern Baptists are going to cooperate. The big question in 2009 is whether Southern Baptists are going to be relevant in the mission of God and the world." A second factor, he pointed out, is that the denomination is not "Going to be able to tell Southern Baptist churches in a new age what you must do and how you must give…We're going to have to at every level make sure that we are worthy of the support."[94] The protracted trend of decline does not bode well for a sudden reversal in the amount of funding through the CP to be expected from the congregations, in order to fund the additional needed missionaries.

Further, as pointed out by John L. Yeats, director of communications for the Louisiana Baptist Convention and recording secretary of the SBC, a long period of discussion about restructuring cannot be the solution: "What's needed is more new fuel in the tank. This means new missions dollars, not reshuffling of old currency.

> "We have problems in terms of the fact that we say we are sold out to missions and yet the closer you look at the actual infrastructure of the Southern Baptist Convention at every level and all the rest of you trace the dollars, only a small portion of that offering plate ever gets close to the International Mission Board."

And the fuel is needed now. It takes significant time and additional resources to change the structure and gain marginal efficiency. The new dollars, however, are needed now."[95]

There has also been a decline in support for the Lottie Moon offering over time. Offering income data was published in various documents for the period 1979 through 2008.[96] During this period, the per member levels of support have been less than a tenth of one percent as a portion of income. From 1979-2008, there was an overall decline of 35% in even the small amount of income that each member invests in the IMB through Lottie Moon. Figure 25 presents the 1979-2008 Lottie Moon Offering per member contribution as a portion of income.

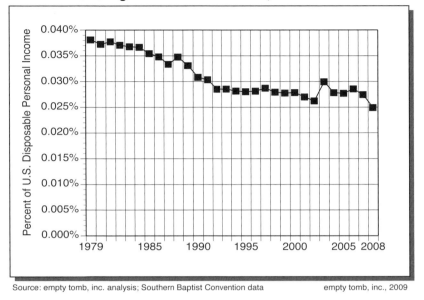

Figure 25: Per Member Contribution to the Lottie Moon Christmas Offering as a Portion of Income, 1979-2008

Source: empty tomb, inc. analysis; Southern Baptist Convention data   empty tomb, inc., 2009

Another analysis can be done related to the request for 2,800 additional missionaries. In 2007, Korean Southern Baptists, through the Council of Korean Southern Baptist Churches, set the goal of having 1,000 missionaries serving through the IMB by 2010. There was celebration at a council meeting in June 2009 when it was announced that the goal had been met a year early: 300 missionaries were presently in service, 200 were in process, and 500 were prepared to go when resources become available.[97]

The good news was dampened, of course, by the fact that the 500 who were prepared to go could not do so for lack of funds.

Table 45 considers the cost per Southern Baptist to expand the global mission force. There are two parallel analyses. The column on the left considers the cost per Korean Southern Baptist to send the 500 missionaries for which there are currently no funds. The column on the right calculates the cost per non-Korean Southern Baptist to send the balance of 2,300 missionaries needed to expand the total IMB staff to engage the remaining unreached people groups. The calculations indicate that it would cost an additional $195 per attender to

Table 45: Cost Per Southern Baptist Attender to Fund Additional Needed Missionaries

Southern Baptist Convention	Korean	Non-Korean
Additional Missionaries to be Funded	500	2,300
Cost per Missionary	x $40,931.64	x $40,931.64
Total Funding Needed	$20,465,820	$94,142,772
Number of Congregations	÷ 760	÷ 44,088
Cost per Congregation	$26,929	$2,135
Average Number of Attenders	÷ 138	÷ 138
Cost per Attender per Year	$195	$15

Data may not compute to the numbers shown due to rounding
Sources: empty tomb, inc. analysis; SBC data

fund the 500 additional Korean missionaries. For the non-Korean Southern Baptists, it would cost each attender $15 a year to fund the 2,300 missionaries needed.

Observations. The stated goal of the Southern Baptist Convention is the Great Commission, which involves taking the Gospel to everyone on earth. To do that, its International Mission Board has said that it needs an additional 2,800 missionaries. When this need was publicized, additional missionary candidates applied. The cost to fund the additional missionaries was not publicized. The money to fund the additional missionaries was not received.

The Cooperative Program structure would require that several times the dollar amount needed to support the additional missionaries would have to be donated by the congregations in order for sufficient additional funds to be allocated to the IMB as a percent of the CP. The additional money could be donated directly through the Lottie Moon offering. However, there has been no organized publicity campaign to increase the offering, perhaps out of concern that the CP be fully funded.

The analysis in Table 45 indicates that the cost would be in the neighborhood of $15 a year per attender to field most of the additional missionaries. However, there apparently is no organizing center within the SBC to promote the idea that this relatively modest amount be given.

> The analysis in Table 45 indicates that the cost would be in the neighborhood of $15 a year per attender to field most of the additional missionaries.

The Great Commission Resurgence. A fairly recent development in the SBC is the Great Commission Resurgence Task Force. What began as an April 2009 sermon by Danny Aiken, president of Southeastern Baptist Theological Seminary, turned into a "declaration" with the assistance of SBC President Johnny Hunt. Attracting support from a variety of Southern Baptist leaders and laypeople, a task force was approved at the June 2009 Convention annual meeting. In an interview about the document, "Akin said it is 'irresponsible' for anyone to 'pretend we're not in a crisis moment, that we're not facing some very difficult times, and it would be irresponsible for us not to take a good, hard look' at the denomination." One of the original articles of the declaration, Article IX, was rewritten to be less critical of the structure, particularly the state convention offices, although Akin stated that the purpose was, "for every sphere in Southern Baptist life—churches, associations, state convention and national entities—to be 'self-critical in asking the question: Are we maximizing the resources entrusted to us by Southern Baptists for the fulfilling of the Great Commission?' "[99]

In addressing the 2009 Convention annual meeting, Johnny Hunt, president, said, "We will have to give an account for what we have done with what God has given us." He described the Great Commission Resurgence proposal: "It's about all of us, starting with the local church, taking a look to see if we're doing the best we've ever done in our lifetime to fulfill the Great Commission."[100]

An article on the Baptist Press Web site combined several published interviews with Hunt that occurred before the June 2009 Convention annual meeting, where Hunt was re-elected to serve as president for a second term. In the interviews, Hunt expressed views that, although not often highlighted, may reflect the strains between the pastors and denominational officials in many different communions. Although some of Hunt's comments specifically address the congregation-based structure of the

SBC, the general themes are relevant for understanding aspects of the congregation-denomination relationship in any communion.

> "It's sort of like I almost feel like I have to ask permission to ask a question about the agencies I support. That gives me major, major heartburn." Hunt went on to comment on the negative reaction from some denominational officials about the GRC document calling for changes: "Why all the ruckus? Why so much self-preservation? Why so much 'shame on you to think that we're not doing the best we can'? I mean, who are we? Are we a bunch of perfectionists?"

Having noted earlier in one of the interviews that in the Southern Baptist structure, the congregation is considered to be the "king" to which denominational structures at each level are answerable, Hunt asked, "Should it be the church holding denominations accountable...or should they be holding us accountable?...If the church is a king, anyone else that speaks to us is a prince speaking to the king." [101]

Hunt's comments highlight the mutual respect that is necessary among all levels of the church in order to organize for addressing global physical and spiritual needs. In fact, without a strong commitment to a larger vision, congregations as well as denominations may develop an unhealthy inward focus. Certainly, the giving patterns outlined in chapter 1 demonstrate a growing inward emphasis in congregations that are spending a larger portion of their income on Congregational Finances, funding the internal operations of the church. Jimmy Draper, retired president of the SBC LifeWay Christian Resources, served in many denominational capacities, and now is a resource preacher for congregations. In an article that surveyed the opinions of denominational leaders about the Great Commission Resurgence declaration, Draper was quoted as saying that the GRC might help with some SBC dynamics he has observed: "lack of baptisms, lack of real discipleship, still losing 80 percent of our kids when they graduate from high school before they get out of college." Later in the article, his comments were again conveyed: " '...by and large, we're not really passionate about reaching the lost,' Draper said. 'I preach in about 50 different churches every year. It is rare to find a church that has a real concern for the lost. It's rare to find a church that's not having some real disruptive things in the fellowship.' " [102]

> "Are we saying that five thousand missionaries are enough ... to evangelize the rest of the world while we support over 100,000 pastors, church staff, and denominational workers in our own country?"

The trends in the SBC noted by Draper were echoed by Ronnie Floyd, chair of the Great Commission Resurgence Task Force. A reporter, covering an address by Floyd to a group of Southern Baptist pastors and laypeople, wrote, "Floyd said the reality is that many churches in the United States are plateaued or declining in membership and the denomination baptized fewer people in 2008 than far fewer congregations baptized in 1950. 'We have more people and more resources than we have ever had and we are doing less with it to reach the lost, unchurched people of America,' Floyd said." The same article quoted Floyd's agenda for the Great Commission Resurgence Task Force: "As chairman, I have one commitment: I am going to keep our focus on getting the Gospel of Jesus Christ to every nation, every people group in the world." [103]

The difference between the stated goal of the denomination, to reach a lost world, and its practice was summarized by Jerry Rankin, president of the IMB, this way: "Are we saying that five thousand missionaries are enough ... to evangelize the rest of the world while we support over 100,000 pastors, church staff, and denominational workers in our own country?" [104]

In reviewing reports of SBC officials' views, the Great Commission Resurgence is being promoted as a time to regroup and improve the communion's outreach. Some church leaders have expressed hope that the SBC is ready to act on a larger goal.

Southern Seminary President Al Mohler, acknowledging the fact that the SBC was formed in 1845 "for the solitary purpose of getting the Gospel to the ends of the earth," declared, "There is a generation ready and waiting to be challenged to do something great for the cause of Christ. I say we take this opportunity."[105]

At the 2009 Convention, Johnny Hunt told the delegates who are called "messengers," "Instead of seeking a program to follow, Southern Baptists long for a vision to embrace that will draw all of the nations to honor God."[106]

The difficulty is, to be most practical, the vision will need to be made real through programming. In a published interview, Hunt suggested that any increased giving by Southern Baptist members to expand mission work might have to be accompanied by changes in the structure. The article quoted Hunt:

> "I would like to see churches give more money than ever before. But as it gives it, I would like to see bureaucracy ceasing to grow so much larger," Hunt said, describing a future scenario in which a state convention would determine it has enough funds to do its ministry and can give more to national and international mission causes.
>
> "I hope it would come to the point they say, 'You know what, we don't need to grow the bureaucracy any larger. Let's just send the money on.' "[107]

The initial formation of the Southern Baptist Convention was viewed as a "sacred effort." The challenge for both denominations and congregations is to separate the sacred from the comfortably familiar. The structure of the SBC provides a detailed budgeting process for each agency, including the IMB. It is not clear if Section II-C of the SBC Business and Financial Plan would allow any agency, including the IMB, to develop a budget large enough to fund the vision that Johnny Hunt suggests that SBC members need. That section of the plan limits budgets to the current allocation "plus any other anticipated receipts which can be substantiated by previous experience, not including wills, bequests, and special gifts for special purposes…"[108]

A Wholesale Billionaire Strategy Scenario. The case study of the Southern Baptist Convention describes a denomination with a clearly stated goal, that is not effectively meeting that goal. The difference between the Southern Baptist Convention and many other denominations and multi-denominational groups, is that the Southern Baptist Convention has a large, at-scale clearly stated goal around which congregations can gather.

Leaders in the SBC are taking what might be constructive steps to revise the working relationships at all levels of the church to serve the overarching purpose more fully. The report from the Great Commission Resurgence Task Force is due at the June 2010 Convention.

The difficulty with that schedule, of course, is the lost mission work in the meantime. Families who gave up jobs and sold homes are in limbo. Those on the front lines do not receive the help they need. The trend to turn inward at the congregational level is unaddressed, and becomes more imbedded as time passes.

"There is a generation ready and waiting to be challenged to do something great for the cause of Christ. I say we take this opportunity."

The concept of mobilizing the "retail billionaires" who have traditionally funded the mission work of the SBC is compatible with the SBC's stated goal. There does not seem to be a question that increased donations to field the 2,800 additional missionaries, many of whom apparently are already on hold in the pipeline, would be welcomed by the denominational structure. The only question seems to be how to attract the increased giving.

The CP structure would require over two hundred million dollars more be given, over and above the $115 million needed for the additional missionaries. Since church members did not fully fund the 2008 Lottie Moon Offering goal, 100% of which was to go to the IMB, it is not likely that church members will provide almost three times the amount in order to cover the cost through the CP.

The situation is presently at a standstill. Therefore, it may not be inappropriate to suggest an intervention be made by one or more "hyperagents," as Paul Schervish referred to the very wealthy who can undertake actions that normally would require whole social movements.

A scenario might be as follows. One or more wholesale billionaires could announce their intention to match every dollar of the 2009 Lottie Moon offering that exceeds the previous year's offering, up to a specified amount of dollars. The stated goal of the effort would be to increase the Lottie Moon offering to a level sufficient to fully fund IMB current operations, recover the ground lost with the decline in the 2008 offering, and especially to field the additional 2,800 missionaries needed to engage all unreached people groups. Based on publicly available numbers, the new total might be $265 million. That would be the $141 million base equal to what was received in 2008, the $9 million shortfall from the 2007 level of $150 million, and the $114.6 million estimated cost for the additional 2,800 missionaries. Half of the $124 million increase over the $141 million 2008 Lottie Moon offering, or $62 million, would come from increased giving from the congregations, and half, up to $62 million, would come from one or more wholesale billionaires. The increased offering from the congregations would cost each member about $3.82 extra to raise the $62 million to be matched, using the 2008 membership figure.

The role for the Great Commission Resurgence Task Force could then be to explore how to sustain the increased energy and giving in future years. The Task Force members would probably find that it is easier to guide a moving train than to start one from a stopped position.

Would this proposal work within the SBC structure? The SBC Business and Financial Plan is very strict about prohibiting agency fundraising in the congregations as stated in Section VI.D.: "In no case shall any Convention entity approach a church for inclusion in its church budget or appeal for financial contributions."[109]

However, there is no restriction that would prevent the already established Lottie Moon offering from exceeding its goal, set for $175 million in 2009.[110]

Further, Section VII. of the SBC Business and Financial Plan explicitly states: "The Convention binds itself and its entities faithfully to apply and use such gifts as designated by the donor."[111]

Donations to match increased Lottie Moon funds, explicitly designated for the work of the IMB, would therefore fit perfectly well within the present SBC structure.

The stated goal of the effort would be to increase the Lottie Moon offering to a level sufficient to fully fund IMB current operations, recover the ground lost with the decline in the 2008 offering, and especially to field the additional 2,800 missionaries needed to engage all unreached people groups.

It is not improbable that the "money follows vision" theorem would, in faith, be found to be true for the support of the general CP, thus providing for the denominational entities other than the IMB. Church members are willing to support the general structure of the denomination, as demonstrated by the current ongoing donations to the CP. However, as noted, the percent of CP donations leaving the congregation has been declining since the 1980s. Denominational officials may take courage in the Biblical affirmation that "perfect love casts out fear" (1 John 4:18), and choose to love those in desperate spiritual and physical need at the risk of the preservation of their own structures. Current giving trends suggest that continuing in the same pattern will not protect those structures. The perceived risks associated with expanding missions may be well worth taking.

This scenario recommends itself in that some of the internal dynamics outlined earlier in this chapter, at both the denominational and congregational levels, would not have to be engaged by the wholesale billionaires in order to move quickly. The matching of the 2009 Lottie Moon Offering would also mean that the donations would be available in early 2010, thus reducing the period of time when present IMB efforts are restricted. The boldness could also provide a needed, strengthening jolt to the vision of church members who, as earlier discussed, may be prone to learned helplessness.

There is one caveat. It would be important to make clear the expectation that the increased Lottie Moon funds would not be taken from what otherwise would have been donated for the CP or the congregational mission outreach, a process called "equalization" in church circles, or more appropriately, "robbing Peter to pay Paul." Congregations would need to understand that, if CP funding does not stay at or exceed current levels, then the IMB will, in fact, not be any better off as a result of the increased Lottie Moon funds. If the IMB funding through the CP decreases, due to an overall decline in CP income, then the IMB will still not receive enough income to fund the additional 2,800 missionaries needed, even if the Lottie Moon offering increases.

However, it is hoped that one may count on the good will and intention of Southern Baptist church members in their desire to see the stated goal of taking the Gospel to the whole world fulfilled within the coming weeks and months.

Application for Other Denominations. The wholesale billionaire scenario described above focuses specifically on the Southern Baptist Convention. A similar plan could be applied in other denominations or denominational groupings as well. A key factor would be for the denominations to have a broadly accepted, attractive, large, at-scale goal around which the retail billionaire church members in that communion could mobilize.

Wholesale billionaire philanthropist Ted Turner initiated a mobilization effort with United Methodists and Lutherans in what he terms the Malaria Partnership. Through the United Nations Foundation, he is working with The United Methodist Church, and Lutheran World Relief, which counts the Evangelical Lutheran Church in America and the Lutheran Church-Missouri Synod among its constituents. The goal is for the denominations to raise $200 million to assist with ending malaria over five years.[112]

It would be important to make clear the expectation that the increased Lottie Moon funds would not be taken from what otherwise would have been donated for the CP or the congregational mission outreach, a process called "equalization" in church circles, or more appropriately, "robbing Peter to pay Paul."

146

What can be learned from a review of his foray into denominational mobilization? Several factors in the Malaria Partnership are different than the scenario described above. First, Ted Turner is working through an outside secular organization, the United Nations Foundation, which could have an effect on how church members perceive the effort. Second, no matching money is involved, perhaps limiting the level of urgency present on the part of the denominational leadership and the church members. Third, the specific financial goal of the campaign is not placed in a larger context. Is $200 million enough to eliminate malaria in the world? Is it enough to impact malaria in a particular country? As noted earlier in this chapter, people want to know that the help they offer will make a significant difference. What difference will this $200 million make? The cost model presented earlier in this chapter suggests that $481 million dollars is needed to address 95% of the global under-5 child deaths from malaria.[113] Information such as that, or a focus on addressing malaria deaths in a particular country or region, might be helpful. Use of a strategy such as the Yoking Map® might create a geographical focus between churches in an area of the U.S. and a country or region of the world.[114]

Another key factor in working with denominations to mobilize retail billionaires seems to be that the intervention focuses on a goal that the denomination has identified. Asked what she and her husband had learned from their grantmaking activities, wholesale multimillionaire philanthropist Roberta Green Ahmanson responded: "Also, you can't make people do for money what they don't want to do anyway. If you see things you think need to be done in the world, you look around to find the people who share the vision and have the skills, ability, and drive to do those things, and come alongside them. Those have been our most successful grants, and our blessings."[115] Put another way, a wholesale billionaire philanthropist cannot impose an agenda on retail billionaires. However, Christians from all economic levels ought to be able to agree on some fairly broad and impressive agendas built on loving God, and then loving neighbors in need, agendas that are worthy of major investment of both money and lives.

Moving to the Level of True Riches

Based on Luke 16:11, Jesus regards "worldly wealth" as a set of training wheels to be prepared to handle "true riches." Giving patterns, then, are important indicators of the level of spiritual maturity and readiness on the part of the church in the U.S. for more responsibility in God's agenda.

A wholesale billionaire who helps mobilize retail billionaires to give more to missions is not only helping to meet dire physical and spiritual needs of people around the globe. That wholesale billionaire is also involved in strengthening the church.

Many individuals who have made significant worldly wealth may feel out of their comfort zones, engaging church structures in order to pursue such a mobilization agenda. At that point, it might be worthwhile to consider how the shepherd David was trained to take over the kingship of Israel. The Bible indicates that God was not happy with the way that the kingdom was going, and wanted to make a change (1 Samuel 13:13-14, 15:26). God's alternative, David, was found tending sheep. Soon after Samuel anoints him as the new king, David is killing Goliath, serving the present king at court, and winning battles at the head of a well-prepared army. It would have been easy for God to keep David at court, learning "how it was done," mastering all

> A wholesale billionaire who helps mobilize retail billionaires to give more to missions is not only helping to meet dire physical and spiritual needs of people around the globe. That wholesale billionaire is also involved in strengthening the church.

the skills and strategies he would need to eventually take over the kingdom. Instead, God has David spending years living in caves, running for his life, turning a rag-tag crew of malcontents into a disciplined army. When he eventually becomes king, he brings an outsider's perspective that allows God to move in a fresh direction.

A key factor was that David was a person after God's heart (1 Samuel 13:14). The church in the U.S. does not need another power center promoting another agenda. The church needs servant leadership to figure out how to better pursue God's agenda. It might be possible that there are wholesale billionaires who have been in training, gaining worldly wealth and practical knowledge, that could now help God bring a fresh energy and perspective to the fulfillment of the Great Commission and Great Commandment that Jesus Christ has given the church. Not having seminary training would not be a limitation to such leadership; not having a heart yielded to God would.

Of course, the wholesale billionaire has numerous options other than engaging the church in mobilizing missions dollars. The wealthy can pursue personal entertainment or focus on making even more money, while not doing anything great with it. David's son, Solomon, built on his father's start with the kingdom, exceeding him in wealth and power. Yet Solomon ends up concluding that it is all pretty meaningless (Eccl. 2:2). Perhaps the Psalmist who wrote Psalm 49 was observing Solomon at the end of his life in verse 20: "A man who has riches without understanding is like the beasts that perish" (NIV).

> The church in the U.S. does not need another power center promoting another agenda. The church needs servant leadership to figure out how to better pursue God's agenda.

That lack of understanding can have dire consequences for everyone on earth. National and international leaders are willing to pursue their own agendas regardless of the risks for humanity. For example, some scientists are worried that new artificial intelligence developments may produce self-directed robots and future computer viruses that will challenge the ability of humans to control them.[116] Other scientists continue to express concern that the Hadron Collider, designed to smash atoms, may create a black hole that would swallow the entire earth, but the collider was put into operation until a "bad accident" that was "probably due to human error" shut it down.[117]

From a Christian perspective, which is presumably built on God's perspective, there is an even greater threat. Benedict XVI spoke of Abbot Aupert's conclusion that greed is at the root of all vices, and then continued: "I underline this because in light of the current worldwide economic crisis it reveals itself as being (a) timely (message). We see that this crisis arose precisely from this root of greed."[118]

The Fall turned humans inward and away from God. That event may be part of the reason people find it so hard to understand their own potential for good. Greed, which is idolatry (Eph. 5:5, Col. 3:5), leads to lack of love for others, which leads to lack of oneness of mind and heart, which leads to the world not knowing that God sent Jesus (John 17:20-21). Greed is not a sin that affects only the heart of the one who practices it. Greed and a lack of love are a deadly combination for the dying children and the unevangelized of the world. The good that is not done has fatal consequences. From a secular ethicist's point of view, Peter Singer, after describing self-indulgent spending displays by wholesale billionaires, observed, "It's time we stopped thinking of these ways of spending money as silly but harmless displays of vanity, and started thinking of them as evidence of a grievous lack of concern for others. We need an ethical culture that takes account of the consequences of what each of us does for the world in which we are living, and that judges accordingly."[119]

Many verses in the Bible provide the ethic that Singer says is needed. It appears at least some wealthy people are reading them. Ron Blue, author and financial counselor, founded a group called "Kingdom Advisors." The purpose is to provide a fellowship for Christian financial advisors. At its February 2009 meeting, Tim Mohns was given a "Kingdom Advisor of the Year Award." Mohns and his wife made a decision to cap their personal income at $125,000 and give everything else away. A perhaps unexpected side effect of his decision was the different way Mohns says he now approaches advising clients. He said that, since a few clients one way or the other will not impact his income, he finds himself being completely forthright: "It's brought a sense of calling back into my work. I speak into other people's lives without fear."[120]

The wise use of wealth not only blesses those in need who benefit from the donor's generosity. The donor also finds meaning in fulfilling more of God's larger purpose of salvation through Jesus Christ. Interestingly, on April 30, 2009, two comic strips both addressed the issue of reaching individual potential. In "Blondie," Blondie (B) asks Dagwood (D): "What are you doing, dear?" D: "I've just begun to figure out my vast, untapped potential." B: "Your vast, untapped potential for doing what?" D: "That's the part I haven't figured out yet." Then, in "The Born Loser," Brutus Thornapple sits at the dinner table and reflects over three frames: (1) "There's only one thing worse…" (2) "than the thought that I might not have fulfilled my potential in life…" (3) "the thought that I might have."[121]

> The wise use of wealth not only blesses those in need who benefit from the donor's generosity. The donor also finds meaning in fulfilling more of God's larger purpose of salvation through Jesus Christ.

In faith, for the Christian, there is a purpose and plan of God's making. Even the cynical Solomon poetically frames the fact that, "There is a time for everything, and a season for every activity under heaven" (Eccl. 3:1, NIV).

For the Christian wholesale billionaire, the task is to consider whether or not to act as a "hyperagent" by leveraging his or her available resources to mobilize retail billionaires' potential for impacting word and deed need in Jesus' name.

For Christian retail billionaires, the task is to consider whether now is the time to unlearn "helplessness" and step out in faith on an agenda that addresses global word and deed need.

For denominational leaders and pastors, the task is to consider whether to step out in faith and risk the preservation of institutions in an effort to accomplish the 2,000-year old responsibility of global evangelization, even while preventing the deaths of millions of children.

For those children who are dying around the globe from preventable causes, and for those who would like a Bible but cannot obtain one, their task is to cry out to God for someone to recognize in them the true riches that Jesus Christ described in Luke 16:11, so that someone will love them at their points of need, for Christ's sake.

Notes for Chapter 8

[1] John Ronsvalle and Sylvia Ronsvalle, *The State of Church Giving through 2006: Global Triage, MDG 4, and Unreached People Groups*, 18th edition (Champaign, IL: empty tomb, inc., 2008), chapter 8, pp. 107-148.

[2] "The 2007 *Slate* 60"; 2/11/2008; <http://specials.slate.com/slate60/2007/>; pp. 1-8 of 5/1/2009 9:24 AM printout.

[3] "The Philanthropy 50: at a Glance" and "The Philanthropy 50: America's Most-Generous Donors in 2008," *The Chronicle of Philanthropy*, January 29, 2009, pp. 10, 8-9.

[4] Matthew Miller and Duncan Greenberg, eds.; "The Forbes 400"; 9/17/2008 6:00 PM ET; <http://www.forbes.com/2008/09/16/richest-american-billionaires-lists-400list08-cx_mm_dg_0917richintro_print.html>; p. 1 of 3/12/2009 5:23 PM printout.

[5] Noelle Barton and Suzanne Perry, "Foundations Urged to Collaborate and Find New Ways to Solve Problems," *The Chronicle of Philanthropy*, May 17, 2007, p. 14.

[6] Matthew Bishop and Michael Green, *Philanthrocapitalism: How the Rich Can Save the World* (New York: Bloomsbury Press, 2008), p. 51.

[7] Bishop and Green, *Philanthrocapitalism*, p. 5.

[8] John Ronsvalle and Sylvia Ronsvalle, *Behind the Stained Glass Windows: Money Dynamics in the Church* (Grand Rapids, MI: Baker Books, 1996), pp. 274, 275.

[9] Max M. Fisher, et al., "Commentary on Page 133," *Giving in America: Toward a Stronger Voluntary Sector* (n.p.: Commission on Private Philanthropy and Public Needs, 1975), p. 203.

[10] Nancy Frazier O'Brien, "Washington Letter: Voter Guides Confuse or Clarify?" *The (Peoria, Ill.) Catholic Post*, November 2, 2008, p. 4, col. 3-6.

[11] General Board of Church and Society of The United Methodist Church; U.S. Presidential Election 2008 Bulletin Insert: "Comparison of Political Party Platforms and The United Methodist Church"; <http://www.umc-gbcs.org/site/c.frLJKLqF/b.4565653/>; 11/4/2008 3:22 PM printout.

[12] Southern Baptist Convention Ethics & Religious Liberty Commission and North American Mission Board; "40/40 Prayer Guide, 40 Day Prayer Vigil"; <ilivevalues.com/documents/prayer/40_Day_Guide-full.pdf>.

[13] "Presbyterians, Lutherans Cut Jobs, Reduce Budgets," *Christian Century*, May 5, 2009, p. 17, and Associated Press; "Denomination Makes Cuts Amid Economic Slump"; OneNewsNow.com; 3/7/2009 4:00 PM; <http://onewnesnow.com/Printer.aspx?id=438992>; p. 1 of 3/7/2009 10:37 AM printout.

[14] For a more detailed discussion of this concept, see John Ronsvalle and Sylvia Ronsvalle, *The State of Church Giving through 2005: Abolition of the Institutional Enslavement of Overseas Missions* (Champaign, IL: empty tomb, inc., 2007), chapter 8, pp. 105-131.

[15] David Neff, "Global Is the New Local," *Christianity Today*, June 2009, p. 39.

[16] Melissa Deming; " 'Love Affair' with Freedom Can Become 'a False God," *World* Founder Tells Editors"; Baptist Press; 2/26/2009; <http://www.bpnews.net/printerfriendly.asp?ID=29967>; pp. 4, 5 of 2/27/2009 10:05 AM printout.

[17] Gallup "Religion"; December 2008; <http://www.gallup.com/poll/1690/religion.aspx>; pp. 1-2 of 8/22/2009 1:37 PM printout.

[18] Tammi Reed Ledbetter; "There's Gold in Them There Pews,' Hunt Tells Pastors"; Baptist Press; 6/23/2009; <http://www.bpnews.net/printfriendly.asp?ID=30741>; p. 2 of 6/24/2009 8:49 AM printout.

[19] A Religion News Service article appearing as "Southern Baptists Seek to Shake Membership Malaise," *Christian Century*, July 28, 2009, p. 15.

[20] Erin Roach; "Culture Digest: Spiritual Immaturity Stymies Church, Research Barna Says"; Baptist Press; 6/1/2009; <http://www.bpnews.net/printerfriendly.asp?ID=30593>; p. 1 of 6/1/2009 5:15 PM printout.

[21] Michelle A. Vu; "U.S. Evangelicals Pessimistic about Christianity in America"; Christian Post; 6/3/2009 1:21 PM EDT; <http://www.christianpost.com/article/20090603/u-s-evangelicals-pessimistic-about-christianity-in-america/index.html>; p. 1 of 6/4/09 9:17 AM printout.

[22] Archbishop Charles J. Chaput; "Rendering Unto Caesar: The Catholic Political Vocation"; Catholic News Agency; 2/23/2009; <http://www.catholicnewsagency.com/document.php?n=790>; p. 3 of 2/252009 10:16 AM printout.

[23] Steve Gray; "Author Challenges Absurd Religion – Suggests Common Sense Alternatives to Powerless Christianity"; Press Release; 2008; <http://www.steveandkathygray.com/whatshappening/religiousChallenge.php?press=1>; p. 1 of 10/17/2008 3:57 PM printout.

[24] Rusty Leonard and Warren Cole Smith, "Profound Witness, Giving Money in Tough Times Says Much about Christian Security," *World* magazine, January 31, 2009, p. 64.

[25] Audrey Barrick; "Most Protestants Fall Short of Spiritual Maturity"; Christian Post; 10/14/2008 3:19 PM EDT; <http://www.christianpost.com/article/print/20081014/most-protestants-fall-short-of-spiritual-maturity-pageall.htm>; p. 1 of 10/14/2008 3:27 PM printout.

[26] L. Gregory Jones, "Faith Matters: Undermanaged," *Christian Century*, August 11, 2009, p. 35.

[27] Mark Oppenheimer, "The Utility of Peter Singer: Who Lives? Who Dies?" *Christian Century*, July 3-10, 2002, pp. 24,

[28] Peter Singer, *The Life You Can Save: Acting Now to End World Poverty* (New York: Random House, 2009), pp. 52-53.

[29] Val J. Peter, *Seven Secular Challenges Facing 21st Century Catholics* (New York: Paulist Press, 2009), p. 118.

[30] Aldous Huxley, *Brave New World and Brave New World Revisited* (New York: Harper Perennial, 2005), p. 162.

[31] Eric Frazier, "Easing Their Burdens: New Efforts Seek to Assist Stressed-out Clergy Members," *The Chronicle of Philanthropy*, November 29, 2007, p. 23.

[32] Lindsay Perna, "Many Clergy Vulnerable to Health Insurance Loss," a Religion News Service article appearing in *Christian Century*, August 25, 2009, p. 16.

[33] Sarah Eekhoff Zylstra, "Church Life: Blessed Insurance, Many Pastors Lack Access to Adequate Health Benefits," *Christianity Today*, August 2008, p. 14, and Frazier, "Easing Their Burdens: New Efforts Seek to Assist Stressed-out Clergy Members," p. 23.

[34] "Denominational Research Report: Indiana Kentucky UCC Clergy Financial Issues," *Review of Religious Research 2009*, June 2009, Volume 50(4), p. 481.

[35] Ronsvalle, *Behind the Stained Glass Windows*, p. 56.

[36] Frank S. Page, "The Maginot Line," *SBC Life*, August 2007, p. 3.

[37] *There Will Be Blood*, writer and director Paul Thomas Anderson, producers Paul Thomas Anderson, Daniel Lupi, Joanne Sellar, Paramount Vantage and Miramax Films, 2007.

[38] A. W. Tozer; "The Inseparability of Faith and Obedience"; Christian Post; 11/17/2008 4:46 PM EST; <http://www.christianpost.com/article/20081117/the-inseparability-of-faith-and-obedience.htm>; p. 1 of 11/18/2008 7:56 AM printout.

[39] Bishop and Green, *Philanthrocapitalism*, pp. 48-49.

[40] Marvin Olasky, "Nothing to Fear," *World* magazine, December 13/20, 2008, p. 27.

[41] Micah Challenge Teleconference; September 22, 2008; <http://www.micahchallenge.us/press_files/press_teleconference.zip>; transcribed from <080922_press_teleconf.Michah.mp3> on 8/21/2009.

[42] "Hunger+Thirst"; Willow Creek Church; n.d.; http://www.willowcreek.org/coh/challenge/>; accessed 8/23/09 11:18 AM. See also <http://www.willowcreeknorthshore.org/compassion/celebration-of-hope/>; accessed 8/23/2009 11:16 AM.

[43] Kay Warren, "Needed: More 'Miracles'," *Christianity Today*, December 2008, p. 57.

44 Junior Achievement; "2008 JA Worldwide®/Deloitte Teen Ethics Survey"; October 2008; <http://ja.org/files/polls/2008-JA-Deloitte-Teen-Ethics-Survey-Data.pdf>; pp. 1-4 of August 23, 2009 3:45 PM printout.

45 Josephson Institute Center for Youth Ethics; "The Ethics of American Youth — 2008 Summary"; 2009; <http://charactercounts.org/programs/reportcard/index.html>; pp. 1-2 of 8/23/2009 5:36 PM printout.

46 Christian retailers are serving an older clientele; as author and speaker Josh McDowell was quoted as saying at a Christian retailers convention, "there is an onslaught of young people leaving the Church because they don't believe it's true or relevant." Lillian Kwon; "Christian Retailers, Publishers Convene for 60th Convention"; Christian Post; 7/13/2009 12:43 PM EDT; <http://www.christianpost.com/article/20090713/Christian-retailers-publishers-convene-for-60th-convention/index.html>; p. 1 of 7/21/2009 8:31 AM printout. A 2009 Pew research poll found that "one-fourth of Americans ages 18-29 said they were atheists, agnostics or had no religion." "Poll: 'Religion Gap' Growing," a Catholic News Service article appearing in *The (Peoria, Ill.) Catholic Post*, July 5, 2009, p. 3, col. 1-3. Harvard political scientist Robert Putnam, discussing findings from the new book he coauthored with David Campbell of Notre Dame, stated that youth are " 'vastly more secular…That is a stunning development…The youth are the future. Some of them are going to get religious over time, but most of them are not." Daniel Burke, a Religion News Service story appearing as "Congregants Make Better Citizens, Says New Study," in *Christian Century*, 6/16/2009, p. 16.

47 John Hall; "Christian 'Brand' Turning Off Younger Generation, Author Insists"; Baptist Standard; 10/16/2008; <http://baptiststandard.com/index2.php?option=com_content&task=view&id=8652&pop=1&page=01&Itemid=53>; p. 1 of 10/24/2008 10:38 AM printout.

48 Daniel Burke, *The Christian Century*, 6/16/2009, p. 16.

49 Lisa Lambert; "Cost of Locking Up Americans Too High: Pew Study"; Reuters; 3/2/2009 2:49 PM EST; <http://www.reuters.com/articlePrint?articleId=USTRE5215TW20090302>; pp. 1, 2 of 3/2/2009 3:42 PM printout.

50 Don Dodson, "Prof, Son Reveal Keys to Happiness," *The Champaign (Ill.) News-Gazette*, 10/21/2008, p. A-3, col. 1-4.

51 The Supreme Pontiff Benedict XVI; *Caritas In Veritate*; Libreria Editrice Vaticana; 6/29/2009; <http://www.vatican.va/holy_father/benefict_xvi/encyclicals/documents/hf_ben-xvi_enc_20090629_caritas-in-veritate_en.html>; pp. 5-6 of 8/15/2009 2:52 PM printout.

52 Ronsvalle, *The State of Church Giving through 2006*.

53 "Millennium Development Goals: About the Goals"; World Bank; 2004; <http://ddpext.worldbank.org/ext/MDG/homePges.do>; pp.1-2 of 4/19/2005 8:36 AM printout.

54 Mark Newman; "Images of the Social and Economic World"; 2006; <http://www-personal.umich.edu/~mejn/cartograms/>; pp. 2-3 of 8/27/2009 10:30 AM printout.

55 Peter Singer, *The Life You Can Save*, pp. 115.

56 Bill & Melinda Gates Foundation; "Grantmaking Stages – Step One: Develop Strategy"; 2009; <http://www.gatesfoundation.org/about/Pages/our-approach-step-one-develop-strategy.aspx>; p. 1 of 8/27/2009 11:52 AM printout.

57 *The State of the World's Children 2009* (New York: UNICEF, December 2008), pp. 118-21.

58 *Countdown to 2015: Maternal, Newborn & Child Survival; Tracking Progress in Maternal, Newborn & Child Survival: the 2008 Report*; UNICEF; 4/2/2008; <http://www.childinfo.org/files/Countdown2015Publication.pdf>; pp. i-xi and 1-207 of 5/5/2009 printout.

59 Karin Stenberg, Benjamin Johns, Robert W. Scherpbier, & Tessa Tan-Torres Edejer; "A Financial Road Map to Scaling Up Essential Child Health Interventions in 75 Countries"; Bulletin of the World Health Organization; April 2007, 85 (4); <http://www.who.int/bulletin/volumes/85/4/06-032052.pdf>; p. 1 of 8/8/2009 printout.

[60] "Guinea Worm 'Almost Eradicated'"; BBC News; 12/6/2008 11:13 GMT; <http://news.bbc.co.uk/2/hi/africa/7768871.stm>; p. 1 of 12/8/2008 9:23 AM printout.

[61] S. Michael Craven; "Sending Our Children"; Christian Post; 8/17/2009 10:33 EDT; <http://www.christianpost.com/article/20090817/sending-our-children/pageall.html>; pp. 1, 2 of 8/17/2009 5:21 PM printout.

[62] James A. Scherer, "Edinburgh II — A New Springtime for Ecumenical Mission?" *International Bulletin of Missionary Research*, Vol. 31, No. 4, October 2007, pp. 195, 196.

[63] Kenneth Scott Latourette, *A History of Christianity* (New York: Harper & Brothers, 1953), p. 1163.

[64] Ronsvalle, *Behind the Stained Glass Windows*, pp. 184-185.

[65] Associated Press, "Afghanistan: Opium Addiction Enveloping Whole Families," appearing in *The Champaign (Ill.) News-Gazette*, 8/10/2009, p. A-6, col. 1-5.

[66] For a review of the early *Yearbook* series, see John Ronsvalle and Sylvia Ronsvalle; "Giving Trends and the Church's Priorities"; *The State of Church Giving through 2003*, empty tomb, inc.; 2005; <http://www.emptytomb.org/SCG03Priorities.pdf>; pp. 107-111.

[67] David Broder, "Outgoing Health Chief Has Good Advice for Successor," *The Champaign (Ill.) News-Gazette*, 1/16/2009, p. A-6, col. 1-3.

[68] Eric Young; "Bible Translators Campaign Draws Over $117M in Support"; Christian Post; 4/13/2009 8:28 AM; <http://www.christianpost.com/Mission/Non-Profit/2009/04/bible-translators-campaign-draws-over-117m-in-support-13/print.html>; p. 1 of 4/14/2008 8:38 AM printout.

[69] Allie Martin; "Bible Translators Combat Malaria Spread"; OneNewsNow.com; 9/4/2008 8:50 AM; <http://www.onenewsnow.com/Printer.aspx?id=238546>; p. 1 of 9/4/2008 9:48 AM printout.

[70] Jennifer Riley; "Anonymous Donor Gives $50M to Translate Bible"; Christian Post; 11/14/2008 2:15 EST; <http://www.christianpost.com/article/print/20081114/anonymous-donor-gives-50m-to-translate-bible.htm>; p. 1 of 11/14/2008 2:00 PM printout.

[71] "Within Reach": Wycliffe Last Languages Campaign; n.d.; <http://www.lastlanguagescampaign.org/LLC/LLCmain/WithinReach.aspx>; p. 1 of 11/14/2008 2:31 PM printout.

[72] "There Has Been Great Support: More Is Needed": Wycliffe Last Languages Campaign; n.d.; <http://www.lastlanguagescampaign.org/LLC/LLCmain/GreatSupport.aspx>; p. 1 of 11/14/2008 2:19 PM printout.

[73] Jennifer Riley; "Anonymous Donor Gives $50M to Translate Bible"; p. 1 of 11/14/2008 2:00 PM printout.

[74] Eric Young; "Bible Translators Campaign Draws Over $117M in Support; p. 1 of 4/14/2008 8:38 AM printout.

[75] Jennifer Riley; "Anonymous Donor Gives $50M to Translate Bible"; p. 1 of 11/14/2008 2:00 PM printout.

[76] "Within Reach": Wycliffe Last Languages Campaign; p. 1 of 11/14/2008 2:31 PM printout.

[77] Bishop and Green, *Philanthrocapitalism*, p. 52.

[78] Staff; "SBC Cooperative Program: A Sacred Effort"; Baptist Press; 4/24/2009; <http://www.bpnews.net/printerfriendly.asp?ID=30289>; pp. 1, 2 of 4/27/2009 3:43 PM printout.

[79] John D. Floyd and Jerry A. Rankin; "International Mission Board, One Hundred Sixty-Third Annual Report"; Annual of the 2008 Southern Baptist Convention; 9/16/2008; < http://sbcec.org/bor/2008/default.asp>; pp. 159 of 8/24/2009 printout. An article on a March 2007 IMB trustees meeting noted: "By the end of the decade, Rankin hopes to see 10,000 Southern Baptist churches involved in strategic partnerships overseas. Other goals include expanding the missionary force from a little more than 5,000 to 8.000 and engaging unreached people groups." Shawn Hendricks; "Lottie Moon Set to Break Record"; Baptist Press; 3/23/2007; <http://www.bpnews/printerfriendly.asp?ID=25243>; p. 1 of 3/26/2007 8:21 AM printout.

[80] "The SBC Exhibit Hall," *SBC Life*, June/July 2008, p. 6.

[81] "How Missions Is Funded"; Southern Baptist Convention International Missions Board; 2009; <http://www.imb.org/main/give/page.asp?StoryID=4426&LanguageID=1709>; p. 2 of 7/13/2009 5:01 PM printout.

[82] The 2008 SBC membership was published as 16,228,438. "Annual Church Profile: 2008 Southern Baptist Convention Statistical Summary"; SBC LifeWay Christian Resources; n.d.; <http://www.lifeway.com/lwc/images/lwcl_corp_news_SCP2008_HR.jpg>; p. 1 of 7/14/2009 3:31 PM printout.

[83] "Your Missions funding Questions Answered"; SBC; 2009; <http://www.imb.org/main/give/page.asp?StoryID=4427&LanguageID=1709>; p. 1 of 5/26/2009 8:43 AM printout.

[84] Art Toalston, "The SBC Exhibit Hall," *SBC Life*, June/July 2008, p. 1.

[85] "Your Missions Funding Questions Answered"; SBC; p. 1 of 5/26/2009 8:43 AM printout.

[86] David Steverson; "First Person: A Time for Humility & Thanks"; Baptist Press; 8/14/2009; <http://www.bpnews.net/printerfriendly.asp?ID=31802>; p. 1 of 8/16/2009 12:01 PM printout.

[87] Paul Chitwood; "History Suggests Sacrifice for Lottie Moon Offering Needed Now"; Baptist Press; 12/1/2008; <http://bpnews.net/printerfriendly.asp?ID=29435>; p. 1 of 12/2/2008 8:30 AM printout.

[88] Don Graham; "Lottie Shortfall Leaves Missionaries on Hold"; Baptist Press; 8/14/2009; <http://www.bpnews.net/printer/friendly.asp?ID=31803>; pp. 1, 2 of 8/15/2009 9:47 AM printout.

[89] Tammi Reed Ledbetter, "Increased CP Support Unfolding Nationwide," *SBC Life*, December 2006, p. 8.

[90] Tammi Reed Ledbetter, "Increased CP Support Unfolding Nationwide," p. 8.

[91] The figure of $40,931.64 cost per missionary may not include all IMB support service costs: "These adjustments are vital since 70 percent of the organization's budget and financial resources go toward the support of missionary personnel, IMB officials said." Shawn Hendricks & Erich Bridges; "Trustees: Troubled Economy Causes IMB to Scale Back Missionary Appointments"; Baptist Press; 5/21/2009; http://www.bpnews.net/printerfriendly.asp?ID=30535; p. 2 of 5/22/2009 9:01 AM printout. If the $40,931.64 figure represents only 70% of the full cost for each of the additional 2,800 missionaries, the total additional funds needed for both direct missionary support and the IMB support services for 2,800 would total $164 million instead of $114.6 million.

[92] Trennis Henderson; "Cooperative Program Definition Sparks Messenger Debate"; Kentucky Western Recorder; 6/13/2007; <http://www.biblicalrecorcder.org/content/news/2007/06_13_2007/ne130607cooperative.shtml>; p. 1 of 8/21/07 8:15 AM printout.

[93] Executive Committee "Trend in Giving"; Annual of the 2008 Southern Baptist Convention; 9/16/2008; <http://sbcec.org/bor/2008/default.asp >; p. 109 of 7/14/2009 printout.

[94] Jeff Robinson; "Mohler: SBC Must Be Willing to Change or Face Decline"; Baptist Press; 8/20/2009; <http://www.bpnews.not/printfriendly.asp?ID=31110>; p. 3 of 8/21/2009 9:19 AM printout.

[95] John L. Yeats; "First Person: New Fuel Needed"; Baptist Press; 8/6/2009; <http://www.bpnews.net/printerfriendly.asp?ID=31030>; p. 1, 2 of 8/6/2009 5:15 PM printout.

[96] The Lottie Moon Christmas Offering totals were found in the following documents:

1979-1997: *SBC Life*, December 1998, p. 3.

1998-2000: "Lottie Moon Christmas Offering Receipts: 1994-2001"; International Mission Board, Southern Baptist Convention; published 2002; <http://www.imb.org/core/results7.htm>; p. 1 of 10/30/2002 2:42 PM printout.

2001: "Fast Facts: Lottie Moon Christmas Offering: Amount Southern Baptists Gave to the Offering in 2001"; International Mission Board, Southern Baptist Convention; published 2002; <http://www.imb.org/lmco/fastfacts.asp>; p. 1 of 10/30/2002 2:39 PM printout.

2002: "Fast Facts: LMCO receipts for Christmas 2002"; International Mission Board, Southern Baptist Convention; published 2003; <http://www.imb.org/core/fastfacts.asp>; p. 1 of 9/9/2003 4:43 PM printout.

2003: "Fast Facts: LMCO receipts for Christmas 2003"; International Mission Board, Southern Baptist Convention; published 2003; <http://www.imb.org/core/fastfacts.asp>; p. 1 of 7/29/2004 10:40 AM printout.

2004: "Fast Facts: LMCO receipts for Christmas 2004"; International Mission Board, Southern Baptist Convention; published 2005; <http://www.imb.org/core/fastfacts.asp>; p. 1 of 8/11/2006 10:40 AM printout.

2005: Don Graham; "Southern Baptist giving breaks Lottie Moon record, hits 'historic' high of $137.9 million;" Baptist Press; published June 2, 2006; <http://www.bpnews.net/bpnews.asp?ID=23381>; p. 1 of 6/3/2006 7:25 AM printout.

2006: Shawn Hendricks; "Record $150 million offering to result in more missionaries"; Baptist Press; published June 5, 2007; <http://www.bpnews.net/printerfriendly.asp?ID=25786>; p. 1 of 1/2/2008 11:22 AM printout.

2007: Erich Bridges; "Lottie Moon offering gifts total $150.4 million for missions"; Baptist Press; published June 5, 2008; <http://www.bpnews.net/printerfriendly.asp?ID=28206>; p. 1 of 8/20/2008 1:23 PM printout.

2008: Shawn Hendricks; "141M Lottie Moon offering short of goal"; Baptist Press; published June 4, 2009; <http://www.bpnews.net/printerfriendly.asp?ID=30616>; p. 1 of 6/5/2009 9:43 AM printout.

[97] Karen L. Willoughby; "Korean Baptists Reach Goal 1 Year Early"; Baptist Press; 6/30/2009; <http://www.bpnews.net/printerfriendly.asp?ID=30804>; p. 1 of 6/30/2009 5:54 PM printout.

[98] "Final 2008: Primary worship attendance: 6,184,317" and "Final 2008: Churches: 44,848" from: "2008 Southern Baptist Convention Statistical Summary"; Annual Church Profile; LifeWay Christian Resources Technology Division, Southern Baptist Convention; <http://www.lifeway.com/lwc/images/lwcl_corp_news_ACP2008_HR.jpg>; p. 1 of 7/14/2009 3:31 PM printout.

[99] James A. Smith Sr.; "GCR: Akin Discusses Its History, Intent"; Baptist Press; 5/5/2009; <http://www.bpnews.net/printerfriendly.asp?ID=30430>; pp. 1, 2 of 5/6/2009 9:13 AM printout.

[100] Tammi Reed Ledbetter, "There's Gold in Them There Pews," p. 2.

[101] Staff; "Hunt: SBC Needed 'Shock' of GCR Declaration"; Baptist Press; 5/19/2009; <http://www.bpnews.net/printerfriendly.asp?ID=30522>; pp. 2, 3 of 5/20/2009 9:15 AM printout.

[102] Mark Kelly; "GCR: Signers of the Document Say 'Great Commission Resurgence' Needed"; 5/5/2009; <http://www.bpnews.net/printerfriendly.asp?ID=30424>; p. 1, 2 of 5/6/2009 9:12 AM printout.

[103] Mark Kelly; "GCR's Floyd: Take 'Honest Look" at SBC"; Baptist Press; 8/26/2009; <http://www.bpnews.net/printerfriendly.asp?ID=31145>; p. 1 of 8/26/2009 6:47 PM printout.

[104] Michel Foust, "Southern Baptist Convention Wrap-Up: Love Loud: Actions Speak Louder Than Words," *SBC Life*, August/September 2009, p. 5.

[105] Baptist Press reports, "A Great Commission Resurgence," *SBC Life*, August-September 2009, p. 1.

[106] Tammi Reed Ledbetter, "There's Gold in Them There Pews," p. 2.

[107] Staff; "Hunt: SBC Needed 'Shock' of GCR Declaration"; p. 3 of 5/20/2009 9:15 AM printout.

[108] "Business and Financial Plan"; Southern Baptist Convention; 2009; <http://www.sbc.net/aboutus/legal/bussfinanceplan.asp>; pp. 1, 2 of 8/24/2009 7:08 PM printout.

[109] "Business and Financial Plan"; Southern Baptist Convention; p. 3.

[110] "Who's Missing? Whose Mission?"; SBC IMB; 2009; <http://www.imb.org/main/give/page.asp?StoryID=5523&LanguageID=1709>; p. 1 of 8/29/2009 8:30 PM printout.

[111] "Business and Financial Plan"; Southern Baptist Convention; p. 3.

[112] Ronsvalle, *The State of Church Giving through 2006*, pp. 125-126, 127-128.

[113] The figure of $481 million represents the cost estimate to address malaria to prevent under-5 child deaths. An article in the World Health Organization *Bulletin* estimated an average annual cost of $3.8 to $4.5 billion a year to reach agreed-on targets for malaria control for entire global populations, citing "optimistic and pessimistic scenarios." Anthony Kiszewski, et al.; "Estimated Global Resources Needed to Attain International Malaria Control Goals"; *Bulletin of the World Health Organization*; 8/8/2007; <http://www.who.int/bulletin/volumes/85/8/06-039529/en/index. html>; p. 4 of 8/9/2009 12:33 PM printout.

[114] "The Yoking Map"; empty tomb, inc.; <www.emptytomb.org/yoking.html>.

[115] Marvin Olasky, "Wealth Effects, Passionate Lives 2: Roberta Green Ahmanson on Poverty, Affluence, Faith, Art, and Journalism," *World* magazine, March 28, 2009, p. 26.

[116] John Markhoff; "Scientists Worry Machines May Outsmart Man"; The New York Times; 7/25/2009; <http://www.nytimes.com/2009/07/26/schience/26robot.html?_r=2&hp>; p. 1 of 7/26/2009 11:22 AM printout.

[117] Alexander G. Higgins, "Particle Collider: Black Hole or Crucial Machine?" an Associated Press story appearing in *The Champaign (Ill.) News-Gazette*, 8/10/2009, p. A-11, col. 1-6.

[118] Carol Glatz, "Pope: Greed Is at Root of the Economic Crisis," *The (Peoria, Ill.) Catholic Post*, Sunday, April 26, 2009, p. 3, col. 1-3.

[119] Peter Singer, *The Life You Can Save*, p. 159.

[120] Warren Cole Smith, "Fearing Not," *World* magazine, March 14, 2009, p. 68.

[121] Dean Young and John Marshall, "Blondie," and Chip Sansom, "The Born Loser," appearing in *The Champaign (Ill.) News-Gazette*, April 30, 2009, p. C-5.

APPENDIXES

APPENDIX A: *List of Denominations*

Church Member Giving, 1968-2007, Composite Set

American Baptist Churches in the U.S.A.
The American Lutheran Church (through 1986)
Associate Reformed Presbyterian Church
  (General Synod)
Brethren in Christ Church
Christian Church (Disciples of Christ)
Church of God (Anderson, Ind.) (through 1997)
Church of God General Conference (Oregon, Ill., and
  Morrow, Ga.)
Church of the Brethren
Church of the Nazarene
Conservative Congregational Christian Conference
Cumberland Presbyterian Church
Evangelical Congregational Church
Evangelical Covenant Church
Evangelical Lutheran Church in America
  The American Lutheran Church (merged 1987)
  Lutheran Church in America (merged 1987)
Evangelical Lutheran Synod
Fellowship of Evangelical Bible Churches
Fellowship of Evangelical Churches (formerly
  Evangelical Mennonite Church)
Free Methodist Church of North America
Friends United Meeting (through 1990)
General Association of General Baptists
Lutheran Church in America (through 1986)
Lutheran Church-Missouri Synod
Mennonite Church USA (1999)
  Mennonite Church (merged 1999)
  Mennonite Church, General Conference (merged
  1999)
Moravian Church in America, Northern Province
North American Baptist Conference (through 2006)
The Orthodox Presbyterian Church
Presbyterian Church (U.S.A.)
Reformed Church in America
Seventh-day Adventist Church, North American Division of
Southern Baptist Convention
United Church of Christ
Wisconsin Evangelical Lutheran Synod

Church Member Giving, 2006–2007

The Composite Set Denominations included in the
  1968-2007 analysis with data available for both
  years, plus the following:
Allegheny Wesleyan Methodist Connection
The Antiochian Orthodox Christian Archdiocese
Baptist Missionary Association of America
Bible Fellowship Church
Brethren Church (Ashland, Ohio)
Christ Comunity Church (Evangelical-Protestant)
Christian and Missionary Alliance
Church of Christ (Holiness) U.S.A.
Church of the Lutheran Brethren of America
Church of the Lutheran Confession
Churches of God General Conference
The Episcopal Church
International Pentecostal Holiness Church
Missionary Church, The
Presbyterian Church in America
Primitive Methodist Church in the U.S.A.
The United Methodist Church
The Wesleyan Church

By Organizational Affiliation: NAE, 1968-2007

Brethren in Christ Church
Church of the Nazarene
Conservative Congregational Christian Conference
Evangelical Congregational Church
Fellowship of Evangelical Bible Churches
Fellowship of Evangelical Churches (formerly
  Evangelical Mennonite Church)
Free Methodist Church of North America
General Association of General Baptists

By Organizational Affiliation: NCC, 1968-2007

American Baptist Churches in the U.S.A.
Christian Church (Disciples of Christ)
Church of the Brethren
Evangelical Lutheran Church in America
Moravian Church in America, Northern Province
Presbyterian Church (U.S.A.)
Reformed Church in America
United Church of Christ

11 Denominations, 1921-2007

American Baptist (Northern)
Christian Church (Disciples of Christ)
Church of the Brethren
The Episcopal Church
Evangelical Lutheran Church in America
  The American Lutheran Church
    American Lutheran Church
    The Evangelical Lutheran Church
    United Evangelical Lutheran Church
    Lutheran Free Church
  Evangelical Lutheran Churches, Assn. of
  Lutheran Church in America
    United Lutheran Church
      General Council Evangelical Lutheran Ch.
      General Synod of Evangelical Lutheran Ch.
      United Synod Evangelical Lutheran South
    American Evangelical Lutheran Church
    Augustana Lutheran Church
    Finnish Lutheran Church (Suomi Synod)
Moravian Church in America, Northern Province
Presbyterian Church (U.S.A.)
  United Presbyterian Church in the U.S.A.
    Presbyterian Church in the U.S.A.
    United Presbyterian Church in North America
  Presbyterian Church in the U.S.
Reformed Church in America
Southern Baptist Convention
United Church of Christ
  Congregational Christian
    Congregational
  Evangelical and Reformed
    Evangelical Synod of North America/German
    Reformed Church in the U.S.
The United Methodist Church
  The Evangelical United Brethren
  The Methodist Church
    Methodist Episcopal Church
    Methodist Episcopal Church South
    Methodist Protestant Church

Trends in Membership, 11 Mainline Protestant Denominations, 1968-2007

American Baptist Churches in the U.S.A.
Christian Church (Disciples of Christ)
Church of the Brethren
The Episcopal Church
Evangelical Lutheran Church in America

Friends United Meeting
Moravian Church in America, Northern Prov.
Presbyterian Church (U.S.A.)
Reformed Church in America
United Church of Christ
The United Methodist Church

Trends in Membership, 15 Evangelical Denominations, 1968-2007

Assemblies of God
Baptist General Conference
Brethren in Christ Church
Christian and Missionary Alliance
Church of God (Cleveland, Tenn.)
Church of the Nazarene
Conservative Congregational Christian Conference
Evangelical Congregational Church
Fellowship of Evangelical Churches (formerly
  Evangelical Mennonite Church)
Fellowship of Evangelical Bible Churches
Free Methodist Church of North America
General Association of General Baptists
Lutheran Church-Missouri Synod
Salvation Army
Southern Baptist Convention

Trends in Membership, 37 Protestant Denominations and the Roman Catholic Church, 1968-2007

11 Mainline Protestant Denominations (above)
15 Evangelical Denominations (above)
The Roman Catholic Church
11 Additional Composite Denominations:
Associate Reformed Presbyterian Church (General
  Synod)
Church of God (Anderson, Ind.)
Church of God General Conference (Oregon, Ill.
  and Morrow, Ga.)
Cumberland Presbyterian Church
Evangelical Covenant Church
Evangelical Lutheran Synod
Mennonite Church USA
North American Baptist Conference
The Orthodox Presbyterian Church
Seventh-day Adventist Church, North American
  Division of
Wisconsin Evangelical Lutheran Synod

APPENDIX B SERIES: *Denominational Data Tables*

Introduction

The data in the following tables is from the *Yearbook of American and Canadian Churches* (*YACC*) series unless otherwise noted. Financial data is presented in current dollars.

Data in italics indicates a change from the previous edition in *The State of Church Giving* (*SCG*) series.

The Appendix B tables are described below.

Appendix B-1, Church Member Giving, 1968-2007: This table presents aggregate data for the denominations which comprise the data set analyzed for the 1968 through 2007 period.

Elements of this data are also used for the analyses in chapters two through seven.

In Appendix B-1, the data for the Presbyterian Church (U.S.A.) combined data for the United Presbyterian Church in the U.S.A. and the Presbyterian Church in the United States for the period 1968 through 1982. These two communions merged to become the Presbyterian Church (U.S.A.) in 1983, data for which is presented for 1983 through 2007.

Also in Appendix B-1, data for the Evangelical Lutheran Church in America (ELCA) appears beginning in 1987. Before that, the two major component communions that merged into the ELCA—the American Lutheran Church and the Lutheran Church in America—are listed as individual denominations from 1968 through 1986.

In the Appendix B series, the denomination listed as the Fellowship of Evangelical Bible Churches was named the Evangelical Mennonite Brethren Church prior to July 1987.

For 1999, the Mennonite Church (Elkhart, IN) provided information for the Mennonite Church USA. This communion is the result of a merger passed at a national convention in July 2001 between the Mennonite Church and the Mennonite Church, General Conference. The latter's 1968-1998 data has been added to the composite set series. The Mennonite Church USA dollar figures for 1999, and membership through 2001, combine data for the two predecessor communions.

The 1999, 2000, 2001, and 2002 data for the Southern Baptist Convention used in the 1968-2007 analysis includes data only for those State Conventions that provided a breakdown of total contributions between Congregational Finances and Benevolences for that year. For the 11 Denominations 1921-2007 analysis, 1999, 2000, 2001, and 2002, Southern Baptist Convention Total Contributions is $7,772,452,961, $8,437,177,940, $8,935,013,659, and $9,461,603,271 respectively. For the 11 Denominations 1921-2007 analysis, and the Membership Trends analysis, 1999, 2000, 2001, and 2002, Southern Baptist Convention Membership is 15,581,756, 15,960,308, 16,052,920, and 16,137,736 respectively.

Data for the American Baptist Churches in the U.S.A. has been obtained directly from the denominational office as follows. In discussions with the American Baptist Churches Office of Planning Resources, it became apparent that there had been no distinction made between the membership of congregations reporting financial data, and total membership for the denomination, when reporting data to the *Yearbook of American and Canadian Churches*. Records were obtained from the denomination for a smaller membership figure that reflected only those congregations reporting financial data. While this revised membership data provided a more useful per member giving figure for Congregational Finances, the total Benevolences figure reported to the *YACC*, while included in the present data set, does reflect contributions to some Benevolences categories from 100% of the American Baptist membership. The membership reported in Appendix B-1 for the American Baptist Churches is the membership for congregations reporting financial data, rather than the total membership figure provided in editions of the *YACC*. However, in the sections that consider membership as a percentage of population, the Total Membership figure for the American Baptist Churches is used.

Appendix B-2, Church Member Giving for 44 Denominations, 2006-2007: Appendix B-2 presents the Full or Confirmed Membership, Congregational Finances and Benevolences data for the 15 additional denominations included in the 2006-2007 comparison.

Appendix B-3, Church Member Giving for 11 Denominations, 1921-2007: This appendix presents additional data which is not included in Appendix B-1 for the 11 Denominations.

The data from 1921 through 1928 in Appendix B-3.1 is taken from summary information contained in the *Yearbook of American Churches, 1949 Edition*, George F. Ketcham, ed. (Lebanon, PA: Sowers Printing Company, 1949, p. 162). The summary membership data provided is for Inclusive Membership. Therefore, giving as a percentage of income for the years 1921 through 1928 may have been somewhat higher had Full or Confirmed Membership been used. The list of denominations that are summarized for this period is presented in the *Yearbook of American Churches, 1953 Edition*, Benson Y. Landis, ed. (New York: National Council of the Churches of Christ in the U.S.A., 1953, p. 274).

The data from 1929 through 1952 is taken from summary information presented in the *Yearbook of American Churches, Edition for 1955*, Benson Y. Landis, ed. (New York: National Council of the Churches of Christ in the U.S.A., 1954, pp. 286-287). A description of the list of denominations included in the 1929 through 1952 data summary on page 275 of the *YACC Edition for 1955* indicated that the Moravian Church, Northern Province is not included in the 1929 through 1952 data.

The data in Appendix B-3.2 for 1953 through 1964 was obtained for the indicated denominations from the relevant edition of the *YACC* series. Giving as a percentage of income was derived for these years by dividing the published Total Contributions figure by the published Per Capita figure to produce a membership figure for each denomination. The Total Contributions figures for the denominations were added to produce an aggregated Total Contributions figure. The calculated membership figures were also added to produce an aggregated membership figure. The aggregated Total Contributions figure was then divided by the aggregated membership figure to yield a per member giving figure which was used in calculating giving as a percentage of income.

Data for the years 1965 through 1967 was not available in a form that could be readily analyzed for the present purposes, and therefore data for these three years was estimated by dividing the change in per capita Total Contributions from 1964 to 1968 by four, the number of years in this interval, and cumulatively adding the result to the base year of 1964 and the succeeding years of 1965 and 1966 to obtain estimates for the years 1965 through 1967.

In most cases, this procedure was also applied to individual denominations to avoid an artificially low total due to missing data. If data was not available for a specific year, the otherwise blank entry was filled in with a calculation based on surrounding years for the denomination. For example, this procedure was used for the American Baptist Churches for the years 1955 and 1996, the Christian Church (Disciples of Christ) for the years 1955 and 1959, and the Evangelical United Brethren, later to merge into The United Methodist Church, for the years 1957, 1958 and 1959. Data for the Methodist Church was changed for 1957 in a similar manner.

Available Total Contributions and Full or Confirmed Members data for The Episcopal Church and The United Methodist Church for 1968 through 2007 is presented in Appendix B-3.3. These two communions are included in the 11 Denominations. The United Methodist Church was created in 1968 when the Methodist Church and the Evangelical United Brethren Church merged. While the Methodist Church filed summary data for the year 1968, the Evangelical United Brethren Church did not. Data for these denominations was calculated as noted in the appendix. However, since the 1968 data for The Methodist Church would not have been comparable to the 1985 and 2007 data for The United Methodist Church, this communion was not included in the more focused 1968-2007 composite analysis.

Appendix B-4, Membership for Seven Denominations, 1968-2007: This appendix presents denominational membership data used in the membership analyses presented in chapter five that is not available in the other appendices. Unless otherwise indicated, the data is from the *YACC* series.

Appendix B-5, Overseas Missions Income, 2003, 2004, 2005, 2006, and 2007: This appendix presents numbers provided on the four lines of the Overseas Missions Income form completed by the respective denominations. Also provided is Overseas Missions Income for three denominations which are not included in the analyses (see chapter 6, note 9).

Appendix B-6, Estimates of Giving: This appendix provides the data used in the comparison presented in chapter 7 of the Consumer Expenditure Survey, the Form 990 series, and the *Giving USA* series, for 1989-2005.

APPENDIX B-1: *Church Member Giving 1968-2007*

Key to Denominational Abbreviations: Data Years 1968-2007

Abbreviation	Denomination
abc	American Baptist Churches in the U.S.A.
alc	The American Lutheran Church
arp	Associate Reformed Presbyterian Church (General Synod)
bcc	Brethren in Christ Church
ccd	Christian Church (Disciples of Christ)
cga	Church of God (Anderson, IN)
cgg	Church of God General Conference (Oregon, IL and Morrow, GA)
chb	Church of the Brethren
chn	Church of the Nazarene
ccc	Conservative Congregational Christian Church
cpc	Cumberland Presbyterian Church
ecc	Evangelical Congregational Church
ecv	Evangelical Covenant Church
elc	Evangelical Lutheran Church in America
els	Evangelical Lutheran Synod
emc	Evangelical Mennonite Church
feb	Fellowship of Evangelical Bible Churches
fec	Fellowship of Evangelical Churches
fmc	Free Methodist Church of North America
fum	Friends United Meeting
ggb	General Association of General Baptists
lca	Lutheran Church in America
lms	Lutheran Church-Missouri Synod
mch	Mennonite Church
mgc	Mennonite Church, General Conference
mus	Mennonite Church USA
mca	Moravian Church in America, Northern Province
nab	North American Baptist Conference
opc	The Orthodox Presbyterian Church
pch	Presbyterian Church (U.S.A.)
rca	Reformed Church in America
sda	Seventh-day Adventist, North American Division of
sbc	Southern Baptist Convention
ucc	United Church of Christ
wel	Wisconsin Evangelical Lutheran Synod

Appendix B-1: Church Member Giving 1968-2007 (continued)

	Data Year 1968			Data Year 1969			Data Year 1970		
	Full/Confirmed Members	Congregational Finances	Benevolences	Full/Confirmed Members	Congregational Finances	Benevolences	Full/Confirmed Members	Congregational Finances	Benevolences
abc	1,179,848 a	95,878,267 a	21,674,924 a	1,153,785 a	104,084,322	21,111,333	1,231,944 a	112,668,310	19,655,391
alc	1,767,618	137,260,390	32,862,410	1,771,999	143,917,440	34,394,570	1,775,573	146,268,320	30,750,030
arp	28,312 a	2,211,002 a	898,430 a	28,273	2,436,936 a	824,628 a	28,427 a	2,585,974 a	806,071 a
bcc	8,954	1,645,256	633,200 a	9,145	1,795,859	817,445	9,300 a	2,037,330 a	771,940 a
ccd	994,683	105,803,222	21,703,947	936,931	91,169,842	18,946,815	911,964	98,671,692	17,386,032
cga	146,807	23,310,682	4,168,580	147,752	24,828,448	4,531,678	150,198	26,962,037	4,886,223
cgg	6,600	805,000	103,000	6,700	805,000	104,000	6,800	810,000	107,000
chb	187,957	12,975,829	4,889,727	185,198	13,964,158	4,921,991	182,614	14,327,896	4,891,618
chn	364,789	59,943,750 a	14,163,761 a	372,943	64,487,669 a	15,220,339 a	383,284	68,877,922 a	16,221,123 a
ccc	15,127	1,867,978	753,686	16,219	1,382,195	801,534	17,328	1,736,818	779,696
cpc	87,044 a	6,247,447 a	901,974 a	86,435 a	7,724,405 a	926,317 a	86,683 a	7,735,906 a	1,011,911 a
ecc	29,582 a	3,369,308 a	627,731 a	29,652 a	3,521,074 a	646,187 a	29,437 a	3,786,288 a	692,428 a
ecv	66,021	14,374,162 a	3,072,848	67,522	14,952,302 a	3,312,306	67,441	15,874,265 a	3,578,876
elc	ALC & LCA	ALC & LCA	ALC & LCA	ALC & LCA	ALC & LCA	ALC & LCA	ALC & LCA	ALC & LCA	ALC & LCA
els	10,886 a	844,235 a	241,949 a	11,079	1,003,746	315,325	11,030	969,625	242,831 a
emc	2,870 a	447,397	232,331	NA	NA	NA	NA	NA	NA
feb	1,712 a	156,789 a	129,818 a	3,324	389,000	328,000	3,698	381,877	706,398
fec	see EMC	see EMC	see EMC	see EMC	see EMC	see EMC	see EMC	see EMC	see EMC
fmc	47,831 a	12,032,016 a	2,269,677 a	47,954 a	13,187,506 a	2,438,351 a	64,901	9,641,202	7,985,264
fum	55,469	3,564,793	1,256,192	55,257	3,509,509	1,289,026	53,970	3,973,802	1,167,183
ggb	65,000	4,303,183 a	269,921 a	NA	NA	NA	NA	NA	NA
lca	2,279,383	166,337,149	39,981,858	2,193,321	161,958,669	46,902,225	2,187,015	169,795,380	42,118,870
lms	1,877,799	178,042,762	47,415,800	1,900,708	185,827,626	49,402,590	1,922,569	193,352,322	47,810,664
mch	85,682 a	7,078,164 a	5,576,305 a	85,343	7,398,182	6,038,730	83,747 a	7,980,917 a	6,519,476 a
mgc	36,337 a	2,859,340 a	2,668,138 a	35,613	2,860,555 a	2,587,079 a	35,536	3,091,670	2,550,208
mus	MCH & MGC	MCH & MGC	MCH & MGC	MCH & MGC	MCH & MGC	MCH & MGC	MCH & MGC	MCH & MGC	MCH & MGC
mca	27,772	2,583,354	444,910	27,617	2,642,529	456,182	27,173	2,704,105	463,219
nab	42,371 a	5,176,669 a	1,383,964 a	55,100	6,681,410	2,111,588	55,080	6,586,929	2,368,288
opc	9,197	1,638,437	418,102	9,276	1,761,242	464,660	9,401 a	1,853,627 a	503,572 a
pch	4,180,093	375,248,474	102,622,450	4,118,664	388,268,169	97,897,522	4,041,813	401,785,731	93,927,852
rca	226,819 b	25,410,489 b	9,197,642 b	224,992 b	27,139,579 b	9,173,312 b	223,353 b	29,421,849 b	9,479,503 b
sda	395,159 a	36,976,280	95,178,335	407,766	40,378,426	102,730,594	420,419	45,280,059	109,569,241
sbc	11,332,229 a	666,924,020 a	128,023,731 a	11,487,708	709,246,590	133,203,885	11,628,032	753,510,973	138,480,329
ucc	2,032,648 a	152,301,536	128,869,136	1,997,898	152,791,512	27,338,543	1,960,608	155,248,767	26,934,289
wel	259,649 a	18,982,244 a	6,572,250 a	264,710 a	20,761,838 a	6,414,099 a	270,073 a	22,525,244 a	6,781,600 a
Total	27,852,248	2,126,599,624	569,206,727	27,738,884	2,200,875,738	595,650,854	27,879,411	2,310,446,837	599,147,126

a Data obtained from denominational source.

b empty tomb review of RCA directory data.

Appendix B-1: Church Member Giving 1968-2007 (continued)

	Data Year 1971			Data Year 1972			Data Year 1973		
	Full/Confirmed Members	Congregational Finances	Benevolences	Full/Confirmed Members	Congregational Finances	Benevolences	Full/Confirmed Members	Congregational Finances	Benevolences
abc	1,223,735 a	114,673,805	18,878,769	1,176,092 a	118,446,573	18,993,440	1,190,455 a	139,357,611	20,537,388
alc	1,775,774	146,324,460	28,321,740	1,773,414	154,786,570	30,133,850	1,770,119	168,194,730	35,211,440
arp	28,443 a	2,942,577 a	814,703 a	28,711 a	3,329,446 a	847,665 a	28,763 a	3,742,773 a	750,387 a
bcc	9,550	2,357,786	851,725	9,730	2,440,400	978,957	9,877 a	2,894,622 a	1,089,879 a
ccd	884,929	94,091,862	17,770,799	881,467	105,763,511	18,323,685	868,895	112,526,538	19,800,843
cga	152,787	28,343,604	5,062,282	155,920	31,580,751	5,550,487	157,828	34,649,592	6,349,695
cgg	7,200	860,000	120,000	7,400	900,000	120,000	7,440	940,000	120,000
chb	181,183	14,535,274	5,184,768	179,641	14,622,319 c	5,337,277 c	179,333	16,474,758	6,868,927
chn	394,197	75,107,918 a	17,859,332 a	404,732	82,891,903 a	20,119,679 a	417,200	91,318,469 a	22,661,140 a
ccc	19,279 a	1,875,010 a	930,485 a	20,081 a	1,950,865 a	994,453 a	20,712 a	2,080,038 a	1,057,869 a
cpc	86,945 a	7,729,131 a	1,009,657 a	88,200 a	8,387,762 a	1,064,831 a	88,203 a	9,611,201 a	1,220,768 a
ecc	29,682 a	4,076,576 a	742,293 a	29,434 a	4,303,406 a	798,968 a	29,331 a	4,913,214 a	943,619 a
ecv	68,428	17,066,051 a	3,841,887	69,815	18,021,767 a	4,169,053	69,922	18,948,864 a	4,259,950
elc	ALC & LCA	ALC & LCA	ALC & LCA	ALC & LCA	ALC & LCA	ALC & LCA	ALC & LCA	ALC & LCA	ALC & LCA
els	11,426 a	1,067,650 a	314,335 a	11,532	1,138,953	295,941 a	12,525	1,296,326	330,052 a
emc	NA	NA	NA	NA	NA	NA	3,131	593,070	408,440
feb	NA	NA	NA	NA	NA	NA	NA	NA	NA
fec	see EMC	see EMC	see EMC	see EMC	see EMC	see EMC	see EMC	see EMC	see EMC
fmc	47,933 a	13,116,414 a	2,960,525 a	48,400 a	14,311,395 a	3,287,000 a	48,763 a	15,768,216 a	3,474,555 a
fum	54,522	3,888,064	1,208,062	54,927	4,515,463	1,297,088	57,690	5,037,848	1,327,439
ggb	NA	NA	NA	NA	NA	NA	NA	NA	NA
lca	2,175,378	179,570,467	43,599,913	2,165,591	188,387,949	45,587,481	2,169,341	200,278,486	34,627,978
lms	1,945,889	203,619,804	48,891,368	1,963,262	216,756,345	50,777,670	1,983,114	230,435,598	54,438,074
mch	88,522	8,171,316	7,035,750	89,505	9,913,176	7,168,664	90,967	9,072,858	6,159,740
mgc	36,314	3,368,100	2,833,491	36,129	3,378,372	3,219,439	36,483	3,635,418	3,392,844
mus	MCH & MGC	MCH & MGC	MCH & MGC	MCH & MGC	MCH & MGC	MCH & MGC	MCH & MGC	MCH & MGC	MCH & MGC
mca	26,101	2,576,172	459,447	25,500	2,909,252	465,316	25,468	3,020,667	512,424
nab	54,997	7,114,457	2,293,692	54,441	7,519,558	2,253,158	41,516	6,030,352	1,712,092
opc	9,536 a	2,054,448 a	533,324 a	9,741 a	2,248,969 a	602,328 a	9,940 a	2,364,079 a	658,534 a
pch	3,963,665	420,865,807	93,164,548	3,855,494	436,042,890	92,691,469	3,730,312 d	480,735,088 d	95,462,247 d
rca	219,915 b	32,217,319 b	9,449,655 b	217,583 b	34,569,874 b	9,508,818 b	212,906 b	39,524,443 b	10,388,619 b
sda	433,906	49,208,043	119,913,879	449,188	54,988,781	132,411,980	464,276	60,643,602	149,994,942
sbc	11,824,676	814,406,626	160,510,775	12,065,333	896,427,208	174,711,648	12,295,400	1,011,467,569	193,511,983
ucc	1,928,674	158,924,956	26,409,521	1,895,016	165,556,364	27,793,561	1,867,810	168,602,602	28,471,058
wel	274,635 a	24,315,801 a	7,456,829 a	277,628 a	26,585,530 a	8,204,262 a	282,355 a	29,377,447 a	8,623,460 a
Total	27,958,221	2,434,469,498	628,423,554	28,043,907	2,612,675,352	667,708,168	28,170,075	2,873,536,079	714,366,386

a Data obtained from denominational source.

b empty tomb review of RCA directory data.

c YACC Church of the Brethren figures reported for 15 months due to fiscal year change: adjusted here to 12/15ths.

d The Presbyterian Church (USA) data for 1973 combines United Presbyterian Church in the U.S.A. data for 1973 (see YACC 1975) and an average of Presbyterian Church in the United States data for 1972 and 1974, since 1973 data was not reported in the YACC series.

Appendix B-1: Church Member Giving 1968-2007 (continued)

	Data Year 1974			Data Year 1975			Data Year 1976		
	Full/Confirmed Members	Congregational Finances	Benevolences	Full/Confirmed Members	Congregational Finances	Benevolences	Full/Confirmed Members	Congregational Finances	Benevolences
abc	1,176,989 a	147,022,280	21,847,285	1,180,793 a	153,697,091	23,638,372	1,142,773 a	163,134,092	25,792,357
alc	1,764,186	173,318,574	38,921,546	1,764,810	198,863,519	75,666,809	1,768,758	215,527,544	76,478,278
arp	28,570	3,935,533 a	868,284 a	28,589	4,820,846 a	929,880 a	28,581	5,034,270 a	1,018,913 a
bcc	10,255	3,002,218	1,078,576	10,784	3,495,152	955,845	11,375	4,088,492	1,038,484
ccd	854,844	119,434,435	20,818,434	859,885	126,553,931	22,126,459	845,058	135,008,269	23,812,274
cga	161,401	39,189,287	7,343,123	166,259	42,077,029	7,880,559	170,285	47,191,302	8,854,295
cgg	7,455	975,000	105,000	7,485	990,000	105,000	7,620	1,100,000	105,000
chb	179,387	18,609,614	7,281,551	179,336	20,338,351	7,842,819	178,157	22,133,858	8,032,293
chn	430,128	104,774,391	25,534,267 a	441,093	115,400,881	28,186,392 a	448,658	128,294,499	32,278,187 a
ccc	21,661 a	2,452,254 a	1,181,655 a	22,065 a	2,639,472 a	1,750,364 a	21,703 a	3,073,413 a	1,494,355 a
cpc	87,875 a	9,830,198 a	1,336,847 a	86,903 a	11,268,297 a	1,445,793 a	85,541 a	10,735,854 a	1,540,692 a
ecc	29,636 a	4,901,100 a	1,009,726 a	28,886 a	5,503,484 a	1,068,134 a	28,840 a	6,006,621 a	1,139,209 a
ecv	69,960	21,235,204 a	5,131,124	71,808	23,440,265 a	6,353,422	73,458	25,686,916 a	6,898,871
elc	ALC & LCA	ALC & LCA	ALC & LCA	ALC & LCA	ALC & LCA	ALC & LCA	ALC & LCA	ALC & LCA	ALC & LCA
els	13,097	1,519,749	411,732 a	13,489 a	1,739,255	438,875 a	14,504	2,114,998	521,018 a
emc	3,123	644,548	548,000	NA	NA	NA	3,350	800,000	628,944
feb	NA	NA	NA	NA	NA	NA	NA	NA	NA
fec	see EMC	see EMC	see EMC	see EMC	see EMC	see EMC	see EMC	see EMC	see EMC
fmc	49,314 a	17,487,246 a	3,945,535 a	50,632	19,203,781 a	4,389,757 a	51,565	21,130,066 a	4,977,546 a
fum	NA	NA	NA	56,605	6,428,458	1,551,036	51,032	6,749,045	1,691,190
ggb	NA	NA	NA	NA	NA	NA	NA	NA	NA
lca	2,166,615	228,081,405	44,531,126	2,183,131	222,637,156	55,646,303	2,187,995	243,449,466	58,761,005
lms	2,010,456	249,150,470	55,076,955	2,018,530	266,546,758	55,896,061	2,026,336	287,098,403	56,831,860
mch	92,930 a	13,792,266	9,887,051	94,209	15,332,908	11,860,385	96,092 a	17,215,234	12,259,924
mgc	35,534	4,071,002 a	4,179,003 a	35,673 a	3,715,279 a	3,391,943 a	36,397	4,980,967	4,796,037 a
mus	MCH & MGC	MCH & MGC	MCH & MGC	MCH & MGC	MCH & MGC	MCH & MGC	MCH & MGC	MCH & MGC	MCH & MGC
mca	25,583	3,304,388	513,685	25,512	3,567,406	552,512	24,938	4,088,195	573,619
nab	41,437	6,604,693	2,142,148	42,122	7,781,298	2,470,317	42,277	8,902,540	3,302,348
opc	10,186 a	2,627,818 a	703,653 a	10,129 a	2,930,128 a	768,075 a	10,372	3,288,612 a	817,589 a
pch	3,619,768	502,237,350	100,966,089	3,535,825	529,327,006	111,027,318	3,484,985	563,106,353	125,035,379
rca	210,866 b	41,053,364 b	11,470,631 b	212,349 b	44,681,053 b	11,994,379 b	211,628 b	49,083,734 b	13,163,739 b
sda	479,799	67,241,956	166,166,766	495,699	72,060,121	184,689,250	509,792	81,577,130	184,648,454
sbc	12,513,378	1,123,264,849	219,214,770	12,733,124	1,237,594,037	237,452,055	12,917,992	1,382,794,494	262,144,889
ucc	1,841,312	184,292,017	30,243,223	1,818,762	193,524,114	32,125,332	1,801,241	207,486,324	33,862,658
wel	286,083 a	32,596,319 a	9,974,758 a	292,431 a	35,807,415 a	11,173,226 a	297,037 a	39,932,827 a	11,260,203 a
Total	28,221,828	3,126,649,528	792,432,543	28,466,918	3,371,964,491	903,376,672	28,578,340	3,690,813,518	963,759,610

a Data obtained from denominational source.

b empty tomb review of RCA directory data.

Appendix B-1: Church Member Giving 1968-2007 (continued)

	Data Year 1977			Data Year 1978			Data Year 1979		
	Full/Confirmed Members	Congregational Finances	Benevolences	Full/Confirmed Members	Congregational Finances	Benevolences	Full/Confirmed Members	Congregational Finances	Benevolences
abc	1,146,084 a	172,710,063	27,765,800	1,008,495 a	184,716,172	31,937,862	1,036,054 a	195,986,995	34,992,300
alc	1,772,227	231,960,304	54,085,201	1,773,179	256,371,804	57,145,861	1,768,071	284,019,905	63,903,906
arp	28,371 a	5,705,295 a	1,061,285 a	28,644	6,209,447 a	1,031,469 a	28,513	6,544,759 a	1,125,562 a
bcc	11,915 a	4,633,334 a	957,239 a	12,430 a	4,913,311 a	1,089,346 a	12,923	5,519,037	1,312,046
ccd	817,288	148,880,340	25,698,856	791,633	166,249,455	25,790,367	773,765	172,270,978	27,335,440
cga	171,947	51,969,150	10,001,062	173,753	57,630,848	11,214,530	175,113	65,974,517	12,434,621
cgg	7,595	1,130,000	110,000	7,550	1,135,000	110,000	7,620	1,170,000	105,000
chb	177,534	23,722,817	8,228,903	175,335	25,397,531	9,476,220	172,115	28,422,684	10,161,266
chn	455,100	141,807,024	34,895,751 a	462,124	153,943,138	38,300,431 a	473,726	170,515,940 a	42,087,862 a
ccc	21,897 a	3,916,248 a	1,554,143 a	22,364 a	4,271,435 a	1,630,565 a	23,481 a	4,969,610 a	1,871,754 a
cpc	85,227 a	11,384,825 a	1,760,117 a	84,956 a	13,359,375 a	1,995,388 a	85,932 a	13,928,957 a	2,192,562 a
ecc	28,712 a	6,356,730 a	1,271,310 a	28,459 a	6,890,381 a	1,454,826 a	27,995 a	7,552,495 a	1,547,857 a
ecv	74,060	28,758,357 a	7,240,548	74,678	32,606,550 a	8,017,623	76,092	37,118,906 a	9,400,074
elc	ALC & LCA	ALC & LCA	ALC & LCA	ALC & LCA	ALC & LCA	ALC & LCA	ALC & LCA	ALC & LCA	ALC & LCA
els	14,652	2,290,697	546,899 a	14,833	2,629,719	833,543 a	15,081	2,750,703	904,774 a
emc	NA	NA	NA	3,634	1,281,761	794,896	3,704	1,380,806	828,264
feb	NA	NA	NA	3,956	970,960	745,059	NA	NA	NA
fec	see EMC	see EMC	see EMC	see EMC	see EMC	see EMC	see EMC	see EMC	see EMC
fmc	52,563	23,303,722 a	5,505,538 a	52,698 a	25,505,294 a	5,869,970 a	52,900 a	27,516,302 a	6,614,732 a
fum	52,599	6,943,990	1,895,984	53,390	8,172,337	1,968,884	51,426	6,662,787	2,131,108
ggb	72,030	9,854,533	747,842	NA	NA	NA	73,046	13,131,345	1,218,763
lca	2,191,942	251,083,883	62,076,894	2,183,666	277,186,563	72,426,148	2,177,231	301,605,382	71,325,097
lms	1,991,408	301,064,630	57,077,162	1,969,279	329,134,237	59,030,753	1,965,422	360,989,735	63,530,596
mch	96,609	18,540,237	12,980,502	97,142	22,922,417	14,124,757 a	98,027	24,505,346	15,116,762
mgc	35,575 a	5,051,708 a	4,619,590 a	36,775 a	5,421,568 a	5,062,489 a	36,736 a	6,254,850 a	5,660,477 a
mus	MCH & MGC	MCH & MGC	MCH & MGC	MCH & MGC	MCH & MGC	MCH & MGC	MCH & MGC	MCH & MGC	MCH & MGC
mca	25,323	4,583,616	581,200	24,854	4,441,750	625,536	24,782	4,600,331	689,070
nab	42,724	10,332,556	3,554,204	42,499	11,629,309	3,559,983	42,779	13,415,024	3,564,339
opc	10,683 a	3,514,172	931,935	10,939	4,107,705	1,135,388	11,306 a	4,683,302	1,147,191
pch	3,430,927	633,187,916	130,252,348	3,382,783	692,872,811	128,194,954	3,321,787	776,049,247	148,528,993
rca	210,637 b	53,999,791 b	14,210,966 b	211,778 b	60,138,720 b	15,494,816 b	210,700 b	62,997,526 b	16,750,408 b
sda	522,317	98,468,365	216,202,975	535,705	104,044,989	226,692,736	553,089	118,711,906	255,936,372
sbc	13,078,239	1,506,877,921	289,179,711	13,191,394	1,668,120,760	316,462,385	13,372,757	1,864,213,869	355,885,769
ucc	1,785,652	219,878,772	35,522,221	1,769,104	232,593,033	37,789,958	1,745,533	249,443,032	41,100,583
wel	301,125 a	44,378,032 a	11,600,902 a	303,134 a	50,123,714 a	12,907,953 a	305,454 a	54,789,339 a	14,178,008 a
Total	28,712,962	4,026,289,028	1,022,117,088	28,531,163	4,414,992,094	1,092,914,696	28,723,160	4,887,695,615	1,213,581,556

a Data obtained from denominational source.
b empty tomb review of RCA directory data.

Appendix B-1: Church Member Giving 1968-2007 (continued)

	Data Year 1980			Data Year 1981			Data Year 1982		
	Full/Confirmed Members	Congregational Finances	Benevolences	Full/Confirmed Members	Congregational Finances	Benevolences	Full/Confirmed Members	Congregational Finances	Benevolences
abc	1,008,700 a	213,560,656	37,133,159	989,322 a	227,931,461	40,046,261	983,580 a	242,750,027	41,457,745
alc	1,763,067	312,592,610	65,235,739	1,758,452	330,155,588	96,102,638	1,758,239	359,848,865	77,010,444
arp	28,166 a	6,868,650 a	1,054,229 a	28,334 a	7,863,221 a	1,497,838 a	29,087 a	8,580,311 a	1,807,572 a
bcc	13,578 a	6,011,465 a	1,490,334 a	13,993	6,781,857	1,740,711	14,413 a	7,228,612 a	1,594,797 a
ccd	788,394	189,176,399	30,991,519	772,466	211,828,751	31,067,142	770,227	227,178,861	34,307,638
cga	176,429	67,367,485	13,414,112	178,581	78,322,907	14,907,277	184,685	84,896,806	17,171,600
cgg	NA	NA	NA	5,981	1,788,298	403,000	5,781 a	1,864,735 a	418,000 a
chb	170,839	29,813,265	11,663,976	170,267	31,641,019	12,929,076	168,844	35,064,568	12,844,415
chn	483,101	191,536,556	45,786,446 a	490,852	203,145,992	50,084,163 a	497,261	221,947,940	53,232,461 a
ccc	24,410 a	6,017,539 a	2,169,298 a	25,044 a	8,465,804	2,415,233	26,008	9,230,111	2,574,569
cpc	86,941 a	15,973,738 a	2,444,677 a	87,493 a	16,876,846 a	2,531,539 a	88,121 a	17,967,709 a	2,706,361 a
ecc	27,567 a	8,037,564 a	1,630,993 a	27,287 a	8,573,057 a	1,758,025 a	27,203 a	9,119,278 a	1,891,936 a
ecv	77,737	41,888,556 a	10,031,072	79,523	45,206,565 a	8,689,918	81,324	50,209,520 a	8,830,793
elc	ALC & LCA	ALC & LCA	ALC & LCA	ALC & LCA	ALC & LCA	ALC & LCA	ALC & LCA	ALC & LCA	ALC & LCA
els	14,968	3,154,804	876,929 a	14,904	3,461,387	716,624	15,165	3,767,977	804,822
emc	3,782	1,527,945	1,041,447	3,753	1,515,975	908,342	3,832	1,985,890	731,510
feb	4,329	1,250,466	627,536	NA	NA	NA	2,047	696,660	1,020,972
fec	see EMC	see EMC	see EMC	see EMC	see EMC	see EMC	see EMC	see EMC	see EMC
fmc	54,145 a	30,525,352 a	6,648,248 a	54,764 a	32,853,491 a	7,555,713 a	54,198 a	35,056,434	8,051,593
fum	51,691	9,437,724	2,328,137	51,248	9,551,765	2,449,731	50,601	10,334,180	2,597,215
ggb	74,159	14,967,312	1,547,038	75,028	15,816,060	1,473,070	NA	NA	NA
lca	2,176,991	371,981,816	87,439,137	2,173,558	404,300,509	82,862,299	2,176,265	435,564,519	83,217,264
lms	1,973,958	390,756,268	66,626,364	1,983,198	429,910,406	86,341,102	1,961,260	468,468,156	75,457,846
mch	99,511	28,846,931	16,437,738	99,651	31,304,278	17,448,024	101,501	33,583,338	17,981,274
mgc	36,644 a	6,796,330 a	5,976,652 a	36,609 a	7,857,792 a	7,203,240 a	37,007 a	8,438,680 a	7,705,419 a
mus	MCH & MGC	MCH & MGC	MCH & MGC	MCH & MGC	MCH & MGC	MCH & MGC	MCH & MGC	MCH & MGC	MCH & MGC
mca	24,863	5,178,444	860,399	24,500	5,675,495	831,177	24,669	6,049,857	812,015
nab	43,041	12,453,858	3,972,485	43,146	15,513,286	4,420,403	42,735	17,302,952	4,597,515
opc	11,553 a	5,235,294	1,235,849	11,884 a	5,939,983	1,382,451	11,956 a	6,512,125 a	1,430,061 a
pch	3,262,086	820,218,732	176,172,729	3,202,392	896,641,430	188,576,382	3,157,372	970,223,947	199,331,832
rca	210,762	70,733,297	17,313,239 b	210,312	77,044,709	18,193,793 b	211,168	82,656,050	19,418,165 b
sda	571,141	121,484,768	275,783,385	588,536	133,088,131	297,838,046	606,310	136,877,455	299,437,917
sbc	13,600,126	2,080,375,258	400,976,072	13,782,644	2,336,062,506	443,931,179	13,991,709	2,628,272,553	486,402,607
ucc	1,736,244	278,546,571	44,042,186	1,726,535	300,730,591	48,329,399	1,708,847	323,725,191	52,738,069
wel	307,810 a	60,458,213 a	15,989,577 a	310,553 a	67,830,319 a	18,198,804 a	311,364 a	71,611,865 a	18,608,914 a
Total	28,906,733	5,402,773,866	1,348,940,701	29,020,810	5,953,679,479	1,492,832,600	29,102,779	6,517,015,172	1,536,193,341

a Data obtained from denominational source.

b empty tomb review of RCA directory data.

Appendix B-1: Church Member Giving 1968-2007 (continued)

	Data Year 1983			Data Year 1984			Data Year 1985		
	Full/Confirmed Members	Congregational Finances	Benevolences	Full/Confirmed Members	Congregational Finances	Benevolences	Full/Confirmed Members	Congregational Finances	Benevolences
abc	965,117 a	254,716,036	43,683,021	953,945 a	267,556,088	46,232,040	894,732 a	267,694,684	47,201,119
alc	1,756,420	375,500,188	84,633,617	1,756,558	413,876,101	86,601,067	1,751,649	428,861,660	87,152,699
arp	31,738	10,640,050 a	2,180,230 a	31,355	11,221,526 a	3,019,456 a	32,051	12,092,868 a	3,106,994 a
bcc	14,782	7,638,413	1,858,632	15,128	8,160,359	2,586,843	15,535 a	8,504,354 a	2,979,046 a
ccd	761,629	241,934,972	35,809,331	755,233	263,694,210	38,402,791	743,486	274,072,301	40,992,053
cga	182,190	81,309,323	13,896,753	185,404	86,611,269	14,347,570	185,593	91,078,512	15,308,954
cgg	5,759	1,981,300		4,711	2,211,800	504,200	4,575	2,428,730	582,411
chb	164,680	39,726,743	14,488,192	161,824	37,743,527	15,136,600	159,184	40,658,904	16,509,718
chn	506,439	237,220,642	57,267,073 a	514,937	253,566,280	60,909,810 a	520,741	267,134,078	65,627,515 a
ccc	26,691 a	9,189,221 a	2,980,636	28,383	10,018,982	3,051,425	28,624	11,729,365	3,350,021
cpc	87,186 a	19,252,942 a	3,028,953 a	86,995 a	20,998,768 a	3,331,065 a	85,346 a	22,361,332 a	3,227,932 a
ecc	26,769 a	9,505,479 a	2,019,373 a	26,375 a	10,302,554 a	2,220,852 a	26,016	8,134,641 a	1,777,172
ecv	82,943	53,279,350 a	10,615,909	84,185	60,295,634 a	11,243,908	85,150	63,590,735 a	13,828,030
elc	ALC & LCA	ALC & LCA	ALC & LCA	ALC & LCA	ALC & LCA	ALC & LCA	ALC & LCA	ALC & LCA	ALC & LCA
els	15,576	3,842,625	838,788	15,396	4,647,714	931,677 a	15,012	4,725,783	791,586
emc	3,857	1,930,689	738,194	3,908	2,017,565	862,350	3,813	2,128,019	1,058,040
feb	2,094	622,467	1,466,399	NA	NA	NA	2,107 a	1,069,851 a	402,611 a
fec	see EMC	see EMC	see EMC	see EMC	see EMC	see EMC	see EMC	see EMC	see EMC
fmc	56,442 a	36,402,355 a	8,334,248 a	56,667 a	39,766,087 a	8,788,189 a	56,242	42,046,626 a	9,461,369 a
fum	49,441	11,723,240	2,886,931	48,713	11,549,163	2,875,370	48,812	12,601,820	3,012,658
ggb	75,133	17,283,259	1,733,755	75,028	17,599,169	1,729,228	73,040	18,516,252	1,683,130
lca	2,176,772	457,239,780	88,909,363	2,168,594	496,228,216	99,833,067	2,161,216	539,142,069	103,534,375
lms	1,984,199	499,220,552	76,991,991 a	1,986,392	539,346,935	81,742,006 a	1,982,753	566,507,516	83,117,011 a
mch	103,350 a	34,153,628	17,581,878	90,347	37,333,306	16,944,094	91,167	34,015,200	25,593,500
mgc	36,318 a	8,702,849 a	7,661,415 a	35,951 a	9,197,458 a	7,795,680 a	35,356 a	9,217,964 a	7,070,700 a
mus	MCH & MGC	MCH & MGC	MCH & MGC	MCH & MGC	MCH & MGC	MCH & MGC	MCH & MGC	MCH & MGC	MCH & MGC
mca	24,913	6,618,339	911,787	24,269	7,723,611	1,183,741	24,396	8,698,949	1,170,349
nab	43,286	18,010,853	5,132,672	43,215	19,322,720	5,724,552	42,863	20,246,236	5,766,686
opc	12,045	6,874,722	1,755,169	12,278 a	7,555,006	2,079,924	12,593 a	8,291,483	2,204,998
pch	3,122,213	1,047,756,995	197,981,080	3,092,151	1,132,098,779	218,412,639	3,057,226 a	1,252,885,684 a	232,487,569 a
rca	211,660	92,071,986	20,632,574	209,968 b	100,378,778	21,794,880	209,395	103,428,950	22,233,299
sda	623,563	143,636,140	323,461,439	638,929	155,257,063	319,664,449	651,594	155,077,180	346,251,406
sbc	14,178,051	2,838,573,815	528,781,000	14,341,822	3,094,913,877	567,467,188	14,477,364	3,272,276,486	609,868,694
ucc	1,701,513	332,613,396	55,716,557	1,696,107	385,786,198	58,679,094	1,683,777	409,543,989	62,169,679 a
wel	312,974 a	75,825,104 a	24,037,480 a	314,559 a	82,507,020 a	22,845,856 a	315,374 a	86,879,662 a	22,275,822 a
Total	29,345,743	6,974,997,453	1,638,426,440	29,459,327	7,589,485,763	1,726,941,611	29,476,782	8,045,641,883	1,841,797,146

a Data obtained from denominational source.

b empty tomb review of RCA directory data.

169

Appendix B-1: Church Member Giving 1968-2007 (continued)

	Data Year 1986			Data Year 1987			Data Year 1988		
	Full/Confirmed Members	Congregational Finances	Benevolences	Full/Confirmed Members	Congregational Finances	Benevolences	Full/Confirmed Members	Congregational Finances	Benevolences
abc	862,582 a	287,020,378 a	49,070,083 a	868,189 a	291,606,418 a	55,613,855	825,102 a	296,569,316 a	55,876,771
alc	1,740,439	434,641,736	96,147,129	See ELCA	See ELCA	See ELCA	See ELCA	See ELCA	See ELCA
arp	32,438 a	12,336,321 a	3,434,408 a	32,289	13,553,176 a	3,927,030 a	31,922	13,657,776 a	5,063,036 a
bcc	15,911	10,533,883	2,463,558	16,136	11,203,321	3,139,949	16,578 a	13,522,101 a	4,346,690 a
ccd	732,466	288,277,386	42,027,504	718,522	287,464,332	42,728,826	707,985	297,187,996	42,226,128
cga	188,662	91,768,855	16,136,647	198,552	124,376,413	20,261,687	198,842	132,384,232	19,781,941
cgg	NA	NA	NA	4,348	2,437,778	738,818	4,394 a	2,420,600 a	644,000 a
chb	155,967	43,531,293	17,859,101	154,067	45,201,732	19,342,402	151,169	48,008,657	19,701,942 a
chn	529,192	283,189,977	68,438,998 a	541,878	294,160,356	73,033,568 a	550,700	309,478,442	74,737,057 a
ccc	28,948	15,559,846 a	3,961,037	29,429	15,409,349 a	3,740,688	29,015	13,853,547	4,120,974
cpc	84,579 a	22,338,090 a	3,646,356 a	85,781	22,857,711	3,727,681	85,304	23,366,911 e	3,722,607
ecc	25,625	10,977,813 a	2,422,879 a	25,300	14,281,140 a	2,575,415 a	24,980	12,115,762	2,856,766 a
ecv	86,079	67,889,353 a	14,374,707	86,741	73,498,123 a	14,636,000	87,750	77,504,445 a	14,471,178
elc	ALC & LCA	ALC & LCA	ALC & LCA	3,952,663	1,083,293,684	169,685,942	3,931,878	1,150,483,034	169,580,472
els	15,083 a	4,996,111 a	1,050,715 a	15,892	5,298,882	1,082,198	15,518 a	5,713,773 a	1,043,612 a
emc	NA	NA	NA	3,841	2,332,216	1,326,711	3,879	2,522,533	1,438,459
feb	NA	NA	NA	NA	NA	NA	NA	NA	NA
fec	see EMC	see EMC	see EMC	see EMC	see EMC	see EMC	see EMC	see EMC	see EMC
fmc	56,243	46,150,881	9,446,120	57,262	47,743,298	9,938,096	57,432	48,788,041	9,952,103
fum	48,143	12,790,909	2,916,870	47,173	13,768,272	3,631,353	48,325	14,127,491	3,719,125
ggb	72,263	19,743,265	1,883,826	73,515	20,850,827	1,789,578	74,086	21,218,051	1,731,299
lca	2,157,701	569,250,519	111,871,174	See ELCA	See ELCA	See ELCA	See ELCA	See ELCA	See ELCA
lms	1,974,798	605,768,688	87,803,646 a	1,973,347	620,271,274	86,938,723 a	1,962,674	659,288,332	88,587,175 a
mch	91,467 a	40,097,500 a	24,404,200 a	92,673 a	43,295,100	25,033,600	92,682	47,771,200	27,043,900
mgc	35,170	10,101,306 a	7,717,998 a	34,889	11,560,998	8,478,414	34,693	11,399,995	9,638,417
mus	MCH & MGC	MCH & MGC	MCH & MGC	MCH & MGC	MCH & MGC	MCH & MGC	MCH & MGC	MCH & MGC	MCH & MGC
mca	24,260	8,133,127	1,155,350	24,440	9,590,658	1,174,593	23,526	9,221,646	1,210,476
nab	42,084	20,961,799	5,982,391	42,150 a	23,773,844 a	7,873,096 a	42,629	24,597,288	6,611,840
opc	12,919 a	9,333,328 a	2,347,928 a	13,013 a	9,884,288	2,425,480	13,108 a	10,797,786 a	2,648,375 a
pch	3,007,322	1,318,440,264	249,033,881	2,967,781	1,395,501,073	247,234,439	2,929,608	1,439,655,217	284,989,138
rca	207,993	114,231,429	22,954,596	203,581	114,652,192 b	24,043,270	200,631	127,409,263	25,496,802 b
sda	666,199	166,692,974	361,316,753	675,702	166,939,355	374,830,065	687,200	178,768,967	395,849,223
sbc	14,613,638	3,481,124,471	635,196,984	14,722,617	3,629,842,643	662,455,177	14,812,844	3,706,652,161	689,366,904
ucc	1,676,105	429,340,239	63,808,091	1,662,568	451,700,210	66,870,922	1,644,787	470,747,740	65,734,348
wel	315,510 a	92,309,279 a	22,354,781 a	316,393 a	97,179,349 a	22,112,031 a	316,098 a	101,545,536 a	22,323,451 a
Total	29,499,786	8,517,531,020	1,931,227,711	29,640,732	8,943,528,012	1,960,389,607	29,605,339	9,270,777,839	2,054,514,209

a Data obtained from denominational source.

b empty tomb review of RCA directory data.

e A YACC prepublication data table listed 23,366,911 for Congregational Finances which, added to Benevolences, equals the published Total of 27,089,518.

Appendix B-1: Church Member Giving 1968-2007 (continued)

	Data Year 1989			Data Year 1990			Data Year 1991		
	Full/Confirmed Members	Congregational Finances	Benevolences	Full/Confirmed Members	Congregational Finances	Benevolences	Full/Confirmed Members	Congregational Finances	Benevolences
abc	789,730 a	305,212,094 a	55,951,539	764,890 a	315,777,005 a	54,740,278	773,838 a	318,150,548 a	52,330,924
alc	See ELCA	See ELCA	See ELCA	See ELCA	See ELCA	See ELCA	See ELCA	See ELCA	See ELCA
arp	32,600	16,053,762 a	4,367,314 a	32,817 a	17,313,355 a	5,031,504 a	33,494 a	17,585,273 a	5,254,738 a
bcc	16,842	12,840,038	3,370,306	17,277	13,327,414	3,336,580	17,456 a	14,491,918 a	3,294,169 a
ccd	690,115	310,043,826	42,015,246	678,750	321,569,909	42,607,007	663,336	331,629,009	43,339,307
cga	199,786	134,918,052	20,015,075	205,884	141,375,027	21,087,504	214,743 a	146,249,447 a	21,801,570 a
cgg	4,415	3,367,000	686,000	4,399	3,106,729	690,000	4,375	2,756,651	662,500
chb	149,681	51,921,820	19,737,714 a	148,253	54,832,226	18,384,483 a	147,954 a	55,035,355 a	19,694,919 a
chn	558,664	322,924,598	76,625,913 a	563,756 a	333,397,255 a	77,991,665 a	572,153	352,654,251	82,276,097 a
ccc	28,413	18,199,823	4,064,111	28,355	16,964,128	4,174,133	28,035	17,760,290	4,304,052
cpc	84,994 a	25,867,112 a	4,086,994 a	85,025 a	27,027,650 a	4,139,967 a	84,706 a	28,069,681 a	5,740,846 a
ecc	24,606	13,274,756 a	2,703,095 a	24,437	12,947,150 a	2,858,077 a	24,124 a	13,100,036 a	3,074,660 a
ecv	89,014	80,621,293 a	15,206,265	89,735	84,263,236 a	15,601,475	89,648	87,321,563 a	16,598,656
elc	3,909,302	1,239,433,257	182,386,940	3,898,478	1,318,884,279	184,174,554	3,890,947	1,375,439,787	186,016,168
els	15,740	6,186,648	1,342,321	16,181	6,527,076	1,193,789	16,004	6,657,338	1,030,445
emc	3,888	2,712,843	1,567,728	4,026	2,991,485	1,800,593	3,958	3,394,563	1,790,115
feb	NA	NA	NA	NA	NA	NA	2,008 a	1,398,968 a	500,092 a
fec	see EMC	see EMC	see EMC	see EMC	see EMC	see EMC	see EMC	see EMC	see EMC
fmc	59,418 a	50,114,090 a	10,311,535 a	58,084	55,229,181	10,118,505	57,794	57,880,464	9,876,739
fum	47,228	16,288,644	4,055,624	45,691	10,036,083	2,511,063	50,803 f	NA	NA
ggb	73,738	23,127,835	1,768,804	74,156	23,127,835	1,737,011	71,119 a	22,362,874 a	1,408,262 a
lca	See ELCA	See ELCA	See ELCA	See ELCA	See ELCA	See ELCA	See ELCA	See ELCA	See ELCA
lms	1,961,114	701,701,168 a	90,974,340 a	1,954,350	712,235,204	96,308,765 a	1,952,845	741,823,412	94,094,637 a
mch	92,517	55,353,313	27,873,241	92,448 a	65,709,827	28,397,083	93,114 a	68,926,324	28,464,199
mgc	33,982	12,096,435	9,054,682	33,535	13,669,288	8,449,395	33,937	13,556,484	8,645,993 a
mus	MCH & MGC	MCH & MGC	MCH & MGC	MCH & MGC	MCH & MGC	MCH & MGC	MCH & MGC	MCH & MGC	MCH & MGC
mca	23,802	10,415,640	1,284,233	23,526	10,105,037	1,337,616	22,887	10,095,337	1,205,335
nab	42,629	28,076,077	3,890,017	44,493	31,103,672	7,700,119	43,187 a	27,335,239 a	7,792,876 a
opc	12,573 a	11,062,590 a	2,789,427 a	12,177 a	10,631,166 a	2,738,295 a	12,265	11,700,000	2,700,000
pch	2,886,482	1,528,450,805	295,365,032	2,847,437	1,530,341,707	294,990,441	2,805,548	1,636,407,042	311,905,934 a
rca	198,832	136,796,188 b	29,456,132 b	197,154	144,357,953 b	27,705,029 b	193,531 b	147,532,382 b	26,821,721 b
sda	701,781	196,204,538	415,752,350	717,446	195,054,218	433,035,080	733,026	201,411,183	456,242,995
sbc	14,907,826	3,873,300,782	712,738,838	15,038,409	4,146,285,561	718,174,874	15,232,347	4,283,283,059	731,812,766
ucc	1,625,969	496,825,160	72,300,698	1,599,212	527,378,397	71,984,897	1,583,830	543,803,752	73,149,887
wel	316,163 a	110,112,151 a	22,717,491 a	315,840 a	115,806,027 a	23,983,079 a	315,853 a	121,159,792 a	24,160,350 a
Total	29,581,844	9,793,502,338	2,134,659,005	29,616,221	10,261,375,080	2,166,982,861	29,718,062	10,658,972,022	2,225,990,952

a Data obtained from denominational source.

b empty tomb review of RCA directory data.

f Inclusive membership, obtained from the denomination and used only in Chapter 5 analysis; not included in the Total sum on this page.

Appendix B-1: Church Member Giving 1968-2007 (continued)

	Data Year 1992			Data Year 1993			Data Year 1994		
	Full/Confirmed Members	Congregational Finances	Benevolences	Full/Confirmed Members	Congregational Finances	Benevolences	Full/Confirmed Members	Congregational Finances	Benevolences
abc	730,009 a	310,307,040 a	52,764,005	764,657 a	346,658,047 a	53,562,811	697,379 a	337,185,885 a	51,553,256 a
alc	See ELCA	See ELCA	See ELCA	See ELCA	See ELCA	See ELCA	See ELCA	See ELCA	See ELCA
arp	33,550	18,175,957 a	5,684,008 a	33,662 a	20,212,390 a	5,822,845 a	33,636	22,618,802 a	6,727,857
bcc	17,646 a	15,981,118 a	3,159,717 a	17,986	13,786,394	4,515,730 a	18,152	14,844,672	5,622,005
ccd	655,652	333,629,412	46,440,333	619,028	328,219,027	44,790,415	605,996	342,352,080	43,165,285
cga	214,743	150,115,497	23,500,213	216,117	158,454,703	23,620,177	221,346 a	160,694,760 a	26,262,049 a
cgg	4,085	2,648,085	509,398	4,239	2,793,000	587,705	3,996	2,934,843	475,799
chb	147,912	57,954,895	21,748,320	146,713	56,818,998	23,278,848	144,282	57,210,682	24,155,595
chn	582,804 a	361,555,793 a	84,118,580 a	589,398	369,896,767	87,416,378 a	595,303	387,385,034	89,721,860
ccc	30,387	22,979,946	4,311,234	36,864	24,997,736 a	5,272,184	37,996 a	23,758,101 a	5,240,805 a
cpc	85,080 a	27,813,626 a	4,339,933 a	84,336 a	27,462,623 a	4,574,550 a	83,733 a	29,212,802 a	4,547,149 a
ecc	24,150	13,451,827 a	3,120,351 a	23,889	13,546,159 a	3,258,595 a	23,504	13,931,409	3,269,986
ecv	90,985 a	93,071,869 a	16,732,701 a	89,511	93,765,006 a	16,482,315	90,919 a	101,746,341 a	17,874,955 a
elc	3,878,055	1,399,419,800 a	189,605,837	3,861,418	1,452,000,815	188,393,158	3,849,692	1,502,746,601	187,145,886
els	15,929 a	6,944,522 a	1,271,058 a	15,780	6,759,222 a	1,100,660	15,960	7,288,521	1,195,698
emc	4,059	3,839,838 a	1,403,001 a	4,130 a	4,260,307 a	1,406,682 a	4,225 a	4,597,730 a	1,533,157 a
feb	1,872 a	1,343,225 a	397,553 a	1,866 a	1,294,646 a	429,023 a	1,898 a	1,537,041 a	395,719 a
fec	see EMC	see EMC	see EMC	see EMC	see EMC	see EMC	see EMC	see EMC	see EMC
fmc	58,220	60,584,079	10,591,064	59,156	62,478,294	10,513,187	59,354 a	65,359,325 a	10,708,854 a
fum	50,005 f	NA	NA	45,542 f	NA	NA	44,711 f	NA	NA
ggb	72,388 a	21,561,432 a	1,402,330 a	73,129 a	22,376,970 a	1,440,342 a	71,140 a	19,651,624 a	2,052,409 a
lca	See ELCA	See ELCA	See ELCA	See ELCA	See ELCA	See ELCA	See ELCA	See ELCA	See ELCA
lms	1,953,248	777,467,488	97,275,934 a	1,945,077	789,821,559	96,355,945 a	1,944,905	817,412,113	96,048,560 a
mch	94,222 a	68,118,222	28,835,719	95,634	71,385,271	27,973,380	87,911 a	64,651,639	24,830,192
mgc	34,040	14,721,813 a	8,265,700	33,629	14,412,556	7,951,676	32,782	16,093,551 a	8,557,126 a
mus	MCH & MGC	MCH & MGC	MCH & MGC	MCH & MGC	MCH & MGC	MCH & MGC	MCH & MGC	MCH & MGC	MCH & MGC
mca	22,533	10,150,953	1,208,372	22,223	9,675,502	1,191,131	21,448	9,753,010	1,182,778
nab	43,446	28,375,947	7,327,594	43,045	30,676,902	7,454,087	43,236	32,800,560	7,515,707
opc	12,580 a	12,466,266 a	3,025,824 a	12,924 a	13,158,089 a	3,039,676 a	13,970	14,393,880	3,120,454
pch	2,780,406	1,696,092,968	309,069,530	2,742,192	1,700,918,712	310,375,024	2,698,262	1,800,008,292	307,158,749
rca	190,322 b	147,181,320 b	28,457,900 b	188,551 b	159,715,941 b	26,009,853 b	185,242	153,107,408	27,906,830
sda	748,687	191,362,737	476,902,779	761,703	209,524,570	473,769,831	775,349	229,596,444	503,347,816
sbc	15,358,866	4,462,915,112	751,366,698	15,398,642	4,621,157,751	761,298,249	15,614,060	5,263,421,764	815,360,696
ucc	1,555,382	521,190,413	73,906,372	1,530,178	550,847,702	71,046,517	1,501,310	556,540,722	67,269,762
wel	315,062 a	127,139,400 a	26,239,464 a	314,757 a	136,405,994 a	24,403,323 a	314,141 a	142,238,820 a	23,825,002 a
Total	29,756,320	10,958,560,600	2,282,981,522	29,730,434	11,313,481,653	2,287,334,297	29,791,127	12,195,074,456	2,367,771,996

a Data obtained from denominational source.

b empty tomb review of RCA directory data.

f Inclusive membership, obtained from the denomination and used only in Chapter 5 analysis; not included in the Total sum on this page.

Appendix B-1: Church Member Giving 1968-2007 (continued)

	Data Year 1995			Data Year 1996			Data Year 1997		
	Full/Confirmed Members	Congregational Finances	Benevolences	Full/Confirmed Members	Congregational Finances	Benevolences	Full/Confirmed Members	Congregational Finances	Benevolences
abc	726,452 a	365,873,197 a	57,052,333 a	670,363 a	351,362,401	55,982,392 a	658,731 a	312,860,507 a	54,236,977 a
alc	See ELCA	See ELCA	See ELCA	See ELCA	See ELCA	See ELCA	See ELCA	See ELCA	See ELCA
arp	33,513	23,399,372 a	5,711,882 a	34,117	23,419,989 a	5,571,337 a	34,344	25,241,384	6,606,829
bcc	18,529	16,032,149	5,480,828	18,424	16,892,154	4,748,871	19,016 a	17,456,379 a	5,934,414 a
ccd	601,237	357,895,652	42,887,958	586,131	370,210,746	42,877,144	568,921	381,463,761	43,009,412
cga	224,061	160,897,147	26,192,559	229,240	180,581,111	26,983,385	229,302	194,438,623	29,054,047
cgg	3,877	2,722,766	486,661	3,920	2,926,516	491,348	3,877	2,987,337	515,247
chb	143,121	60,242,418	22,599,214	141,811	60,524,557 a	19,683,035 a	141,400	60,923,817 a	19,611,047 a
chn	598,946	396,698,137	93,440,095	608,008	419,450,850	95,358,352	615,632	433,821,462	99,075,440
ccc	38,853 a	24,250,819 a	5,483,659 a	38,469 a	25,834,363 a	4,989,062 a	38,956	28,204,355	5,167,644
cpc	81,094 a	31,072,697 a	4,711,934 a	80,122 a	31,875,061 a	5,035,451 a	79,576 a	32,152,971 a	5,152,129 a
ecc	23,422	14,830,454	3,301,060	23,091	14,692,608	3,273,685	22,957	15,658,454	3,460,999
ecv	91,458	109,776,363 a	17,565,085 a	91,823 a	115,693,329 a	18,726,756 a	93,414	127,642,950	20,462,435
elc	3,845,063	1,551,842,465	188,107,066	3,838,750	1,629,909,672	191,476,141	3,844,169	1,731,806,133	201,115,441
els	16,543	7,712,358 a	1,084,136	16,511	8,136,195	1,104,996	16,444	8,937,103	1,150,419
emc	4,284 a	5,321,079 a	1,603,548 a	4,201	5,361,912 a	1,793,267 a	4,348 a	7,017,588 a	2,039,740 a
feb	1,856 a	1,412,281 a	447,544 a	1,751 a	1,198,120 a	507,656 a	1,763 a	1,120,222 a	518,777 a
fec	see EMC	see EMC	see EMC	see EMC	see EMC	see EMC	see EMC	see EMC	see EMC
fmc	59,060	67,687,955	11,114,804	59,343 a	70,262,626	11,651,462	62,191 a	78,687,325	12,261,465
fum	43,440 f	NA	NA	42,918 f	NA	NA	41,040 f	NA	NA
ggb	70,886 a	24,385,956 a	1,722,662 a	70,562 a	27,763,966 a	1,832,909 a	72,326	28,093,944	1,780,851
lca	See ELCA	See ELCA	See ELCA	See ELCA	See ELCA	See ELCA	See ELCA	See ELCA	See ELCA
lms	1,943,281	832,701,255	98,139,835 a	1,951,730	855,461,015	104,076,876 a	1,951,391	887,928,255	110,520,917
mch	90,139 a	71,641,773	26,832,240	90,959	76,669,365	27,812,549	92,161 a	76,087,609 a	25,637,872 a
mgc	35,852	15,774,961 a	7,587,049 a	35,333	18,282,833	7,969,999	34,731	14,690,904	6,514,761
mus	MCH & MGC	MCH & MGC	MCH & MGC	MCH & MGC	MCH & MGC	MCH & MGC	MCH & MGC	MCH & MGC	MCH & MGC
mca	21,409	10,996,031	1,167,513	21,140	11,798,536	1,237,349	21,108	12,555,760	1,148,478
nab	43,928	37,078,473	7,480,331	43,744 a	37,172,560 a	7,957,860 a	43,850	37,401,175	7,986,099
opc	14,355	16,017,003	3,376,691	15,072 a	17,883,915 a	3,467,207 a	15,072	20,090,259	3,967,490
pch	2,665,276	1,855,684,719	309,978,224	2,631,466	1,930,179,808	322,336,258	2,609,191	2,064,789,378	344,757,186
rca	183,255	164,250,624	29,995,068	182,342	183,975,696 a	31,271,007	180,980 a	181,977,101 a	32,130,943 a
sda	790,731	240,565,576	503,334,129	809,159	242,316,834	524,977,061	825,654	249,591,109	552,633,569
sbc	15,663,296	5,209,748,503	858,635,435	15,691,249 a	5,987,033,115	891,149,403 a	15,891,514	6,098,933,137	930,176,909
ucc	1,472,213	578,042,965	67,806,448	1,452,565	615,727,028	69,013,791	1,438,181	651,176,773	70,180,193
wel	312,898 a	150,060,963 a	33,096,069 a	313,446 a	156,363,694 a	47,334,098 a	314,038 a	163,568,990 a	52,241,401 a
Total	29,818,888	12,404,616,111	2,436,422,060	29,754,842	13,488,960,575	2,530,690,707	29,925,238	13,947,304,765	2,649,049,131

a Data obtained from denominational source.

f Inclusive membership, obtained from the denomination and used only in Chapter 5 analysis; not included in the Total sum on this page.

Appendix B-1: Church Member Giving 1968-2007 (continued)

	Data Year 1998			Data Year 1999			Data Year 2000		
	Full/Confirmed Members	Congregational Finances	Benevolences	Full/Confirmed Members	Congregational Finances	Benevolences	Full/Confirmed Members	Congregational Finances	Benevolences
abc	621,232 a	326,046,153 a	53,866,448 a	603,014 a	331,513,521 a	58,675,160	593,113	359,484,902	63,042,002
alc	See ELCA	See ELCA	See ELCA	See ELCA	See ELCA	See ELCA	See ELCA	See ELCA	See ELCA
arp	34,642 a	28,831,982 a	7,378,121 a	35,643 a	33,862,219 a	7,973,285 a	35,022 a	33,004,995 a	8,048,586 a
bcc	19,577	24,116,889	5,274,612	20,010	22,654,566	5,913,551	20,587	25,148,637	5,703,506
ccd	547,875 a	395,699,954 a	45,576,436 a	535,893	410,583,119	47,795,574	527,363	433,965,354	48,726,390
cga	234,311 f	NA	NA	235,849 f	NA	NA	238,891 f	NA	NA
cgg	3,824	3,087,000	689,756	4,083	3,357,300	503,365	4,037	3,232,160	610,113
chb	140,011 a	57,605,960 a	22,283,498 a	138,304 a	63,774,756 a	21,852,687 a	135,978	67,285,361	25,251,272 a
chn	623,028	460,776,715	104,925,922	626,033 a	487,437,668 a	110,818,743 a	633,264	516,708,125	122,284,083
ccc	38,996	28,976,122	5,194,733	40,414	31,165,218	5,931,456	40,974 a	33,537,589 a	6,360,912 a
cpc	80,829 a	33,623,232 a	5,412,917 a	79,452 a	36,303,752 a	5,879,014 a	86,519	39,533,829	6,591,617
ecc	22,868	15,956,209	3,599,440	22,349	16,574,783	3,587,877	21,939	17,656,789	1,982,328
ecv	96,552	140,823,872	20,134,436	98,526 a	161,361,490 a	23,237,513 a	101,317 a	181,127,526 a	25,983,315 a
elc	3,840,136	1,822,915,831	208,853,359	3,825,228	1,972,950,623	220,647,251	3,810,785	2,067,208,285	231,219,316
els	16,897	9,363,126	1,120,386	16,734	10,062,900	1,129,969	16,569	10,910,109	949,421
emc	4,646 a	6,472,868 a	1,854,222 a	4,511 a	7,528,256 a	1,982,985 a	4,929	8,289,743 a	2,085,475 a
feb	1,828 a	1,433,305 a	502,839 a	1,936 a	1,496,949 a	534,203 a	1,764 a	1,360,133 a	373,057 a
fec	see EMC	see EMC	see EMC	see EMC	see EMC	see EMC	see EMC	see EMC	see EMC
fmc	62,176	82,254,922	12,850,607	62,368 a	86,906,899	12,646,064	62,453	98,853,770	13,430,274
fum	33,908 f	NA	NA	34,863 f	NA	NA	41,297 f	NA	NA
ggb	67,314 a	28,533,439 a	2,594,098 a	55,549 a	22,857,097 a	2,331,087 a	66,296 a	30,470,298 a	2,950,915 a
lca	See ELCA	See ELCA	See ELCA	See ELCA	See ELCA	See ELCA	See ELCA	See ELCA	See ELCA
lms	1,952,020	975,113,229	121,536,226	1,945,846	986,295,136	123,632,549	1,934,057	1,101,690,594	127,554,235
mch	92,002 a	75,796,469 a	26,452,444 a	See MUS	See MUS	See MUS	See MUS	See MUS	See MUS
mgc	36,600	14,786,936 a	5,853,292 a	See MUS	See MUS	See MUS	See MUS	See MUS	See MUS
mus	MCH & MGC	MCH & MGC	MCH & MGC	123,404 a	95,843,112 a	34,821,702 a	120,381 l	NA	NA
mca	20,764	13,082,671	1,131,742	20,400	11,527,684	849,837	20,925 a	13,224,765 a	1,014,314 a
nab	43,844 a	41,939,978 a	7,731,550 a	45,738	47,207,867	9,055,128	47,097	54,866,431	9,845,352
opc	15,936	22,362,292	4,438,333	17,279 a	24,878,935	4,920,310	17,914	28,120,325	5,978,474
pch	2,587,674	2,173,483,227	355,628,625	2,560,201	2,326,583,688	384,445,608	2,525,330	2,517,278,130	398,602,204
rca	179,085	189,390,759	33,890,048	178,260 a	216,305,458 a	36,158,625 a	177,281	226,555,821	37,221,041
sda	839,915	269,679,595	588,227,010	861,860	301,221,572	629,944,965	880,921	316,562,375	675,000,508
sbc	15,729,356	6,498,607,390	953,491,003	14,001,690 g	6,001,443,051 g	795,207,316 g	15,221,959 g	7,037,516,273 g	936,520,388 g
ucc	1,421,088	678,251,694	74,861,463	1,401,682	700,645,114	76,550,398	1,377,320	744,991,925	78,525,195
wel	314,265 a	177,633,393 a	44,584,079 a	314,217 a	181,513,283 a	49,143,360 a	314,941 a	193,625,639 a	52,918,434 a
Total	29,454,980	14,596,645,212	2,719,937,645	27,640,624	14,593,856,016	2,676,169,582	28,680,654	16,162,209,883	2,888,772,727

a Data obtained from denominational source.

f Inclusive membership, obtained from the denomination and used only in Chapter 5 analysis; not included in the Total sum on this page.

g The 1999 and 2000 data for the Southern Baptist Convention used in the 1968-2002 analysis includes data only for those State Conventions that provided a breakdown of Total Contributions between Congregational Finances and Benevolences for that year. For the Eleven Denominations 1921-2005 analysis, 1999 and 2000 Southern Baptist Convention Total Contributions are $7,772,452,961 and $8,437,177,940, respectively. For the Eleven Denominations 1921-2005 analysis, and the Membership Trends analysis, 1999 and 2000 Southern Baptist Convention Membership is 15,851,756 and 15,960,308, respectively.

l Data obtained from denominational source and used only in Chapter 5 analysis; not included in Total sum on this page.

Appendix B-1: Church Member Giving 1968-2007 (continued)

	Data Year 2001			Data Year 2002			Data Year 2003		
	Full/Confirmed Members	Congregational Finances	Benevolences	Full/Confirmed Members	Congregational Finances	Benevolences	Full/Confirmed Members	Congregational Finances	Benevolences
abc	631,771 a	381,080,930 a	74,228,212 a	617,034	396,380,200	65,103,943	572,218	391,456,166	60,965,853
alc	See ELCA	See ELCA	See ELCA	See ELCA	See ELCA	See ELCA	See ELCA	See ELCA	See ELCA
arp	35,181	36,976,653	7,707,456	35,556	37,394,125	8,091,930	35,418	36,664,331	7,615,661
bcc	20,739	29,566,287	6,864,936	20,579 a	29,069,369 a	5,619,911 a	21,538 a	30,219,066 a	6,090,287 a
ccd	518,434	437,447,942	48,609,107	504,118	438,378,385	46,708,737	491,085 a	456,513,192 a	45,243,300 a
cga	237,222 l	NA	NA	247,007 k	NA	NA	250,052 l	NA	NA
cgg	4,155	3,436,200	477,457	3,860 k	NA	NA	3,694 a	3,786,000 a	511,394 a
chb	134,828	68,790,933	22,869,690	134,844	70,524,998	22,730,417	132,481	73,120,173	20,756,646
chn	639,296 a	557,589,101 a	121,203,179 a	639,330	587,027,991	132,183,078	616,069	595,552,079	133,379,908
ccc	40,857	34,483,917	6,754,192	40,041	36,747,983	8,190,510	42,032 a	46,340,288 a	6,232,465 a
cpc	85,427	41,216,632	6,744,757	84,417	42,570,586	6,876,097	83,742	41,950,671	7,218,214
ecc	21,463	17,932,202	2,011,619	21,208	18,195,387	2,002,028	20,743	17,648,320	1,980,327
ecv	103,549 a	198,202,551 a	25,137,813 a	105,956 a	211,733,299 a	22,644,569 a	108,594 a	222,653,578 a	24,786,692 a
elc	3,791,986 a	2,166,061,437 a	239,796,502 a	3,757,723	2,238,773,875	233,875,597	3,724,321	2,285,110,767 a	231,916,904 a
els	16,815	11,361,255	1,246,189	16,849	11,787,432	1,010,416	16,674	12,018,180	995,710
emc	5,278 a	10,563,872 a	2,335,880 a	see FEC	see FEC	see FEC	see FEC	see FEC	see FEC
feb	1,271 a	1,086,582 a	246,296 a	1,896 a	1,651,056 a	512,269 a	1,861 a	1,723,143 a	673,694 a
fec	see EMC	see EMC	see EMC	5,686 a	10,457,231 a	1,811,985 a	5,780 a	11,862,813 a	2,275,726 a
fmc	61,202	111,415,741	14,595,290	62,742 a	117,340,008 a	16,194,960 a	64,726 a	122,723,869 a	14,281,867 a
fum	40,197 f	NA	NA	38,764 f	NA	NA	37,863 f	NA	NA
ggb	66,636 a	30,152,750 a	3,091,252 a	67,231	31,000,633	2,922,004	62,377 a	32,581,954 a	2,846,173 a
lca	See ELCA	See ELCA	See ELCA	See ELCA	See ELCA	See ELCA	See ELCA	See ELCA	See ELCA
lms	1,920,949	1,092,453,907	124,703,387	1,907,923	1,086,223,370	117,110,167	1,894,822	1,131,212,373 a	125,169,844
mch	See MUS	See MUS	See MUS	See MUS	See MUS	See MUS	See MUS	See MUS	See MUS
mgc	See MUS	See MUS	See MUS	See MUS	See MUS	See MUS	See MUS	See MUS	See MUS
mus	113,972 l	NA	NA	112,688 k	NA	NA	111,031 l	NA	NA
mca	21,319 a	13,237,006 a	1,054,515 a	20,583 a	13,037,136 a	971,527 a	19,456	16,939,268	925,302
nab	49,017	50,871,441	9,742,646	47,692	56,813,620	8,952,067	47,812 a	55,566,213 a	9,602,812 a
opc	18,414	30,012,219	6,077,752	18,746	29,251,600	5,216,600	19,725	30,972,500	5,671,600
pch	2,493,781	2,526,681,144	409,319,291	2,451,969	2,509,677,412	392,953,913	2,405,311	2,361,944,688	381,693,067
rca	173,463	228,677,098	39,313,564	171,361	229,560,092	39,393,056	168,801	235,422,160	39,932,078
sda	900,985	329,285,946	707,593,100	918,882	346,825,034	725,180,278	935,428	348,219,525	740,463,422
sbc	15,315,526 g	7,477,479,269 g	980,224,243	15,394,653 g	7,935,692,549 g	1,028,650,682	16,205,050 a	8,546,166,798	1,102,363,842
ucc	1,359,105	772,191,485	80,464,673	1,330,985	789,083,286	78,157,356	1,296,652	802,327,537	76,647,374
wel	314,360 a	203,334,779 a	53,455,670 a	313,690 a	211,121,810 a	49,035,869 a	313,330 a	227,521,597 a	50,687,438 a
Total	28,745,807	16,861,589,279	2,995,868,668	28,691,694	17,486,318,467	3,022,099,966	29,309,740	18,138,217,249	3,100,927,600

a Data obtained from denominational source.

f Inclusive membership, obtained from the denomination and used only in Chapter 5 analysis; not included in the Total sum on this page.

g The 2001 and 2002 data for the Southern Baptist Convention used in the 1968-2002 analysis includes data only for those State Conventions that provided a breakdown of Total Contributions between Congregational Finances and Benevolences for that year. For the Eleven Denominations 1921-2004 analysis 2001 and 2002 Southern Baptist Convention Total Contributions is $8,935,013,659 and $9,461,603,271, respectively. For the Eleven Denominations 1921-2004 analysis, and the Membership Trends analysis, 2001 and 2002 Southern Baptist Convention Membership is 16,052,920 and 16,137,736, respectively.

k Data used only in Chapter 5 analysis; not included in Total sum on this page.

l Data obtained from denominational source and used only in Chapter 5 analysis; not included in Total sum on this page.

Appendix B-1: Church Member Giving 1968-2007 (continued)

	Data Year 2004			Data Year 2005			Data Year 2006		
	Full/Confirmed Members	Congregational Finances	Benevolences	Full/Confirmed Members	Congregational Finances	Benevolences	Full/Confirmed Members	Congregational Finances	Benevolences
abc	498,407 a	372,241,219 a	60,493,722 a	375,917	277,122,001 a	59,772,842	343,301 a	261,159,450	51,325,563
alc	See ELCA	See ELCA	See ELCA	See ELCA	See ELCA	See ELCA	See ELCA	See ELCA	See ELCA
arp	35,640 a	43,324,132 a	5,965,950 a	35,209 a	41,256,621 a	9,664,612 a	34,939 a	40,305,680 a	8,286,494 a
bcc	22,818 a	27,218,450 a	5,016,990 a	23,498 a	34,920,636 a	4,879,420 a	25,866 a	35,492,373 a	5,904,127 a
ccd	479,075 a	447,535,858 a	45,841,497 a	431,365 a	453,623,467 a	49,421,931 a	450,057 a	489,840,866 a	49,271,591 a
cga	252,419 k	NA	NA	255,771 l	NA	NA	249,845 k	NA	NA
cgg	3,267 a	3,966,000 a	479,000 a	3,200 a	4,115,400 a	381,422 a	3,080 a	4,030,000 a	391,793 a
chb	131,201	71,402,128	19,038,122	128,820	73,982,601	23,958,373	126,994 a	72,676,903	20,157,405
chn	623,774	610,902,447	132,624,279	630,159	622,257,466	143,177,276	633,154	655,937,953	136,893,238
ccc	42,725	51,335,963	8,459,095	42,838 j	50,845,153 j	8,501,074 j	42,862 a	55,997,723 a	9,419,501 a
cpc	83,007 a	42,431,192	7,368,979	81,464 a	45,769,458 a	8,379,379 a	81,034	46,396,330	8,331,581
ecc	20,745 a	19,402,040 h	3,429,948 h	20,169 a	17,880,135 a	3,528,552 a	19,166 a	18,741,363 a	3,432,641 a
ecv	113,002 a	244,040,438 a	23,226,589	114,283 a	266,614,225 a	25,232,786 a	120,030 a	290,965,669 a	22,805,559 a
elc	3,685,987	2,329,793,744	238,220,062	3,636,948	2,348,010,569 a	256,787,436 a	3,580,402	2,413,738,345 a	250,408,865
els	16,407	11,808,028	1,118,456	15,917	12,581,651	1,250,120 a	16,319	15,105,802	1,306,478
emc	See FEC	See FEC	See FEC	See FEC	See FEC	See FEC	See FEC	See FEC	See FEC
feb	1,844 a	2,023,545 a	511,470 a	1,664 a	2,043,940 a	595,313 a	1,434 a	2,265,710 a	427,685 a
fec	6,496	13,855,056 a	2,670,733	6,694 a	15,751,410 a	2,675,422 a	6,786 a	16,301,682 a	2,729,537 a
fmc	65,272	131,576,527	15,440,418	65,816	138,619,962	15,905,067	65,802	142,861,676	15,958,866
fum	34,323 f	NA	NA	38,121 f	NA	NA	43,612 f	NA	NA
ggb	78,863 a	30,631,505 a	3,140,132 a	60,559 a	36,990,479 a	3,156,104 a	52,279 a	32,918,373 a	2,987,587 a
lca	See ELCA	See ELCA	See ELCA	See ELCA	See ELCA	See ELCA	See ELCA	See ELCA	See ELCA
lms	1,880,213	1,186,000,747	121,763,263	1,870,659	1,176,649,592	120,169,146	1,856,783	1,229,305,441	126,153,117 a
mch	See MUS	See MUS	See MUS	See MUS	See MUS	See MUS	See MUS	See MUS	See MUS
mgc	See MUS	See MUS	See MUS	See MUS	See MUS	See MUS	See MUS	See MUS	See MUS
mus	110,420 i	NA	NA	109,808 l	NA	NA	109,385 l	NA	NA
mca	19,021	17,545,228	969,697	18,529	16,738,701	1,096,554	17,955	16,729,153 a	1,051,451
nab	46,995 a	59,832,412 a	10,342,080 a	46,671 l	NA	NA	47,150	62,175,197	10,104,273
opc	19,993 a	32,760,800 a	5,899,500 a	19,965	34,520,600	6,215,800	20,850	38,642,300	7,241,000
pch	2,362,136	2,387,317,945	387,589,903	2,313,662	2,425,999,953	388,271,070	2,267,118	2,459,679,132	395,040,718
rca	166,761	256,915,687	39,941,147	164,697	267,082,267	43,827,424	163,160	286,075,445	42,718,072
sda	948,787 a	347,797,864 a	773,751,848 a	964,811	427,285,012	846,114,329	980,551	426,686,109	863,635,364
sbc	16,267,494	8,971,390,824	1,199,806,224	16,270,315	9,487,900,433	1,233,644,135	16,306,246	10,086,992,362	1,285,616,031
ucc	1,266,129 a	822,172,566	73,481,544	1,224,297	827,237,883	81,488,911	1,218,541	846,482,513 a	73,611,594 a
wel	313,088 a	245,098,070 a	51,692,943 a	311,950 a	244,718,123 a	54,606,362 a	310,338 a	250,589,183 a	63,427,503 a
Tota	29,199,147	18,780,320,415	3,238,283,591	28,833,405	19,350,517,738	3,392,700,860	28,792,197	20,298,092,733	3,458,637,634

a Data obtained from denominational source.

f Inclusive membership, obtained from the denomination and used only in Chapter 5 analysis; not included in the Total sum on this page.

h Data obtained from the denomination included the following note: "2004 figures differ substantially due to change in accounting procedures."

i 2004 membership data is an average of 2003 and 2005 data obtained from the denomination; used only in Chapter 5 analysis; not included in Total sum on this page.

j The denomination stated that the data appearing in YACC 2007 as 2004 data was actually for 2005.

k Data used only in Chapter 5 analysis; not included in Total sum on this page.

l Data obtained from denominational source and used only in Chapter 5 analysis; not included in Total sum on this page.

Appendix B-1: Church Member Giving 1968-2007 (continued)

Data Year 2007

	Full/Confirmed Members	Congregational Finances	Benevolences
abc	345,588 a	272,304,732 a	53,636,473
alc	See ELCA	See ELCA	See ELCA
arp	34,954 a	40,442,600 a	8,981,600 a
bcc	26,468 a	40,826,470 a	5,980,438 a
ccd	447,340	473,677,625	45,405,339
cga	252,905 k	NA	NA
cgg	3,039 a	4,066,200 a	312,545 a
chb	125,418	68,434,534	20,233,969
chn	635,526	677,586,886	140,135,344
ccc	41,772	64,471,078	9,996,077
cpc	78,451	49,306,468	8,460,302
ecc	19,339	15,731,559 a	1,449,196 a
ecv	123,150 a	301,961,227 a	21,955,749 a
elc	3,533,956	2,470,777,573 a	254,571,455 a
els	15,734	14,738,808	1,365,828
emc	See FEC	See FEC	See FEC
feb	1,248 a	2,261,292 a	400,589 a
fec	6,834 a	17,646,038 a	2,300,708 a
fmc	67,259	149,855,328	18,778,761 a
fum	43,647 k	NA	NA
ggb	46,242 a	27,179,045 a	4,206,088 a
lca	See ELCA	See ELCA	See ELCA
lms	1,835,064	1,278,836,855	120,937,847
mch	See MUS	See MUS	See MUS
mgc	See MUS	See MUS	See MUS
mus	108,651 l	NA	NA
mca	17,554	17,869,301	1,152,271
nab	NA	NA	NA
opc	21,031	38,486,700	7,243,700
pch	2,209,546	2,518,402,119	398,386,295
rca	162,182	294,008,651	44,438,226
sda	1,000,472	368,356,521	890,924,215
sbc	16,266,920	10,779,240,776	1,327,856,082
ucc	1,145,281	859,744,628	77,117,434
wel	309,658 a	255,887,929 a	67,194,722 a
Total	28,520,026	21,102,100,943	3,533,421,253

a Data obtained from denominational source.

k Data used only in Chapter 5 analysis; not included in Total sum on this page.

l Data obtained from denominational source and used only in Chapter 5 analysis; not included in Total sum on this page.

Appendix B-2: Church Member Giving for 44 Denominations, 2006-2007

	Data Year 2006			Data Year 2007		
	Full/Confirmed Members	Congregational Finances	Benevolences	Full/Confirmed Members	Congregational Finances	Benevolences
Allegheny Wesleyan Methodist Connection (Original Allegheny Conference)	1,471	3,767,239	1,124,588	1,414	3,851,469	1,122,120
Baptist Missionary Association	185,256 [a]	52,924,252 [a]	15,381,554 [a]	177,463 [a]	52,048,000 [a]	13,138,820 [a]
Bible Fellowship Church	7,585 [a]	13,069,984 [a]	3,373,362 [a]	7,605	12,633,422	3,514,772
Christ Community Church (Evangelical-Protestant)	676	1,380,332 [a]	597,598 [a]	684 [a]	1,105,079 [a]	382,723 [a]
Christian and Missionary Alliance	189,969	390,679,845 [a]	67,383,338 [a]	195,481	395,920,208	71,891,940
Church of Christ (Holiness) U.S.A.	10,816 [a]	12,051,781 [a]	727,432 [a]	11,468	12,855,697	715,581
Church of the Lutheran Brethren of America	8,907	18,576,152	1,989,752	9,347 [a]	18,684,672 [a]	2,072,752 [a]
Church of the Lutheran Confession	6,298 [a]	5,966,978 [a]	998,166 [a]	6,262 [a]	6,152,034 [a]	1,055,678 [a]
Churches of God General Conference	33,208	27,504,509	5,556,842	33,083	29,468,091	5,638,765
The Episcopal Church	1,749,073 [a]	1,871,109,504 [a]	316,199,294 [a]	1,720,477	1,895,165,434	326,002,004
The Missionary Church	34,196 [a]	69,241,216 [a]	18,611,947 [a]	43,026	81,494,766	10,080,425
Presbyterian Church in America	266,166	532,611,674	117,479,754	270,605	561,594,911	124,736,766
Primitive Methodist Church in the U.S.A.	3,833	4,434,026	646,459	3,635 [a]	4,027,817 [a]	604,214 [a]
The United Methodist Church	7,976,985 [a]	4,825,846,715	1,186,532,183	7,899,147 [a]	5,080,054,998 [a]	1,215,887,457 [a]
The Wesleyan Church	117,493 [a]	252,374,528 [a]	40,451,722 [a]	116,985 [a]	279,692,216 [a]	41,769,766 [a]

[a] Data obtained from denominational source.

Appendix B-3.1: Church Member Giving for 11 Denominations, 1921-1952, in Current Dollars

Year	Total Contributions	Members	Per Capita Giving
1921	$281,173,263	17,459,611	$16.10
1922	345,995,802	18,257,426	18.95
1923	415,556,876	18,866,775	22.03
1924	443,187,826	19,245,220	23.03
1925	412,658,363	19,474,863	21.19
1926	368,529,223	17,054,404	21.61
1927	459,527,624	20,266,709	22.67
1928	429,947,883	20,910,584	20.56
1929	445,327,233	20,612,910	21.60
1930	419,697,819	20,796,745	20.18
1931	367,158,877	21,508,745	17.07
1932	309,409,873	21,757,411	14.22
1933	260,366,681	21,792,663	11.95
1934	260,681,472	22,105,624	11.79
1935	267,596,925	22,204,355	12.05
1936	279,835,526	21,746,023	12.87
1937	297,134,313	21,906,456	13.56
1938	307,217,666	22,330,090	13.76
1939	302,300,476	23,084,048	13.10
1940	311,362,429	23,671,660	13.15
1941	336,732,622	23,120,929	14.56
1942	358,419,893	23,556,204	15.22
1943	400,742,492	24,679,784	16.24
1944	461,500,396	25,217,319	18.30
1945	551,404,448	25,898,642	21.29
1946	608,165,179	26,158,559	23.25
1947	684,393,895	27,082,905	25.27
1948	775,360,993	27,036,992	28.68
1949	875,069,944	27,611,824	31.69
1950	934,723,015	28,176,095	33.17
1951	1,033,391,527	28,974,314	35.67
1952	1,121,802,639	29,304,909	38.28

Appendix B-3.2: Church Member Giving for Eleven Denominations, 1953-1967

	Data Year 1953		Data Year 1954		Data Year 1955	
	Total Contributions	Per Capita Total Contributions	Total Contributions	Per Capita Total Contributions	Total Contributions	Per Capita Total Contributions
American Baptist (Northern)	$66,557,447 a	$44.50 b	$65,354,184	$43.17	$67,538,753 d	$44.19 d
Christian Church (Disciples of Christ)	60,065,545 c	32.50 b	65,925,164	34.77	68,611,162 d	35.96 d
Church of the Brethren	7,458,584	43.78	7,812,806	45.88	9,130,616	53.00
The Episcopal Church	84,209,027	49.02	92,079,668	51.84	97,541,567 d	50.94 b
Evangelical Lutheran Church in America						
The American Lutheran Church						
American Lutheran Church	30,881,256	55.24	34,202,987	58.83	40,411,856	67.03
The Evangelical Lutheran Church	30,313,907	48.70	33,312,926	51.64	37,070,341	55.29
United Evangelical Lutheran Ch.	1,953,163	55.85	2,268,200	50.25	2,635,469	69.84
Lutheran Free Church	Not Reported: YACC 1955, p. 264		2,101,026	44.51	2,708,747	55.76
Evan. Lutheran Churches, Assn. of	Not Reported: YACC 1955, p. 264		Not Reported: YACC 1956, p. 276		Not Reported: YACC 1957, p. 284	
Lutheran Church in America						
United Lutheran Church	67,721,548	45.68	76,304,344	50.25	83,170,787	53.46
General Council Evang. Luth. Ch.						
General Synod of Evan. Luth. Ch.						
United Syn. Evang. Luth. South						
American Evangelical Luth. Ch.	Not Reported: YACC 1955, p. 264		Not Reported: YACC 1956, p. 276		Not Reported: YACC 1957, p. 284	
Augustana Lutheran Church	18,733,019	53.98	22,203,098	62.14	22,090,350	60.12
Finnish Lutheran Ch. (Suomi Synod)	744,971	32.12	674,554	29.47	1,059,682	43.75
Moravian Church in Am. No. Prov.	1,235,534	53.26	1,461,658	59.51	1,241,008	49.15
Presbyterian Church (U.S.A.)						
United Presbyterian Ch. in U.S.A.	141,057,179	56.49	158,110,613	61.47	180,472,698	68.09
Presbyterian Church in the U.S.A.	13,204,897	57.73	14,797,353	62.37	16,019,616	65.39
United Presbyterian Ch. in N.A.	56,001,996	73.99	59,222,983	75.54	66,033,260	81.43
Presbyterian Church in the U.S.	13,671,897	68.57	14,740,275	71.87	17,459,572	84.05
Reformed Church in America						
Southern Baptist Convention	278,851,129	39.84	305,573,654	42.17	334,836,283	44.54
United Church of Christ						
Congregational Christian	64,061,866	49.91	71,786,834	54.76	80,519,810	60.00
Congregational						
Evangelical and Reformed	31,025,133	41.24	36,261,267	46.83	41,363,406	52.74
Evangelical Synod of N.A./German						
Reformed Church in the U.S.						
The United Methodist Church						
The Evangelical United Brethren	36,331,994	50.21	36,609,598	50.43	41,199,631	56.01
The Methodist Church	314,521,214	34.37	345,416,448	37.53	389,490,613	41.82
Methodist Episcopal Church						
Methodist Episcopal Church South						
Methodist Protestant Church						
Total	$1,318,601,306		$1,446,219,640		$1,600,655,226	

a In data year 1953, $805,135 has been subtracted from the 1955 *Yearbook of American Churches* (Edition for 1956) entry. See 1956 *Yearbook of American Churches* (Edition for 1957), p. 276, n.1.

b This Per Capita Total Contributions figure was calculated by dividing (1) revised Total Contributions as listed in this Appendix, by (2) Membership that, for purposes of this report, had been calculated by dividing the unrevised Total Contributions by the Per Capita Total Contributions figures that were published in the *YACC* series.

c In data year 1953, $5,508,883 has been added to the 1955 *Yearbook of American Churches* (Edition for 1956) entry. See 1956 *Yearbook of American Churches* (Edition for 1957), p.276, n. 4.

d Total Contributions and Per Capita Total Contributions, respectively, prorated based on available data as follows: American Baptist Churches, 1954 and 1957 data; Christian Church (Disciples of Christ), 1954 and 1956 data; and The Episcopal Church, 1954 and 1956 data.

Appendix B-3.2: Church Member Giving for Eleven Denominations, 1953-1967 (continued)

	Data Year 1956		Data Year 1957		Data Year 1958	
	Total Contributions	Per Capita Total Contributions	Total Contributions	Per Capita Total Contributions	Total Contributions	Per Capita Total Contributions
American Baptist (Northern)	$69,723,321 e	$45.21 e	$71,907,890	$46.23	$70,405,404	$45.03
Christian Church (Disciples of Christ)	71,397,159	37.14	73,737,955	37.94	79,127,458	41.17
Church of the Brethren	10,936,285	63.15	11,293,388	64.43	12,288,049	70.03
The Episcopal Church	103,003,465	52.79	111,660,728	53.48	120,687,177	58.33
Evangelical Lutheran Church in America						
The American Lutheran Church						
American Lutheran Church	45,316,809	72.35	44,518,194	68.80	47,216,896	70.89
The Evangelical Lutheran Church	39,096,038	56.47	44,212,046	61.95	45,366,512	61.74
United Evangelical Lutheran Ch.	2,843,527	73.57	2,641,201	65.46	3,256,050	77.38
Lutheran Free Church	2,652,307	53.14	3,379,882	64.70	3,519,017	66.31
Evan. Lutheran Churches, Assn. of	Not Reported: YACC 1958, p. 292		Not Reported: YACC 1959, p. 277		Not Reported: YACC 1960, p. 276	
Lutheran Church in America						
United Lutheran Church	93,321,223	58.46	100,943,860	61.89	110,179,054	66.45
General Council Evang. Luth. Ch.						
General Synod of Evan. Luth. Ch.						
United Syn. Evang. Luth. South						
American Evangelical Luth. Ch.	Not Comparable YACC 1958, p. 292		935,319	59.45	1,167,503	72.98
Augustana Lutheran Church	24,893,792	66.15	28,180,152	72.09	29,163,771	73.17
Finnish Lutheran Ch. (Suomi Synod)	1,308,026	51.56	1,524,299	58.11	1,533,058	61.94
Moravian Church in Am. No. Prov.	1,740,961	67.53	1,776,703	67.77	1,816,281	68.14
Presbyterian Church (U.S.A.)						
United Presbyterian Ch. in U.S.A.					243,000,572	78.29
Presbyterian Church in the U.S.A.	204,208,085	75.02	214,253,598	77.06		
United Presbyterian Ch. in N.A.	18,424,936	73.30	19,117,837	74.24		
Presbyterian Church in the U.S.	73,477,555	88.56	78,426,424	92.03	82,760,291	95.18
Reformed Church in America	18,718,008	88.56	19,658,604	91.10	21,550,017	98.24
Southern Baptist Convention	372,136,675	48.17	397,540,347	49.99	419,619,438	51.04
United Church of Christ						
Congregational Christian	89,914,505	65.18	90,333,453	64.87	97,480,446	69.55
Congregational						
Evangelical and Reformed	51,519,531	64.88	55,718,141	69.56	63,419,468	78.56
Evangelical Synod of N.A./German						
Reformed Church in the U.S.						
The United Methodist Church						
The Evangelical United Brethren	44,727,060	60.57	45,738,332 e	61.75 e	46,749,605 e	62.93 e
The Methodist Church	413,893,955	43.82	462,826,269 e	48.31 e	511,758,582	52.80
Methodist Episcopal Church						
Methodist Episcopal Church South						
Methodist Protestant Church						
Total	$1,753,253,223		$1,880,324,622		$2,012,064,649	

e Total Contributions and Per Capita Total Contributions, respectively, prorated based on available data as follows: American Baptist Churches, 1954 and 1957 data; The Evangelical United Brethren, 1956 and 1960 data; and The Methodist Church, 1956 and 1958 data.

Appendix B-3.2: Church Member Giving for Eleven Denominations, 1953-1967 (continued)

	Data Year 1959		Data Year 1960		Data Year 1961	
	Total Contributions	Per Capita Total Contributions	Total Contributions	Per Capita Total Contributions	Total Contributions	Per Capita Total Contributions
American Baptist (Northern)	$74,877,669	$48.52	$73,106,232	$48.06	$104,887,025	$68.96
Christian Ch (Disciples of Christ)	Not Comparable (YACC 1961, p. 273)		$86,834,944	$63.26	$89,730,589	$65.31
Church of the Brethren	$12,143,983	$65.27	$12,644,194	$68.33	$13,653,155	$73.33
The Episcopal Church	$130,279,752	$61.36	$140,625,284	$64.51	$154,458,809	$68.30
Evangelical Lutheran Church in Am.						
The American Lutheran Church					$113,645,260	$73.28
American Lutheran Church	$50,163,078	$73.52	$51,898,875	$74.49		
The Evangelical Lutheran Church	$49,488,063	$65.56	$51,297,348	$66.85		
United Evangelical Lutheran Ch.	Not Reported: YACC 1961, p. 273		Not Reported: YACC 1963, p. 273			
Lutheran Free Church	$3,354,270	$61.20	$3,618,418	$63.98	$4,316,925	$73.46
Evan. Lutheran Churches, Assn of	Not Reported: YACC 1961, p. 273		Not Reported: YACC 1963, p. 273			
Lutheran Church in America						
United Lutheran Church	$114,458,260	$68.29	$119,447,895	$70.86	$128,850,845	$76.18
General Council Evang Luth Ch						
General Synod of Evan Luth Ch						
United Syn Evang Luth South						
American Evangelical Luth. Ch	$1,033,907	$63.83	$1,371,600	$83.63	$1,209,752	$74.89
Augustana Lutheran Church	$31,279,335	$76.97	$33,478,865	$80.88	$37,863,105	$89.37
Finnish Luth. Ch (Suomi Synod)	$1,685,342	$68.61	$1,860,481	$76.32	$1,744,550	$70.60
Moravian Church in Am. No. Prov.	$2,398,565	$89.28	$2,252,536	$82.95	$2,489,930	$90.84
Presbyterian Church (U.S.A.)						
United Presbyterian Ch in U.S.A.	$259,679,057	$82.30	$270,233,943	$84.31	$285,380,476	$87.90
Presbyterian Ch in the U.S.A.						
United Presbyterian Ch in N.A.						
Presbyterian Church in the U.S.	$88,404,631	$99.42	$91,582,428	$101.44	$96,637,354	$105.33
Reformed Church in America	$22,970,935	$103.23	$23,615,749	$104.53	$25,045,773	$108.80
Southern Baptist Convention	$453,338,720	$53.88	$480,608,972	$55.68	$501,301,714	$50.24
United Church of Christ						
Congregational Christian	$100,938,267	$71.12	$104,862,037	$73.20	$105,871,158	$73.72
Congregational						
Evangelical and Reformed	$65,541,874	$80.92	$62,346,084	$76.58	$65,704,662	$80.33
Evangelical Synod of N.A./German						
Reformed Church in the U.S.						
The United Methodist Church						
The Evangelical United Brethren	$47,760,877 d	$64.10	$48,772,149 d	$65.28	$50,818,912 d	$68.12
The Methodist Church	$532,854,842 d	$53.97	$553,951,102 d	$55.14	$581,504,618	$57.27
Methodist Episcopal Church						
Methodist Episcopal Ch South						
Methodist Protestant Church						
Total	$2,042,651,427		$2,214,409,136		$2,365,114,612	

d Total Contributions averaged from available data as follows: Evangelical United Brethren, 1956 and 1960 data; The United Methodist Church, 1958 and 1960 data.

Appendix B-3.2: Church Member Giving for Eleven Denominations, 1953-1967 (continued)

	Data Year 1962		Data Year 1963		Data Year 1964	
	Total Contributions	Per Capita Total Contributions	Total Contributions	Per Capita Total Contributions	Total Contributions	Per Capita Total Contributions
American Baptist (Northern)	$105,667,332	$68.42	$99,001,651	$68.34	$104,699,557	$69.99
Christian Church (Disciples of Christ)	91,889,457	67.20	96,607,038	75.81	102,102,840	86.44
Church of the Brethren	14,594,572	77.88	14,574,688	72.06	15,221,162	76.08
The Episcopal Church	155,971,264	69.80	171,125,464	76.20	175,374,777	76.66
Evangelical Lutheran Church in America						
The American Lutheran Church	114,912,112	72.47	136,202,292	81.11	143,687,165	83.83
The Evangelical Lutheran Church						
United Evangelical Lutheran Ch.						
Lutheran Free Church	4,765,138	78.68				
Evan. Lutheran Churches, Assn. of						
Lutheran Church in America	185,166,857	84.98	157,423,391	71.45	170,012,096	76.35
United Lutheran Church						
General Council Evang. Luth. Ch.						
General Synod of Evan. Luth. Ch.						
United Syn. Evang. Luth. South						
American Evangelical Luth. Ch.						
Augustana Lutheran Church						
Finnish Lutheran Ch. (Suomi Synod)						
Moravian Church in Am. No. Prov.	2,512,133	91.92	2,472,273	89.29	2,868,694	103.54
Presbyterian Church (U.S.A.)						
United Presbyterian Ch. in U.S.A.	288,496,652	88.08	297,582,313	90.46	304,833,435	92.29
Presbyterian Church in the U.S.A.						
United Presbyterian Ch. in N.A.						
Presbyterian Church in the U.S.	99,262,431	106.96	102,625,764	109.46	108,269,579	114.61
Reformed Church in the U.S.	25,579,443	110.16	26,918,484	117.58	29,174,103	126.44
Southern Baptist Convention	540,811,457	53.06	556,042,694	53.49	591,587,981	55.80
United Church of Christ	164,858,968	72.83	162,379,019	73.12	169,208,042	75.94
Congregational Christian						
Congregational						
Evangelical and Reformed						
Evangelical Synod of N.A./German						
Reformed Church in the U.S.						
The United Methodist Church						
The Evangelical United Brethren	54,567,962	72.91	49,921,568	67.37	56,552,783	76.34
The Methodist Church	599,081,561	58.53	613,547,721	59.60	608,841,881	59.09
Methodist Episcopal Church						
Methodist Episcopal Church South						
Methodist Protestant Church						
Total	$2,448,137,339		$2,486,424,360		$2,582,434,095	

Note: Data for the years 1965 through 1967 was not available in a form that could be readily analyzed for the present purposes, and therefore data for 1965-1967 was estimated as described in the introductory comments to Appendix B. See Appendix B-1 for 1968-1991 data except for The Episcopal Church and The United Methodist Church, available data for which is presented in the continuation of Appendix B-3 in the table immediately following.

Appendix B-3.3: Church Member Giving for 11 Denominations,
The Episcopal Church and The United Methodist Church, 1968-2007

The Episcopal Church			The United Methodist Church		
Data Year	Total Contributions	Full/Confirmed Membership	Data Year	Total Contributions	Full/Confirmed Membership
1968	$202,658,092 [c]	2,322,911 [c]	1968	$763,000,434 [a]	10,849,375 [b]
1969	209,989,189 [c]	2,238,538	1969	800,425,000	10,671,774
1970	248,702,969	2,208,773	1970	819,945,000	10,509,198
1971	257,523,469	2,143,557	1971	843,103,000	10,334,521
1972	270,245,645	2,099,896	1972	885,708,000	10,192,265
1973	296,735,919 [c]	2,079,873 [c]	1973	935,723,000	10,063,046
1974	305,628,925	2,069,793	1974	1,009,760,804	9,957,710
1975	352,243,222	2,051,914 [c]	1975	1,081,080,372	9,861,028
1976	375,942,065	2,021,057	1976	1,162,828,991	9,785,534
1977	401,814,395	2,114,638	1977	1,264,191,548	9,731,779
1978	430,116,564	1,975,234	1978	1,364,460,266	9,653,711
1979	484,211,412	1,962,062	1979	1,483,481,986	9,584,771
1980	507,315,457	1,933,080 [c]	1980	1,632,204,336	9,519,407
1981	697,816,298	1,930,690	1981	1,794,706,741	9,457,012
1982	778,184,068	1,922,923 [c]	1982	1,931,796,533	9,405,164
1983	876,844,252	1,906,618	1983	2,049,437,917	9,291,936
1984	939,796,743	1,896,056	1984	2,211,306,198	9,266,853
1985	1,043,117,983	1,881,250	1985	2,333,928,274	9,192,172
1986	1,134,455,479	1,772,271 [c]	1986	2,460,079,431	9,124,575
1987	1,181,378,441	1,741,036	1987	2,573,748,234	9,055,145
1988	1,209,378,098	1,725,581	1988	2,697,918,285	8,979,139
1989	1,309,243,747	1,714,122	1989	2,845,998,177	8,904,824
1990	1,377,794,610	1,698,240	1990	2,967,535,538	8,853,455
1991	1,541,141,356 [c]	1,613,825 [c]	1991	3,099,522,282	8,789,101
1992	1,582,055,527 [c]	1,615,930 [c]	1992	3,202,700,721 [c]	8,726,951 [c]
1993	1,617,623,255 [c]	1,580,339 [c]	1993	3,303,255,279	8,646,595
1994	1,679,250,095 [c]	1,578,282 [c]	1994	3,430,351,778	8,584,125
1995	1,840,431,636 [c]	1,584,225 [c]	1995	3,568,359,334 [c]	8,538,808 [c]
1996	1,731,727,725 [c]	1,637,584 [c]	1996	3,744,692,223	8,496,047 [c]
1997	1,832,000,448 [c]	1,757,972 [c]	1997	3,990,329,491 [c]	8,452,042 [c]
1998	1,977,012,320 [c]	1,807,651 [c]	1998	4,219,596,499 [c]	8,411,503 [c]
1999	2,146,835,718 [c]	1,843,108 [c]	1999	4,523,284,851	8,377,662
2000	2,143,238,797 [c]	1,877,271 [c]	2000	4,761,148,280	8,340,954
2001	2,070,493,919 [c]	1,897,004 [c]	2001	5,043,693,838 [c]	8,298,460 [c]
2002	2,090,536,512 [c]	1,902,525 [c]	2002	5,242,691,229	8,251,042
2003	2,133,772,253	1,866,157	2003	5,376,057,236 [c]	8,186,274 [c]
2004	2,132,774,534	1,834,530	2004	5,541,540,536	8,120,186 [d]
2005	2,180,974,503 [c]	1,796,017 [c]	2005	5,861,722,397 [c]	8,040,577 [c]
2006	2,187,308,798 [c]	1,749,073 [c]	2006	*6,012,378,898* [c]	7,976,985 [c]
2007	2,221,167,438	1,720,477	2007	6,295,942,455 [c]	7,899,147 [c]

a The Evangelical United Brethren Data Not Reported: YACC 1970, p. 198-200. This figure is the sum of The Methodist Church in 1968, and the Evangelical United Brethren data for 1967.

b This membership figure is an average of the sum of 1967 membership for The Methodist Church and the Evangelical United Brethren and 1969 data for The United Methodist Church.

c Data obtained directly from denominational source.

d Data obtained from the denomination included this note: "Combines 2004 local church data with 2004 clergy data. In the past 2004 lay would be combined with 2005 clergy. We've been delayed in finalizing clergy figures for 2005… [Based on a check of] the past few years, that will mean a difference of less than 300 for the total number."

Appendix B-4: Membership for Seven Denominations, 1968-2007

Year	American Baptist Churches (Total Mem.)	Assemblies of God	Baptist General Conference	Christian and Missionary Alliance	Church of God (Cleveland, TN)	Roman Catholic Church	Salvation Army
1968	1,583,560	610,946	100,000	71,656	243,532	47,468,333	329,515
1969	1,528,019	626,660	101,226	70,573	257,995	47,872,089	331,711
1970	1,472,478	625,027	103,955	71,708	272,276	48,214,729	326,934
1971	1,562,636	645,891	108,474	73,547	287,099	48,390,990	335,684
1972	1,484,393	679,813	111,364	77,991	297,103	48,460,427	358,626
1973	1,502,759	700,071	109,033	77,606	313,332	48,465,438	361,571
1974	1,579,029	751,818	111,093	80,412	328,892	48,701,835	366,471
1975	1,603,033	785,348	115,340	83,628	343,249	48,881,872	384,817
1976	1,593,574	898,711	117,973	83,978	365,124	49,325,752	380,618
1977	1,584,517	939,312	120,222	88,763	377,765	49,836,176	396,238
1978	1,589,610	932,365	131,000	88,903	392,551	49,602,035	414,035
1979	1,600,521	958,418	126,800	96,324	441,385	49,812,178	414,659
1980	1,607,541	1,064,490	133,385	106,050	435,012	50,449,842	417,359
1981	1,621,795	1,103,134	127,662	109,558	456,797	51,207,579	414,999
1982	1,637,099	1,119,686	129,928	112,745	463,992	52,088,774 [a]	419,475
1983	1,620,153	1,153,935	131,594 [a]	117,501	493,904	52,392,934	428,046
1984	1,559,683	1,189,143	131,162 [a]	120,250	505,775	52,286,043	420,971
1985	1,576,483	1,235,403	130,193 [a]	123,602	521,061 [b]	52,654,908	427,825
1986	1,568,778 [a]	1,258,724	132,546 [a]	130,116	536,346 [b]	52,893,217	432,893
1987	1,561,656 [a]	1,275,146	136,688 [a]	131,354	551,632 [b]	53,496,862	434,002
1988	1,548,573 [a]	1,275,148	134,396 [a]	133,575	556,917 [b]	54,918,949 [a]	433,448
1989	1,535,971 [a]	1,266,982	135,125 [a]	134,336	582,203	57,019,948	445,566
1990	1,527,840 [a]	1,298,121	133,742 [a]	138,071	620,393	58,568,015	445,991
1991	1,534,078 [a]	1,324,800	134,717 [a]	141,077	646,201 [b]	58,267,424	446,403
1992	1,538,710 [a]	1,337,321	134,658 [a]	142,346	672,008	59,220,723	450,028 [a]
1993	1,516,505	1,340,400	134,814 [a]	147,367	700,517	59,858,042	450,312 [a]
1994	1,507,934 [a]	1,354,337	135,128	147,560 [a]	722,541	60,190,605	443,246
1995	1,517,400	1,377,320	135,008	147,955	753,230	60,280,454	453,150
1996	1,503,267 [a]	1,407,941	136,120	143,157	773,483 [a]	61,207,914	462,744 [a]
1997	1,478,534 [a]	1,419,717	134,795	146,153	815,042 [a]	61,563,769 [a]	468,262 [a]
1998	1,507,824 [a]	1,453,907	141,445	163,994	839,857 [a]	62,018,436	471,416
1999	1,454,388	1,492,196	142,871 [a]	164,196	870,039	62,391,484	472,871
2000	1,436,909	1,506,834	141,781 [a]	185,133	895,536	63,683,030 [a]	476,887 [a]
2001	1,442,824	1,532,876	144,365 [a]	191,318	920,664 [a]	65,270,444	454,982
2002	1,484,291	1,585,428	145,148	190,573	944,857	66,407,105	457,807 [a]
2003	1,433,075	1,584,076	145,436 [a]	194,074	961,390	67,259,768	449,634 [a]
2004	1,418,403 [a]	1,594,062	145,000 [a]	197,764	989,965	67,820,833	427,027
2005	1,396,700	1,612,336	140,494 [a]	201,009	1,013,488	69,135,254	422,543 [a]
2006	1,371,278	1,627,932	140,000 [a]	189,969	1,032,550	67,515,016	414,054 [a]
2007	1,358,351 [a]	1,641,341	147,500	195,481	1,053,642	67,117,016	413,028

[a] Data obtained from a denominational source.
[b] Extrapolated from YACC series.
  Note regarding American Baptist Churches in the U.S.A. Total Membership data: Total Membership is used for the American Baptist Churches in the U.S.A. for analyses that consider membership as a percentage of U.S. population. The ABC denominational office is the source for this data in the years 1968 and 1970. The year 1978 Total Membership data figure is an adjustment of YACC data based on 1981 YACC information.
Additional Note: North American Baptist Conference 2007 memebership data is calculated from Data Year 2005 and Data Year 2006; used only in Chapter 5 analysis.

Appendix B-5.1: Overseas Missions Income, 34 Denominations, 2003 and 2004

Denomination	2003 Overseas Missions Income				2004 Overseas Missions Income			
	Line 1.	Line 2.	Line 3.	Line 4.	Line 1.	Line 2.	Line 3.	line 4.
Allegheny Wesleyan Methodist Connection	$262,260	$0	$0	$262,260	$266,299	$0	$0	$266,299
American Baptist Churches in the U.S.A.	$20,562,505	$12,048,667	$0	$8,513,838	$17,250,939	$7,759,091	$0	$9,491,848
Associate Reformed Presbyterian Church (General Synod)	$3,508,682	$0	$175,690	$3,332,992	$4,453,573	$15,183	$483,815	$3,954,575
Brethren in Christ Church	$1,651,911	$45,000	$0	$1,606,911	$1,850,963	$50,000	$0	$1,800,963
Christian Church (Disciples of Christ)	$5,960,892	$1,881,873	$0	$4,079,019	$5,347,401	$1,515,309	$0	$3,832,092
Christian and Missionary Alliance [1]	$43,160,960	$0	$0	$43,160,960	$43,534,066	$0	$0	$43,534,066
Church of the Brethren [2]	$1,767,447	$203,824	$0	$1,563,623	$1,702,267	$143,947	$0	$1,558,320
Church of God General Conf. (Oregon, Ill., and Morrow, Ga.)	$67,193	$0	$0	$67,193	$113,497	$0	$0	$113,497
Church of the Lutheran Confession	$182,156	$27,000	$0	$155,156	$246,896	$40,000	$0	$206,896
Church of the Nazarene	$46,334,499	$694,019	$0	$45,640,480	$49,715,273	$1,542,188	$0	$48,173,085
Churches of God General Conference	$899,679	$0	$0	$899,679	$1,068,665	$21,517	$0	$1,047,148
Conservative Congregational Christian Conference [3]	$147,805	$0	$0	$147,805	$149,299	$0	$0	$149,299
Cumberland Presbyterian Church	$303,000	$12,236	$0	$290,764	$338,314	$14,974	$0	$323,340
The Episcopal Church [4]	$21,120,265	$3,507,225	$4,419,185	$13,193,855	$23,281,000	$3,000,000	$5,500,000	$14,781,000
Evangelical Congregational Church	$1,264,969	$219,732	$0	$1,045,237	$1,135,224	$193,815	$0	$941,409
Evangelical Covenant Church	$7,913,682	$0	$0	$7,913,682	$8,591,574	$0	$0	$8,591,574
Evangelical Lutheran Church in America	$22,590,206	$2,952,825	$0	$19,637,381	$27,173,066	$3,741,985	$0	$23,431,081
Evangelical Lutheran Synod	$912,460	$665,873	$0	$246,587	$945,470	$679,229	$0	$266,241
Fellowship of Evangelical Churches	$912,689	$0	$0	$912,689	$847,526	$0	$0	$847,526
Free Methodist Church of North America	$9,848,924	$727,325	$0	$9,121,599	$10,817,138	$630,519	$0	$10,186,619
General Association of General Baptists	*$1,893,585*	*$34,719*	*$0*	*$1,858,866*	*$1,817,715*	*$49,178*	*$0*	*$1,768,537*
Lutheran Church-Missouri Synod [5]	$14,960,928	$1,881,887	$0	$13,079,041	$15,548,240	$2,370,861	$0	$13,177,379
Moravian Church in America, Northern Province [6]				$467,570				$528,733
The Orthodox Presbyterian Church	$1,254,678	$40,229		$1,214,449	$1,417,758	$43,504	$0	$1,374,254
Presbyterian Church in America	$24,070,885	$0	$0	$24,070,885	$24,319,185	$0	$0	$24,319,185
Presbyterian Church (U.S.A.) [7]	$34,348,000	$11,046,000	$47,000	$23,255,000	$36,900,000	$12,190,000	$122,000	$24,588,000
Primitive Methodist Church in the U.S.A.	$542,252	$5,349	$0	$536,903	$532,337	$5,697	$0	$526,640
Reformed Church in America [8]	$8,159,552	$307,088	$0	$7,852,464	$7,610,120	$325,560	$0	$7,284,560
Seventh-day Adventist, North Am. Division [9]	$50,790,392	$2,565,158	$0	$48,225,234	$48,209,196	$1,456,611	$0	$46,752,585
Southern Baptist Convention	$239,663,000	$0	$0	$239,663,000	$242,140,000	$0	$0	$242,140,000
United Church of Christ	$12,990,011	$4,616,927	$0	$8,373,084	$12,125,594	$4,189,916	$0	$7,935,678
The United Methodist Church [10]	$124,800,000	$20,000,000	$22,800,000	$82,000,000	$138,700,000	$19,800,000	$27,700,000	$91,200,000
The Wesleyan Church	$8,507,914	$0	$0	$8,507,914	$8,881,386	$0	$0	$8,881,386
Wisconsin Evangelical Lutheran Synod	$11,534,079	$754,916	$0	$10,779,164	$10,707,496	$402,633	$0	$10,304,863

See Notes on page 180.

Appendix B-5.2: Overseas Missions Income, 34 Denominations, 2005 and 2006

Denomination	2005 Overseas Missions Income				2006 Overseas Missions Income			
	Line 1.	Line 2.	Line 3.	Line 4.	Line 1.	Line 2.	Line 3.	Line 4.
Allegheny Wesleyan Methodist Connection	$399,514	$0	$0	$399,514	$286,781	$0	$0	$286,781
American Baptist Churches in the U.S.A.	$18,837,736	$7,741,255	$0	$11,096,481	$14,701,486	$5,922,316	$0	$8,779,170
Associate Reformed Presbyterian Church (General Synod)	$4,920,208	$139,231	$264,675	$4,516,302	$4,682,925	$689,152	$172,476	$3,821,297
Brethren in Christ Church	$1,980,000	$60,000	$0	$1,920,000	$2,200,000	$82,406	$0	$2,117,594
Christian Church (Disciples of Christ)	$5,810,205	$1,587,428	$0	$4,222,777	$6,134,200	$1,712,531	$0	$4,421,669
Christian and Missionary Alliance [1]	$54,267,422	$0	$0	$54,267,422	$52,505,044	$0	$0	$52,505,044
Church of the Brethren [2]	$2,417,349	$147,215	$0	$2,270,134	$2,087,021	$199,819	$0	$1,887,202
Church of God General Conf. (Oregon, Ill. and Morrow, Ga.)	$80,000	$0	$0	$80,000	$63,355	$0	$0	$63,355
Church of the Lutheran Confession	$329,823	$20,000	$0	$309,823	$314,804	$125,987	$0	$188,817
Church of the Nazarene	$54,653,601	$1,899,919	$0	$52,753,682	*$52,721,095*	$1,751,130	$0	$50,969,965
Churches of God General Conference	*$1,146,044*	$15,944	$0	*$1,130,100*	*$1,282,333*	*$48,490*	$0	*$1,233,843*
Conservative Congregational Christian Conference [3]	$166,875	$0	$0	$166,875	$123,509	$0	$0	$123,509
Cumberland Presbyterian Church	$306,428	$13,082	$0	$293,346	$306,035	$15,728	$0	$290,307
The Episcopal Church [4]	$23,871,967	$3,000,000	$5,500,000	$15,371,967	$24,334,083	$3,000,000	$6,527,290	$14,806,793
Evangelical Congregational Church	$767,359	$42,270	$0	$725,089	$1,326,393	$0	$0	$1,326,393
Evangelical Covenant Church	$9,008,719	$0	$0	$9,008,719	$8,530,245	$0	$0	$8,530,245
Evangelical Lutheran Church in America	$29,109,564	$3,025,562	$0	$26,084,001	$25,484,714	$3,942,905	$0	$21,541,809
Evangelical Lutheran Synod	$1,211,101	$988,897	$0	$222,204	$1,214,815	$884,164	$0	$330,651
Fellowship of Evangelical Churches	$785,676	$0	$0	$785,676	$700,159	$0	$0	$700,159
Free Methodist Church of North America	$10,831,707	$111,467	$0	$10,720,240	$12,578,589	$699,714	$0	$11,878,875
General Association of General Baptists	*$1,945,215*	*$20,707*	*$0*	*$1,924,508*	*$2,082,916*	*$34,346*	*$0*	*$2,048,570*
Lutheran Church-Missouri Synod [5]	$18,897,894	$1,722,316	$0	$17,175,578	$16,170,108	$2,737,162	$0	$13,432,946
Moravian Church in America, Northern Province [6]	$568,497	$86,340	$0	$482,157	$561,849	$49,021	$0	$512,828
The Orthodox Presbyterian Church	$2,212,525	$355,996	$0	$1,856,529	$2,064,820	$358,528	$0	$1,706,292
Presbyterian Church in America	$25,890,591	$0	$0	$25,890,591	$27,627,770	$0	$0	$27,627,770
Presbyterian Church (U.S.A.) [7]	$47,223,000	$15,540,000	$65,000	$31,618,000	$35,539,000	$14,575,000	$0	$20,964,000
Primitive Methodist Church in the U.S.A.	$503,286	$5,441	$0	$497,845	$568,032	$1,916	$0	$566,116
Reformed Church in America [8]	$10,727,347	$0	$0	$10,727,347	$7,891,745	$405,218	$0	$7,486,527
Seventh-day Adventist, North Am. Division [9]	$53,745,101	$1,614,134	$0	$52,130,967	$51,459,266	$2,553,650	$0	$48,905,616
Southern Baptist Convention	$259,394,000	$0	$0	$259,394,000	$275,747,000	$0	$0	$275,747,000
United Church of Christ	$11,299,684	$3,647,313	$0	$7,652,371	$10,834,552	$3,295,428	$0	$7,539,124
The United Methodist Church [10]	$177,000,000	$23,400,000	$26,000,000	$127,600,000	$120,400,000	$21,600,000	$15,700,000	$83,100,000
The Wesleyan Church	$9,769,938	$0	$0	$9,769,938	$13,105,882	$0	$0	$13,105,882
Wisconsin Evangelical Lutheran Synod	$8,957,945	$163,652	$0	$8,794,293	$10,886,785	$418,225	$0	$10,468,560

See Notes on page 180.

Appendix B-5.2: Overseas Missions Income, 34 Denominations, 2007

Denomination	2005 Overseas Missions Income			
	Line 1.	Line 2.	Line 3.	Line 4.
Allegheny Wesleyan Methodist Connection	$332,511	$0	$0	$332,511
American Baptist Churches in the U.S.A.	$15,703,238	$5,837,228	$0	$9,866,010
Associate Reformed Presbyterian Church (General Synod)	$5,088,825	$254,533	$14,670	$4,819,622
Brethren in Christ Church	$2,264,672	$92,850	$0	$2,171,822
Christian Church (Disciples of Christ) [1]	$55,964,407	$0	$0	$55,964,407
Christian and Missionary Alliance	*$6,645,790*	$1,871,786	$0	*$4,774,004*
Church of the Brethren	$103,495	$0	$0	$103,495
Church of God General Conf. (Oregon, Ill. and Morrow, Ga.) [2]	$1,943,631	$206,977	$0	$1,736,654
Church of the Lutheran Confession	*$313,700*	*$36,100*	*$0*	*$277,600*
Church of the Nazarene	$52,195,781	$1,604,626	$0	$50,591,155
Churches of God General Conference	$1,148,045	$29,124	$0	$1,118,921
Conservative Congregational Christian Conference [3]	$169,508	$0	$0	$169,508
Cumberland Presbyterian Church	$368,334	$15,690	$0	$352,644
The Episcopal Church [4]	$26,940,269	$3,400,000	$8,511,710	$15,028,559
Evangelical Congregational Church	$1,464,523	$0	$0	$1,464,523
Evangelical Covenant Church	$7,954,834	$0	$0	$7,954,834
Evangelical Lutheran Church in America	$26,161,433	$4,414,055	$0	$21,747,378
Evangelical Lutheran Synod	$1,389,221	$885,203	$0	$504,018
Fellowship of Evangelical Churches	$700,590	$0	$0	$700,590
Free Methodist Church of North America	$13,705,466	$1,226,998	$0	$12,478,468
General Association of General Baptists	$2,246,653	$67,605	$0	$2,179,048
Lutheran Church-Missouri Synod [5]	$16,086,361	$2,899,441	$0	$13,186,920
Moravian Church in America, Northern Province [6]	$542,968	$18,819	$0	$524,149
The Orthodox Presbyterian Church	$22,337,000	$13,429,000	$0	$8,908,000
Presbyterian Church in America [7]	$28,456,453	$0	$0	$28,456,453
Presbyterian Church (U.S.A.)	$568,612	$1,802	$0	$566,810
Primitive Methodist Church in the U.S.A.	$7,931,523	$319,910	$0	$7,611,613
Reformed Church in America [8]	$53,772,765	$1,734,653	$0	$52,038,112
Seventh-day Adventist, North Am. Division [9]	$278,313,000	$0	$0	$278,313,000
Southern Baptist Convention	$1,899,674	$75,285	$0	$1,824,389
United Church of Christ	$9,600,591	$2,493,501	$0	$7,107,090
The United Methodist Church [10]	$126,600,000	$21,400,000	$25,700,000	$79,500,000
The Wesleyan Church	$13,554,996	$0	$0	$13,554,996
Wisconsin Evangelical Lutheran Synod	$11,173,147	$500,952	$0	$10,672,195

See Notes on next page.

Overseas Missions Income Data for Three Additional Denominations, 2003-2007 (see Chapter 6, Note 9)

Denomination	2003 Overseas Missions Income, Line 4	2004 Overseas Missions Income, Line 4	2005 Overseas Missions Income, Line 4	2006 Overseas Missions Income, Line 4	2007 Overseas Missions Income, Line 4
Friends United Meeting	$1,314,527	$276,887 (partial year)	$863,445	$859,750	$937,142
Mennonite Church USA	$4,155,596	$3,854,139	$3,937,548	$3,876,657	$4,054,734
North American Baptist Conference	$4,092,633	$3,569,567	$2,535,946 (partial year)	$2,501,513	NA

Line Descriptions on empty tomb, inc. Overseas Missions Income Data Request Form:

Line 1.: What was the amount of income raised in the U.S. during the calendar or fiscal year indicated for overseas ministries?

Line 2.: How many dollars of the total amount on Line 1. came from endowment, foundation, and other investment income?

Line 3.: Of the total amount on Line1., what is the dollar value of government grants, either in dollars or in-kind goods for distribution?

Line 4.: Balance of overseas ministries income: Line 1. minus Lines 2. and 3.

Notes to Table B-5: Overseas Missions Income, 34 Denominations, 2003, 2004, 2005, 2006, and 2007

[1] Christian and Missionary Alliance: "Since both domestic and overseas works are budgeted through the same source (our 'Great Commission Fund'), the amount on lines 1 and 4 are actual amounts spent on overseas missions."

[2] Church of the Brethren: "This amount is national denominational mission and service, i.e., direct staffing and mission support, and does not include other projects funded directly by congregations or districts, or independent missionaries sponsored by congregations and individuals that would not be part of the denominational effort."

[3] Conservative Congregational Christian Conference: The structure of this communion limits the national office coordination of overseas ministries activity. By design, congregations are to conduct missions directly, through agencies of their choice. The national office does not survey congregations about these activities. The one common emphasis of affiliated congregations is a focus on Micronesia, represented by the reported numbers.

[4] The Episcopal Church: "The Episcopal Church USA Domestic and Foreign Missionary Society does not specifically raise money to support our non-domestic ministries. Many of the activities included in our budget are, however, involved, directly or indirectly, with providing worldwide mission...Many other expenditures (e.g., for ecumenical and interfaith relations; for military chaplaincies; for management's participation in activities of the worldwide Anglical Communion) contain an overseas component; but we do not separately track or report domestic vs. overseas expenses in those categories."

[5] Lutheran Church-Missouri Synod: "Since 1968, many of the Lutheran Church-Missouri Synod (LCMS) 35 geographic districts now sponsor mission fields directly. The money does not flow through LCMS World Mission and LCMS World Relief, but through various mission societies. In 1996, the LCMS also established the Association of Lutheran Mission Agencies which includes 'recognized service agencies' of LCMS World Mission. They work in places where LCMS World Mission used to work (or might work today), but they direct and fund the work on their own. Millions of dollars of support from LCMS members is raised and spent by these 75+ mission societies. The Congregation Statistics Reports do not include information about missions spending other than that sent to LCMS World Mission and LCMS World Relief. The dollars that support the mission societies and the Lutheran Mission Agencies would not be included in the Congregation Statistics Reports. Nothing outside of the money that flows through the mission accounting department is verifiable, and no central accounting is made of mission societies spending. District support is only a small portion of the World Mission Support figure, with most of the budget coming from direct gifts from individuals."

[6] Moravian Church, Northern Province: The Overseas Missions Income figure was estimated for the Northern Province by the Board of World Mission of the Moravian Church. The Northern Province is the only one of the three Moravian Provinces that reports Total Contributions to the Yearbook of American and Canadian Churches series.

[7] Presbyterian Church (U.S.A.): #1 & 4 Year 2005 higher for Asian Tsunami Relief

[8] Reformed Church in America: "We do not know how much money was given to missions outside the RCA structure." Also, the staff submitting the 2005 data wrote: "The Reported 2003 and Reported 2004 totals listed could not be substantiated."

[9] Seventh-day Adventist, North American Division: This estimate, prepared by the General Conference Treasury Department, is for the U.S. portion of the total donated by congregations in both Canada and the U.S.

[10] The United Methodist Church: "The above represents total income received by the General Board of Global Ministries, The United Methodist Church." For 2005 data: "Increase due to funding received for Tsunami."

Appendix B-6: Estimates of Giving

Year	A. Form 990 Direct Public Support '000s $	B. Form 990 Indirect Public Support '000s $	C. Form 990-EZ Contributions, Gifts and Grants '000s $	D. *Giving USA* Gifts to Foundations Billion $s	E. *Giving USA* Giving by Corporations Billion $s	F. *Giving USA* Giving by Foundations Billion $s	G. *Giving USA* Giving to Bequests Billion $s	H. *Giving USA* Individual Giving, Million $s	I. IRS Other than Cash Contributions '000s	J. CE Giving to "Church, Religious Organizations" '000s
1989	35,828,100	7,008,648	463,432	4.41	5.46	6.55	6.84	79,450	7,550,914	31,739,713
1990	39,395,074	8,055,551	644,613	3.83	5.46	7.23	6.79	81,040	7,494,016	30,673,887
1991	40,282,952	7,717,705	685,538	4.46	5.25	7.72	7.68	84,270	9,681,786	36,444,100
1992	43,986,785	9,110,478	813,604	5.01	5.91	8.64	9.54	87,700	9,632,779	35,159,679
1993	47,507,722	8,335,206	769,751	6.26	6.47	9.53	8.86	92,000	12,278,893	35,495,384
1994	49,238,498	8,722,141	780,896	6.33	6.98	9.66	11.13	92,520	14,739,299	37,189,109
1995	64,148,723	9,746,924	820,036	8.46	7.35	10.56	10.41	95,360	13,521,937	39,741,542
1996	69,419,764	10,230,304	988,638	12.63	7.51	12.00	12.03	107,560	21,298,819	39,053,447
1997	74,681,875	10,945,060	977,961	13.96	8.62	13.92	16.25	124,200	27,961,174	41,201,034
1998	83,359,695	12,711,938	1,053,669	19.92	8.46	17.01	12.98	138,350	29,255,985	44,831,015
1999	91,696,783	13,519,909	1,011,289	28.76	10.23	20.51	17.37	154,630	38,286,580	49,102,106
2000	103,453,445	15,176,512	1,086,099	24.71	10.74	24.58	19.88	174,510	47,256,104	48,737,216
2001	108,065,595	14,561,940	1,087,365	25.67	11.66	27.22	19.80	173,350	37,997,546	57,321,111
2002	102,802,550	15,223,713	1,095,317	19.16	10.79	26.98	20.90	174,440	34,293,125	62,476,667
2003	112,808,019	16,330,097	1,188,783	21.62	11.06	26.84	18.19	181,960	38,041,067	65,108,080
2004	124,575,951	16,947,398	1,397,630	20.32	11.36	28.41	18.46	201,360	43,373,209	65,712,121
2005	140,348,374	21,624,408	1,469,440	27.46	16.59	32.41	23.45	220,750	48,056,520	82,948,394

Source:

Columns A. and B.

1989	"Form 990 Returns of Nonprofit Charitable Section 501(c)(3) Organizations: Selected Income Statement and Balance Sheet Items, by Size of Total Assets, 1989"; <http://www.irs.gov/pub/irs-soi/89eo01as.xls>; p. 2 of 6/13/2007 12:26 PM printout.
1990	"Table 1.--1990, Form 990 Returns of Organizations Tax-Exempt Under Internal Revenue Code Sections 501(c)(3)-(9): Selected Income Statement and Balance Sheet Items, by Code Section"; <http://www.irs.gov/pub/irs-soi/90np01fr.xls>; p. 3 of 6/13/2007 1:48 PM printout.
1991	"Form 990 Returns of Nonprofit Charitable Internal Revenue Code Section 501(c)(3) Organizations: Selected Income Statement and Balance Sheet Items, by Asset Size, 1991"; <http://www.irs.gov/pub/irs-soi/91eo01as.xls>; p. 2 of 6/13/2007 2:48 PM printout.
1992-1999	"Table 1.--[Year], Form 990 Returns of Nonprofit Charitable Internal Revenue Code Section 501(c)(3) Organizations: Selected Income Statement and Balance Sheet Items, by Asset Size"
1992	<http://www.irs.gov/pub/irs-soi/92eo01as.xls>; p. 2 of 6/13/2007 3:21 PM printout.
1993	<http://www.irs.gov/pub/irs-soi/93eo01as.xls>; p. 2 of 6/13/2007 3:39 PM printout.
1994	<http://www.irs.gov/pub/irs-soi/94eo01as.xls>; p. 2 of 6/13/2007 4:12 PM printout.
1995	<http://www.irs.gov/pub/irs-soi/95eotab1.xls>; p. 2 of 6/14/2007 9:25 AM printout.
1996	<http://www.irs.gov/pub/irs-soi/96eo01c3.xls>; p. 1 of 6/14/2007 9:55 AM printout.
1997	<http://www.irs.gov/pub/irs-soi/97eotb1.xls>; p. 1 of 6/14/2007 10:09 AM printout.
1998	<http://www.irs.gov/pub/irs-soi/98eo01as.xls>; p. 1 of 6/14/2007 10:17 AM printout.
1999	<http://www.irs.gov/pub/irs-soi/99eo01as.xls>; p. 1 of 6/14/2007 10:29 AM printout.
2000	"Table 1.--2000, Form 990 Returns of Nonprofit Charitable Section 501(c)(3) Organizations: Selected Balance Sheet and Income Statement Items, by Size of Total Assets"; <http://www.irs.gov/pub/irs-soi/00eo01ta.xls>; p. 2 of 6/14/2007 10:43 AM printout.
2001-2003	"Table 1.--Form 990 Returns of Nonprofit Charitable Section 501(c)(3) Organizations: Selected Balance Sheet and Income Statement Items, by Asset Size, Tax Year [Year]"
2001	<http://www.irs.gov/pub/irs-soi/01eo01as.xls>; p. 1 of 6/14/2007 10:55 AM printout.
2002	<http://www.irs.gov/pub/irs-soi/02eo01as.xls>; p. 2 of 6/14/2007 4:31 PM printout.
2003	<http://www.irs.gov/pub/irs-soi/03eo01as.xls>; p. 1 of 6/14/2007 4:42 PM printout.
2004-2005	"Table 1.--Form 990 Returns of Nonprofit Charitable Section 501(c)(3) Organizations: Balance Sheet and Income Statement Items, by Asset Size, Tax Year [Year]"
2004	<http://www.irs.gov/pub/irs-soi/04eo04ty.xls>; p. 1 of 3/15/2008 9:59 AM printout.
2005	<http://www.irs.gov/pub/irs-soi/05eo01as.xls>; p. 1 of 3/5/2009 3:59 PM printout.

Appendix B-6: Estimates of Giving

Col. C.

1989	"Form 990EZ Returns of Organizations Tax-Exempt Under Internal Revenue Code Sections 501(c)(3)-(9): Selected Income Statement and Balance Sheet Items, by Code Section, 1989"; <http://www.irs.gov/pub/irs-soi/89eo04cs.xls>; p. 1 of 6/16/2007 8:56 AM printout
1990	"Table 2.--1990, Form 990EZ Returns of Organizations Tax-Exempt Under Internal Revenue Code Sections 501(c)(3)-(9): Selected Income Statement and Balance Sheet Items, by Code Section"; <http://www.irs.gov/pub/irs-soi/90np02ro.xls>; p. 1 of 6/16/2007 9:11 AM printout.
1991	"Form 990EZ Returns of Organizations Tax-Exempt Under Internal Revenue Code Sections 501(c)(3)-(9): Selected Income Statement and Balance Sheet Items, by Code Section, 1991"; <http://www.irs.gov/pub/irs-soi/91eo04cs.xls>; p. 1 of 6/16/2007 9:22 AM printout.
1992-1994	"Table 4.--[Year], Form 990EZ Returns of Organizations Tax-Exempt Under Internal Revenue Code Sections 501(c)(3)-(9): Selected Income Statement and Balance Sheet Items, by Code Section"
1992	<http://www.irs.gov/pub/irs-soi/92eo04cs.xls>; p. 1 of 6/16/2007 9:39 AM printout.
1993	<http://www.irs.gov/pub/irs-soi/93eo04as.xls>; p. 1 of 6/16/2007 9:48 AM printout.
1994	<http://www.irs.gov/pub/irs-soi/94eo04cs.xls>; p. 1 of 6/16/2007 9:58 AM printout.
1995	"Table 4.--1995, Form 990-EZ Returns of Organizations Tax-Exempt Under Internal Revenue Code Sections 501(c)(3)-(9): Selected Balance Sheet and Income Statement Items, by Code Section"; <http://www.irs.gov/pub/irs-soi/eotab4.xls>; p. 1 of 6/16/2007 10:09 AM printout.
1996	"Table 3.--1996, Form 990-EZ Returns of Nonprofit Charitable Section 501(c)(3) Organizations: Selected Balance Sheet and Income Statement Items, by Asset Size"; <http://www.irs.gov/pub/irs-soi/96eo03c3.xls>; p. 1 of 6/16/2007 10:28 AM printout.
1997-2000	"Table 4.--[Year], Form 990-EZ Returns of Organizations Tax-Exempt Under Internal Revenue Code Sections 501(c)(3)-(9): Selected Balance Sheet and Income Statement Items, by Code Section"
1997	<http://www.irs.gov/pub/irs-soi/97eotb4.xls>; p. 1 of 6/16/2007 10:36 AM printout.
1998	<http://www.irs.gov/pub/irs-soi/98eo04cs.xls>; p. 1 of 6/16/2007 10:43 AM printout.
1999	<http://www.irs.gov/pub/irs-soi/99eo04cs.xls>; p. 1 of 6/16/2007 11:22 AM printout.
2000	<http://www.irs.gov/pub/irs-soi/00eo04cs.xls>; p. 1 of 6/16/2007 11:29 AM printout.
2001	"Form 990-EZ Returns of Organizations Tax-Exempt Under Internal Revenue Code Sections 501(c)(3)-(9): Selected Balance Sheet and Income Statement Items, by Code Section, Tax Year 2001"; <http://www.irs.gov/pub/irs-soi/01eo04cs.xls>; p. 1 of 6/16/2007 11:34 printout.
2002-2003	"Table 4.--Form 990-EZ Returns of Organizations Tax-Exempt Under Internal Revenue Code Sections 501(c)(3)-(9): Selected Balance Sheet and Income Statement Items, by Code Section, Tax Year [Year]"
2002	<http://www.irs.gov/pub/irs-soi/02eo04ty.xls>; p. 1 of 6/17/2007 7:50 AM printout.
2003	<http://www.irs.gov/pub/irs-soi/03eo04ty.xls>; p. 1 of 6/17/2007 8:07 AM printout.
2004-2005	"Table 4: Form 990-EZ Returns of 501(c)(3)-(9) Organizations: Balance Sheet and Income Statement Items, by Code Section, Tax Year [Year]"; IRS, Statistics of Income Division
2004	<http://www.irs.gov/pub/irs-soi/04eo04ty.xls>; p. 1 of 3/14/2008 3:50 PM printout.
2005	<http://www.irs.gov/pub/irs-soi/05eo04ty.xls>; p. 1 of 3/5/2009 4:11 PM printout.

Col. D.

1989-2003	*Giving USA 2007* (Glenview, Ill.: Giving USA Foundation, 2007), p. 215.
2004	*Giving USA 2008* (Glenview, Ill.: Giving USA Foundation, 2008), p. 213.
2005	*Giving USA 2009* (Glenview, Ill.: Giving USA Foundation, 2009), p. 213.

Columns E., F., and G.

1989-2003	*Giving USA 2007*, p. 212
2004	*Giving USA 2008*, p. 210
2005	*Giving USA 2009*, p. 210

Col. H.

1989-2005	*Giving USA 2009*, p. 210

Col. I.

1989	Internal Revenue Service, Statistics of Income—1989, Individual Income Tax Returns, "Table 2.1—Returns with Itemized Deductions: Sources of Income, Adjustments, Itemized Deductions by Type, Exemptions, and Tax Items by Size of Adjusted Gross Income (Internsl Revenue Service: Washington, DC, 1992), p. 41.
1990-2001	"Table 1.--Individual Income Tax Returns, Selected Deductions, 1990-2001;" IRS Statistics of Income Winter 2003-2004 Bulletin, Publication 1136; <http://www.irs.gov/pub/irs-soi/01in01sd.xls>; pp. 1-2 of 9/6/2005 8:59 AM printout.
2002	"Table 3.--2002, Individual Income Tax Returns with Itemized Deductions, by Size of Adjusted Gross Income"; IRS, Statistics of Income Bulletin, Fall 2004, Publication 1136, (Rev. 12-04) <http://www.irs.gov/pub/irs-soi/02in03ga.xls>; p. 5 of 9/6/2005 10:58 AM printout.
2003	"Table 3.--2003, Individual Income Tax Returns with Itemized Deductions, by Size of Adjusted Gross Income;" IRS, Statistics of Income Bulletin, Fall 2005, Publication 1136, (Rev. 12-05) <http://www.irs.gov/pub/irs-soi/03in03ag.xls>; p. 5 of 6/6/2006 3:38 PM printout.
2004	"Table 3.--Returns with Itemized Deductions: Sources of Income, Adjustments, Itemized Deductions by Type, Exemptions, and Tax Items, by Size of Adjusted Gross Income, Tax year 2004"; IRS, Statistics of Income Division, July 2006; <http://www.irs.gov/pub/irs-soi/04in03id.xls>; p. 3 of 8/12/2007 1:33 PM printout.
2005	"Table 3.--Returns with Itemized Deductions: Itemized Deductions by Type and by Size of Adjusted Gross Income, Tax Year 2005"; IRS; <http://www.irs.gov/pub/irs-soi/05in03id.xls>; p. 3 of 4/10/2008 7:07 PM printout.

Col. J.

1989-2005	U.S. Department of Labor, Bureau of Labor Statistics, "Table 1800.Region of residence: Average annual expenditures and characteristics, Consumer Expenditure Survey, [Year]"

APPENDIX C: *Income, Deflators, and U.S. Population*

Appendix C: *Income, Deflators, and U.S. Population*

Appendix C.1 presents U.S. Per Capita Disposable Personal Income for 1921 through 2008.

The Implicit Price Index for Gross National Product is provided for 1921 through 2008. The deflator series keyed to 2000 dollars provided deflators from 1929, only, through 2008. Therefore, the 1921 through 1928 data was converted to inflation-adjusted 1958 dollars using the series keyed to 1958=100, and the inflation-adjusted 1958 dollar values were then converted to inflation-adjusted 2000 dollars using the series keyed to 2000 dollars.

Appendix C.2 presents U.S. Population for 1921 through 2008.

SOURCES

Income, 1921-1928, Deflator 1921-1928, and U.S. Population, 1921-1928

Historical Statistics of the United States: Colonial Times to 1970, Bicentennial Edition, Part 1 (Washington, DC: Bureau of the Census, 1975):

   1921-28 Per Capita Disposable Personal Income: Series F 9, p. 224 (F 6-9).

   1921-28 Implicit Price Index GNP (1958=100): Series F 9, p. 224 (F 6-9).

   1921-28 U.S. Population: Series A-7, p. 8 (A 6-8).

Income, 1929-2008

   Per Capita Disposable Personal Income in Current Dollars: U.S. Department of Commerce, Bureau of Economic Analysis; "Table 7.1. Selected Per Capita Product and Income Series in Current and Chained Dollars"; Line 4: "Disposable personal income"; National Income and Product Accounts Tables; <http://www.bea.gov/national/nipaweb/SS_Data/Section7All_xls.xls>; Data Published on March 26, 2009.

Deflator, 2000 Dollars, 1929-2008

   Gross National Product: Implicit Price Deflators for Gross National Product [2000=100]: U.S. Bureau of Economic Analysis; "Table 1.1.9. Implicit Price Deflators for Gross Domestic Product"; Line 25: "Gross national product"; National Income and Product Accounts Tables; <http://www.bea.gov/national/nipaweb/SS_Data/Section1All_xls.xls>; Data Published on March 26, 2009.

Population, 1929-2008

   U.S. Bureau of Economic Analysis; "Table 7.1. Selected Per Capita Product and Income Series in Current and Chained Dollars"; Line 16: "Population (midperiod, thousands)"; National Income and Product Accounts Tables; <http://www.bea.gov/national/nipaweb/SS_Data/Section7All_xls.xls>; Data Published on March 26, 2009.

Appendix C-1: Per Capita Disposable Personal Income and Deflators, 1921-2008

Year	Current $s Per Capita Disposable Personal Income	Implicit Price Deflator GNP [1958=100]	Implicit Price Deflator GNP [2000=100]	Year	Current $s Per Capita Disposable Personal Income	Implicit Price Deflator GNP [2000=100]
1921	$555	54.50		1965	$2,563	22.52
1922	$548	50.10		1966	$2,734	23.16
1923	$623	51.30		1967	$2,895	23.87
1924	$626	51.20		1968	$3,114	24.89
1925	$630	51.90		1969	$3,324	26.13
1926	$659	51.10		1970	$3,587	27.51
1927	$650	50.00		1971	$3,860	28.89
1928	$643	50.80		1972	$4,140	30.15
1929	$684		11.96	1973	$4,616	31.83
1930	$606		11.52	1974	$5,010	34.70
1931	$518		10.33	1975	$5,498	37.98
1932	$394		9.11	1976	$5,972	40.18
1933	$366		8.87	1977	$6,517	42.73
1934	$418		9.36	1978	$7,224	45.74
1935	$466		9.55	1979	$7,967	49.53
1936	$526		9.66	1980	$8,822	54.02
1937	$560		10.07	1981	$9,765	59.10
1938	$512		9.78	1982	$10,426	62.70
1939	$545		9.68	1983	$11,131	65.18
1940	$581		9.79	1984	$12,319	67.63
1941	$703		10.45	1985	$13,037	69.70
1942	$879		11.26	1986	$13,649	71.23
1943	$990		11.87	1987	$14,241	73.18
1944	$1,072		12.14	1988	$15,297	75.68
1945	$1,088		12.47	1989	$16,257	78.55
1946	$1,141		13.97	1990	$17,131	81.59
1947	$1,188		15.49	1991	$17,609	84.44
1948	$1,300		16.36	1992	$18,494	86.38
1949	$1,276		16.33	1993	$18,872	88.38
1950	$1,385		16.51	1994	$19,555	90.26
1951	$1,497		17.69	1995	$20,287	92.11
1952	$1,550		18.00	1996	$21,091	93.86
1953	$1,621		18.22	1997	$21,940	95.42
1954	$1,627		18.39	1998	$23,161	96.48
1955	$1,714		18.72	1999	$23,968	97.87
1956	$1,801		19.37	2000	*$25,473*	100.00
1957	$1,867		20.01	2001	*$26,243*	102.40
1958	$1,898		20.47	2002	*$27,183*	104.18
1959	$1,979		20.73	2003	*$28,076*	106.40
1960	$2,022		21.02	2004	*$29,592*	109.46
1961	$2,078		21.26	2005	*$30,611*	*113.03*
1962	$2,171		21.55	2006	*$32,263*	*116.67*
1963	$2,246		21.78	2007	*$33,706*	*119.81*
1964	$2,410		22.11	2008	$34,946	122.41

Appendix C-2: U.S. Population, 1921-2008

Year	U.S. Population	Year	U.S. Population
1921	108,538,000	1965	194,347,000
1922	110,049,000	1966	196,599,000
1923	111,947,000	1967	198,752,000
1924	114,109,000	1968	200,745,000
1925	115,829,000	1969	202,736,000
1926	117,397,000	1970	205,089,000
1927	119,035,000	1971	207,692,000
1928	120,509,000	1972	209,924,000
1929	121,878,000	1973	211,939,000
1930	123,188,000	1974	213,898,000
1931	124,149,000	1975	215,981,000
1932	124,949,000	1976	218,086,000
1933	125,690,000	1977	220,289,000
1934	126,485,000	1978	222,629,000
1935	127,362,000	1979	225,106,000
1936	128,181,000	1980	227,726,000
1937	128,961,000	1981	230,008,000
1938	129,969,000	1982	232,218,000
1939	131,028,000	1983	234,333,000
1940	132,122,000	1984	236,394,000
1941	133,402,000	1985	238,506,000
1942	134,860,000	1986	240,683,000
1943	136,739,000	1987	242,843,000
1944	138,397,000	1988	245,061,000
1945	139,928,000	1989	247,387,000
1946	141,389,000	1990	250,181,000
1947	144,126,000	1991	253,530,000
1948	146,631,000	1992	256,922,000
1949	149,188,000	1993	260,282,000
1950	151,684,000	1994	263,455,000
1951	154,287,000	1995	266,588,000
1952	156,954,000	1996	269,714,000
1953	159,565,000	1997	272,958,000
1954	162,391,000	1998	276,154,000
1955	165,275,000	1999	279,328,000
1956	168,221,000	2000	*282,413,000*
1957	171,274,000	2001	*285,294,000*
1958	174,141,000	2002	*288,055,000*
1959	177,130,000	2003	*290,729,000*
1960	180,760,000	2004	*293,348,000*
1961	183,742,000	2005	*296,036,000*
1962	186,590,000	2006	*298,820,000*
1963	189,300,000	2007	*301,737,000*
1964	191,927,000	2008	304,529,000

Notes

120636

<u>Notes</u>